Issues in Modern Foreign Languages Teaching

Edited by Kit Field

London and New York

First published 2000
by RoutledgeFalmer
2 Park Square, Milton Park, Abingdon, Oxon, OX14 4RN

Simultaneously published in the USA and Canada
by RoutledgeFalmer
270 Madison Ave, New York NY 10016

RoutledgeFalmer is an imprint of the Taylor & Francis Group

Transferred to Digital Printing 2005

Typeset in Goudy by Exe Valley Dataset Ltd, Exeter

British Library Cataloguing in Publication Data
A catalogue record for this book is available
from the British Library

Library of Congress Cataloging in Publication Data
Issues in modern foreign languages teaching / edited by Kit Field.
      p. cm.—(Issues in subject teaching series)
   Includes bibliographical references and index.
   1. Languages, Modern—Study and teaching.   I. Field, Kit.
   II. Issues in subject teaching

PB35.I85 2000
418'.0071–dc21   00-034463

ISBN 0–415–23717–3 (hbk)
ISBN 0–415–23064–0 (pbk)

Issues in Modern Foreign Languages Teaching

Issues in Modern Foreign Languages Teaching draws together many eminent writers in the field to address the key issues associated with Modern Foreign Languages teaching and learning.

The issues addressed include:

- the development of Modern Foreign Language teaching
- the content and definition of Modern Foreign Languages
- how Modern Foreign Languages are taught in English schools
- issues concerned with pupils and their learning
- the relationship of the subject to the curriculum as a whole

Issues in Modern Foreign Languages Teaching will provide stimulating references for newly qualified teachers, student teachers and experienced teachers to build on existing good practice and to develop a theoretical perspective which may be lacking in Initial Teacher Training courses. It is important reading for students and teachers of Modern Foreign Languages at both primary and secondary level.

Kit Field is a principal lecturer at Canterbury Christ Church University College and the deputy director of Continuing Professional Development.

Issues in Subject Teaching series
Series edited by Susan Capel, Jon Davison,
James Arthur and John Moss

Other titles in the series:

Contents

PART 3

Issues associated with pedagogy

PART 4

Broader issues

Illustrations

Figures

Tables

Contributors

Julie Adams is a senior lecturer in Teacher Education and course tutor for the PGCE Modern Languages programme at the University of North London. Julie has a particular research interest in, and has published on, assessment in Modern Foreign Languages teaching. Julie professes to be an evangelist for course work and continuous assessment.

Douglas Allford is Lecturer in Languages in Education at the Institute of Education, University of London, where he teaches on the MA in Modern Languages in Education. He holds a PhD and has many years' experience teaching German for commercial, economic and other applied purposes at most levels from *ab initio* to postgraduate. In this connection he became interested in translation not only as a skill but also as a pedagogic tool. His current research and writing interests include, as well as aspects of mfl teaching, independent language learning, literature and language teaching, discourse analysis, aspects of language and cognition. Douglas is currently joint editor of the *Language Learning Journal*.

Jim Anderson has worked as Head of Languages in two multilingual London comprehensive schools and, as well as teaching French, German and Spanish, has taken a particular interest in supporting bilingual learners both in developing their home languages and their competence in English. In the 1980s he coordinated cross-curricular Language Awareness programmes involving colleagues teaching English, English as an Additional Language and Community, as well as Foreign Languages. Since 1996, Jim has been working as PGCE MFL tutor at Goldsmiths College. A current research focus is the potential of ICT in enhancing the learning and teaching of Community Languages.

Stephen Bax is a principal lecturer in the Department of Language Studies at Canterbury Christ Church University College. His main interest is the use of ICT in Modern Languages Teaching. Stephen's principal role is leading and teaching programmes for native and non-native teachers of English as a foreign language. Stephen has published academic texts and curriculum materials, as well as computer based language learning activities.

Do Coyle is teacher educator at the University of Nottingham. She has taught French German and Russian in schools and also English as a foreign language in France. Do leads and teaches on initial teacher education programmes, and now co-ordinates a European programme leading to joint Anglo–French and Anglo–Austrian qualifications. She has also set up the first bilingual teacher training programme in the UK. Do has a particular interest in content-based learning, which is linked to her research and publications in the field of teacher and learner autonomy in MFL teaching and learning. This has led Do to becoming a key figure in national and international projects and networks.

Patricia Driscoll has been engaged in research in the field of early Modern Foreign Language teaching and learning for more than 5 years. She has taught MFL in secondary schools and also taught English as a foreign language across the whole age range. For a number of years she worked in industry both in Britain and abroad. She participates in a network of ETML researchers under the European Commission Training and Mobility of Researchers Programme.

Kit Field works as a principal lecturer at Canterbury Christ Church University College. Kit is the Deputy Director of Continuing Professional Development, and has an interest in Subject Leadership. As a modern linguist, Kit has published in the field of Modern Foreign Languages teaching and learning, as well as Subject Leadership, mentoring and Ofsted inspections.

Vee Harris taught French in a number of comprehensive schools before becoming a PGCE MFL tutor at Goldsmiths College, University of London. Her publications draw on her experience of working in the classroom with practising and trainee teachers and include 'Modern Languages and Learning Strategies: In Theory and Practice' (with Dr. M. Grenfell, Routledge), a book on Learning Strategies in the CILT Pathfinder series as well as articles on learner autonomy. She is currently coordinating a European project on teaching Learning Strategies.

Barry Jones is a principal lecturer at Homerton College, University of Cambridge, where he is responsible for two Modern Languages teacher training programmes: the PGCE and the European Teacher programme. All his students take part in several projects during their training year, one of which has been to organise the exchange of shoe boxes by secondary school children in the UK and other countries in an attempt to portray cultural identity by what the pupils choose to put in them. He has published books and many articles on other aspects of Modern Language teaching and learning, three in the CILT Pathfinder series, and is co-author of a four-part French course 'Spirale', published by Hodder and Stoughton.

Jane Jones is Head of MFL in the School of Education, King's College, University of London. She taught French and Latin in comprehensive schools for many years and worked in collaboration with several higher education institutions on teacher training. Her research interests include primary MFLs (she is a member of the National Primary Languages Network), language across the curriculum, issues of school leadership and governance and comparative education frameworks. Jane co-ordinates a range of EU-funded research projects, some concerning language learning, others focusing on educational management and leadership.

Shirley Lawes taught French in secondary, further and adult education, as well as in industry. She was also involved for many years in training teachers of Modern Foreign Languages before joining the staff of the Faculty of Education at Canterbury Christ Church University College. Her current role is lead tutor for Modern Foreign Languages on the Secondary PGCE Course and course tutor for the PGCE/Maitrise FLE programme in partnership with the Université du Littoral Côte Opale in France. Shirley has published a number of articles and contributions to books on post-compulsory education, teaching Modern Foreign Languages at advanced level and aspects of teacher training. Her current research interests include a comparative study of European initial teacher training and a transnational project on school and social exclusion.

Ernesto Macaro taught languages in secondary schools for 15 years. Since 1990 he has been involved with the training of teachers both at an initial level and at an in-service level. He has a PhD in language teacher education and is currently a lecturer in the Department of Educational Studies at the University of Oxford. He has research interests in classroom interaction and learning strategies.

Norbert Pachler is a senior lecturer in Languages in Education at the Institute of Education, University of London, with responsibility for the Secondary PGCE in Modern Foreign Languages and the MA in Modern Languages in Education. His research interests include all aspects of Modern Foreign Languages teaching and learning, comparative (teacher) education, as well as the application of new technologies in teaching and learning. He has published widely in these fields. In 1997 *Learning to Teach Modern Foreign Languages in the Secondary School*, which he co-authored with Kit Field, was published by Routledge. More recently he edited *Teaching Modern Foreign Languages at Advanced Level* and co-edited *Learning to Teach Using ICT in the Secondary School* with Marilyn Leask. He holds a Dr. phil. degree, has taught in secondary and further education and has worked for the inspectorate and advisory service of a local education authority on curriculum development and in-service training. Norbert is currently joint editor of the *Language Learning Journal*.

Cathy Pomphrey taught MFLs and English in schools in London for many years. She became the tutor with responsibility for the MFLs and English (PGCE) programme before being appointed as the PGCE Course Director at the University of North London. Cathy has written texts within the

Pathfinder series for CILT and many articles in refereed journals. She has an interest in learning styles and learning strategies, as well as the need to understand and contribute to pupils' cultural development.

Ana Redondo is currently Curriculum Manager for Modern Languages in a London comprehensive school and is interested in a wide range of issues in education and ITE in general and the teaching and learning of Modern Foreign Languages in particular. Ana has been working as a mentor with various HEIs and has been involved in a number of projects and INSET provision with various LEAs. She has written stories for the teaching of Spanish and she contributed to *Learning to Teach Modern Foreign Languages in the Secondary School* published by Routledge in 1997.

Keith Sharpe is Professor of Education and Head of the Education Department at the University of Liverpool. He taught in primary and middle schools for many years and until recently was the Director of Primary Education at Canterbury Christ Church University College. He played a leading role in the development of a primary MFL programme for Kent Local Education Authority and has published a number of papers on the subject.

Acknowledgements

It is important for me to thank all the contributors. All are eminent in the field of Modern Foreign Languages teaching and learning, and it is the ideas and arguments of these colleagues which has helped me to develop my own approach. Thanks must also go to the numerous teachers and other colleagues who have helped to shape the views expressed in this text. The many student teachers, most of whom are now successful teachers, have provided me and many colleagues with the opportunities to reflect on the subject, which has helped to structure this text. My colleagues who have contributed to this text have acknowledged sources and inspirations for their work within their own chapters. Thanks must also go to the Series Editors, in particular to John Moss who was assigned MFLs along with other subject areas. His patience and understanding is much appreciated. Last, but not least, my thanks to the editorial staff at RoutledgeFalmer for all their support and help.

Introduction to the Series

Modern Foreign Languages

This book, *Issues in Teaching*, is one of a series of books entitled *Issues in Subject Teaching*. The series has been designed to engage with a wide range of issues relaed to subject teaching. Types of issues vary among subjects, but may include, for example: issues that impact on Initial Teacher Education in the subject; issues addressed in the classroom through the teaching of the subject; issues to do with the content of the subject and its definition; issues to do with subject pedagogy; issues to do with the relationship between the subject and broader educational aims and objectives in society, and the philosophy and sociology of education; and issues to do with the development of the subject and its future in the twenty-first century.

Each book consequently presents key debates that subject teachers will need to understand, reflect on and engage in as part of their professional development. Chapters have been designed to highlight major questions, to consider the evidence from research and practice and to arrive at possible answers. Some subject books or chapters offer at least one solution or a view of the ways forward, whereas others provide alternative views and leave readers to identify their own solution or view of the ways forward. The editors expect readers of the series to want to pursue the issues raised, and so chapters include suggestions for further reading, and questions for further debate. The chapters and questions could be used as stimuli for debate in subject seminars or department meetings, or as topics for assignments or classroom research. The books are targeted at all those with a professional interest in the subject, and in particular: student teachers learning to teach the subject in the primary or secondary school; newly qualified teachers; teachers with a subject co-ordination or leadership role, and those preparing for such responsibility; mentors, tutors, trainers and advisers of the groups mentioned above.

Each book in the series has a cross-phase dimension. This is because the editors believe it is important for teachers in the primary and secondary phases to look at subject teaching holistically, particularly in order to provide for continuity and progression, but also to increase their understanding of how children learn. The balance of chapters that have a cross-phase relevance, chapters that focus on issues which are of particular concern to primary teachers and chapters that focus on issues which secondary teachers are more likely to need to address, varies according to the issues relevant to different subjects. However, no matter where the emphasis is, authors have drawn out the relevance of their topic to the whole of each book's intended audience.

Because of the range of the series, both in terms of the issues covered and its cross-phase concern, each book is an edited collection. Editors have commissioned new writing from experts on particular issues who, collectively, will represent many different perspectves on subject teaching. Readers should not expect a book in this series to cover a full range of issues relevant to the subject, or to offer a completely unified view of subject teaching, or that every issue will be dealt with discretely, or that all aspects of an issue will be covered. Part of what each book in this series offers to readers is the opportunity to explore the inter-relationships between positions in debates and, indeed, among the debates themselves, by identifying the overlapping concerns and competing arguments that are woven through the text.

The editors are aware that many initiatives in subject teaching currently originate from the centre, and that teachers have decreasing control of subject content, pedagogy and assessment strategies. The editors strongly believe that for teaching to remain properly a vocation and a profession, teachers must be invited to be part of a creative and critical dialogue about subject teaching, and encouraged to reflect, criticize, problem-solve and innovate. This series is intended to provide teachers with a stimulus for democratic involvement in the development of subject teaching.

Susan Capel,
Jon Davison,
James Arthur and
John Moss
May 1999

Introduction

It is the intention of this book to stimulate thought and ideas which will enable student teachers and teachers to build on existing good practice, and to develop a theoretical perspective which may be lacking in current and recent Initial Teacher Training courses. Many of the issues contained within this volume are addressed in a range of texts, including books and journal articles. This book draws together many eminent writers in the field, and my role has been to invite them to develop their thoughts on a range of themes related to modern foreign language teaching and learning. This has led to a comprehensive list of topics being covered, but a thread of an argument running through each of the chapters. This permeating argument is a plea that theorists and practitioners join together to re-examine the so-called communicative approach to foreign language teaching and learning, which has developed and benefited learners over the last twenty years. My colleagues do not condemn and reject the approach, which has developed to the extent that it can be seen to underpin the recommendations contained in the National Curriculum documentation, but see a need to develop it further to prevent the devaluing of the subject as an academic discipline.

The book is divided into four sections. The first section, an *Historical Overview* contains two Chapters. Firstly, Field tracks the development of an approach to MFL teaching and learning, which, as it stands in the National Curriculum, represents an eclectic assortment of methods, which teachers have found to be successful. The chapter points out, too, how an approach to MFL teaching and learning has always led to heated discussions amongst educationalists. Pachler in the second chapter presents a critique of what he calls the British variant of communicative language teaching (CLT). He explains that teachers do have options and choices, and that even within the overarching label 'Communicative' there are alternatives available to the teacher.

The second section retains a theoretical perspective, yet focuses on classroom issues. *Issues Concerned with the Content of and a Definition of, Modern Foreign Languages* captures the content of many staffroom discussions, in which MFL teachers find themselves embroiled. Why are teachers of MFLs so committed to the teaching and learning of the subject in a Britain which appears to resist everything European, and why should the school system restrict itself to the main European languages when a large proportion of our population are already speakers of other languages? Lawes and Anderson address these questions with great authority and enthusiasm. Britain is almost unique in that it delays the learning of foreign languages until children are of secondary school age, and Sharpe and Driscoll question the impact of this policy decision, and the appropriateness of adopting secondary style approaches to teaching on a voluntary basis to younger children. Despite this array of issues, which weigh heavily on teachers, Lawes galvanises the views of many in a chapter explaining the unique contribution learning MFLs makes to young people's development.

In the section *Issues Associated with Pedagogy*, colleagues maintain a very positive and forward looking outlook. Schools make many decisions which impact upon the quality of learning. The grouping of pupils according to ability as opposed to mixed ability teaching remains a heated debate. Girls seem to be better at MFLs than boys. Many argue that able learners' needs have been neglected, as MFL teachers' doors have been opened to a wider range of learner types. The types of learners faced by teachers has also contributed to the development of a 'best fit' approach to the teaching of the subject. This section also includes an examination of issues which should not be forgotten. Barry Jones and Jane Jones provide timely reminders of the place of cultural awareness and grammar in MFL programmes. They do so in a way which does not look back to a golden age, but which presents exciting and stimulating methods and techniques which will appeal to both learners and teachers. Macaro questions the dogmatic approach to exclusive use of the target language, and recommends that teachers optimise the use, yet consider occasions when learners will gain form use of their native language in terms of learning, rather than in terms of expediency. Macaro provides a conceptual framework for all teachers. Bax considers an appraisal of the use of ICT and warns against viewing computers and technology as a salvation. He identifies the value of technology, and points out the need for teachers to be selective in its use. There has been a quiet revolution in assessment methods and external examination systems over the past decade, and Adams recommends careful analysis of pupils' needs and the matching of appropriate assessment methods. She carefully explains that assessment is part and parcel of the teaching and learning process, and therefore presents the advantages and disadvantages of different approaches on this basis. Pachler and Allford examine the potential of literature at a time when many teachers are lamenting the loss of extended reading in particularly A level classes. Harris notes the need for independent use of languages in all skills, and condemns over reliance on the teacher for the practice of receptive and productive language skills. Her response is to encourage teachers to build in a progression of autonomous language learning skills into programmes of study. Harris sees the need to teach how to learn, despite the pressure from assessment performance tables to teach what to learn.

The last section, *Broader Issues*, overlaps with the content of preceding sections to a degree. It picks up on many of the questions and issues raised, yet provides a positive look to the future. Coyle looks at ways of making MFLs more relevant and stimulating to the learner. Her position is that MFLs can and should link up with other areas of the curriculum more. The very content of the curriculum, taken as a whole can be seen to promote such an approach, rather than to require teachers to retain a rigid, compartmentalised approach to planning teaching and learning. Pomphrey adopts a similar stance, less from a 'content' point of view, but more in examining the transferability of skills and learning processes.

The book as whole does have a theme and a message; to re-examine the communicative approach. As yet, complete answers are not presented, but teachers should be aware of the questions posed. The book is not a manifesto; it is an invitation to engage in professional debate and dialogue.

How to use this book

Each chapter is focused on a particular issue. Section headings and chapter titles should assist the reader to identify those of interest. At the end of each chapter, their is a short summary of questions raised in the form of an *Editor's note*. The editor has also provided some guidance to readers, as to which chapters within this book are linked to the content of the chapter being read. This serves as a indicator for useful 'further reading' to enable the reader to develop a wider perspective on specific concerns. A reference list follows each chapter, again serving to acknowledge the source of ideas and information, but also to guide the reader to other relevant texts.

Readers should not feel obliged to read this book from beginning to end. It is a complement to practice, and also a means of informing practice. As issues arise in the classroom and outside the classroom, this text should serve as a way of informing teachers, and helping them to devise answers of their own. All the contributors are experts in their field, and each chapter provides an introduction to the key issues associated with MFL teaching and learning.

Part 1
An historical overview

1 The changing place of Modern Foreign Languages in the curriculum

Kit Field

Introduction

There is no tradition of pedagogy in the history of compulsory education in England and Wales. From Victorian times, when MFLs first appeared on the school curriculum, no formal teacher training was required, and native speakers were employed to service the perceived needs of the British upper middle classes. In a mood of desperation, and in face of pedagogical studies emerging from their home countries, native speaking teachers resorted to self help by forming their own 'Société Nationale des Professeurs de Français en Angleterre'. This legacy of eclecticism has remained a striking feature of education in the form of conflict and confusion of thought as theorists have striven to relate aims and purposes of education to teaching, learning and pedagogy (Simon, 1994 in Moon and Mayes). Judge (1974) states that the tensions between a traditional academic emphasis and a notion of communication and international understanding have never been more at odds than in discussions centring around MFLs. Undoubtedly there has been a series of trends and recommended methodologies, and within the field of MFL teaching and learning more than in most other subject disciplines. The pragmatic alternative to following a stipulated pedagogy has led to a polarisation of teaching and learning styles, linked inextricably to the perceived purposes of teaching and learning MFLs in secondary schools. Richardson (1981) asserts that recommended approaches to teaching foreign languages have always been linked to the perceived purposes. With no formal direction until 1988, teachers have been able to determine their own aims and objectives, resulting in the view that '. . . there is no such thing as a new idea in language teaching' (Swarbrick, 1994: 1).

Reform and counter-reform movements throughout the century have led commentators to draw on the metaphor of 'pendulum swings' (see Hawkins 1987, Goodson 1985, Richardson 1981). In articulating recommended approaches, theorists make reference to general learning theories and theories of language learning and acquisition, which in turn are promoted and supported by governmental backing in the form of reports and education acts. At the same time, teachers have struggled to cater for an ever-changing 'clientele' relying on their own collective and individual intuition. The obvious need to motivate and stimulate learners is a key to success as a language teacher, in both a pragmatic and philosophical sense. Palmer (1922) a theorist with ideas before his time, attempted to identify features and principles from a range of methodologies, upon which teachers could build their own understanding of good practice. Palmer noted that no course of language study could be designed until much is known about the students for whom the course is intended. However, a respect for practitioners' views, and the role of the professionals has never been formalised, although groups and movements have evolved. As a consequence methodological standpoints have become increasingly entrenched. As 'Action Research' (see Elliott 1991, McNiff, 1988 and others) is seen as individuals' and groups' means of improving practice, this notion of interpreting frameworks and guidance is perpetuated as the best way to progress.

New approaches develop as a reaction to existing practices, and lessons from the past have been incorporated into new recommendations. Periodically attempts have been made to crystallise thoughts and beliefs by institutionalising dogma associated with periods of time in the history of MFL teaching and learning. The most important such event has been the implementation of the National Curriculum orders. The national criteria for GCSE (DES/WO, 1985) represented a consensus between teachers, examiners and government. The confusion between different factions of the profession continued into the late 1980s and early 1990s, evident in the publication of the National Curriculum Statutory Orders. A set of purposes for teaching and learning MFLs emerged, and appeared to be a compromise between conflicting parties, rather than as a consensus. The purposes contain aspects which appeal to all teachers, yet at the same time, contentious issues to the very same body of professionals.

The purposes (DES/WO, 1990: 3) attempt to be all things to all teachers. In an age of accountability and of inspection mania, one sign of good practice is the visible fulfilment of the stated purposes.

The place of a brief historical study is to analyse the validity, consistency and coherence of such a diverse set of aims. Again, electric pragmatism is the only solution for practising teachers. They are compelled to muddle through and to develop and interpret good practice in their own way. Each 'purpose' owes its presence in the National Curriculum documentation to the power of arguments justifying its position in conflicting theories and consequent ratification by government actions.

The educational purposes of learning foreign languages

The purposes (DES/WO 1990: 3) listed below are subsequently explained. Their position in the official documentation is justified historically. The purposes are:

- to develop the ability to use language effectively for purposes of practical communication;
- to form a sound base of the skills, language and attitudes required for further study, work and leisure;

- to offer insights into the culture and civilisation of the countries where the target language is spoken;
- to develop an awareness of the nature of language and language learning;
- to provide enjoyment and intellectual stipulations;
- to encourage positive attitudes to foreign language learning and to speakers of foreign languages and a sympathetic approach to other cultures and civilisations;
- to promote learning of skills of more general application (e.g. analysis, memorising, drawing of inferences).

To develop the ability to use the language effectively for purposes of practical communication

The place of communication has not always been valued in MFL teaching and learning. Indeed the acceptance of what has been seen as a purely practical, functional purpose, has been treated as a devaluing of the subject in academic terms. This has placed the notion of practical communication in conflict with that of developing 'an awareness of the nature of language and language learning' (DES/WO, 1990: 3). Nevertheless, philosophers throughout time have related foreign language learning to the acquisition of the mother tongue. John Locke (1690) applied the empiricist philosophy of learning through experience, and this recommendation for immersion techniques can be found in the views of (John Stuart Mill, 1867), and indeed (Bertrand Russell, 1940).

The acceptance of phonetics as a discipline worthy of study in the late nineteenth century placed sound systems at the core of language learning. The understanding and production of sounds, inevitably led to a belief that oral communication is at the heart of the language learning process. Viëtor's, (1882) seminal work '*Der Sprachunterricht muß umkehren*' criticised the prominent 'grammar/translation' methods, recommending the need to hear and speak the target language as a starting point. Native speakers of French, frustrated by the approach in schools formed their own society, demanding that French should be taught as a living language. The development of the Direct Method – instructions in the target language, and maximum exposure to it in the classroom – quickly became accepted as an alternative approach. The conflict between those promoting a functional approach with the universities representing academic centres quickly evolved. Progress was hindered by the non-acceptance of oral methods by the examinations boards. The works of (Palmer, 1917, 1921, 1922) influenced linguists in the mid-twentieth century. The insistence of many modern theorists that the learning of language should be based around the conveyance of meaning and that meaningless grammar-based drills should be abandoned, owes much to the works of Palmer.

The Direct Method did not go so far as to reject grammatical explanation, although Gouin (1853), representing advocates of '*The Natural Method*', did recommend the application of language in vocational, professional and personal contexts, which became accepted as the major motivational factor in the learning process.

The Incorporated Association of Assistant Masters' (IAAM, 1956) public-ation *The Teaching of Modern Foreign Languages* is another example of teachers acting independently in the face of adversity. The paper concluded that more able linguists were required in day to day workings in commerce. The 'vocational' needs gave even greater credence to the demand for effective communication skills.

Developments in technology in the period following the Second World War provided the advocates of communication with new ammunition. Tape recorders and language laboratories became commonplace and associated practices led to the formation in 1962 of the Audio Visual Language Association. Once again a greater emphasis was placed on the spoken word. In its early days, this behaviourist approach could be seen to recommend many techniques contained within the later communicative approach, which in turn, would replace the audio-visual methods. The main tenets of the audio-lingual method were that there is a primacy of the spoken word over written text, that the four language skills of speaking, listening, reading and writing could be separated, and that grammar is a set of structures which should be learnt inductively.

Audio-visual methods were not a natural precursor to the communicative approach. Indeed, in contrast to the post-war BBC broadcasts, audio-visual techniques did not draw on colloquial language in authentic situations. The stimulus/response approach received due criticism, even at the time. The Incorporated Association of Head Masters (IAHM) recommended in 1966, at their annual conference, that communication, not habit formation, should underpin discussions of method, course and materials design. Nevertheless the method did establish the spoken word and a sound system as a viable alternative to the study of grammatical rules.

These beliefs and values fed into the examination system. In 1962, the Secondary Schools Examination Council (SSEC) disbanded and was replaced by first the Curriculum Study Group, and in 1964 by the Schools Council. The Nuffield Foundation, which had pioneered audio-visual techniques and was assisted by the DES secured agreement that the vocabulary presented in courses such as 'En Avant', and 'Vorwärts' would be incorporated in the forthcoming CSE syllabuses.

Just as phonetics influenced the Direct Method, new linguistic theories in the 1960s eased the development of the Communicative Approach. *The Speech Act Theory* (see Searle, 1969) shifted attention from habit formation through rote learning to the conveyance of meaning by dint of an illocutionary force underpinning language use. Searle argued that speakers use language for a purpose, which is more powerful than simply the meanings of words. Utterances carry a force – whether it is an apology, a question, a demand, a request etc. This new description of linguistic competence led to the evolution of functional/ notional syllabuses, central to the communicative approach.

Entry to the Common Market, and subsequent analyses of British business' rate of success in Europe (e.g. Barclays Banks International *Factors for International Success (The Barclays Bank Report on Export Development in France,*

Germany and the UK, 1979), and (BETRO *Language and Export Performance: A Study prepared for the BETRO Committee*, RSA, London, 1979), placed communication and language learning firmly in a functional context.

Work in the Council of Europe, led by John Trim, and the publication of Threshold Levels (Van Ek, 1972) led to a tighter definition of adult learner needs, and a system of credit transfer. Both of these developments were transferred to secondary education contexts in the form of short-term communicative goals and defined syllabuses. These in turn were the two key features of the Graded Objectives Movement, and the explosion of local organisations offering graded assessments in the late 1970s and early 1980s. GOML (Graded Objectives in Modern Languages) signalled a full implementation of the so-called communicative approach. Teachers took control of the syllabuses and assessment methods in an attempt to meet the needs of the ever-broadening range of learner types.

The audio-visual approach collapsed. In 1977 the Audio Visual Language Association renamed itself the British Association of Language Teachers (BALT). The design and implementation of the statutory National Curriculum Orders acknowledged the work of GOML and institutionalised the communicative approach. Practical communication became a formal purpose of modern language teaching. However the Direct Method, and the audio-visual revolution influenced developments. Strategies and teaching techniques have been drawn into the newer language teaching methods, and they have contributed enormously to the shift in emphasis from mental, linguistic agility to a focus on the message and the spoken word. Successful application of the communicative approach, and the fulfilment of the aim 'to develop the ability to use the language for purposes of practical communication' do, therefore, require a sound professional knowledge and understanding of a range of linked modern foreign language teaching trends.

To form a sound base of the skills, language and attitudes required for further study, work and leisure

The Cartesian principles of logic and reason at the centre of meaning was applied to language teaching and learning in the sixteenth century. Swarbrick (1994) regards this philosophy as the root of the grammar/translation method. Grammar is a set of basic rules embedded in language. The manipulation of universals is consequently a basis for learning and mastery. Hawkins (1987) coined the phrase 'apprenticeship' in relation to language learning. Formal language teaching has only ever occupied a small proportion of curriculum time in England and Wales. The process of learning a foreign language is merely an introduction to strategies and techniques upon which s/he can draw at a later date, when proficiency in the given language becomes more necessary.

The learning of Latin, from the Middle Ages onwards fits in with this analogy. Swarbrick (1994) notes that it was not so much the lingua franca of Europe, but more the key to scholarship. The study of Latin was not valid in its own right, but in the sense that it was a means of disciplining the mind.

This vantage point has never been accepted blindly (Comenius, 1648), quoted in Jelinek (1953) presented a system and process for language learning. The recommended process involved the presentation of exemplars leading to a precept and imitation. Short chunks of language should be mastered before long, simple before complex, and general applications should be understood before the particular. Regular patterns precede the irregular. Such a pedagogy provides support to the learner as well as to the teacher.

It is interesting to note that the work of Comenius was not translated until 1896, at a time when pedagogy was on the agenda for educationalists. Whether or not teachers adhered to Comenius' philosophy is not the question. The very justification of a modern language as a curriculum subject, and the discussions on the merits of immersion and grammar/translation methods placed the issue on the agenda, and articulated the skills and strategies necessary for effective teaching and learning.

As early as 1862, a Royal Commission examined the value of foreign language teaching. Its conclusion that oral proficiency served no educational purpose, and that grammar and reading skills facilitated future study placed the mastery of grammar as a justifiable educational goal. Dr Hiley, in the Journal of Education responded to the newly formed 'Société des Professeurs de Français en Angleterre' by stating categorically that grammar is a mental discipline and is the 'pith and marrow' of a language.

On the other hand, the advent of the newer Direct Method presented a different picture. Grammar remained as essential, but language learning was self-perpetuating. Inductive grammar learning was not a belittling of grammar, but of the traditional, systematic method of teaching it. Government reports from the 1860s confirmed this stance. The publication of the Clarendon Commission Report (Public Schools Commmission, 1864) and the Schools Enquiry Commission (1868) reaffirmed the superiority of Latin as a school subject, in that it provided less of a utilitarian outcome, and more of a mental discipline. Modern Foreign Languages could only justify its position on the curriculum if it could challenge Latin as a form of mental gymnastics. Evidently, the basis of skills for future study was a sound mastery of the grammar of a language at the turn of the century.

The assessment of learners of a foreign language at the beginning of the century served to reinforce the supremacy of grammar. Despite the advances made by the proponents of the Direct Method, the establishment of the School Certificate, and the Higher School Certificate perpetuated the triumvirate of grammar, translation and literature. This examination system lasted until 1950.

Indeed, as new GCE examinations replaced the existing system in 1952, the IAAM issued guidance in the form of The Teaching of Modern Languages. Whitehead, (1996) clearly feels that the advice to new examination boards to build on the practice of the School Certificate, ensured that the key skills required for language study were those of grammar mastery. Evidently the main purpose of language learning was to master the grammar, before attaining a high level of communicative competence.

Assessment techniques were overtaken by a series of events. The comprehensivisation of schools from 1965, and the development of audio-visual materials by the Nuffield Foundation meant that new learners, with new skills, had to be assessed. The fourteen CSE examination boards, consisting of panels of practising teachers broke the autonomy of the universities. Use of language and oral proficiency grew in status. The ensuing Mode 2 examinations and Mode 3 course work options led to learners being compelled to develop skills and to undergo different learning processes. Imitation, repetition and therefore exposure to the language became the buzz words. Audio-visual materials emanating from France (TAVOR), and increased opportunities for foreign travel offered the learner a new set of challenges.

Corder (1981) accepted errors as a natural part of the learning process. Experimentation was the key. Krashen's (1981) work continued to demote the place of grammar. Indeed a focus on grammar was seen to inhibit learning. A willingness to attempt to communicate, and an ability to learn from one's mistakes were now the key skills required for future continual language development.

The development of learning skills is inextricably linked to the shift towards communicative competence. Successful communication motivates, and learners' growing awareness of effective strategies is paramount if linguistic and communicative competence is to continue to develop. Two strands of development are clear. Both communication and grammatical knowledge form the basis for future study and language use. The challenge is, of course, to offer both to learners, when historically the two are presented as mutually exclusive.

To offer insights into the culture and civilisation of the countries where the target language is spoken

An understanding and appreciation of the culture of the countries where essentially French is spoken has never been high on the agenda. Cultural awareness has been seen as a by-product of learning a language. Early in the century advocates of the Direct Method stressed how improved French and German learning would contribute to international goodwill, if the subjects were regarded as part of a modern humanist curriculum.

The insistence in the first half of the century on grammatical accuracy removed the need for cultural understanding. Languages as a mental discipline did not include intentional presentations of cultural aspects. Nevertheless, the SSEC (Secondary Schools Examination Council, 1963, Examination Bulletin No. 1: 62) assumed that as pupils embarked upon the new CSE he language. European studies courses offered the opportunity to learners to become acquainted with different cultures through formal study, as an alternative to language study.

As a progression from the graded objectives qualifications offered by St Martin's College, Lancaster, a vocational slant was provided by materials for older pupils. Such an approach provided a British context for language use.

Pupils continued with a communicative approach, yet were situated in petrol stations, café's and tourist information offices dealing with imaginary French/German/Spanish tourists to this country.

The opportunity to encounter insights to the culture and civilisation is now for the first time a fixed and set element of language study. Once again teachers are faced with fresh challenges. To date the extra-curricular opportunities associated with language study have become an entitlement to all. The need is, therefore, to incorporate new style materials and activities to meet such demands.

To develop an awareness of the nature of language and language learning

One of the age old reasons for justifying MFLs on the school timetable has been that it offers an insight into the structure of language in general terms. Indeed, the move to introduce modern languages into the curriculum has not intentionally been to offer an alternative to the study of Latin. Even as early as 1632, Comenius (in *Didactica Magna*) recommended a sequence of language learning, first students should master the mother tongue, second a modern foreign language, and last Latin (and/or Greek). From the outset, a modern foreign language was deemed to be a useful, practical skill, which in fact widened its acceptance as an academic discipline. It was, in effect, the collapse of Latin as the lingua franca in Europe that had the effect of elevating MFLs as a school subject. Language teaching expertise had developed through the reading of Latin, and a conservative force to use Modern Foreign Languages to fill the vacuum created by the decline of Latin. In 1879, H.W. Eve, quoted by Hawkins, (1981: 113) asserted at a Headteachers conference that 'your (MFL teachers) first object is to discipline the mind, your second to give a knowledge of French or German'.

Nevertheless, towards the late nineteenth century the Direct Method did gather force, despite considerable opposition from academics. Indeed in 1912 (Circular 797), the Board of Education recommended the continuation of the grammar/translation method, as the staff in schools appeared unequal to the task of delivering a foreign language through the Direct Method. Gilbert (1953) in 'The Origins of the Reform Movement', cites examples of exercises from text books published early in the century. Sentences designed for translation were presented in a disconnected way, in ways that learners can identify units of grammar in manipulating the language.

The acceptance of phonetics and the building of language study around phonetics clearly impacted on the learners' experience. With the emphasis on exposure to the target language inevitably learners were able to focus on the sound systems, including pronunciation. The approach was supported by practising teachers, and was reflected by developments in Europe, which also referred to the 'Reform Method' stressing phonetics, communication, and association of words with objects and ideas (Jesperson, 1904). Although writers, such as Jesperson were not denouncing the value of grammar, but recommending an inductive approach, the establishment view was still clearly that unless grammatical structures were not presented overtly, then the status and profile of MFLs was not on a par with Latin. Scholarships offered in classics at university outnumbered those offered in a Modern Language ten to one.

The continued decline of Latin did lead to concern being expressed at governmental level. The Crowther Report (HMI, 1959) noted that as Latin died out, the whole basis of language teaching needed a rethink.

Until very recently, of course, the study of Modern Foreign Languages was restricted to the most able. After 1944, the eleven plus served to segregate children who had scored highly on verbal reasoning tests from those who had not. The right to learn a language was earnt by those with high level language skills. It was therefore no real surprise that the study of MFLs was not viewed as a means of improving pupils awareness of language. However the newer methodologies, including audio-visual schemes presented a process of learning based on mother tongue acquisition in order to justify the approval.

Following the Crowther Report (1959), a programme entitled 'Linguistics and English Teaching' was set up under Professor M. Halliday. The outcomes of the project were not published until 1971, by Doughty, P., Pearce, J. and Thornton, G. (eds). The aim of the project was to develop in pupils an awareness of what language is and how it is used, and at the same time extend their competence in using it.

At the same time as attention was focused on children's language development, Chomsky (1957) challenged Skinner's behaviourist approach to foreign language learning. The mind numbing effect of constant repetition was denounced in favour of the belief that all speakers had an innate ability to generate language through the absorption of examples (Language Acquisition Device, LAD). This revolutionised the world of linguistics. Through experience of language, learners automatically developed a sense of creativity, and could transform samples of language into personalised outputs (Bruner, 1975) built on this discovery, developing a theory based around a 'Language Acquisition Support System'. Teachers are thereby encouraged to focus on strategies for learning to enable the LAD (Chomsky, 1957) to be activated. Inevitably learners are made more aware of the learning process as teachers strive to develop a communicative competence into an 'analytic' competence.

The academic establishment could not fail to be influenced. The change of examination formats began in 1963 when the Modern Language Association Examinations Project, sponsored by the Nuffield Foundation designed experimental examinations, which through the inclusion of oral, pronunciation, multiple choice and aural comprehension allowed pupils to demonstrate skills acquired throughout the programme of study, as opposed to demonstrating a knowledge of course content. Otter (1968), the director of the project went as far as to recommend a separation of guided composition exercises from objective grammar tests. Learners following such courses, inevitably focused on the development of skills, and gained a different perspective in terms of an understanding of language.

The Bullock Report (HMI, 1975) continued the theme of needing to address learners' language skills, and the media reported outcries in response to ten years of comprehensivisation. The report recognised the 'horizontal' structure of a language curriculum, in that language is used in all subjects, and a consistent approach by teachers – all subjects was of immense help. It was, though, almost unbelievable that Modern Languages departments received no acknowledgements, and no recommendations in the whole report. Once again, it seems, the establishment did not recognise MFL departments as major contributors to the development of language skills.

Despite the demise of audio-visual techniques, the underpinning philosophy of second language acquisition skill holds firm. The paradigm of 'presentation, explication, repetition, exploitation' (CREDIF, 1963) does structure the process of language learning. One problem for learners was that the examination systems gave no credit for undergoing the process. In 1977, HMI commented that teachers should '. . . offer pupils a terminal objective that they can perceive for themselves' (HMI, 1977: 2)

The Graded Objectives Movement in Languages (GOML) gave pupils the opportunity to recognise and use short-term learning strategies. The National Co-ordinating Committee (for GOML) circulated newsletters and disseminated the outcomes of research projects at annual conferences from 1979. The structures for developing learning strategies stemmed from the very negative HMI report on MFL teaching in eighty-three comprehensive schools (1977). A three year project, funded by Nuffield to identify good practice in response to the HMI report, identified aspects of good practice, included focused attention paid to general language development.

The Kingman (HMI, 1988) and Cox (HMI, 1989) reports recognised the influence of foreign language learning on pupils' language development for the first time. Clear recommendations were made that MFL teachers should join forces with English teachers to develop whole school language across the curriculum projects.

It seems almost absurd now that one could not recognise the value of learning a foreign language in terms of increasing language awareness and learning skills. However the supremacy of Latin early in the century, and the continued belief that Modern Languages were utilitarian failed to lead to a culture of interdisciplinary co-operation. Only from 1981 were MFLs seen as an entitlement to all pupils, and indeed was viewed by many as a hindrance to pupils with general language problems. Only now, following the National Curriculum Statutory Requirements is MFL teaching and learning seen as a means of improving the whole education of children.

To provide enjoyment and intellectual stimulation

Modern Foreign Languages teaching has undergone periods of great enthusiasm, and subsequent periods of disillusionment. Indeed the short periods of time when the subject has enjoyed popularity and a sense of future hope share historical features. During the late nineteenth century, discoveries in the field of linguistics, technological inventions (telephone and phonograph) increased opportunities for foreign travel, and a broadening of the range of pupils to be taught the subject, mirror similar developments in the 1960s. The 1902 Education Act led to the growth of maintained grammar schools signalling a period of exuberance. The introduction and partial acceptance of The Direct Method, based on findings in the field of phonetics presented a form of a solution to the new pupils to be taught. The success of MFL teaching was acknowledged in Circular 7.97 (Board of Education, 1912), which Hawkins (1984) quotes as a major contribution to '. . . raising modern languages to a position of dignity in the curriculum' (p. 133).

The success, however was short lived. The First World War put a stop to educational development, and the introduction of the School Certificate and Higher School Certificate reverted to the assessment of skills necessary to cope with a grammar/translation method. The insistence that Modern Foreign Languages contained serious academic rigour, perpetuated the belief that MFLs were a subject to be restricted to the most able of pupils. Expansion beyond the grammar schools was slow, and even as late as 1963, Newsom (HMI 1963) that only 30 per cent of pupils in half of the secondary modern schools studied French.

Anthony Crossland's Circular 10/65 (DES, 1965), launching comprehensive schools as the norm, triggered another period of development. Coupled with the technological boom, and what turned out to be false hopes for the tape recorder and the language laboratory, offered an exciting prospect for the growing number of pupils. CREDIF (1963) launched a series of materials for audio-visual methods which built on (Skinner, 1957) new behaviourist learning theories. All had confidence in the Nuffield Foundation/Schools Council Pilot Scheme, which further extended the study of French to pupils of primary and secondary school age. This (Nuffield Foundation Schools Council, 1969) and the establishment of the National Association of Language Advisors in the same year confirmed this feeling of confidence and hope.

All teachers recognise the importance of motivation. External forces (i.e. the proposed entry into the Common Market and easy access to mainland Europe), as well as the buzz of excitement within the world of education could not help but have an impact on the sense of enjoyment experienced by pupils.

However, by the end of the 1960s the popularity of the subject began to fizzle out. Despite the formal acknowledgement (HMI, 1949) – that MFLs were important for vocational reasons, little was done to improve provision. In 1967, the universities gave up the MFL requirement for degree study. The Schools Council Working Paper No. 28 recognised MFL study to be a middle-class prerogative, and that oral work in courses concentrated on potential home to home exchanges. Emmans *et al.* (1974) surveyed the career destinations of MFL graduates, and concluded that proficiency in a foreign language was a useful adjunct, but that there was little demand for specialists. Numbers of candidates for 'A' level study, particularly amongst boys, dropped significantly between 1970 and 1975. Numbers entering French examinations dropped by 17 per cent but more significant was the drop in other subjects (German 31 per cent, Spanish 11 per cent, and Russian 46 per cent); reversing the hopes and aspirations articulated in the Annan Report (1962).

The Burstall Report (HMI, 1974) brought the Primary French Project to an abrupt end, citing the tape recorder as an object of detestation. Technological advances proved not to be the saviour of language learners. In 1977, the HMI report 'Modern Languages in Comprehensive Schools' discredited MFLs as a comprehensive school subject. The press jumped on allegations in the reports that the 'failures' were attributable in part to bad planning, the non-existence of schemes of work, unclear objectives and inappropriate teaching approaches. Amid such a climate, it is hard to imagine how pupils could feel inspired!

The advent of the Graded Objectives Movement offered some form of a rescue. Mitchell (1994) in Swarbrick suggests that the communicative approach was a pragmatic response to the failure of the two dominant approaches to date. Supported by new linguistic theories, the GOML movement gathered momentum. Page (1996) reported that in so-called GOML areas, the post-14 uptake rose to 66 per cent in 1981. Swarbrick (1994) attributed this success to GOML, and the new joint 16+ examinations, demonstrating that teachers themselves, working collaboratively were able to assess and motivate the whole ability range in schools. The success of a more student-centred, short-term goal-oriented and functional language programme is well documented in Buckby (1981) and the Graded Objectives for Modern Languages (Schools Council).

Due recognition to the movement was paid in the National Criteria for GCSE (DES/WO, 1985) and lastly in the production of the National Curriculum Orders (DES/WO, 1990).

Motivation comes in many forms. To oblige teachers to stimulate and provide enjoyment is a tall order. The effect of external factors must be taken into account, and teachers can learn lessons from the past. Teachers do have the expertise, and evidently carefully planned courses and programmes based upon realistic and authentic needs without an over-reliance on new technology do hold an appeal. Good practice involves the sharing of ideas and a flexibility of approach enabling a meeting of pupils' and society's needs.

To encourage positive attitudes to foreign language learning and to speakers of foreign languages and a sympathetic approach to other cultures and civilisations

From 1882, and the formation of the 'Société Nationale des Professeurs de Francais en Angleterre', there has always been a sense of betrayal for the French in terms of how and to what level their language has been taught in England. Two outcomes of the first annual conference of the society sum up the views of French teachers. First, it recommended that the subject be taught as a living language, and second that it be taught by native speakers. The resistance by the academic institutions to accept French as a language worthy of academic status undoubtedly harmed international relations. Elsewhere in the world greater emphasis has been placed on the value of MFL learning, and particularly learning languages at an earlier age.

If pre-puberty learning opportunities are lost, ground may never be made up. The open-mindedness of children to new cultures is well understood, as is the resistance to new ideas and ways by adolescents seeking to establish their own identity. The abandonment of the Primary French project following the Burstall Report (HMI, 1974) has had a lasting effect on attitudes of learners to MFL learning ever since.

In Europe, Stern (1963) noted that the growing interdependence of European countries was a stimulus for foreign language learning, in his report of the 1962 UNESCO conference. Indeed from 1962–1973, a 35 per cent increase in the number of pupils studying French took place, although there is no evidence of a similar improvement of attitudes. The HMI Report (1977) revealed considerable dissatisfaction of learners with the subject.

Nevertheless, during the same ten years, access to European cultures did improve. The transferral of responsibility for language assistants in 1964 from the DES to the CBEVE triggered a 50 per cent increase in assistantships in England and Wales over ten years. At the same time the CBEVE set up more and more programmes facilitating teachers' visits, itself leading to a greater number of trips and exchanges.

Presenting the culture of countries where the target language is spoken is inevitably enhanced by direct contact with native speakers, both at home and abroad. The status of such cultures is inevitably dependent upon pictures painted by the press, and international economic and political relations. Good practice by teachers is to offer opportunities for contact, which have, and will inevitably continue to increase.

To promote learning of skills of more general application (e.g. analysis, memorising, drawing of inferences)

In learning and developing language learning skills, pupils inevitably develop skills which can be applied in other areas of learning. Pupils not following MFL courses are therefore denied the opportunities to reinforce and even develop new learning skills.

The compartmentalisation of subject learning in the secondary school is by no means an accident. As early as 1904, the Board of Education recommended against curriculum overlap, and brought to an end the admirable work on vocational programmes begun in the elementary schools.

The belief that studying a modern foreign language can have a positive effect on the learning of other subject disciplines has been researched in Canada and Wales. In the USA, Shelton (1957) noted the benefits to the mother tongue of MFL learning by comparing 'freshmen' test scores at Alabama Polytechnic Institute. Lopato (1961) came to a similar conclusion in his study of younger, third grade children.

Exactly how MFL learning can enhance broader learning skills is not fully known. Nevertheless, Mattingley (1972) concludes that successful language study is attributable, not to an innate capability, but to what he calls secondary learning strategies. If this is the case, MFL learning offers further opportunities to reinforce pre-existing learning techniques. An acceptance of the learner at the centre of the curriculum is therefore a key to success. If the learner is aware of the value of MFL learning as a means of assisting developing other curriculum areas, then inevitably the level of motivation will rise.

The argument supports the view that MFLs should be made available to non-specialist learners. The elitist nature of MFL learning through to the 1970s has persuaded teachers of the need to set by ability. Teacher-centred teaching methods encouraged a culture of reliance, and compartmentalisation led to a focus on higher level language learning skills. Nevertheless, the by-products of language learning have been officially recognised. 'Curriculum 11–16' (HMI, 1977) included a recommendation for a 'linguistic experience' and advised 10 per cent of curriculum time should be devoted to it.

Circular 14/77 (DES/WO, 1977) reiterated the recommendation for such a policy, and the subsequent 'Better Schools' (DES, 1985a) proposed that all pupils should have an entitlement to foreign language learning.

Donaldson (1978) suggests that MFL study leads to a language 'awareness', similar to the notion of 'analytic competence' in Bruner (1975). Bruner argued that language competence is not an automatic response but is stimulated through focused study. Three issues are therefore relevant. First, the GOML movement promoted a less teacher and more learner centred curriculum – demanding greater independence of pupils. Second, since the introduction of A/S levels (1987) non-specialists are encouraged to continue with MFL study, and therefore have the opportunity to improve general learning skills. Third, the need to teach strategies, i.e. how to learn, is currently being researched. Recent publications (e.g. Pomphrey 1996; Harris 1997) advocate the making public of 'how to learn', rather than teachers relying on pupils developing such skills as a by-product of language learning.

To develop pupils understanding of themselves and their own culture

Lado (1957) concluded that positive and negative transfer between languages relies on systematic comparison. The cross-over points, where languages and cultures coincide with others make learning easy. Points of difference, however are more problematic. Inevitably learners of an MFL make comparisons – it is how one learns. Such comparisons obviously heighten one's awareness of oneself and one's own culture. The contribution a MFL makes to inter-cultural awareness has already been covered, but it is important to note its value beyond learning about the foreign culture.

Learning an MFL is an experience. It requires particular social, as well as learning skills. Whitehead (1996) quite rightly notes that 'during the period 1904–1964, the value of modern languages in developing social skills was neglected at the expense of the development of mental cultivation and dis-cipline and the almost exclusive study of their written form.'

More contemporary approaches to the teaching of MFLs place the learning in a different context. The coverage of communicative acts in public situations requires an examination of cultural aspects – such as how to behave. Exposure to the country, customs and relationships, invites the learner to relate 'foreign' experiences to his/her own.

Hawkins (1996: 33) quotes Yuen Ren Chao (1968) who stated that '. . . the foreign language makes a different contribution from the mother tongue, and one that is complementary to it'.

The contribution of an MFL to general and language learning skills has been accounted for. Once again, however the application of learning processes acquired through MFL learning, in other curricular areas is undoubtedly valued. The inclusion of MFL in TVEI curricular modules justifies the inclusion of this particular aim in the National Curriculum documentation. Indeed the majority of pupils learning an MFL will not become fluent speakers. The principal outcomes are that they will develop in terms of communication, collaboration, co-operation and flexible, versatile learning skills.

Conclusion

Throughout the century a series of events and research projects have shaped the nature of MFL teaching and learning. Periodically authorities in the form of teacher associations and the government have taken stock, which has led to action which has tied together loose ends. Indeed the National Curriculum documentation has attempted to do this for education as a whole. The 1990 National Curriculum proposals provided useful points of reference, and delineated purposes for MFL teaching (DES/WO 1990). It is by tracing these purposes back that the origins of good practice can be identified. A definite historical process, supported by improved theoretical understanding can be seen in the developments. A shift in emphasis from the grammar/translation method, to a communicative approach is inevitably centred around the perceived aims and purposes of teaching MFLs. The need for proficiency in foreign languages for vocational purposes increased as Britain has become more involved with the economic affairs of Europe (see Emmans *et al.*, 1974). Vocational syllabuses and examinations (London Chamber of Commerce and Industry, RSA, BTEC, Institute of Linguists) throughout the 1980s stand testament to this need. From the early 1970s, universities have provided degree courses linked to social, political, economic and business programmes. Evidently good practice in the secondary school is, in part, measurable by the extent to which these demands are met.

Political and social issues are also of concern to the MFL teacher. From 1963 (Newsom Report, HMI, 1963) educationalists have had to consider the impact of travel opportunities and the need to provide a 'tourist knowledge' (p. 161) of another language. The Annan Report (1962) recommended a diversification of languages to be taught, notably the inclusion of Russian on the curriculum. The exuberance of the 1960s, coupled with the perceived political value of proficiency in languages led to the proliferation of language teachers' associations (1958 – Association of German Teachers, 1959 – Association of Italian teachers). It is clear that lessons from the past have been learnt. Leathes (1918) had stated in the first publication of Modern Studies that an ignorance of German culture and language had hampered preparation for and the prosecution of conflict (World War I).

The educational value of MFLs was hotly contested early in the century. The place of the subject as a replacement for Latin established its profile as a means of disciplining the mind. Phonetics, the Direct Method and technological advances appeared to facilitate learning through different methods. Eventually the functional value of proficiency in an MFL appears to have won the day. It is, though interesting to observe huddles of MFL teachers at in-service conferences lamenting the demise of grammatical study in modern courses. Such a concern is addressed, in part, by the post-Dearing National Curriculum Orders for MFLs.

There is undoubtedly a British resistance to foreign language learning. Teachers have to battle against a linguistic rationalism, and focus much attention on motivating pupils.

Good practice means learning lessons from the past. Fulfilling the stated purposes requires professional understanding, and the ability to make and justify decisions about how and what to teach pupils in one's charge.

Editor's note

Field traces the history of MFL reading and learning, pointing out how the metaphor of pendulum swings is appropriate. Teaching practices have emerged, as theorists and teachers have asserted their opinions and views, and as new needs have emerged, in the form of learners of differing needs and abilities. As the world outside the school environment has changed, then teaching technologies and methods have followed suit.

Without any dominant pedagogy structuring teaching and learning process, teachers have always adopted commonsense approaches which 'feel right', yet which can also be justified professionally in terms of the most recent dominant theory. The emergence of a so-called communicative approach in the 1980s, has not proven to be the answer to all problems. Theorists and teachers are now very ready to criticise the justification for a situational and functional approach, as in practice teachers have adapted and amended the model presented to them.

Linked chapters

This chapter serves as a historical introduction and therefore links with all chapters.

References

Annan, N. (1962) *Report on the Teaching of Russian* (The Annan Report), London: HMSO.

Barclays Bank International (1979) *Factors for International Success*, The Barclays Bank Report on Export Development in France, Germany and the UK.

BETRO (1979) *Language and Export Performance:* A study prepared for the BETRO Committee, London: RSA.

Board of Education (1902) *The Education Act*, London: HMSO.

—— (1912) *Memorandum on the Teaching of Modern Languages: Circular 7.97*, London: HMSO.

Bruner, J. S. (1975) 'Language as an instrument of thought', in A. Davies (ed.) *Problems of Language and Learning*, London: Heinemann.

Buckby, M. (1981) *Graded Objectives for Modern Languages Schools Council.*

Centre de Recherches et Etudes pour la Diffusion du Francais (1963) *Voix et Images*, Paris: CREDIF.

Chomsky, N. (1957) *Syntactic Structure*, Netherlands: Mouton.

Comenius, J. (1632 [1910, 1917]) *Didactica Magna, The Great Didactic of John Amos Comenius*, translated into English by A. W. Keatinge, London: A & C Black.

Corder, S. P. (1981) *Analysis and Inter Language*, Oxford: Oxford University Press.

DES (1959) *15–18 Report of Central Advisory Council for Education* (The Crowther Report) London: HMSO.

—— (1963) *Half our Future* (Newsom Report), London: HMSO.

—— (1965) *Circular 10/65*, London: HMSO.

—— (1974) *Primary French in the Balance* (The Burstall Report), London: HMSO.

—— (1975) *A Language for Life* (The Bullock Report), London: HMSO.

—— (1977) *Curriculum 11–16*, London: HMSO.

—— (1977) *Circular 14/77*,London: HMSO.

—— (1977) *Modern Languages in Comprehensive Schools*, London: HMSO.

—— (1985) *GCSE The National Criteria for French*, London: HMSO.

—— (1985a) *Better Schools*, London: HMSO.

—— (1988) *Report of the Committee of Inquiry into the Teaching of English Language* (The Kingman Report), London: HMSO.

—— (1989) *English for Ages 5–16* (The Cox Report), London: HMSO.

—— (1990) *Modern Foreign Languages for Ages 11–16* (National Curriculum), London: HMSO.

Donaldson, M. (1978) *Children's Minds*, London: Fontana.

Doughty, P., Pearce, J. and Thornton, G. (eds) (1971) *Language in Use*, London: Edward Arnold.

Elliott, J. (1991) *Action Research for Educational Change*, Milton Keynes: Open University Press.

Emmans, K., Hawkins, E. and Westley, A. (1974) *The Use of Foreign Languages in the Private Sector of Industry and Commerce*, York: York University Teaching Centre.

Gilbert, M. (1953) *The Origins of the Reform Movement in Modern Language Teaching, Research Review*, 4 (5+6).

Goodson, I. F. (1985) *Social Histories of the Secondary Curriculum*, Lewes: Falmer Press.

Gouin, F. (1853) *Language as a Means of Mental Culture and International Communication*, (see Hawkins 1984).

Harris, V. (1997) *Teaching Learners How to Learn: Strategy training in the ML classroom*, London: CILT.

Hawkins, E. (1981) *Modern Languages in the Curriculum*, London: Cambridge: Cambridge University Press.

—— (1984) *Awareness of Language: An Introduction*, Cambridge, Cambridge University Press.

—— (1987) *Modern Languages in the Curriculum*, Cambridge: Cambridge University Press (revised edition).

HMI (1949) *Teacher Education and Training, Report of a Committee of Inquiry*, London: HMSO.

—— (1977) *Maths, Science and Modern Languages in Maintained Schools*, London: HMSO.

IAAM (1956) *The Teaching of Modern Foreign Languages*, London: Incorporated Association of Assistant Masters.

IAHM (1966) *Conference Report*, London: IAHM.

Jelinek, I. (ed.) (1953) *The Analytic Didactic of Comenius*, Chicago: University of Chicago Press.

Jesperson, J. O. H. (1904) *How to Teach a Foreign Language*, Stockholm: Swan, Sonnenschein and Co.

Judge, H. (1974) *School is Not Yet Dead*, London: Longman.

Krashen, S. (1981) *Second Language Acquisition and Second Language Learning*, Oxford: Oxford University Press.

Lado, R. (1957) *Linguistics Across Cultures*, US: University of Michigan Press.

Leathes Committee (1918) *Modern Studies*, London: HMSO.

Locke, J. (1690) *Some Thoughts Concerning Education* (Yolton, J. W. and J. S., eds) Oxford: Clarendon Press.

Lopato, E. (1961) 'An experience to determine the effect of learning conversational French on academic development of third grade children', PhD dissertation, New York: New York University.

Mattingley, I. G. (1972) 'Language by ear and by eye', in J. F. Kavanagh and I. G. Mattingley (eds) (1972) *Language*, Cambridge, Mass: MIT Press.

McNiff, J. (1988) *Action Research: Principles and Practice*, London: Routledge.

Mill, J. S. (1867) *Inaugural Lecture*, Scotland: St Andrews.

Mitchell, R. (1994) 'The communicative approach to language teaching: an introduction', in A. Swarbrick (ed.) *Teaching Modern Foreign Languages*, 32–42, London: Routledge.

Nuffield Foundation Schools Council (1969) *Working Paper 19 (Development of Modern Languages Teaching in Secondary Schools*.

Otter, H.S. (1968) *A Functional Language Examination*, Oxford: Oxford University Press.

Page, B. (1996) 'Graded objectives in ML (GOMC)', in E. Hawkins (ed.) *30 Years of Language Teaching*, London: CILT.

Palmer, H. E. (1917) *The Scientific Study and Teaching of Languages*, London: Harrap.

—— (1921) *The Oral Method of Teaching Languages*, Cambridge: Hether.

—— (1922) *The Principles of Language Study*, London: Harrap

Pomphrey, C. (1996) 'Towards a New Parnership' in E. Hawkins (ed.), *30 Years of Language Teaching*, London: CILT.

Public Schools Commission (1864) *Clarendon Commission Report*, London: Eyre and Spottiswood.

Richardson, G. (1981) 'A hundred years of language revolutions', in G. Richardson (ed.) (1981) *Modern Language Teaching in the 1980s*, Hull: University of Hull: Institute of Education.

Russell, B. (1940) *An Enquiry into Meaning and Truth*, London: George Allen and Unwin.

Schools Council (1967) *Working Pages 28*, London: HMSO.

Schools Enquiry Commission (1868) *An Enquiry into the Teaching of French*, London: Eyre and Spottiswood.

Searle, J. (1969) *The Speech Act Theory*, Cambridge: Cambridge University Press.

Shelton, R. B. (1957) *The Effect of High School Foreign Language Study on Freshmen Test Scores at Alabama Polytechnic Institute School and Society LXXXV*, Alabama Institute, pp. 203–5.

Simon, B. (1994) 'Why no pedagogs in England?' in B. Moon and A. Shelton Mayes (1994), *Teaching and Learning in the Secondary School*, Milton Keynes: Open University.

Skinner, B. (1957) *Verbal Behaviour*, New Jersey: Prentice Hall.

SSEC (1963) *Secondary Schools Examination Council Bulletin No. 1*, London: HMSO.

Stern, H. H. (1963) *Foreign Languages in Primary Education*, Hambury: UNESCO Institute for Education.

Swarbrick, A. (ed.) (1994) *Teaching Modern Languages*, London: Routledge/Open University.

Van Ek, J. (1972) *The Threshold Level*, Strasbourg: Council of Europe.

Viëtor, W. (1882) *Der Sprachunterricht muß umkehren*, Reisland: Leipzig, OR.

Whitehead, M. (1996) 'Materials and methods 1966–1996', in E. Hawkins (ed.) *30 Years of Language Teaching*, London: CILT.

Wringe. C. (1976) *Developments in Language Teaching*, London: Open London Books.

Yuen Ren Chao (1966) quoted in E. Hawkins (ed.) 'Introduction: language teaching in perspective', in *30 Years of Language Teaching*, London: CILT.

2 Re-examining communicative language teaching[1]

Norbert Pachler

Introduction

In recent years critical comments about the prevalent approach to foreign language (FL) teaching in secondary education in the UK, i.e. particular interpretations of Communicative Language Teaching (CLT) implicit in grass-roots developments of the late 1970s and 1980s (i.e. the Graded Objectives movement leading to the GCSE), as well as national policy in the 1990s (i.e. the National Curriculum Modern Foreign Languages Orders), are increasingly being voiced by commentators and practitioners alike.

In this chapter, I aim to explore how useful the notion of communicative competence and associated methodological approaches still are to FL education in general and to FL teaching in UK secondary education in particular.

Conceptualising communicative competence and CLT

One difficulty in any discussion of CLT is doing justice to the eclectic nature of the concept: CLT 'is a broad assembly of ideas, from a range of sources (some linguistic, others more broadly educational), which have together come to be accepted as 'good practice' by many contemporary teachers' Mitchell (1994: 33). Rather than a method, such as *The Silent Way*, *Total Physical Response* or *Suggestopedia*, which according to Ted Rodgers (1996: 3) tend to be characterised by 'a central, founding-father-figure guru', to 'assume a universal applicability', to be 'idiosyncratic, and . . . commercially packaged and marketed', CLT is best viewed as an approach with different permutations derived from a multidisciplinary perspective including, at least, linguistics, psychology, philosophy, sociology, and educational research (see e.g. Savignon 1991: 265). This reflects to some extent the realisation that the search for one definitive method to FL teaching is futile. Instead, researchers and practitioners alike have tended to look of late for appropriate organising principles (see e.g. Herschensohn 1990: 451, or Mitchell and Myles 1998: 195). In the UK, something approaching a consensus has developed which I outline below.

The key concern for proponents of CLT is the development of 'communicative competence'. The emphasis on communicative competence was prompted by a redefinition and broadening of the concept of linguistic proficiency from structural knowledge of language towards a focus on the language functions linguistic items perform. The implicit theory of communicative competence is that of language as communication. Of particular influence, without claiming (and seeking) direct applicability to FL teaching, were J. L. Austin's (1962) and John Searle's (1969) work on speech acts and Michael Halliday's theory of the functions of language (1975). Halliday (1975) distinguished seven basic functions of actual language use including that of communication:

1   the instrumental function: using language to get things;
2   the regulatory function: using language to control the behaviour of others;
3   the interactional function: using language to create interaction with others;
4   the personal function: using language to express personal feelings and meanings;
5   the heuristic function: using language to learn and to discover;
6   the imaginative function: using language to create a world of the imagination;
7   the representational function: using language to communicate information.
          (Halliday 1975 as summarised in Richards and Rodgers 1986: 70–1)

Communication became widely understood to have the following characteristics: it

a   is a form of social interaction, and is therefore normally acquired and used in social interaction;
b   involves a high degree of unpredictability and creativity in form and message;
c   takes place in discourse and socio-cultural contexts which provide constraints on appropriate language use and also clues as to correct interpretations of utterances;
d   is carried out under limited psychological and other conditions such as memory constraints, fatigue and distractions;
e   always has a purpose (for example, to establish social relations, to persuade, or to promise);
f   involves authentic, as opposed to textbook-contrived language; and
g   is judged as successful or not on the basis of actual outcomes.
          (Canale 1983: 3–4)

Given this view of language and language use, the emphasis in FL teaching has become *meaning* rather than *form* and the *ability to use* language rather than knowledge about language. 'Communication' has become the buzzword in FL teaching and the tenet of learning to communicate through communication has become established. A methodology developed which emphasises a focus on the learner by endeavouring to provide her with the necessary language and communication skills to use language effectively and in a purposeful way, i.e. to satisfy personal needs and to 'carry out the functions we want it to perform' (Thompson 1996: 15), as well as active learner participation in pair-work and group-work around information-gap or problem-solving activities (see also Pachler and Field, 1997). Characteristic of CLT is also a concern with the world beyond the classroom, i.e. the linguistic preparation of learners for real-time target language (TL) use with other TL speakers (see Thompson 1996: 15).

The UK variant of CLT has been summarised by Rosamond Mitchell as follows:

1   Classroom activities should maximise opportunities for learners to use the target language for meaningful purposes, with their attention on the messages they are creating and the tasks they are completing, rather than on correctness of language and language structure.
2   Learners trying their best to use the target language creatively and unpredictably are bound to make errors; this is a normal part of language learning, and constant correction is unnecessary, and even counterproductive.
3   Language analysis and grammar explanation may help some learners, but extensive experience of target language use helps everyone!
4   Effective language teaching is responsive to the needs and interests of the individual learner.
5   Effective language learning is an active process, in which the learner takes increasing responsibility for his or her progress.
6   The effective teacher aims to facilitate, not control, the language learning process.

(Mitchell 1994: 38f.)

Richard Johnstone describes 'communicative' methodology, as opposed to more traditional methodologies, in the context of FL learning as a school subject in terms of:

- an increase in the amount of foreign language used for everyday classroom and personal purposes;
- the introduction of functions (asking for, offering, refusing, etc.) and general notions (food, hobbies, time, travel, etc.) as constituents of a language syllabus, in addition to grammar, vocabulary and situations;
- a gradual move beyond course books as sole or even principal determiners of the language syllabus and towards the use of authentic texts and other personalised inputs selected by teachers and pupils themselves;
- an extension of group, paired and individual activity, to complement whole-class work;
- the gradual introduction of information exchange based on role play and simulation, and to a lesser extent of practical skills activities . . . and of communicative games;
- the introduction of assessment, in many cases related to graded objectives, for purposes of 'diagnosis' and of 'formative evaluation'.

(Johnstone, 1988: 12)

The ability to communicate is, therefore, predominantly conceptualised as the skill of using language in real-time and performing specific functions and speech acts.

It is worth noting here that the underlying notion of 'competence' differs significantly from the concept of competence used by Noam Chomsky in his 1965 book *Aspects of the Theory of Syntax*.

> By competence, Chomsky is referring to the abstract and hidden represent-ation of language knowledge held inside our heads, with its potential to create and understand original utterances in a given language.
>
> (Mitchell and Myles, 1998: 6)

Chomsky, who deals with the construct at levels of rarefied abstraction and who has noted that his ideas probably have little directly to offer to FL teaching, viewed competence essentially as knowledge of grammar.

In the UK context, however, the term 'competence' has tended not to include the (explicit) teaching of grammar. This despite the fact that, whilst not conclusive, there is increasingly evidence that explicit grammar teaching contributes substantially to high levels of grammatical and sociolinguistic competence (see Pachler 1999a).

This restricted view of competence can be seen to be partly due to a mis-guided theoretical basis of likening L1 acquisition with second/foreign language learning, in particular the appeal of Stephen Krashen's (1981 and 1987) notion of 'comprehensible input' as a major guiding principle in FL teaching and his belief in the limited usefulness of the formal study of rules, as well as to the impact of Dell Hymes' views stressing both grammaticality and sociocultural appropriateness:

> [some] occasions call for being appropriately ungrammatical. We have . . . to account for the fact that a normal (*sic!*) child acquires knowledge of sentences, not only as grammatical, but also as appropriate. He or she acquires competence as to when to speak, when not, and as to what to talk about with whom, when, where, in what manner. In short, a child becomes able to accomplish a repertoire of speech acts, to take part in speech events, and to evaluate their accomplishment by others. This competence, moreover, is integral with attitudes, values, and motivations concerning language, its features and uses, and integral with competence for, and attitude towards, the interrelation of language with the other code of communicative conduct. . . . I should take *competence* as the most general term for the capabilities of a person. (This choice is in the spirit, if at present against the letter, of the concern in linguistic theory for underlying capability.) Competence is dependent upon both (tacit) *knowledge* and (ability for) *use*.
>
> (Hymes 1972: 277–82, italics in original)

In the UK a variant developed which viewed CLT as limited to the early stages of language learning and (involving) essentially a vague mixture of direct method, use of visuals, games and other oral activities, with a nod in the direction of inductive approaches to grammar learning, but little mention of systematic reinforcement or practice. The tacit assumption seems to be that communicative competence is no more than a low-level, threshold ability, formulaic and almost behaviorist in character, and that as such it is both an appropriate and sufficient objective for sub-A level language work.

(Klapper, 1997: 27)

This view was influenced, amongst other factors, by: certain theories of Second Language Acquisition/Learning, (Applied) Linguistics and educational research discussed above; the constraints of foreign language education in a predominantly comprehensive school environment from the mid-1960s and associated curriculum development work, i.e. the Graded Objectives movement; as well as the influence of Van Ek's Threshold levels designed (for adults) to 'get by' in a FL by the Council of Europe in the 1970s.

The considerable widening of the target audience, the lack of status of FLs on the school curriculum and the limited time available as well as the context-reduced nature of school-based learning (as opposed to natural acquisition) have led, during the 1970s and 1980s, to the so-called 'Graded Objectives' movement, which developed defined syllabuses around rather narrow topics and specified learning outcomes, often in the form of 'can-do' statements (see also Pachler and Field 1997, Chapter 3). These developments were significantly informed by the so-called Threshold level FL skills, devised by the Council of Europe in the 1970s for migrant workers, adult tourists and visitors to countries where the TL is spoken (see Van Ek 1975) which in turn incorporated the functional/communicative definition of language offered by David Wilkins in 1972 and 1976 who analysed the communicative meanings which FL learners needed to understand and express. These developments have led, by and large, to a narrow transactional–functional orientation in which pupils are prepared for the linguistic (and non-linguistic) needs of tourists, such as making travel arrangements, going to bars, restaurants, museums, booking into hotels, buying petrol for the car etc, with the emphasis on 'getting by'. On the one hand this approach is characterised by a heavy emphasis on recall of often random lexical items and phrases derived from narrowly defined, idealised interactions and exchanges at the cost of transfer of knowledge and skills across topics. On the other hand, it tends to ignore the teenage learner's communicative needs and does not allow her to engage in meaningful and realistic interaction, both supposedly central tenets of communicative methodology.

This narrow view of communicative competence has, rightly, been subjected to considerable criticism:

[in] fact, true communicative competence (in the sense of expressing some-thing that is personally meaningful and which therefore represents an

'original' utterance) denotes a complex and relatively high-level body of skills which presuppose and are predicated on a solid grasp of both structure and lexis. It is not developed solely or even predominantly through repeated 'communicative activities' based on a fairly narrow notional-functional range but depends to a large extent on a learner having ready access to that underlying generative linguistic framework which enables him/her to form substantially new or unique utterances.

(Klapper, 1997: 27)

These insights are not new. Already by the early 1980s there existed a clear conceptual framework proposing that communicative competence consisted of skill, i.e. how well a learner can use language with speed and in real time, as well as knowledge, i.e. what learners know consciously and unconsciously about language and its use. The theoretical framework for communicative competence proposed by Michael Canale (1983: 7–12), based on earlier work with Merrill Swain (see Canale and Swain, 1980) comprises four interacting areas of knowledge and skill:

- grammatical competence: 'mastery of the language code';
- sociolinguistic competence: 'the extent to which utterances are produced and understood *appropriately* in different sociolinguistic contexts depending on contextual factors such as status of participants, purposes of interaction, and norms or conventions of interaction' both regarding meaning and form;
- discourse competence: 'mastery of how to combine grammatical forms and meanings to achieve a unified spoken or written text in different genres' both regarding cohesion (structural links of utterances) and coherence (relationships of meanings in a text); and
- strategic competence: 'mastery of verbal and non-verbal communication strategies . . . (a) to compensate for breakdowns in communication . . .; and (b) to enhance the effectiveness of communication.'

Alas, in mainstream FL teaching and learning in the UK this conceptualisation of communicative competence received insufficient attention despite the work, for instance, of Eric Hawkins (1981 and 1984) and others who argued for approaches that implied a broader view of competence.

Realigning CLT

From this conceptualisation of communicative competence and CLT, then, it follows that a realignment of current practice in keeping with Canale's framework is both desirable and necessary in order to render CLT useful and appropriate for the UK school context in the future.

One important area for realignment is the current lack of attention afforded to awareness of and knowledge about language (for a detailed discussion see Pachler, Norman and Field, 1999). Whilst expectations of what form focussed instruction can achieve in the short and medium term need to be realistic given the non-linear and non-instantaneous nature of language learning, explicit and implicit grammar teaching can, nevertheless, be seen to be effective if combined with sufficient exposure to and ample opportunity to (re)produce TL utterances.

Tony Roberts (1992: 27) rightly points out the difference between learning a FL *for* communication and learning it *through* communication and suggests an approach starting from structure via controlled practice to function, viewing the teaching of grammatical forms as a pre-requisite for language use and stressing that doing is subservient to knowing.

What is needed is not a return to the traditional grammar–translation paradigm as language learning is not just a conscious cognitive process but also experiential predicated on extensive exposure, imitation and adaptation of rich language forms (see e.g. Klapper, 1997: 24). This implies the need for FL teachers to create ample opportunities for learners to 'notice the gap' between TL features and their own language production. Reflection on the TL and the negotiation of meaning during actual language use are very important (for a detailed discussion of grammar teaching see Pachler, 1999a).

The need to increasingly focus on grammatical competence is intimately linked to the need to emphasise how to combine grammatical forms and meanings not only at word, but also at sentence and text, i.e. discourse, level to enable learners to construct and generate structurally cohesive and coherent longer utterances and texts.

The focus of our work as FL teachers should, therefore, not merely be on individual linguistic items but include an emphasis on longer utterances and texts. We need to provide more opportunities for learners to analyse the discourse features and discourse markers of texts, i.e. how texts are structured, with a view to learners modelling their own language production on it by extracting and recombining relevant information than is currently the case in many FL classrooms. Hutchinson and Waters argue that what is needed is 'an interpretation of discourse types in the target situation to discover what competence is required to cope with them' (1984: 110; see also Pachler and Allford later in this volume).

Writing frames, focussing on the process of writing, scaffolded writing, group writing tasks, peer correction, drafting and re-drafting with the teacher as adviser and editor, might provide a useful way forward (see also Lewis 1996: 15).

Tom Hutchinson and Alan Waters (1984: 108) suggest that in FL teaching we should be learning rather than learner centred. They wonder whether we might be trying too hard to mirror 'the performance data of the target situation' rather than focus on 'the capacity to handle communication in the target situation' (Hutchinson and Waters 1984: 109). On the one hand we are overburdening learners with situation-specific language and idealised dialogues and stock written passages to be memorised and reproduced under examination condition rather than develop in them a real understanding of how language works. On the other hand, the prevalent variant of CLT emphasises 'authenticity' of materials and tasks. Materials and tasks are deemed to be authentic if they focus on (the) culture(s) of the TL. Alan Hornsey (1992) rightly argues that 'plausibility' might be a more useful guiding principle than 'authenticity'. This raises the interesting question whether, as FL teachers, we should focus more on tasks and situations which learners encounter in their everyday lives rather than on those requiring suspension of disbelief (e.g. simulations and role-plays located in the target country) and which prepare for potential FL use in the future (e.g. buying petrol in the target country whilst on holiday with your family).

The 'methodological imperative' of *teaching* in the TL, i.e. maximum to exclusive TL use by the teacher for instruction of and interaction with learners (see Pachler and Field, 1997, Chapter 5), characteristic of the view of CLT promoted by the 1992 and 1995 National Curriculum Modern Foreign Languages Orders for England and Wales, is at least partly based on the misguided notion that FL learning is similar to mother tongue learning. (Another lasting influence of this misconception is the interest in meaning at the expense of attention to form discussed above, as well as the neglect of the cognitive development of FL learners.)

This can be seen to be deeply flawed (see also Klapper 1998: 22) and runs counter to one of the five guiding principles derived from Canale's theoretical construct: the need to make 'optimal use of those communication skills that the learner has developed through use of native . . . language' (1983: 19).

> Apart from retarding the FL learning process, dogmatic exclusion of L1 can lead to resentment, frustration and the build-up of affective factors which are well known to be the enemy of effective FL learning.
>
> (Klapper, 1998: 24)

Whilst clearly providing exposure to the FL and bringing it to life, exclusive TL use by the teacher ignores the fact that the mother tongue tends to be the language of thought for many learners and fails to take into account that code switching is natural. Some commentators also point out that the exclusion of the mother tongue from the FL learning process may threaten the very identity of the learner.

Certain current methodological prescriptions seem to overlook the fact that FL input by the teacher, as well as classroom interactions differ significantly from natural settings in terms of input modification by the teacher, the make-believe nature of interactions and their context-reduced settings, which means that their value as input as a basis for intake is strictly limited. Also, from the point of view of interaction/output-based FL learning models, focussing on acquisition through negotiation of meaning by communicating with others, maximum classroom-based TL use by learners can be seen to be insufficient. In an examination of the interactional processes characterising FL teaching in secondary classrooms David Westgate *et al.* (1985: 276), for instance, note that [whereas] teachers of any subject may tend to tell their pupils' 'when to talk, what to talk about, when to stop talking and how well they talked' . . ., FL teachers appear also to prescribe for pupils the very words, even features of words, *with which* to talk [italics in original].

Whilst understandable, given the need to present and practise new linguistic items in a 'context-reduced' environment, this phenomenon is often stifling and demotivating for learners because time (made) available for the reproduction and production phases tends to be very limited. Pressures to cover the examination specifications, i.e. the need to race from one topic to the next and to cover an array of linguistic items and phrases for each of them, can easily lead to a lack of emphasis on transfer across topics and to pupils being unable to engage with old and new language creatively and cyclically. There tends to be a lack of opportunity for learners to engage in hypothesis formulation and testing.

The 'total exclusion position' of the mother tongue promoted by the 1992 and 1995 NC Modern Foreign Languages Orders seems, therefore, unwise and should perhaps be abandoned in favour of the 'optimal use position' which sees some value in use of the mother tongue. The focus on TL use should switch from teaching in the TL to learning in the TL, i.e. from the exclusive/maximum use of the TL by the teacher to the optimum use of the TL by the teacher and the learner coupled with a focus and reflection on (formal aspects of) language (see also Macaro later in this volume).

Furthermore, the TL imperative can make 'real' communication difficult. Ernesto Macaro, for instance, points out that currently in FL teaching in compulsory secondary education, at best, teachers and learners communicate messages to each other, but do not communicate with each other (see Macaro 1997: 125).

The focus on exposure to input is epitomised in the prevalent presentation-practice–production (PPP) model. Whilst undoubtedly very important, exposure and input are increasingly being seen as less important than the internal procedures by which the learner processes the language she is exposed to in order to convert input into intake (see e.g. Skehan 1996: 18).

Recently, the PPP model, central to communicative approaches to FL teaching (as well as others before it), has been criticised on the grounds of failing to reflect both the nature of language and the nature of learning. Instead, the alternative paradigm of 'observe – hypothesise – experiment' has been suggested (see Lewis 1996).

Another aspect of current methodology and practice in need of realignment is the concern with the use of language and with teaching and the relative neglect of the language learning process. Jim Coleman (1999: 333), in the context of MFL teaching and learning in higher education, observes that '(despite) widespread language awareness courses, students frequently possess a fresh and naive view of the language learning process, as untainted by knowledge of second language acquisition research findings as is that of their teachers'.

Knowledge of, as well as the ability to use, communication and learning strategies (strategic competence) needs to be seen, and is increasingly being seen, as a central concern of FL teaching. Throughout the last decade or so a number of publications featuring fairly abstract taxonomies of learning strategies with limited direct applicability to the FL classroom have been published. However, more recently there have been attempts to operationalise them (see e.g. Harris 1997). The focus of FL teaching, I would argue, needs to be on how learners learn, as well as on what they learn. Recent research (see e.g. Graham 1997) suggests that most learners will require detailed and structured guidance in how to learn, i.e. learner training (see e.g. Dickinson 1992).

Hutchinson and Waters take the term 'communicative' to mean 'geared to the competence and expectations of those participating in the learning process' (1984: 108). This, they argue, means that there needs to be negotiation between all the parties involved. The question arises whether this really happens in the context of compulsory FL teaching and learning in secondary education. To what extent are learners' 'needs' taken on board? One could argue that teachers tend to use learner-centred approaches (pair work, group work etc) but the fact remains that topics and linguistic means for expression are highly restricted. One topic is covered after the next, all with clearly defined lexical items but often with little transfer between them. Most importantly in the context of meeting the needs of learners is the issue of how relevant these topics are for them. There appears to be a mismatch between learners' needs and sponsor's needs, i.e. the aims underpinning the NC Modern Foreign Languages Orders and the (GCSE) examination specifications and criteria. To what extent do the topics really trigger in learners a desire to express meaning and communicate personal information? Also, to what extent have we become slaves to the transactional, notional–functional rationale of CLT? Ian Bauckham (1995: 31), leaning heavily on Lev Vygotsky, cogently argues that

> [the] primary aim should be, like the primary aim of literacy, to enhance the learner's semiotic system, to help him/her to abstract his/her thought from the contextual prison of spontaneous concepts in order to make language a more autonomous object, of which the learner is more fully aware and over which greater control can be exercised.

It would seem, therefore, that a re-examination of the current aims of FL teaching in secondary education is desirable and that there is a need for the inclusion of thought-provoking texts and contexts which allow pupils to perform tasks that make appropriate cognitive demands and emphasise (linguistic) creativity, moving learners on from single-word and short-phrase transactions and interactions. Marilyn McMeniman makes an appeal for thinking to be put back into language teaching (see 1996; see also Johnstone 1988: 16). What is called for is a focus on intellectually challenging activities and the avoidance of those that are simple-minded. In its current incarnation, CLT in compulsory FL teaching in the UK tends not to be renowned for exciting activity types despite considerable efforts by FL teachers to make FL learning relevant and enjoyable for learners. This is due to what might be called a 'conspiracy of systemic factors', in particular the lack of encouragement for many years to reflect on, manipulate and generate (complex) language. Hutchinson and Waters suggest overcoming these constraints by building on learners' existing background knowledge of issues and by introducing 'a new and unusual slant to it' (1984: 112). It seems that a focus on the development of the ability in learners to solve communication problems and to avoid and/or overcome breakdown in communication are equally important. An emphasis on spontaneity of language use rather than on scripted dialogues and role plays and predictable texts and contexts in examination specifications would also help.

The final aspect of CLT to be discussed in this chapter is the need to extend the notion of communicative competence to 'intercultural communicative competence', i.e. to 'take account of the ways of living out of which others speak and write' (Byram 1997: 4). In recent years the importance of duly reflecting the cultural component of language in FL teaching and learning has been increasingly noted as language and culture are seen to be inextricably linked to one another. In order to understand language fully and use it fluently, learners need not only linguistic, pragmatic, discourse and strategic competence but also socio-cultural and world knowledge, as some areas of language do reflect culture. This applies to the idiomatic level, as well as to syntax and morphology, but seems particularly important in relation to avoiding socio-pragmatic failure at discourse level, e.g. how to start and conclude conversations, turn-taking, turn-keeping and turn-giving, topic nomination, topic change, etc. In order to become proficient TL speakers, therefore, learners need to be aware of the cultural dimension of language.

Alas, in current CLT methodology insufficient attention is paid to the cultural embeddedness of FL use (partly due to problems of assessing the cultural component through a standardised examination) and there is a real need to include in our schemes-of-work material and tasks which allow learners to become familiar with potential cultural differences at a pragmatic discourse level (see also Pachler 1999b).

In addition to an increased focus on target culture learning, what is needed, researchers, theorists and commentators increasingly argue, is a shift in pedagogy and methodology. Rather than focusing on the differences in TL and target culture systems, Michael Byram, for instance, suggests an emphasis on 'encounters between individuals with their own meanings and cultural capital' (1997: 40). In terms of FL teaching and learning this necessitates an emphasis on first-hand contact and interaction with FL speakers. Byram also suggests that FL learners should not necessarily model themselves on first language speakers 'as this ignores the significance of the social identities and cultural competence of the learner in any intercultural interaction' (1997: 8). In other words, foreign language and culture learning should not be about learners giving up and abandoning their own language and identity in order to become fully accepted by another. Instead, Byram (1997: 12) argues for an outcome of language-and-culture learning which enables learners to see and manage the relationships between themselves and their own cultural beliefs, behaviours and meanings, as expressed in a foreign language, and those of their interlocutors, expressed in the same language – or even in a combination of languages – which may be the interlocutors' native language, or not.

An important pedagogical consequence of this line of argument, for instance, is the need to use competent non-native language in teaching material.

Some alternatives to CLT

There have been proposals for alternatives to CLT in recent years most notably the Lexical Approach (see e.g. Lewis 1993 and 1996) and Task-based Learning (see e.g. Skehan 1996).

Michael Lewis (1996: 10) argues that 'much of our supposedly "original" language use is, in fact, made of prefabricated chunks, often, perhaps usually, much larger than single words'. From this follows for Lewis that memorisation should play a more important role in FL teaching and learning, understanding of 'grammar rules' a less important role and that the majority of the language acquired needs to come from sources other than formal teaching, in particular learner activity, ie observing, hypothesising and experimenting (see 1996: 11 and 13). In this approach:

> [the] teacher's primary role is the selection of materials and tasks and the creation of an appropriate atmosphere. Patience, a teaching style which values questions, and the ability to endorse curiosity, experiment and creativity are essential. . . . Methodologically it implies activities which involve sorting, matching, identifying and describing. . . . The emphasis is not on radically new methods, but on applying a wide range of familiar activities to input selected according to lexical criteria, and with no expectation that any of the new language will be 'learned' in a particular lesson.
>
> (Lewis 1996: 15)

Peter Skehan is one of the main proponents of Task-based Learning who focus on meaning-based activities or tasks which are more or less closely related to real-life language use and can be evaluated in terms of the achievement of tangible outcomes. The learning process is conceived of as one of learning through doing. Learners are required to operate under pressure of real-time language processing and to use communication strategies linked to lexicalised communication hopefully leading to greater fluency and a greater capacity to solve communication problems. The challenge for teachers in such an approach is to ensure learners make longer-term progress in relation to individual and across a range of structures and beyond reliance on prefabricated chunks to solve short-term and situationalised communication problems (see e.g. Skehan 1996: 20, 22 and 28).

Summary

Teachers usually feel (or rather, are made to feel, NP) guilty about something: translating, or explaining grammar, or standing up in front of the class and behaving like teachers, or engaging in some other activity that is temporarily out of favour. Currently teachers feel guilty about not being communicative.

(Swan 1985: 82)

This chapter has attempted to show how, whilst having moved FL learning in the UK on to a new plane by emphasising the communicative potential of language, i.e. the functions language allows us to perform, and by making FL learning more accessible to a much wider ability range of learners, CLT is not the panacea of FL teaching. In particular, in its UK variant, CLT has tended to neglect the generative potential of language by downplaying awareness of and knowledge about language by focussing too narrowly on transactional, situationalised language in narrowly defined contexts and idealised discourse patterns, thereby limiting learners', and in particular more able learners', potential to express personal meaning and to use the FL creatively and spontaneously. As FL teachers we should not be afraid to use a wide range of teaching and learning activities including some which do not seem to have immediate communicative value focussing, in a systematic manner, for instance on memorisation of lexical items, pronunciation and form as well as meaning, within an overall communicative framework.

In short, there is still life in CLT but it needs to be adapted in response to changing cultural, socio-political and societal contexts (see also Wolff 1998) as well as in response to research findings in the fields of education, (Applied) Linguistics and Second Language Acquisition/Learning in order to continue to render it useful for the next generation of FL learners. A current and important paradigm shift is the so-called 'digital revolution' brought about by emerging new technologies which is beginning to influence FL pedagogy and policy (see e.g. Pachler forthcoming, Noss and Pachler 1999, or Leask and Pachler 1999). Alas, there is insufficient space here to examine these developments.

Note

1   Thanks to my colleague Dr Douglas Allford, Institute of Education, University of London for his constructive comments on a draft of this chapter.

Editor's note

Pachler describes what he calls the British variant of communicative language teaching, commending the development of a more meaningful approach than previous methodologies. However, he does lament over-simplistic interpretation of communicative language teaching as a functional, transactional approach, which has been formalised through the Graded Objectives movement, GCSE and National Curriculum documentation. In presenting a critical argument to support a re-examination of teaching methods, Pachler defines communicative and, indeed, linguistic competence. These descriptors serve as criteria for the evaluation of teaching and learning methodologies, enabling the identification of gaps in current, recommended practices. In this way, this chapter is central to the themes of this text as a whole. Pachler questions the foundations of the communicative approach – target language use, and the Presentation, Practice, Production paradigm. The chapter is not, however, negative in tone. Pachler recommends building on good practice and considers a pedagogy which offers learners the opportunity to understand, use and manipulate foreign language forms. Due consideration is given to teachers' and learners' roles in a process of what he perceives to be the next phase of foreign language teaching and learning approaches. Pachler is beginning to provide answers to questions and criticisms voiced in other chapters within this volume.

Linked chapters

This chapter is at the core, and raises questions addressed by all other con-tributors.

References

Austin, J. (1962) *How to Do Things with Words*, Milton Keynes: Open University Press.

Bauckham, I. (1995) 'A Vygotskyan perspective on foreign language teaching', *Languages Forum* 4, Institute of Education, University of London, pp. 29–31.

Byram, M. (1997) *Teaching and Assessing Intercultural Communicative Competence*, Clevedon: Multilingual Matters.

Canale, M. (1983) 'From communicative competence to communicative language pedagogy', in J. Richards and R. Schmidt (eds) *Language and Communication*, Harlow: Longman, pp. 2–27.

Canale, M. and Swain, M. (1980) 'Theoretical bases of communicative approaches to second language teaching and testing', *Applied Linguistics*, 1(1): 1–47.

Chomsky, N. (1965) *Aspects of the Theory of Syntax*, Cambridge, MA: MIT Press.

Coleman, J. (1999) 'Looking ahead: trends in modern foreign languages in higher education', in N. Pachler (ed.) *Teaching Modern Foreign Languages at Advanced Level*, London: Routledge.

Dickinson, L. (1992) *Learner Training for Language Learning*, Dublin: Authentik.

Graham, S. (1997) *Effective Language Learning*, Clevedon: Multilingual Matters.

Halliday, M. (1970) 'Language structure and language function', in J. Lyons (ed.) *New Horizons in Linguistics*, Harmondsworth: Penguin.

—— (1975) *Learning How to Mean: Explorations in the Development of Language*, London: Edward Arnold.

Harris, V. (1997) *Teaching Learners How to Learn. Strategy Training in the ML Classroom*, London: CILT.

Hawkins, E. (1984) *Awareness of Language: an Introduction*, Cambridge: Cambridge University Press.

—— (1981) *Modern Languages in the Curriculum*, Cambridge: Cambridge University Press.

Herschensohn, J. (1990) 'Towards a theoretical basis for current language pedagogy', *The Modern Language Journal*, 74(iv): 451–8.

Hornsey, A. (1992) 'Authenticity in foreign language learning', *Languages Forum* 2/3, Institute of Education, University of London, pp. 6–7.

Hutchinson, T. and Waters, A. (1984) 'How communicative is ESP?', *ELT Journal*, 38(2): 108–13.

Hymes, D. (1972) 'On communicative competence', in J. Pride and J. Holmes (eds) *Sociolinguistics*, Harmondsworth: Penguin, pp. 269–93.

Johnstone, R. (1988) 'Communicative methodology: second generation', in P. Kingston (ed.) *Languages Breaking Barriers*, selected proceedings from The Joint Council of Language Associations' Annual Course/Conference March 1988, London: CILT, pp. 12–21.

Klapper, J. (1997) 'Language learning at school and university: the great grammar debate continues (I)', *Language Learning Journal*, 16: 22–7.

—— (1998) 'Language learning at school and university: the great grammar debate continues (II)', *Language Learning Journal*, 16: 22–8.

Krashen, S. (1987) *Principles and Practice in Second Language Acquisition*, Oxford: Pergamon.

—— (1981) *Second Language Acquisition and Second Language Learning*, Oxford: Pergamon.

Leask, M. and Pachler, N. (1999) *Learning to Teach Using ICT in the Secondary School*, London: Routledge.

Lewis, M. (1996) 'Implications of a lexical view of language', in J. Willis and D. Willis, (eds) *Challenge and Change in Language Teaching*, Oxford: Heinemann, pp. 10–16.

—— (1993) *The Lexical Approach. The State of ELT and a Way Forward*, Hove: Language Teaching Publications.

Macaro, E. (1997) *Target Language, Collaborative Learning and Autonomy*, Clevedon: Multilingual Matters.

McMeniman, M. (1996) 'Putting thinking back into language learning', *Languages Forum*, 5, Institute of Education, University of London, pp. 21–6.

Mitchell, R. (1994) 'The communicative approach to language teaching. An introduction', in A. Swarbrick (ed.) *Teaching Modern Languages*, London: Routledge, pp. 33–42.

Mitchell, R. and Myles, F. (1998) *Second Language Learning Theories*, London: Arnold.

Noss, R. and Pachler, N. (1999) 'The challenge of new technologies: doing old things in a new way, or doing new things?' in P. Mortimore (ed.) *Understanding Pedagogy and Its Impact on Learning*, London: Sage, Chapter 10.

Pachler, N. (1999b) 'Teaching and learning culture', in P. Mortimer (ed.) *Teaching Modern Foreign Languages at Advanced Level*, London: Routledge, Chapter 5.

—— (1999a) 'Teaching and learning grammar', in P. Mortimer (ed.) *Teaching Modern Foreign Languages at Advanced Level*, London: Routledge, Chapter 6.

—— (forthcoming) 'Connecting schools and pupils: to what end? Issues related to the use of ICT in school settings', in M. Leask (ed.) *Using Information and Communications Technologies in Schools: Key Issues*, London: Routledge, Chapter 2.

Pachler, N. and Allford, D. (2000) 'Literature in the communicative classroom', in K. Field (ed.) *Issues in Modern Foreign Languages Teaching*, London: Routledge.

Pachler, N. and Field, K. (1997) *Learning to Teach Modern Foreign Languages in the Secondary School*, London: Routledge.

Pachler, N., Norman, N. and Field, K. (1999) 'A new approach to language study', *Studies in Modern Languages Education*, 7, Leeds: University of Leeds.

Richards, J. and Rodgers, T. (1986) *Approaches and Methods in Language Teaching. A Description and Analysis*, Cambridge: Cambridge University Press.

Roberts, T. (1992) *Towards a Learning Theory in Modern Languages*, Occasional Paper No. 2, London: Institute of Education, University of London.

Rodgers, T. (1996) 'The secret synergy of methods', opening address given at the International ELT Conference entitled *From Diversity to Synergy*, Kara Harp Okulu, Ankara, Turkey, 27 June.

Savignon, S. (1991) 'Communicative language teaching: state of the art,' in *TESOL Quarterly*, 25(2): 261–77.

Searle, J. (1969) *Speech Acts*, Cambridge: Cambridge University Press.

Skehan, P. (1996) 'Second language acquisition research and task-based instruction', in J. Willis and D. Willis (eds) *Challenge and Change in Language Teaching*, Oxford: Heinemann, pp. 17–30.

Swan, M. (1985) 'A critical look at the communicative approach (2)', *ELT Journal*, 39(2): 76–87.

Thompson, G. (1996) 'Some misconceptions about communicative language teaching', *ELT Journal*, 50(1): 9–15.

Van Ek, J. (1975) *The Threshold Level in a European Unit/Credit System for Modern Language Teaching by Adults. Systems Development in Adult Language Learning*, Strasbourg: Council of Europe.

Westgate, D., Batey, J. Brownlee, J. and Butler, M. (1985) 'Some characteristics of interaction in foreign language classrooms', *British Educational Research Journal*, 11(3): 271–81.

Wilkins, D. (1976) *Notional Syllabuses*, Oxford: Oxford University Press.

—— (1972) *The Linguistic and Situational Content of the Common Core in a Unit/Credit System*, Strasbourg: Council of Europe.

Wolff, D. (1998) 'Fremdsprachenlernen in der Informationsgesellschaft: einige Anmerkungen zu gesellschaftlichen und medialen Rahmenbedingungen', *TELL&CALL*, 4: 6–13.

Part 2

The content and definition of Modern Foreign Languages

3   Why learn a foreign language?

Shirley Lawes

Introduction

The justification for and position of modern foreign languages in the school curriculum has reflected different understandings of the aims and purposes of education at different times. There are many good historical accounts of the development of modern foreign languages in the school curriculum (see e.g. Hawkins, 1987 or Rowlinson, 1994) which provide a useful background to the current status of languages in schools. The introduction of the National Curriculum for Modern Foreign Languages 1991, was a landmark in language teaching in that for the first time curriculum content, approaches to teaching and the assessment of learning were all carefully prescribed for the whole compulsory secondary age range. The national curriculum identified the educational purposes of teaching a modern foreign languages as being, among several other things:

> To develop the ability to use the language effectively for purposes of practical communication and to form a sound base of the skills, language and attitudes required for further study, work and leisure.
>
> (MFL Working Group, 1990)

The emphasis on the use of the language and the identifying of purposes for which foreign languages should be taught is important because this confirms a shift from the view that languages were primarily an academic study to the idea that the practical ability to communicate was of more importance.

An examination of the present position and future direction of modern foreign language learning in Britain must be set in the wider context of our current understanding of the value and purposes of education in the face of the growing, if not dominant, influence of vocationalism throughout the British education system. This underlying influence sets a different framework for the content of educational programmes and indeed our very understanding of the word education. The idea that education is good in its own right and should have no end other than to develop knowledge, understanding and critical thinking for its own sake appears to be outmoded and no longer a viable concept. Such a view of education is often considered to be elitist. Vocationalism, on the other hand, is 'inclusive' and purports to respond to the new demands made on individuals to be flexible, multi-skilled and broadly prepared for working life. More specifically, vocational education, which has developed significantly in recently years, is heralded as the model for the future.

However, some observers see the situation somewhat differently. They see the dominance of vocationalism as an expression of a loss of faith in the value of knowledge and ideas and is in fact an impoverished form of education. Whereas it was once the case that the relationship between education and the world of work was seen as contingent, now it is seen as necessary.

What has this fundamental shift meant for modern languages teaching and learning? At first glance, a survey of the ground gained by modern foreign languages in the curriculum seems praiseworthy. The widespread use of the Communicative Approach to modern language teaching and learning in many ways made MFL learning more successful, particularly in the early stages. The emphasis on the active use of the foreign language right from the beginning, the teaching of grammar in context and the focus on the links between language and culture are good examples of how MFL teachers have sought to make language learning effective for a much wider range of learners than ever before. The fact that every young person now learns a modern foreign language up to the age of sixteen is a step forward in that Britain now has a generation of young people who can at the very least 'get by' in a foreign language. It could be argued that the ability to communicate, understand, read and write at a basic level is still all the majority of people ever need. However, in an age of European Union and a more 'global' world, one might expect many more learners to see the need for continuing modern languages beyond the 'first base' of GCSE. But they do not. The numbers of young people studying a modern language at A level and going on to university to study it at degree level is dwindling year by year.

As GCSE has been made more 'accessible' to a wider variety of learners, the gap between GCSE and A level has widened. In an attempt to make the continuation of modern language study beyond GCSE a more attractive option for a greater number of learners, Advanced Supplementary (AS) level courses have been promoted more widely and A level syllabuses have been substantially changed and modularised.

At a time when modern foreign languages should have a higher status in schools, colleges and higher education institutions than ever before, the opposite is in fact true.

The problems of status and popularity of modern foreign languages are arguably greater now than ever given the external pressures to produce competent foreign language speakers. Why is it that, in the midst of so much emphasis on the need for ever more and higher qualifications to get a good job, on the need for better knowledge of foreign languages in industry and commerce, fewer young people are studying languages at university?

Is it that the content of the National Curriculum fails to inspire, stimulate or challenge many learners? The enormous developments that have taken place in information and communication technology have confirmed the position of

English as the dominant world language (see Reeves, 1996 and Hagen, 1998). Is this a key factor? Could it be that the heavy emphasis on the importance of basic skills and 'relevance' of curriculum content to young people has led them to have a much narrower view of what they need to learn for the future? Should the study of modern languages still be seen as an academic discipline in its own right, or as an accompanying skill to other subjects like Law, Media Studies, Business Administration or Leisure and Tourism? Are teachers much more 'qualification-orientated' rather than 'education-orientated' than in the past? Should modern languages continue to be offered to all? These issues are all essential to the question 'why learn a foreign language?' This chapter will examine these questions by looking at current arguments for modern foreign languages in the curriculum and discuss how we might make a more effective case for languages in the future.

Two opposing views

The vocational argument

'Learning a foreign language will help you get a (better) job', is the cliché that modern foreign languages teachers resort to at some time in their careers in an attempt to motivate reluctant learners. However, even if we do not consistently promote modern foreign languages in such a simplistic way, nevertheless, a vocational motive is implicit. After all, the National Curriculum at Key Stage 4 includes an Area of Experience on 'The World of Work'. The National Curriculum Working Group (1990) had previously indicated the importance for the UK as a trading nation of competence in foreign languages. A/AS level syllabuses follow through the vocational theme in various ways. The Dearing Report, The National Curriculum and its assessment (SCAA, 1995) called for an alternative vocational pathway to qualifications at KS4 which led to the introduction of Language Units by the National Council for Vocational Qualifications (NCVQ) and the School Curriculum Assessment Authority (SCAA), based on the NVQ National Language Standards. These Units are competence based for language use in the workplace and are intended as a vocational alternative to the GCSE short course. The Dearing Review of Post-16 qualifications goes much further in its general advocacy of vocational learning. The weight of the vocational argument continues to gain ground. But as Richard Hoggart (1999) suggests:

> Vocationalism is or seems value-free to those who wish to avoid a definition of education which raises troubling questions about social justice, about the needs of a democracy and, an even worse threat, about education as a good in itself, whatever its practical benefits.
>
> Hoggart (1999: 11)

The new underlying purpose of learning a modern foreign language, therefore, is its possible use in a work context. The value of learning a modern foreign language now lies in its potential for increasing the employability of a young person. The study of a language is now seen as a useful skill. This is not the case for some other school subjects, such as History, where the subject is seen as worthy of study *in its* own right. In the school context, the attempt at popularising modern language learning by reducing it to the level of a useful workplace skill like word processing can only diminish its status in the curriculum and will undoubtedly deter able learners from pursuing their studies to higher levels. Moreover, more important educational aspects of modern foreign language learning are either diminished or denied.

Modern foreign languages are very susceptible to vocational arguments because it is undoubtedly the case that a growing number of people do use a foreign language at work. That does not mean, however, that they should be promoted on that basis or that the vocational argument is effective in motivating learners. The marginal position of modern languages within the GNVQ framework suggests a certain ambivalence on the part of NCVQ (now QCA) in their support of languages in a vocational context. Moreover, teachers on GNVQ programmes express a reluctance to include Language Units partly because they are unlikely to be popular with many young people on vocational courses. While learners recognise on one level that proficiency in a foreign language might be of use to them in a job, they nevertheless make their career and study choices largely on the basis of what they like, rather than on what they are told could be useful in the future (see Lawes, 1999). Hawkins (1996) considers that while vocational arguments are now strong, not all vocations require a foreign language skill.

> And how honest is it for the teacher of slow-learning pupils, most of whom will work at manual or semi-skilled jobs, to pretend that French or German or Spanish still be *necessary for employment?* And what do we say to school leavers who face the almost certain prospect of unemployment?
>
> (Hawkins, 1996: 21)

The level of language skills achieved at GCSE in any case, provides only a base line. Where languages are used as part of a job, a much higher level of proficiency is required, often with a very specific orientation. Even at graduate level, languages are mostly needed as an ancillary skill in the majority of jobs. From a school perspective, it is impossible to predict which language a learner might need in the future. The continued predominance of French as the main modern foreign language in UK schools is an anachronism in vocational terms. And yet, if vocational arguments for modern foreign languages are so compelling, why have German, Spanish, Japanese or even Chinese not taken over from the language of the Enlightenment?

Nevertheless, strong economic arguments are continually put forward for improving the foreign language competency of people in the UK. Since 1993 the National Languages for Export Campaign sponsored by the Department of Trade and Industry has been enthusiastic in its support of modern foreign language learning initiatives in the interests of Britain's role in the global market. While the target of these initiatives has been export companies and industry in general, nevertheless, there is now a general understanding that schools also have a significant role to play.

Various studies have produced a wealth of evidence, which support the need for better foreign language expertise in a range of working environments. In his Institute of Linguists Threlford Lecture, Stephen Hagen (1998) draws on data from two large-scale studies, Elucidate (1998) and the DTI Language Study surveys (1994, 1995, 1996, 1997) to provide wide-ranging evidence of UK companies deficiency in modern language competence:

> The UK has the lowest number of companies in Europe with employees with language skills, the fewest companies with executives able to negotiate in a foreign language (apart from Ireland) and its companies are the least likely to include language skills in job adverts.
>
> (Hagen, 1998: 68)

He quotes the Expolangues-Ipsos survey of 1996 in placing Britain bottom of the European league table of foreign languages speakers. From a sample of 5,000 Europeans aged 15 and over, an average of 51 per cent said they were able to speak at least one foreign language. Although 26 per cent of Britons surveyed said they were able to communicate and 10 per cent were 'fluency' in French, Hagen suggests that this only means that the 26 per cent are able to string a few sentences together whilst the 10 per cent have roughly A level standard in the language (Hagen, 1998: 69). Hagen shares the concern with other modern languages specialists that, despite the fact that modern language study is compulsory to the end of Key Stage 4, there is a marked drop in learners continuing to advanced level. 'Most language study in schools is basic, limited to mainly French and non-vocational in content' (Hagen, 1998: 70). This may be true, but is school the best placed to teach modern languages for the workplace, or should the study of modern foreign languages in school have a wider, educational project?

So is a vocational argument an appropriate one to make to the average modern foreign language learner in school? Could it be that to impose the idea that the main reason for learning a foreign language is its practical use in the workplace could be counter-productive if not misleading for most young people? To promote such a functional approach to education in the early years of secondary education is likely to encourage a narrow instrumental view of education. At a later stage, 'I'm not going to need this for the job I want, so why should I bother?' might well be the response from many learners struggling towards GCSE. Whether or not their perception is accurate is not important, but the fact that they may see modern foreign language only in terms of a functional skill is.

Should the possibility that UK companies might be losing business because their employees lack foreign language skills really be the concern of education?

One could put forward a variety of solutions for business and industry to deal with the language learning needs of their employees. To promote a vocational purpose in foreign language learning necessarily leads to a change in curriculum content. Key Stage 4 of the National Curriculum for modern foreign languages is a clear example. It is highly questionable how much 'useful' language can be taught, apart from re-contextualising what has already been learned with the addition of a certain amount of specialist vocabulary. Moreover, within the broader content and requirements of GCSE, the attempt at introducing a vocational element is likely to be somewhat artificial and superficial. It is surely more important, for teachers of modern foreign languages in schools to concentrate on developing in their pupils a sound communicative ability, understanding and knowledge of a foreign language in a general sense, rather than to try to introduce a vocational 'spin' to the curriculum. Language training for specific jobs is best left to specialists and to employers to provide. The most effective languages for work provision is a combination of intensive and on-going courses at work, where learners have real situations to deal with and are consequently highly motivated. The most effective learners in these situations are ones who already have a good basis in the foreign language on which to build.

The academic argument

Attempts at putting forward an academic argument for modern foreign languages in the school curriculum at the present time are often self-conscious, half-hearted and run the risk of being branded as elitist. Yet, it is exactly an elite of modern linguists that Britain lacks at the present time: elite, that is, in the sense of the achievement of excellence. The appreciation and pursuit of excellence is not something we should be ashamed of or let bogus talk of elitism obscure. To promote academic worth is not to promote elitism in a traditional sense, where a privileged few are deemed worthy of accessing certain forms of knowledge. Gone are the days when a foreign language was seen as a subject that only the most able were capable of, because it was an academic pursuit involving acquiring a thorough knowledge of grammar, the ability to translate from one language to the other and to read classical literature. That is not to say that these aspects of modern foreign language learning are not worthwhile, nor that they should be entirely abandoned. However, the recognition that the ability to communicate with speakers of other languages is now rightly seen as being of prime importance.

The opportunity to study modern foreign languages is and should continue to be offered to all young people. However, the study of a modern foreign language should be not only about learning the right words to get across a message although teachers often feel that they have little scope for very much else. Some teachers find the National Curriculum for modern foreign languages somewhat restrictive, and assessment-bound. Others have found the content to be repetitive and unchallenging for more able learners. At the present time, it is uncertain whether the revised National Curriculum will continue to require languages to be compulsory at Key Stage 4. From the point of view of principle, it is difficult to imagine how such a move could be justified; from a practical perspective, it might be easier to make a case in terms of a pragmatic response to the problems raised earlier in this chapter. Should the policy of 'languages for all' be upheld in the name of equality of opportunity, or is it time to concentrate limited resources on those who can most benefit from them?

One of the apparent assumptions underlying a 'languages for all' policy was that curriculum content should be made more relevant and accessible if it were to be applied to the whole ability range. What emerged, was a selection of topic areas which, because they are repeated throughout five years of learning, have proved to be largely uninspiring and unchallenging. Imaginative, creative teachers notwithstanding, it is difficult to maintain motivation up to Year 11 across the range of ability in most topic areas. Differentiation does not compensate for inadequacies of content. The end result is that the real needs of most pupils are not met and the outcomes are disappointing. Nonetheless, if examination results are to be considered as the keystone, Table 3.1 shows the picture seems not too be all bad. In comparison with other subjects, MFLs fare well. Indeed, 17.6 per cent of candidates were awarded A* grade in French: the highest percentage of any subject. The question is: has GCSE been made easier or have standards risen?

Some commentators see the more utilitarian view of the role and value of modern foreign languages together with the implementation of a languages for all policy to the end of Key Stage 4, as being in some ways problematic. Mike Grenfell (1994) suggests that activities such as information gap exercises and role play in GCSE assess learning at a basic level, but amount to little more than phrase-book learning and concludes that 'it is misleading to assume that such exchanges of information represent communication and are hence pedagogically effective' (Grenfell, 1994: 56). Have attempts at combating elitism and democratising in education only led to a levelling down with many young people failing to achieve their potential?

James Milton and Paul Meara's pilot study of achievement in modern foreign languages by British, Greek and German learners (1998) provides disturbing

Table 3.1 GCSE attempts and achievements in MFL 1997–8

	Attempted GCSE			Grade A*–C			Grade A*–G		
	Boys	*Girls*	*Total*	*Boys*	*Girls*	*Total*	*Boys*	*Girls*	*Total*
Any modern foreign language	73	82	77	29	45	37	71	81	76
French	50	57	53	20	32	26	49	56	53
German	21	24	22	10	14	12	20	23	22
Spanish	6	8	7	2	5	3	5	8	7
Other modern languages	3	4	3	2	3	2	3	3	3

Source: Statistical Press Release 557/98 (DfEE 1998).

evidence of lower attainment by British learners compared with those in the other two countries. Milton and Meara conclude from empirical evidence that British learners spent less time learning, were set lower language goals and knew less vocabulary than equivalent learners in Greece and Germany and that there was a considerable difference in attainment. They point out that the poor performance of British learners are 'less the result of deficiencies amongst the teachers and learners, and are far more likely to be connected with the comparatively small amount of time devoted to language learning in Britain and the nature of the course which results from this'. Their final conclusions – that current provision fails both the most and the least able learners – raise grave concerns about modern foreign languages in the school curriculum.

> For the comparatively able British learners, it appears that the national curriculum severely curtails both the speed these learners can learn at, and the language level which they can attain. . . . The current course structure must be demotivating for a good learner. It is in everybody's interests that these learners are stretched to the limits of their abilities. For the less able learners it appears that the nature of the National Curriculum is such that they are notably less successful in languages in a way that the less able learners on the continent are not.
>
> (Milton and Meara, 1998: 76)

When we look beyond GCSE level, the situation becomes more acute. Are learners turning their backs on modern foreign languages at A level because they perceive them as too hard or because they no longer value them as subjects worthy of academic study? Have low expectations and low standards at Key Stages 3 and 4 contributed to the low status and diminishing popularity of languages in the 6th form and in Higher Education? The extensive re-writing of A level syllabuses to ensure a smoother transition from GCSE and to make them more 'relevant' and 'attractive' to learners, has meant that they now offer little more than an extension of the functional content of GCSE with a few 'issues' thrown in.

The main casualty, has been the compulsory study of literature that used to be regarded as an essential window into the culture and people of a foreign country as well as an essential initiation into academic study. The new syllabuses have not so far attracted more young people to study a modern language at A level. Could it be that the old syllabuses in themselves were not the main problem? The study of literature and modern foreign languages is discussed in depth in Chapter. . . . The point to be made here is that the marginalisation of foreign literature in A level syllabuses is an example of low expectations. The justification is made that literature is not really relevant to young people and that learning about a region of the country or using the foreign language to discuss their personal lives or the environment is more important. Behind this lies the suggestion that learners are no longer really capable of studying literature in a foreign language in any depth. Is that true?

The importance of immediate relevance and responding to learners' existing interests might be a starting point, but it is patronising to young people to suppose that they are only capable of exploring relatively practical topics or their subjective feelings. That is not to say that discussions of important social and political issues should not be part of A level syllabuses.

There is no evidence to suggest that young people are now less capable of engaging with different values, ideas, relationships and cultures through literature than they were in the past, or that they cannot be excited and intellectually challenged by what literature has to offer. However, as William Rowlinson points out, 'society determines the content of education in the light of the dominant philosophy . . .' (Rowlinson, 1994: 7).

A popular and influential view in society at the present time is that all knowledge is of equal value. For example, in a modern languages context, one might consider the study of the problem page in a French magazine as being the same as studying Madame Bovary. Both texts are selected on the basis that they consider the problems that people have in relationships. Is there any difference apart from length and complexity of language? On the one hand, the learner is presented with familiar problems within or near to their experience to which they can relate and which are presented in contemporary, often colloquial language. They can empathise and perhaps reflect on their own problems, discuss possible solutions, but they do not move beyond their own subjective experience. In Madame Bovary, on the other hand, they are confronted with more rich and complex language which is not immediately accessible and which requires greater effort to understand. Nor is the context within the learner's experience. But the dilemmas and the issues raised are universal problems of human experience and human relationships that allow the learner to move beyond the subjective. How is it possible to suggest that these two texts are of equal worth, or the knowledge gained from their study to be of equal value? That is not to say that using a problem page as a learning resource is of no value at all. Indeed, it might serve as a useful text for developing language skills and possibly providing preliminary material for discussing the sorts of issues that Madame Bovary raises, but nothing more.

This section started with an assertion that to promote modern foreign languages for their academic value does not necessarily imply elitism. Nor is it an 'old fashioned' view to take. Traditionally, the academic case for modern foreign languages has been seen as one which favours a small section of young people over the rest. As has been shown, there is an increasing body of evidence to suggest that recent attempts to make languages 'inclusive', 'accessible' and 'relevant' to learners has led to a lowering of expectations and achievement. Such a culture of low expectations is likely to favour mediocrity over genuine intellectual achievement. If this is true, then the academic argument is the only case that represents the interests of all young people; that offers the possibility of reclaiming the position of modern foreign languages as an academic discipline worthy of study by all.

What else do modern languages have to offer?

Personal and broader educational benefits

The personal benefits that young people gain from learning modern foreign languages relate to the educational benefits, and in turn, to the contribution an individual makes to society. While sharing many benefits with other subjects in the curriculum, modern foreign languages have nonetheless a unique contribution to make to the development of the individual. In the first place, the majority of learners start to learn a foreign language for the first time when they enter secondary school. Whatever their previous successes or failures in other curriculum areas, in modern languages lessons they all begin on equal terms with no previous history of failure. It is essential that this advantage be seized on. The potential for boosting self-esteem and developing self-confidence in learners through modern language learning is great. The initial enthusiasm and curiosity of the new Year 7 pupils needs to be nurtured as it can be easily lost through boredom, embarrassment or bewilderment within a matter of weeks! On the other hand, the satisfaction that learners feel when they are able to communicate is something that they can, and should, all experience. In schools where modern languages are valued highly, success in this area can have a good motivational effect for learners in other subjects.

Indeed, modern foreign languages as a subject area, are able to have an important influence throughout the school in terms of broadening horizons. Exchange visits and trips abroad are obvious ways in which individuals can broaden their experiences, put their language skills into practice and to get to know other ways of life. When groups of young people from partner schools abroad come to their UK school, ideally the whole school should be involved in hosting the visit. Not all pupils are able to receive exchange guests, but the experiences can be shared in various ways. Moreover, new technologies mean that 'virtual' travel on the world wide web can provide a new sort of window on the world; video-conferencing and e-mail contacts add a new dimension to having a pen-friend. These experiences can greatly increase motivation towards language learning, and also encourage social contact across national boundaries. Hawkins suggests that modern languages have a key role to play in widening the horizons of young people in that they 'can offer the pupil an experience different from that of the mother tongue and so contribute to an understanding of the polyglot world and emancipate the learner from parochialism' Hawkins (1987: 32).

Learning a modern foreign language offers the possibility of breaking down of barriers between people. It is liberating in that it emphasises common humanity in a world more disposed to emphasising difference. It offers the possibility of awakening an interest in other cultures and societies, into other ways of thinking and seeing and of encouraging positive attitudes towards people from other countries. It is enriching to learn other languages and delve into other cultures, but it is enriching not because languages and other cultures are unique, but because making contact across barriers of language and culture allows us to expand our own horizons and become more universal in our outlook. What other peoples and cultures have in common socially and economically is more important than their cultural differences.

'Cultural awareness' has become an important feature of the MFL curriculum. Teachers are encouraged to set language learning within a cultural context since it is recognised that language and culture are inextricably linked. At one level, what is meant by 'culture' relates to traditions, habits and customs of a country. This is an anthropological interpretation that often celebrates the past, that which is static in society and could serve to emphasise differences between people. Culture can also be seen as the best that humanity can aspire to and as providing access to things that are of universal value. From this perspective, 'culture' is dynamic, progressive and potentially a unifying force. In the school curriculum, there is a tendency to focus on the anthropological interpretation of culture and neglect what is of universal cultural value. This might take the form of emphasising trivial differences in daily routines or what food people eat so as to make the 'foreign' culture more foreign than it really is, and possibly to reinforce prejudices and create negative stereotypes. Through making cultural comparisons learners should be encouraged to seek for what people and societies have in common with each other.

In the same way, the study of a foreign language should enhance a learner's understanding of his or her own language. But this does not happen naturally. Walter Grauberg (1997), in discussing the importance of language awareness as a broader educational benefit of modern language learning suggests that

> Young people know that there are other languages besides their own, but when they begin to study a language like French or German, which show both differences and similarities to English, interesting fields of enquiry open up. 'How are languages related? What does a language tell us about its speakers' way of life, in the present or in the past? By what processes are words formed and the relation between words effected?'
>
> (Grauberg, 1997: 241)

He goes on to describe how the study of vocabulary can promote 'language awareness' and concludes that

> The realisation that the vocabulary of a language reflects changes in technology and culture in the widest sense, that such change is a natural feature of every language and that it is sometimes due to influences from abroad should have a broadening effect.
>
> (Grauberg, 1997: 241)

This issue is discussed further in Chapter 6, in relation to the integration of modern foreign languages in other curriculum areas. Clearly, no school subject is learned in isolation, the difficulty is, how to maximise the links between them.

In modern languages there is a heavy emphasis on 'performance' whether it is in real or simulated situations. The sorts of simulated situations that the teacher plans for language practice through role activities also teaches learners how to behave in certain situations, how to address people in particular contexts. When prepared carefully with learners, role activities provide opportunities for exploring a range of aspects of social interaction as well as appropriate forms of communication (see Joy, 1994: 167–179).

We have already touched on how success in the early stages of learning can boost the self-esteem and self-confidence of learners. Written communication and the development of learners' use of language to develop their own creativity is no less important. This could take the form of writing their own stories, poetry or songs. The opportunity to use language in a personal, imaginative, artistic way increases motivation, as well as creativity, and encourages the learner to experiment with language. Learners' own creativity in language use can be stimulated by and partially learned from exposure to the literature, poetry and songs of the target country. Learners are at the same time introduced to important aspects of the target country's cultural works.

Modern language learning, in common with other curriculum subjects provides opportunities for developing many learning skills. The development of learner autonomy is one of the long-term goals of education, that is, the ability to think critically and independently. Modern language learning has an important role to play in the development of learner autonomy in two key ways. First, the whole point of language is communication and as Frederick Engels observed at the end of the last century:

> knowledge of modern languages gives people at least the opportunity of rising above the narrow national standpoint as is the only medium through which the people of different nations can make themselves understood by one another and acquaint themselves with what is happening beyond their own borders.
>
> (Engels, 1894)

That is, speaking a foreign language potentially enables a greater independence of thought through wider and deeper knowledge and experience. Second, the approaches to teaching and learning employed in the modern foreign languages classroom should be aimed essentially at developing learner autonomy through intellectual challenge.

The way ahead?

There are significant changes ahead for the education system as a whole: a new National Curriculum about to be introduced, a transformation of the sixth-form curriculum, far-reaching government initiatives aimed at teachers and teacher training. At the time of writing, the trajectory appears to continue towards increased vocationalisation and emphasis on 'key' skills. As we have already seen, the link between education and work seems inextricable and this has led to a profound shift in emphasis in the school curriculum.

This chapter has examined two opposing ways of justifying the place of modern foreign languages in the secondary curriculum and looked at the broader education benefits of modern language learning. The effects of vocational influences on the school curriculum impinge increasingly on the work of the modern language teacher and the vocational argument is without a doubt attractive and persuasive. It has been argued, however, that the consequence of accepting the notion that education and the world of work are inextricably linked is to the ultimate detriment of modern languages in the school curriculum and can only lead to further marginalisation. More importantly, seen within a broader context, vocationalism offers a much narrower, restrictive view of education. The philosopher, John Anderson concluded in 1980:

> The field of education, then, is a battlefield between liberality and illiberality – between cosmopolitanism and patriotism, between the treatment of the child as 'the heir of all the ages' and the treatment of him as job-fodder.
>
> (Anderson, 1980: 156)

This statement is never truer today.

Editor's note

The purposes of learning MFLs are multifarious. Lawes recognises the value of learning MFLs for personal, social, cultural and vocational reasons. The functional bias associated with the communicative approach has led to an emphasis on the vocational context, corresponding with the recent vocationalisation of the curriculum. Lawes notes the damaging effect of this in terms of learner motivation and broader educational development. Faced with the charge of elitism in the past, teachers of MFLs, and syllabus writers have neglected the full potential offered through the teaching and learning of MFLs, for able learners in particular. She posits that there is a place for grammar and literature, and that through imaginative and creative teaching the benefits of learning MFLs extend beyond the limits of simply coping. Mfls have a powerful contribution to make to the education of young adults, which will hold them in good stead as modern citizens, and as learners.

Linked chapters

Chapter 18, Chapter 15 and Chapter 16.

References

Anderson, J. (1980) *Education and Inquiry*, Oxford: Basil Blackwell.
Dearing, Sir Ron (1994) *The National Curriculum and its Assessment*, London: SCAA.

Department for Education and Employment (1998) Statistical Press Release 557/98.

DTI (1994–97) Unpublished reports prepared by Metra Martech for the DTI national languages for export campaign study.

Elucidate Report (1998) in S. Hagen, *Study of the Needs of European Business*, London: CILT.

Engels, F. (1894) *Anti-Dühring*, London: Lawrence and Wishart (1975).

Grauberg, W. (1997) *The Elements of Foreign Language Teaching*, Clevedon: Multilingual Matters.

Grenfell, M. (1994) 'Communication: sense and nonsense', in A. Swarbrick (ed.) *Teaching Modern Languages*, London: Routledge/Open University.

Hagen, S. (1998) 'Exporting today: policy implications', *The Linguist*, 37(3): 66–70.

Hawkins, E. (1987) *Modern Languages in the Curriculum*, Cambridge: Cambridge University Press.

—— (ed.) (1996) *30 Years of Language Teaching*, London: CILT.

Hoggart, R. (1995) *The Way We Live Now*, London: Pimlico.

Joy, B. (1994) 'Role activities in the foreign language classroom', in A. Swarbrick (ed.) *Teaching Modern Languages*, London: Routledge/Open University.

Lawes, S. (2001) *Young People's Attitudes to Vocational Education*, London: Education & Work Research Group.

Milton, J. and Meara, P. (1998) 'Are the British really bad at learning foreign languages?' *Language Learning Journal*, 18 (Dec.), Rugby: Association for Language Learning.

Modern Foreign Languages Working Group (1990) National Curriculum Initial Advice, Department of Education and Science and the Welsh Office.

Reeves, J.(1996) 'Does Britain need linguistics?', in E. Hawkins (ed.) *30 Years of Language Teaching*, London: CILT.

Rowlinson, W. (1994) 'Historical ball and chain', in A. Swarbrick (ed.) *Teaching Modern Languages*, London: Routledge/Open University.

4 Which language? – An embarrassment of choice

Jim Anderson

Influences and attitudes

At the time of writing this chapter a national inquiry by the Nuffield Foundation (2000) is under way to reassess our current provision for and performance in learning other languages and to identify ways forward. One of the main areas for consideration in the inquiry is which languages we should in fact be teaching in our schools taking into consideration our membership of the European Union, but also the impact of global trade and the fact that the United Kingdom itself is a multilingual, multicultural society. The tension and uncertainty which so evidently characterises the British outlook with regard to each of these factors should serve to remind us that choices made about language in education, whether it be about the teaching of English or about other languages, are made in a context which is anything but neutral or value free.

The relationship between language and power has in fact been particularly transparent in British history and has played a significant part in shaping current attitudes. The imposition of the English language on peoples both within the United Kingdom and throughout the colonies has been used overtly as a means of civilizing and unifying and covertly as a tool of domination and control. Bourne (1997: 64 and 49), reflecting on the way in which language policy has consciously been used as a political tool in Britain, refers to 'the ideology of homogeneity that is so powerfully being constructed' and points out how an 'historical connection is often made between the perceived state of the language and the identity of the nation'. This serves the aims of an 'authoritarian state' which '. . . frequently uses the "national language" as a point of unity and social cohesion and finds linguistic diversity threatening, an element to be contained or even eliminated. In troubled times, when sectors of the community are becoming more deeply divided in terms of material wealth, language can be presented as a bond that unites'.

Moreover, the fact that English has come to be increasingly accepted as an international lingua franca has served to confirm notions of superiority and to encourage the view that if you speak English there is little need to learn other languages. In other words, being truly British has, within the national psyche, come to be synonymous with adopting a monolingual view of the world which sees other languages as inferior and any form of bilingualism as unnatural and potentially subversive. Given these factors it is little wonder that in terms of the proportion of our young people able to speak other languages, we are outper-formed by almost every other country in Europe (European Commission, 1991).

This point is significant here because underpinning any decision about which language(s) should be offered in our schools there needs to be an appreciation of the fact that all language learning is potentially valuable (whether the language be French or Japanese, Turkish or Tamil) and that success or failure will be fundamentally affected by the attitudes and expectations that we bring to the learning process. If we delude ourselves into thinking that our sense of national identity depends on fear and suspicion of all things 'foreign' (especially if they happen to be 'non-white') and if we continue to surrender intellectually to the comfortable stereotypes with which we are incessantly confronted in the media, then we will not create the conditions for that learning process to occur.

The present situation

This is not to suggest that there has been no progress in the teaching and learning of Modern Foreign Languages in Britain over the past fifty years. From a position where the learning of any MFL was reserved for a small elite and where as much, if not more, importance was attached to the study of dead languages than to living ones, it is now a statutory entitlement under the National Curriculum for all pupils from the ages of 11–16 to study at least one MFL. Theoretically the choice is wide, as can be seen from Table 4.1. In practice the number of these languages taught to any significant degree within main-stream schools is very limited indeed.

Under the original National Curriculum regulations (1991) it was agreed that 19 languages would be acceptable as the foundation subject language. The list is deliberately divided into two categories, the first being official languages of the

Table 4.1 List of languages which schools may offer as the foundation subject language

EU languages	Non-EU languages
Danish	Arabic
Dutch	Bengali
French	Gujarati
German	Hindi
Modern Greek	Japanese
Italian	Mandarin or Cantonese Chinese
Irish Gaelic	Modern Hebrew
Portuguese	Panjabi
Spanish	Russian
	Turkish
	Urdu

Source: DES Circular 15/91, p. 10, para. 39.

EU, the second being non-EU languages. From September, 1999 this number will rise to 20 to include Irish Gaelic. Moreover, it is proposed under the QCA (1999) National Curriculum Review that the restriction on which non-EU languages schools may offer should be lifted. There remains, however, the important proviso that students may only choose to study a non-EU language if they have been offered the chance to study an EU one.

In spite of the apparent choice provided under the National Curriculum by far the most commonly taught language remains French although there are also significant numbers taking Spanish and German. Figures 4.1 and 4.2 show the trend in number of entries for these languages (in England and Wales) at GCSE and Advanced level, respectively, over the past five years. Although those entering for French represent by far the highest number, the trend in recent years has been towards decline. Numbers for German, on the other hand, remain steady and for Spanish the trend is upward. It is worth noting, incidentally, that overall entries at Advanced level are low, reflecting the fact that currently the

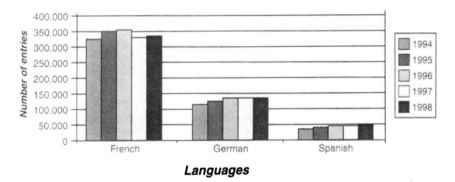

Figure 4.1 Entry numbers 1994–8 for GCSE French, German and Spanish in England and Wales (based on data provided in the CILT Direct 1999 Languages Yearbook) (1999: 41).

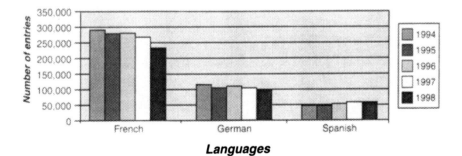

Figure 4.2 Entry numbers 1994–8 for GCE A level French, German and Spanish in England and Wales (based on data provided in the CILT Direct 1999 Languages Yearbook) (1999: 43).

vast majority of pupils, even amongst those who have been successful at GCSE, do not pursue their MFL studies into Key Stage 5.

Turning to other languages for which GCSE and Advanced level examinations are available, figures 4.3 and 4.4 also show the trend in numbers entering over the past five years. Taken in isolation the numbers for each language are low although trends are moving generally in an upwards direction. Of the non-

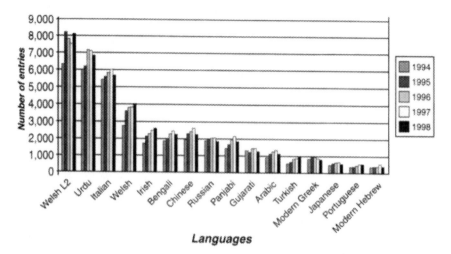

Figure 4.3 Entry numbers 1994–8 for GCSE in lesser taught languages in England and Wales (based on data provided in the CILT Direct 1999 Languages Yearbook) (1999: 40).

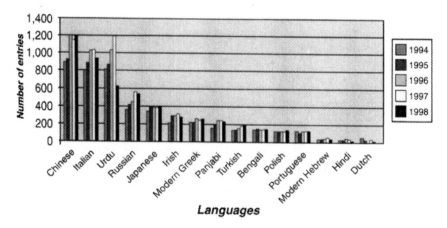

Figure 4.4 Entry numbers 1994–8 for GCE A level in lesser taught languages in England and Wales (based on data provided in the CILT Direct 1999 Languages Yearbook (1999: 43) and the CILT Direct Information Bulletin, No.13 (ed. L. Greenstock) (1999: 3)).

European languages at GCSE, Urdu has by far the highest number of entries followed by Bengali and Chinese and at Advanced level Chinese has the highest number followed by Urdu and then Japanese.

These figures do not, however, give the whole picture by any means. They only provide information on languages for which there is a GCSE or 'A' level examination available. It is in itself a significant fact that no published statistics exist recording what languages are being studied by what number of pupils in mainstream and supplementary sectors in Britain. We know that for decades immigrants to this country have run community classes to support the education of their children and in particular the maintenance of their languages and cultures. According to Rutter (1994: 85), 'Every Saturday morning over 10,000 children can be found learning their mother tongue in classrooms and living rooms throughout Britain'. Languages currently being offered through such community classes, and for which no GCSE or A level examination exist, include Bosnian, Farsi, Kurdish, Pushto, Somali, Tamil, Tigrinya, Vietnamese and Yoruba. There are many others.

Forces for change

As has already been suggested, choices to be made in determining what languages might be offered in our schools can be seen from a number of perspectives – political and economic, social and cultural, linguistic and pedagogical. We shall examine these in turn although it should be noted that the implications arising from each of them clearly overlap at certain points.

Political and economic arguments

Over the past fifty years, Britain has had to come to terms with no longer being a world power and, however reluctantly, has accepted the need to form ever closer ties with her neighbours in Europe. There has been a gradual shift in our trading pattern away from traditionally English-speaking markets and, as Hagen (1998: 15) suggests, over 60 per cent of British exports now go to members of the European Union.

Since the signing of the Treaty on European Union in 1992 it has been clear that the political aims of the EU have assumed increasing importance and that the ultimate goal is the creation of a European superstate able to wield influence on the world stage. In order to fulfil such aims the need has been felt to develop within young people the sense of a common European identity. Thus it is not surprising that the promotion of a European dimension in education, which was adopted in a Resolution by the Council of Ministers of Education in 1988, was strongly supported in the Treaty on European Union. Article 126 of the section on 'Education, vocational training and youth' (Council of the European Communities and Commission of the European Communities, 1992: 47) states that: 'community action shall be aimed at developing the European dimension in education, particularly through the teaching and dissemination of the languages of the Member States'. In order to put this policy into practice substantial funding has been made available. The overall budget of the 1995–1999 education and training programme, Socrates, for instance, amounts to some 850 million ECU.

Integral to the view of European citizenship being proposed is the notion of plurilingualism. The EU White Paper 'Teaching and Learning: towards the learning society' (1996) made one of its general objectives for education and training the development of proficiency in three Community languages. It is significant, however, that due to protests from the governments of several member states, including the United Kingdom, this was not made a binding commitment. Plurilingualism, however, means more than just speaking several languages. According to Draft 2 of the Council of Europe 'Common European Framework' document (1996: 95):

> Plurilingual and pluricultural competence refers to the ability to use languages for the purposes of communication and to take part in intercultural interaction, where a social agent has proficiency, of varying degrees, in several languages and experience of several cultures.

The document suggests that a language portfolio might be introduced in schools where students keep a personal record of all language learning experiences in both formal and informal settings.

As well as these major developments within the EU and the implications they have for language planning in Britain, we also need to be aware that increasingly business is being conducted on a global scale. In relation to the UK's export markets Hagen (1998: 15) argues that, 'the greatest potential for medium- to long-term trade growth lies in areas such as Latin America, Eastern Europe and Asia-Pacific (despite economic difficulties in 1998)' and he goes on to stress the fact that the UK's prosperity in these new markets, '. . . will depend increasingly on developing the capability to acquire not only knowledge of the local language, but also awareness of different cultural norms, values and trading practices, leading to product localisation'.

Whether we think in terms of our economic and political role within Europe or on a more global scale it is clear that the provision we have been making for language learning in this country is inadequate. For decades now the lack of foreign language skills within the world of British business and the detrimental effect that this has had on our economic performance has been widely, if at times reluctantly, accepted. Reeves (1996: 36) refers to a series of reports examining the need for foreign language skills within British industry which strongly indicate that 'there is a correlation between the employment of linguistically qualified personnel and exporting success, and the converse, namely that an absence of linguistic expertise can result in lost business'. He goes on to highlight the problem of the common mismatch of languages that employees can offer compared with actual needs of companies, attributing this to the dominance of French within the MFL curriculum in schools.

This point was, in fact, clearly recognised by the government some ten years ago when it sought to introduce a policy on diversification of the MFL curriculum offer. As a 1988 DES/Welsh Office policy document (1988: 8–9) states:

> LEAs and schools should ensure that a reasonable proportion of their pupils of all abilities study a language other than French as their first foreign language. Although it would be impossible to specify an ideal mix of language provision in schools, the current situation is clearly inappropriate to the needs of a modern trading nation. In trading terms alone, a number of studies suggest that German and French are equally in demand by exporting companies, and there is also a strong need for Italian and Spanish. A capability in German or Spanish is useful not only to firms operating in Western Europe but also to those with markets in Eastern Europe and Latin America, respectively.

Incidentally the document also refers to Britain's trading links outside Europe and to the need for speakers of Arabic, Japanese, Chinese and other Asian languages, but in spite of the fact that some of these are languages of minority groups in Britain it is considered (ibid: 9) 'unlikely to be a cost-effective use of resources to provide them within schools for pupils of compulsory school age'. Just as in the two lists of languages considered acceptable within National Curriculum a clear division is established between EU and non-EU languages. The rationale given for this (ibid: 9) is that, 'On commercial and cultural grounds, priority should be given to the main languages of the European Community'.

Although there was a positive response to the diversification policy initially, a CILT/TES survey carried out in 1996, based on responses from 1,140 schools, indicated that the initiative had quickly run out of steam. The survey examined two forms of diversification: first, the broadening of the range of languages offered as a first MFL in Year 7 and second, languages offered as a second or third MFL. Tables 4.2 and 4.3 reproduce tables contained in the survey.

Table 4.2 Distribution of the most common categories of first foreign language provision

First foreign language offered	Number of schools	% of schools with this offer
French only	624	54.7
French and German (split provision)	223	19.6
French and German (dual provision)	86	7.6
Not applicable/first foreign language not offered	52	4.6
French and Spanish (split provision)	51	4.5
French, German and Spanish (split provision)	21	1.8
French and German alternating each year (wave provision)	11	1.0
French and Spanish (dual provision)	11	1.0
German only	10	0.9
Spanish only	7	0.6

Source: TES/CILT (1996: 8).

Table 4.3 Languages offered as a second or third MFL

Second foreign language	Number of schools offering the language in any combination	Percentage of all schools offering language as second FL
German	720	63.2
Spanish	293	25.7
French	288	25.3
Italian	44	3.9
Russian	27	2.4
Urdu	16	1.4
Punjabi	5	0.4
Japanese	3	0.3
Bengali	3	0.3

Source: TES/CILT (1996: 16).

With regard to the first MFL the survey found that that some schools, having attempted to diversify provision, reverted to offering only French as a first foreign language in Year 7. The major reason given for this was difficulty in recruiting staff qualified in two or more languages, although pressure to build on French being taught in primary schools was also a factor. It is also worth remembering that, since schools were given greater control over the management of their budgets through LMS they have felt less obliged to follow policies promoted by the local education authority.

As far as the second or third MFL is concerned the survey found that, although a majority of schools (80 per cent) offer two languages in Key Stage 3 (34 per cent making the study of two MFLs compulsory), it is only about 5 per cent of students that pursue the study of both languages in Key Stage 4 and most of these attend grant maintained or independent schools. The explanation given for dropping the second language at Key Stage 4 is lack of curriculum time. A further factor may be that where schools make split provision for the first language, i.e. where some pupils study one language and some another, it can become difficult to create viable second language groups.

A recent government initiative which has led to greater diversification of languages taught in mainstream schools has been the creation of Language Colleges of which, according to statistics from CILT, 58 exist in England and Wales at the time of writing. Part of their brief is to 'offer a broad range of modern foreign languages and associated qualifications, which often include less widely taught, but economically and culturally significant languages' (DfEE, 1997: 12). It is expected that all pupils attending these colleges 'should gain a qualification in at least one, and study a second modern foreign language at Key Stage 4'. Apart from French, German and Spanish which are offered in almost all colleges, some eighteen other languages are also being taught. Of these Italian is being taught in 38 colleges, Japanese/Japanese Studies in 36, Russian in 21, Chinese in 18 and Urdu in 8. Patterns of provision for these languages differ considerably. Japanese, for example, may be taught to small groups of sixth formers or to all students in Year 7.

Social and cultural arguments

Although we still lag considerably behind our European neighbours in terms of the provision we make for the learning of MFLs and in ultimate performance, it is clear that economic and political links with the EU have played a major part in shaping government policy. What is equally clear is that opportunities available to us as a multilingual and multicultural society have, for the most part, gone unsupported and unrecognised.

Geach (1996: 151) points out that some 10 per cent of the population of the UK are speakers of Community Languages and estimates that this proportion is likely to remain constant.

Research carried out in 1993 by the University of London's School of Oriental and African Studies estimated that 275 languages were regularly spoken in London. According to Buncombe and MacArthur (1999: 10) further research carried out by the same body indicates a more accurate figure for 1999 to be 300.

Children who grow up bilingual or indeed multilingual are potentially at a tremendous advantage when it comes to language learning not only because each of their languages forms part of their life experience and is therefore embedded psychologically at a deep level, but also because their awareness of language is greater than that of monolinguals and this means that other languages are learnt with greater ease (Swain and Lapkin, 1991; Valencia and Cenoz, 1992). Why is it, then, that a child bringing into school a particular skill in music or drama or sport will have that skill nurtured and encouraged, but that a child whose skill lies in being able to speak Turkish or Chinese or Bengali, as well as English. is likely within our education system to have that skill ignored? Why is such a skill not seen as important for the cognitive and emotional development of that child and as a resource which can promote the language and cultural awareness of all pupils? Why do we not value an outstanding performance in a Gujarati examination as highly as a mediocre one in French? As Boaks (1998: 36–37) points out:

> The presence of many bilingual pupils in schools represents a significant element in our national language capability. The provision of Welsh- and Gaelic-medium state schooling has given considerable status to those languages but the potential contribution of bilingual speakers of Asian languages in the UK remains undervalued.

It is worth recalling that the influential Swann Report (1985), whilst calling on the one hand for strong anti-racist policies and for promoting the teaching of English as a second language argued against bilingual education through minority languages (with the exception of Welsh) on the grounds that it would be socially divisive. Mother tongue maintenance according to the report would best be provided within the communities themselves. Mitchell (1991: 114–15) rightly points out that:

> As linguists we know that minority language maintenance within English-dominant society is hard even with school system support, and almost impossible without, and to say to local groups [as the Swann report did] that their language maintenance efforts are to be respected but be excluded from mainstream schools, is inconsistent if not insincere.

Curiously, it was then argued that these languages should be offered in secondary schools as Modern Foreign Languages. The really important thing, then, it would seem, was to establish that such languages could not be viewed as a legitimate part of mainstream British culture.

The same assimilationist philosophy underlies the National Curriculum introduced several years later. No provision is made for the teaching of languages other than English/Welsh/Gaelic at primary level. At secondary level the opportunity is created for the teaching of some minority languages as Modern Foreign Languages (see Table 4.1), although the split list implies higher status for EU languages.

It is hard to avoid the conclusion made by Verma, Corrigan and Firth (1995: 7) that the planning objective behind the policy was, 'to let the process of attrition affect the heritage languages in the early formative years', with the result that by the secondary stage, 'some minority children are demotivated altogether from opting for their heritage language while the others are convinced that their heritage language has, after all, become a foreign language. Languages such as Panjabi, Bengali and Urdu, then, do not feature in the secondary curriculum as a consequence of any desire to fulfil socio-psychological educational needs – rather they are offered on a par with subjects such as French or German, as if they were new to the student. This highlights one of the means by which the National Curriculum promotes planning for non-preservation'.

So far we have been looking at the teaching of the languages of minority groups mainly from the standpoint of bilingual learners and seeing how the British education system devalues their skills, holds back their linguistic and cognitive development and denies a sense of pride in a cultural allegiance which is part of who they are. This is not to suggest for one moment, however, that these languages are really only of relevance to bilingual learners. All language learning experience is potentially valuable for all children, particularly as it is impossible to predict what languages any individual might need in the future. For many children who do not get the opportunity to go on school journeys or family holidays to France or Germany, the opportunity to learn a language which they can hear in use every day within the local community may well give that language greater relevance and lead to improved levels of achievement in relation both to language skills and cultural understanding.

Clearly there are practical issues here of a logistical and methodological nature and different choices will be appropriate in different circumstances. What is crucial, however, is that all the languages spoken within the school community should be valued and supported and that they should be drawn upon to enrich and enhance the language learning experience of all pupils. There is a body of evidence (Hawkins, 1987; James and Garrett, 1992) showing that Language Awareness courses developed in the 1970s and 1980s contributed significantly to furthering these aims by challenging the blinkered and intolerant attitudes towards other languages and cultures, in particular those of ethnic minorities, which are still prevalent in British society. Unfortunately the narrow subject focus imposed through the introduction of the National Curriculum meant that most of these courses were dropped.

One key way in which mainstream schools can raise the status of the languages of bilingual pupils is by establishing links with mother tongue classes organised in the community. The recently founded Resource Unit for Supplementary and Mother-tongue Schools estimates that there are some 800 such schools in the London area alone. The government is in fact currently promoting links between the mainstream and supplementary sectors through its Study Support initiative for 'out of school hours learning activities'. The policy, set out in a DfEE document (1998: 10–2) is being supported by lottery money through the New Opportunities Fund. It remains to be seen, however, how effective this approach will be.

Linguistic and pedagogical arguments

It has been argued in the introduction to this chapter that, in general terms, the most important factor in determining success in learning other languages is what Spolsky (1989: 25–6) refers to as the 'social context', i.e. those forces in society which over time shape attitudes. However, it is also likely to be true that, depending on one's first language, certain other languages may be relatively easier or harder to learn. In deciding what language(s) should be offered as the first experience of MFL study in Year 7 this is of particular importance because it guarantees the greatest chance of success for all pupils.

James (1979: 19–22) suggests a commonsense method designed for comparing, what he termed the 'linguistic distance' between, in this case, English and the five languages which at that time were most commonly taught in the British education system, i.e. French, German, Italian, Russian and Spanish. To do this, he took five levels of linguistic performance – phonological, grammatical (morphology and syntax), lexical, orthographic and spelling – and rated them for each language on a five-point scale with 1 representing the least difficulty/ distance. The results James arrived at (see Table 4.4 below) indicate that French is a significantly harder language for an English speaker to learn than Spanish or Italian and marginally more difficult than German. His view is that the difficulty of Russian is greatly increased because it is written in a non-Roman script, a factor that also applies to Arabic, Chinese and Japanese and to the languages of the Indian sub-continent. However, it is worth pointing out Macrae and Rix's (1991) claim that Russian can be taught very successfully to mixed-ability classes and that the degree of difficulty of a language depends primarily on the methods used to teach it. Incidentally, his viewpoint is supported by Phillips and Stencel (1983: 44). Commenting on research carried out into pupil perceptions

Table 4.4 Relative difficulty of learning different languages for the native English
speaker

	French	German	Spanish	Italian	Russian
Phonological	4	2	2	1	3
Grammatical	2	3	2	2	3
Lexical	1	2	1	1	4
Orthographic	1	1	1	1	4
Spelling	4	2	1	1	2
Global distances	12	10	7	6	16

Source: James (1979: 19–22).

of and attitudes to different languages, which highlighted the overriding
importance of the teaching method and the teacher, they concluded that, 'To a
large extent . . ., pupils were influenced by the nature of the learning experience
rather than the language itself'.

Later research by Phillips and Filmer-Sankey (1993), comparing the relative
difficulty of French, German and Spanish – the Oxford Project on Diversification of First Foreign Language Teaching (OXPROD) – also suggested that
there were good reasons to question the dominant position of French. This
longitudinal study, carried out between 1987 and 1993 in six mainly mixed
comprehensive schools, set out to test the hypothesis that, 'there is nothing in
the nature of German and Spanish as subjects in the school curriculum that
makes these languages unsuitable as first foreign languages for the whole ability
range' (Phillips and Filmer-Sankey, p. 109).

As far as motivation is concerned, it was found that in the first three years as
a whole, there was a general preference for German and Spanish over French.
Taking levels of attainment into account here, it was found that higher
attaining French and German learners showed more positive attitudes than
lower attainers, but that for Spanish there was no decrease in motivation with
attainment level. With regard to the difficulty of the language, French was
perceived to be more difficult than German or Spanish, the kind of problems
experienced relating to pronunciation, spelling, gender and vocabulary. Learners
of Spanish and German felt that there was a close correspondence between the
way the languages were spoken and written and that they were easy to pro-
nounce. By the third year, however, learners of German were commenting on
the complexities of German grammar, including gender, cases, word order and
verbs. Fewest linguistic problems overall were mentioned by Spanish learners. In
terms of usefulness, the three languages were considered to be equally useful
especially for future careers, given Britain's developing role within Europe. It
was also found that students' attitudes were affected by parents' and siblings'
attitudes to and experience of the three languages.

Unsurprisingly, the conclusions drawn from the research were that, 'the wider
teaching of German and Spanish (in particular) as FL1s would be at least as
successful as the teaching of French' and that there were grounds for thinking
that German and Spanish 'would be more likely to result in success at certain

levels and with certain pupils' (Phillips and Filmer-Sankey, 1993: 164). In a smaller scale study conducted by Kenning (1992 and 1994), which compared responses of Year 7 pupils with the learning of French, German and Italian, the language which was perceived to be most enjoyable and easiest to learn was German. As Kenning (1994: 21) points out, the consistency between her findings and those of the OXPROD project would seem to suggest, 'that the appeal of German has much to do with the language itself'.

The need for a national language policy

In this chapter we have looked at possible choices open to us in deciding which languages should be taught in this country in the next century, as well as major forces affecting the way choices have been made hitherto. The fact that the Nuffield Inquiry is taking place reflects perhaps a growing sense that there is a need, (a) to give greater priority to the teaching of other languages in this country; and (b) to reconsider what range of languages should be offered in our schools.

In considering these issues, there are those whose argument rests primarily on utilitarian principles, in particular the linguistic skills needed by our young people if we are to compete in an increasingly internationalised job market. Reeves (1990, 1996) and Hagen (1988, 1998, 1999) both point to the dangers of complacently assuming that a knowledge of English will be enough in conducting business in the future. They also highlight the fact that the current imbalance in the school curriculum in favour of French is inappropriate and that increasingly we need to be looking towards the development of competence in non-European, as well as European languages.

For Roberts (1994) on the other hand, the narrow economic argument is both unconvincing and educationally unacceptable. He argues that the hegemony of English as the official language of Europe is well underway and that it is likely to extend its influence in future. This, for him, does not in any way diminish the importance of learning other languages though. He shares Hawkins' view that it is impossible to predict what languages students may need in later life and that the study of MFLs at school level should be seen as an 'apprenticeship' through which learners may develop 'a greater sense of cultural and linguistic awareness that will enrich their lives as language-using adults and prepare them for learning any language that might be useful for them at a later stage in their career' (p. 26). As he further points out, once it is accepted that the purpose of Modern Languages study is the development of cultural and linguistic awareness, attempts to prioritise some languages over others becomes redundant since these aims can be achieved through the study of any language. A further advantage identified by Roberts is that this '. . . would permit greater flexibility in choice and would help to secure the role of 'community' languages in our schools which are currently under threat from the National Curriculum's Eurocentric and functional bias' (p. 26).

International travel and communication mean that increasingly our young people have a sense of themselves as citizens of the world. There is perhaps no more powerful symbol of how trans-global links are becoming part of our everyday lives than the Internet. Already this new technology is having a huge impact on education, not least in the field of Modern Languages. One project currently being funded by the European Union (Rainger, 1998) links young people from Guatemala, Spain, Britain and the Western Saharan refugee camps in Algeria. Communication takes place via email, fax, photography, video and newsletters in English and Spanish.

The need, then, is for a broad and creative approach which values all forms of language learning and encourages both sensitivity and sophistication in the way we communicate. As Graddol (1998: 31) points out, 'The key challenge for us is to transform our languages provision into one which supports an ever-increasing diversity of languages, allows for and encourages all levels of proficiency, and provides a flexible basis for introducing new languages into the curriculum'.

The practical implications here are clearly considerable in terms of curriculum time, the training of suitably qualified teachers and the development of appropriate resources. This is why, without an integrated national policy on language learning it is likely that little will change. Brumfit (1999) sees the purpose of such a policy as being to, 'erode deeply entrenched monolingualism' (p. 30) and to instil an awareness of changing social and cultural realities:

> Neither internally nor externally can Britain afford to be monolingual. All major industrial countries are becoming increasingly multilingual, as labour mobility indigenises more and more previously foreign languages, and as a resurgence of support for older mother tongues creates subcultures associated with the languages marginalised by the monolingual policies tacitly espoused by nineteenth century nationalism.
>
> (pp. 30–1)

Whilst recognising the constraints imposed by current legislation and available resources, he (1989 and 1999) urges institutions at all levels of education to embrace a language charter based on four key elements:

1   development of mother tongue or dialect;
2   development of competence in a range of styles of English for educational, work-based, social and public-life purposes;
3   development of knowledge of the nature of language in a multilingual society, including some basic acquaintance with at least two languages from the total range available in education or the community;
4   development of a fairly extensive practical competence in at least one language other than their own.

(Brumfit, 1989: 13)

He sees these as being minimum requirements adding that there should be opportunities for those who wish to specialise to work on more than one foreign language.

Such an integrated approach is, in fact, one which has repeatedly been argued for in successive government reports (Bullock, 1975; Swann, 1985; Kingman, 1988; Cox, 1989), but which has never been carried forward into policy. As has already been argued, the reasons for this doubtless have something to do with the British ambivalence towards other languages and cultures. In deciding what provision needs to be made for language learning in this country we have, in more senses than one, an embarrassment of choice. We can, of course, continue to be embarrassed and to perpetuate the myth of some monolingual and unidimensional British identity, or we can begin to celebrate the insights and opportunities that pluralism and plurilingualism make possible. This, much more than any issue of 'which language?', is the key question to be addressed.

Editor's note

This chapter relates the nation's language skills to political, economic, social and cultural awareness and success. Anderson demonstrates the linguistic wealth within the multi-cultural society in which we live, and laments the poor range of languages on offer to school pupils. He argues strongly for a national policy on all grounds. Which language is taught and learnt should reflect the social and linguistic mix of the British people and Anderson stresses the powerful benefits of such a policy. Cultural awareness and the skills of inter-cultural communication underpin a successful approach. He remarks on a linguistic imperialism of the British which serves to devalue the sub-cultures of ethnic groups and also to reduce the linguistic potential of the nation as a whole. Pedagogic issues are well presented, illustrating the lack of a logical justification for French being the dominant foreign language in schools. It is interesting, too, to note that the difficulty factor is linked to teaching methodology, a further argument for the re-examination of MFL teaching and learning in this country.

Linked chapters

Chapter 17, Chapter 18, Chapter 11.

References

Boaks, P. (1998) 'Languages in schools', in A. Moys (ed.) *Where Are We Going With Languages?*, London: Nuffield Foundation.

Bourne, J. (1997) '"The grown-ups know best": language policy-making in Britain in the 1990s,' in W. Eggington and H. Wren (eds) *Language Policy – Dominant English, Pluralist Challenges*, Canberra: Language Australia Ltd.

Brumfit, C. (1989) 'Towards a policy of multilingual secondary schools', in J. Geach and J. Broadbent (eds) *Coherence in Diversity: Britain's Multilingual Classroom*, London: CILT.

—— (1999) 'A policy for language in British education', in A. Tos and C. Leung (eds) *Rethinking Language Education – From a Monolingual to a Multilingual Perspective*, London: CILT.

Bullock, A. (1975) *A Language for Life – Report of the Committee of Inquiry Appointed by the Secretary of State for Education and Science*, London: HMSO.

Buncombe, A. and MacArthur, T. (1999) 'London: Multilingual Capital of the World', *The Independent*, 29 March 1999.

Centre for Information on Language Teaching and Research (CILT) Direct 1999 Languages Yearbook (1999), London: CILT. (This document is made available to subscribers to the scheme.)

Council for Cultural Co-operation – Education Committee (1996) *Modern Languages: Learning, Teaching, Assessment. A Common European Framework of Reference – Draft 2 of a Framework Proposal*, Strasbourg: Council of Europe.

Council of the European Communities and Commission of the European Communities (1992) *Treaty on European Union*, Luxembourg: Office for Official Publications of the European Communities.

Cox, B. (1989) *English for Ages 5–16 – Final Report of the English Working Group*, London: HMSO.

Department for Education and Employment (1997) *Specialist Schools. Education Partnerships for the 21st Century*, London: DfEE.

—— (1998) *Extending Opportunity: a National Framework for Study Support*, London: DfEE.

Department for Education and Science (1991) *The Education Reform Act 1988: Modern Foreign Languages in the National Curriculum* (Circular 15/91), London: HMSO

—— (1988) *Modern Languages and the School Curriculum – A Statement of Policy*, London: HMSO.

—— (1991) *Modern Foreign Languages in the National Curriculum*, London: HMSO.

European Commission (1991) *Young Europeans in 1990*, Brussels: European Commission.

—— (1996) *Teaching and Learning: Towards a Learning Society*, Brussels: European Commission.

Geach, J. (1996) 'Community languages', in E. Hawkins (ed.) *Modern Languages in the Curriculum*, Cambridge: Cambridge University Press.

Graddol, D. (1998) 'Will English be enough?', in A. Moys (ed.) *Where Are We Going With Languages?*, London: Nuffield Foundation.

Greenstock, L. (ed.) (1999) Centre for Information on Language Teaching and Research (CILT) Direct Information Bulletin, No.13, London: CILT. (This document is made available to subscribers to the scheme.)

Hagen S. (1988) *Languages in British Business. An Analysis of Current Needs*, Newcastle-upon-Tyne Products and CILT.

—— (1998) 'What does global trade mean for UK languages?', in A. Moys (ed.) *Where Are We Going With Languages?*, London: Nuffield Foundation.

—— (1999) 'Overview of European findings', in S. Hagen (ed.) *Business Communication Across Borders. A Study of Language Use and Practice in European Companies*, London: CILT.

—— (1999) 'The communication needs of British companies in an international trading environment', in S. Hagen (ed.) *Business Communication Across Borders. A Study of Language Use and Practice in European Companies*, London: CILT.

Hawkins, E. (1987) *Awareness of Language: An Introduction*, Cambridge: Cambridge University Press.

James, C. (1979) 'Foreign languages in the school curriculum', in G. Perren (ed.) *Foreign Languages in Education, NCLE Papers and Reports*. London: CILT.

James, C. and Garrett, P. (eds) (1991) *Language Awareness in the Classroom*, London: Longman.

Kenning, M.-M. (1992) 'The joint languages diversification model: aspects of a case study', in C. Wringe (ed.) *Language Learning Journal*, 5: 2–5, Rugby: Association for Language Learning.

—— (1994) 'Language preference and time allocation in the joint languages diversification model', in C. Wringe (ed.) *Language Learning Journal*, 9: 19–21, Rugby: Association for Language Learning.

Kingman, J. (1988), *Report of the Committee of Inquiry into the Teaching of English Language*, London: HMSO.

Macrae, J. and Rix, D. (1991) *Russian, Resource Guide for Teachers*, London: CILT.

Mitchell, R. (1991) 'Multilingualism in British schools: future policy directions', in P. Meara and A. Ryan (eds) *Language and Nation*, London: CILT.

The Nuffield Foundation (2000) *Languages: The Next Generation. The Final Report and Recommendations of the Nuffield Languages Inquiry*, Milton Keynes: The English Company (UK) Ltd.

Phillips, D. and Filmer-Sankey, C. (1993) *Diversification in Modern Language Teaching. Choice and the National Curriculum*, London: Routledge.

Phillips, D. and Stencel V. (1983) *The Second Foreign Language*, London: Hodder and Stoughton.

QCA (1999) *National Curriculum Review Consultation Materials*.

Rainger, A. (1998) *Voces Españolas*, London: BBC Educational Publishing.

Reeves, N. (1990) 'The foreign language needs of UK-based corporations', *The annals of the American Academy of Political and Social Science*, 511: 60–73.

—— (1996) 'Does Britain need linguists?', in E. Hawkins (ed.) *30 Years of Language Teaching*, London: CILT.

Roberts, T. (1994) 'Modern languages in perspective', *Languages Forum*, 1(2 and 3).

Rutter, J. (1994) *Refugee Children in the Classroom*, Stoke-on-Trent: Trentham Books.

Spolsky, B. (1989) *Conditions for Second Language Learning*, Oxford: Oxford University Press.

Swain M. and Lapkin, S. (1991) Heritage language children in an English–French bilingual program, *Canadian Modern Languages Review*, 47(4).

Swann, Lord (1985) *Education for All*, London: HMSO

TES/CILT (1996) *Modern Languages Survey*, London: CILT.

Valencia, J. and Cenoz, J. (1992) The role of bilingualism in foreign language acquisition: learning English in the Basque country, *Journal of Multilingual and Multicultural Development* 13(5).

Verma, M.K., Corrigan, K.P. and Firth, S. (1995) 'Death by education: the plight of community languages in Britain', *Language Issues* 7(1).

5   At what age should foreign language learning begin?

Keith Sharpe and Patricia Driscoll

Introduction

Like Shakespeare's enumeration of the ages of man the possible answers to this question are seven-fold:

1   Never
2   In adulthood, at the point of need/desire/interest
3   During adolescence as an option or under compulsion
4   At the beginning of the secondary cycle
5   During the later primary years
6   Throughout the years of primary schooling
7   As early as possible

We consider the implications of each of these in turn.

Never

This answer need not delay us for long. It is essentially grounded in the view that either there is no particular educational or other value in learning a foreign language or that there is no need to learn another language perhaps because one's mother tongue happens to be widely spoken and understood. Either way there is no point in foreign language learning at any age, and the arguments about when and how it should be done are of no consequence. This view is of course fundamentally mistaken. The learning of foreign languages carries immense value both intrinsically and instrumentally for anyone engaged in the process, as indicated in other chapters of this book; and to argue that there is no need to learn other languages, even for speakers of 'world' languages, is to betray massive ignorance of the realities of the globalising world that, for good or ill, we now inhabit.

In adulthood, at the point of need/desire/interest

This position tends to be based on the view that teaching foreign languages in schools is full of problems, mainly surrounding some notion of unwilling, disaffected pupils being forced to learn something they do not like and do not see the point of, and that it would therefore be better to wait until children grow into adults and develop a real life interest in learning a foreign language, perhaps associated with employment or with actual travel plans. Confining the teaching of foreign languages to adults in this way would mean that teachers would only ever have to face motivated and committed learners who would have the advantage also of having acquired a range of learning skills already. Painful encounters in school classrooms could be avoided, the overcrowded school curriculum could be relieved of an element to which considerable time is given, and the general levels of success enjoyed by foreign language teachers would rise. This approach is however based upon a number of assumptions which need to be challenged. We would want to question for example the assumption that foreign language learning in schools is necessarily always problematic as well as the assumption that adults are actually better learners of foreign languages. We suggest that there are valid educational arguments for obliging children to learn foreign languages irrespective of the difficulties involved. These issues will be discussed later in this chapter.

During adolescence, as an option or under compulsion

At this point we begin to enter the argument about critical age, i.e. that in some sense it is better if foreign language learning begins before adulthood, whether through the provision of teaching in the subject as an option or as requirement. What is generally meant by better is that: (a) young learners have advantages in learning foreign languages which are lost if the process is delayed until adulthood (these may be to do with both specific linguistic skills as well as more general capacities toassimilate and process new information and ideas); (b) language learning has a broader value such as promoting tolerance and cross-cultural understanding, and is of such importance that children should be exposed to it during their schooling; (c) in the case of the United Kingdom and other member countries of theEuropean Union, it is important that other European languages are encountered by children during their education as part of their preparation for future life and citizenship. And of course the same argument can be used to make a similar case for all nations and the importance of global citizenship in the twenty-first century.

At the beginning of the secondary cycle

This answer takes all the principles in the section above, but lowers the critical age specifically to 11 years. There are two basic ideas behind this position: first, foreign language learning is of comparable importance to other core subjects such as mathematics or science and should be treated in the same way. Second, for a variety of reasons, it is nevertheless appropriate to make a distinction between foreign languages and other core subjects as far as the primary curriculum is concerned and exclude it on a number of possible grounds, including the belief that young children cannot learn foreign languages as effectively as adolescents; the fact that there are insufficient appropriately qualified primary teachers of MFL; and the conviction that primary schooling should concentrate on basic skills in literacy and numeracy.

During the later primary years

In the final decades of the twentieth century there has been an increasing tendency to raise doubts about the wisdom of the orthodoxy set out in the above section, which has generally held in the education systems of most developed countries. A key argument has been that young children have advantages of linguistic and cognitive flexibility which facilitate success in terms of language learning, and the age of 11 is purely an administrative 'cut off point' for which there is no inherent justification. Another key argument has been that, to the extent that the purpose of teaching foreign languages is to do with impacting upon attitudes, this is better done in the primary years when children are more malleable. It has also been claimed that it is possible to incorporate modern languages into the primary curriculum in such a way that the essential objectives of primary education are still achieved, and by starting earlier, levels of attainment in foreign language learning at the point of assessment in secondary schooling will be raised.

Throughout the years of primary schooling

For the most part, attempts to introduce modern languages into the primary curriculum have been focused on the upper junior years with pupils between the ages of 9 and 11. Many advocates of primary MFL teaching maintain, however, that the arguments in favour of including MFL in primary schools apply to the whole age range, and that 9 is just as much an arbitrary cut off point as 11. Their contention is that modern foreign languages should in some form or other constitute a consistent part of the primary curriculum offered to children between the ages of 5 and 11 in the first 6 years of compulsory schooling.

As early as possible

Real enthusiasts for the teaching of modern foreign languages to young children take the view that exposure should begin as soon as possible. There are a number of projects in different countries designed to introduce a foreign language to nursery age children. There are for example in France some instances of pupils as young as 3 involved in learning English in the *École Maternelle*. Amongst these enthusiasts there is a conviction that the sooner the learning begins the better will be the quality of that learning, not only in relation to measures of linguistic performance but also in relation to the motivational and attitudinal gains claimed for MFL teaching in primary schools.

These seven positions thus span the complete spectrum of opinion in relation to the worthwhileness of teaching MFL. It is possible to view developments during the twentieth century broadly in terms of an overall shift of general opinion, both in England and elsewhere, from position one towards position seven. This drift has not been smooth and progressive; there have been lurches and U-turns, but on the whole the pattern is fairly clear. At the beginning of the century, MFL were not considered suitable curriculum content for inclusion in schooling; at the close of the century they are well established in secondary schools and increasingly being taught in primary schools.

The present situation in England

As far as England is concerned there has been rapid growth of interest in the teaching and learning of foreign languages in primary schools since the mid-1980s (Sharpe, 1991). The Centre for Information on Language Teaching and Research reported that approximately 20 per cent of the state primary schools in at least 40 LEAs (CILT, 1995) in England and Wales and Northern Ireland offer some foreign language provision (CILT, 1995) and following a successful pilot phase, Scotland has embarked on an extension programme to introduce MFL to all primary schools.

The move towards a single market has forged closer links between countries in the European Union thereby creating potentially greater prospects for the workforce. Languages are seen as a key factor in accessing those potential prospects. This recent development of commitment to interdependence in the European marketplace is an important factor lying behind the tendency of parents who want 'the best' for their children increasingly to exert pressure on primary schools to include a foreign language in their curriculum provision (CILT, 1995).

Extending modern languages 'downward' into the primary school has received some official attention, Dearing (1993), SCAA (1997), DfEE, (1998). Although there are no national guidelines of what constitutes good practice, a broad framework of expectations can be found in the Handbook for the Inspection of Primary Schools issued as Guidance for Inspectors (Ofsted, 1998), despite the fact that MFL is not a statutory requirement as part of the National Curriculum for primary schools. This would appear, *prima facie*, to constitute significant evidence of increasing official interest in, and recognition of, the activity.

The underlying rationale for the growth in primary MFL teaching

As suggested above, this growing interest in the teaching of modern foreign languages in the primary school is underpinned and sustained by some key ideas. Broadly speaking there are two central strands to the argument advanced by those in favour of teaching MFL in the primary school. The first strand is concerned with increasing pupils' linguistic proficiency at some future date. It is claimed that, by starting earlier, eventual standards of achievement will be raised. The second strand is concerned with offering a broader education for pupils. It is contended that learning at a formative age about a foreign language and the culture in which it is embedded will enhance the overall quality of pupils' educational experience, specifically developing knowledge, skills and understanding in the areas of socio-cultural empathy, interpersonal skills and language awareness.

The increased linguistic proficiency argument rests on two assumptions. The first is that pupils possess age-specific attributes which allow them to learn languages more efficiently than older pupils, and an 'early start' will profit from this resource and result in raised levels of linguistic attainment later in schooling. We shall call this the age factor assumption.

The second assumption is that by extending the learning time of MFL by a year or more in the primary school, pupils will be able to spend more time practising and learning the language, with the result that they will have achieved higher standards by the time they take public examinations. We shall call this the time factor assumption.

For the sake of clarity, the argument of the age factor will be discussed separately from the time factor, although it is important to emphasise they are complementary rather than mutually exclusive.

The age factor assumption

A critical issue at the heart of the primary MFL debate is whether 'young is best' in relation to foreign language acquisition on the basis that before puberty children possess natural abilities to learn languages efficiently. The idea of there being an optimum age to learn languages was first argued by Penfield and Roberts in 1959, and later supported by Lenneberg's theory of optimal age (1967). The 'critical period hypothesis' suggests that in the years before puberty a child's brain is particularly adaptable for acquiring languages and that language acquisition that takes place after puberty will be different in nature and potentially less successful (Lenneberg, 1967). However, although there has been an abundance of research concerning the 'critical period' the findings are rather complex and as yet there is little conclusive research evidence to support the proposition that there exists a specific critical age for foreign language learning.

Singleton (1989) discusses the evidence and the issues using an analytic framework of four distinct propositions:

1   that young is best in overall attainment
2   that young is best with particular skills such as the oral and aural skills
3   that older is best in general terms
4   that young is best 'in the long run'

No very clear single proposition could be seen to be clearly apparent from the research evidence. The popular general notion that 'catching them young' leads to overall language proficiency, is simply not supported by research findings except in a number of studies in naturalistic settings. For example, the Canadian immersion study by Lapkin *et al.* (1991) found that pupils who started an immersion programme in pre-school showed superiority across the four skills in comparison with pupils who had started an immersion course at the age of 10. Snow and Hofnagel-Hohle (1978), who conducted an extensive study into maturational factors in naturalistic conditions, concluded that younger learners may eventually surpass older beginners in these circumstances. Their findings showed that 12–15-year-old pupils achieved higher scores in all the skills but that the younger group, the 6–10-year-olds caught up and performed better than the older learner on 'story comprehension' and 'spontaneous speech fluency'. Given, however, the huge differences which exist between a naturalist language learning environment and the teaching of a foreign language to pupils in a school classroom setting, it is not possible to use these findings as a valid basis for justifying the earlier teaching of MFL generally.

Research into the effectiveness of The Primary French Pilot Scheme which ran in England between 1964 and 1974 (The National Foundation for Educational Research (NFER) study reported in Burstall, 1974) concluded that there were no overall advantages to be gained from teaching modern languages in the primary school. It was found that the scheme pupils who had been taught French from the age of 8, did not reveal any substantial gain in mastery at the secondary stage over those pupils who started at the age of 11 except in listening comprehension.

Buckby (1976), however, highlighted certain testing discrepancies in the NFER evaluation: for example, the 'experimental pupils' were not tested either for pronunciation or fluency in conversation, both of which had been identified as major advantages for starting French in the primary school. The study was further challenged by Gamble and Smalley, who criticised the 'inadequate questionable, statistical data' (1975: 94). They pointed out that the sample numbers during the nine year study dwindled to unreliable levels; in 1964 there were 11,300 'experimental' pupils and in 1973 the whereabouts of only 1,227 'experimental' pupils were known, yet these small numbers were used as if they could produce reliable and valid results. Above all, the NFER evaluation was seriously weakened by its failure to consider the impact of what the secondary schools did. In most cases they grouped 'experimental' and non-experimental pupils together, ignoring the fact that the former had already studied French for three years. The demotivating effect on these pupils of starting again from scratch was never raised as an issue by the researchers.

Some later researchers have reported evidence indicating a superiority on the part of younger pupils in both oral and aural performance (see Singleton, 1989) where younger children appear to possess a superior 'sound' system (Krashen *et al.*, 1982; Long, 1990). There is also some evidence that as children get older a decline in the quality of native-like pronunciation is evident (Vilke (1988)).

A recent review of European research on early learning in MFL (Blondin *et al.*, 1998), suggests that where primary beginners' attainment is compared in secondary school with the attainment of pupils who have had no primary experience, the primary beginners tend to show an advantage in certain competences such as listening comprehension, although this advantage may be limited to certain pupils such as the faster learners. In the studies reviewed, the outcomes were mostly measured in the early stages of secondary schooling, and therefore the results do not give an indication of long-term effects or advantages. The studies do also show an advantage in reading comprehension in the early stages of secondary schooling (Karl and Knebler, 1996), a slight advantage in broad listening, reading and writing skills, but only in the case of the most able pupils, and the advantage appeared to last only about a year (Genelot, 1996). The teachers perceived an advantage in active listening but not in linguistic knowledge or performance (Favard, 1992). The evaluation of the national pilot scheme in Scotland (Low *et al.*, 1993, 1995) showed that the 'Project pupils' (those pupils who had been taught in the primary school as part of the national scheme) displayed a clear advantage over non-Project pupils in pronunciation and intonation, complexity of structure, length of utterance, ability to sustain interaction, a good level of comprehension and a greater readiness to answer in class. In addition they showed fewer signs of stress and were prepared to use risk-taking strategies in order to sustain interaction.

In terms of the rate of acquisition some studies indicate that older learners tend to be more efficient and effective language learners, and that they generally achieve higher scores on performance tests with an equivalent exposure time (Ausubel, 1964; Asher and Price, 1967; Oller and Nagato, 1974; Snow and Hofnagel-Hohle, 1978). The findings from the NFER report (Burstall *et al.*, 1974) showed that, after 3 years extra tuition, the younger learners displayed virtually no superiority in reading and writing, in comparison with the older beginners, again suggesting that older pupils learn more effectively and quickly 'catch up', although the methodological weaknesses of this study referred to above have always to be borne in mind. The 'experimental' pupils (who had experienced primary French) were also tested at the age of 13 along with pupils who were 2 years older but who had received the same amount of instruction time. It was found that the 15-year-old 'control' pupils' performance on each level of the French tests was consistently superior to that of the 13-year-old 'experimental' pupils (Burstall *et al.*, 1974).

Krashen *et al.* (1982) examined the evidence of child/adult differences by distinguishing between long-term and short-term studies both in informal natural environments and in classroom situations. They suggested that, in light of the research literature, three generalisations can be made in terms of the relationship between age, rate, and eventual attainment in a second language.

1   Adults proceed through early stages of syntactic and morphological develop-
    ment faster than children (where time and exposure are held constant).
2   Older children acquire faster than younger children (again, in early stages
    of syntactic and morphological development where time and exposure are
    held constant).

3   Acquirers who begin natural exposure to second languages during childhood generally achieve higher second language proficiency than those
beginning as adults.

(Krashen *et al.*, 1982: 161)

or as Larsen-Freeman and Long (1991) put it, 'older is faster, but younger is
better' (1991: 155).

There are a number of possible reasons as to why older learners appear to outperform younger learners in the rate of language acquisition. They have a better
knowledge of language patterns, are better at more cognitively demanding tasks,
have more developed general learning strategies and skills, and they have more
experience of acquiring facts and concepts (McLaughlin, 1985; Collier, 1989;
Johnstone, 1994). Also, the majority of research evidence concerning the
comparative rate of acquisition between younger and older learners relates to
outcomes as measured by tests, which arguably favour older learners, either
because the tests are cognitively too demanding for younger age groups or
because the testing techniques are unfamiliar to younger pupils. Johnstone
(1994) notes that, in order to control the variables, some research projects use
the same teaching methods for all age groups, but he suggests that this is
probably an inappropriate practice for any single age group and that studies
based on this approach may not in fact be 'fair' tests.

The time factor

It is sometimes claimed that the amount of time actively spent learning the
foreign language is a significant factor in achieving high levels of proficiency
(see Radnai, 1996 for example). Advocates of an earlier start would contend
that primary provision can promote specific competences which are then able to
be developed at a more sophisticated level in the secondary school as well as
offering to the young child a rich holistic learning experience which is
qualitatively different in kind to the secondary provision. However, if the
argument is simply that, by increasing the number of hours of exposure to MFL
teaching better results overall can be obtained, it might well be the case that the
increase would be better made during secondary schooling, and that this
argument has little of substance that is relevant to primary MFL per se. Indeed
some would maintain that, by using up precious time in primary education on
MFL, young children would not be spending as much time on acquiring basic
skills in numeracy, literacy and an understanding of their mother tongue as they
should, and indeed that, without a secure grounding in these areas, their
capacity to learn anything effectively at the secondary stage, including MFL is
impaired.

With respect to the time factor, there is little conclusive evidence to show
that the extra early years yield better results in linguistic proficiency later in
schooling; however other variables should perhaps be examined before firm
conclusions are drawn. The lack of linguistic superiority could also be a result of

inappropriate teaching methods for young pupils within the primary school, a lack of relevant subject knowledge on behalf of primary teachers, or a lack of differentiation in the materials and methods to suit pupils of varying abilities. The lack of liaison between the primary and secondary schools, may inhibit pupils' progression, and therefore could mask the advantages of the time factor. As has already been pointed out, in the Primary French Project (1964–73) the 'experimental' pupils who had studied French for 3 years were grouped in the same class and taught alongside the 11-year-old beginners. As Buckby observed at the time that 'in this situation one would expect initial gains to be quickly lost' (Buckby, 1976: 16). It would consequently be quite invalid to deduce from this experience that additional years of teaching make no difference.

Does an early start carry benefits?

So then what can be concluded about the benefits of an early start for future linguistic proficiency? Studies have failed to show any clear long-lasting benefit for the young learner except in naturalistic settings. It may be that there is a level of 'actual' overall learning time that needs to be spent in naturalistic contexts before younger beginners show their superiority to older beginners, and it may be that this can never be replicated in formal classroom settings (Singleton, 1987). In general the findings are confusing, sometimes appear contradictory, and do not reveal discernible consistent patterns. Where in some studies there is evidence to support apparent gains in oral and aural skills, other studies show advantages only in listening or in reading and writing. As Singleton suggested in 1987 'Second language acquisition research which, because of its relatively recent beginnings, is not in any case an abundant provider of answers' (1989: 250). In the subsequent decade this position has not substantially changed.

The real issue

It is certainly advantageous for young children to learn another language early when there is something approximating to a 'naturalistic' setting. For example, the child may have a parent who speaks another language, or may be living in a country where more than one language is widely spoken. However, the hard benefits specifically in terms of improved foreign language competence from formalised teaching in primary schools appear to be much more elusive. The arguments in favour of starting foreign languages in the primary school therefore cannot with certainty be built upon the claim that better levels of foreign language competence will necessarily be the automatic result. They have instead to be framed by what is referred to in the beginning of this chapter as the second strand in the debate, which refers more generally to the contribution of MFL to the educational experience of young children.

Foreign language provision makes a valuable contribution to the primary child's overall personal development and should not be seen purely as a foundation for future MFL learning. It cultivates childrens' communication skills and their understanding of human cultures. It plays a significant role in introducing children to new discoveries and the 'world of sound' (Vivet, 1995). A key aspect of primary schooling is the provision of opportunities for children to learn about language, and particularly the opportunity to understand that their mother tongue is only one human language and not the only human language, however widely it happens to be spoken (Driscoll, 1999). As was suggested at the beginning of this chapter, we would wish to argue that primary MFL learning promotes tolerance and cross-cultural understanding. It helps children to understand that they live in a multilingual and multicultural society and that the country they live in is a member state of the European Union which is itself multilingual and multicultural (Sharpe, 1992). In this way the broader educational value of primary MFL at such a formative time of schooling is a crucial element in the case for 'starting them young'. We now explore some of these benefits in more detail.

Cultural awareness and intercultural awareness

The cultural aims of language teaching encompass the development of pupils' interest in and understanding of cultures, an appreciation of ways of life in other countries as well as within the multicultural society of their home nation. Fennes and Hapgood (1997), set out a view of what they call 'the iceberg concept of culture' where only a small part of it is visible but where the major part is beyond our consciousness. Above the waterline are cultural elements such as eating customs, national costumes, music and lifestyle, and below the waterline are aspects of culture such as taken-for-granted notions of correct behaviour, social expectations, modesty, the concept of personal space, body language, appropriate relationships to persons, animals and objects, etc. By learning about the concept of culture, the learner can recognise the importance of culture on people's lives and reflect on their own identity in a more detailed way. Intercultural awareness implies an openness towards others, where the pupil's own critical perspective of their own cultural conventions, attitudes and values is developed, through a process of change and self-development (Byram, 1989).

The development of cultural understanding is a complex process of acquiring multidimensional knowledge, skills and attitudes, some of which undoubtedly can be beneficially pursued in the primary phase of schooling through the work of MFL learning. Professor Michael Byram's work on the concept of intercultural competence is helpful here (Byram, 1997). Byram and colleagues put forward the idea of a series of *'savoirs'* as a useful framework for considering the attitudes, knowledge and skills involved in teaching and assessing the cultural dimension. The *savoir être* is concerned with the cultivation of attitudes such as curiosity, openness and a willingness to accept the other person's perspective as normal. Second, there is a concern with the acquisition of knowledge of different social groups, social classes, customs and norms in one's own and other societies and includes such concepts as national culture and ethnic identity. Third, *savoir comprendre* is crucial to the skills of interpretation of documents which have to be understood in their context. Fourth, *savoir apprendre/faire* is concerned with the skills of discovery and interaction which enable the learner to acquire new knowledge as well as an understanding of the beliefs, meanings and behaviours of any interlocutor. Finally, *savoir s'engager* is concerned with the way learners evaluate foreign behaviours, beliefs and meanings by contrast with their own. Although some of these concepts, skills and attitudes go beyond the cognitive and developmental maturity of a novice learner in the primary school (Byram and Morgan et al., 1994; Morgan, 1995), young learners can be provided with opportunities to perceive the world differently so that they are less likely to accept surface appearance and more likely to see beyond the cultural stereotype. MFL can develop a greater capacity in younger learners to see the world from someone else's point of view and to develop an openness and acceptance of differences in others. Gangl (1997) found that by learning foreign language through an interactive approach in the primary school children developed more open attitudes to other cultures. This element of cultural awareness contributes towards pupils' own personal and social development; it therefore might influence their own sense of identity, as well as influence their perceptions of the people they are learning about. Cultural understanding is a long-term goal and primary schools can begin the process by developing pupils' curiosity, tolerance and appreciation towards other cultures, ways of life and people, as well as developing pupils' insight into the roots of their own culture.

Language awareness

To develop an awareness of the nature of language and a greater sense of the roots of words is part of developing that general overall literacy which is such a key element in primary schooling. There is some evidence that pupils who experienced foreign languages in primary school develop an interest in the differences between languages, and greater metalinguistic awareness (see Bailly and Luc, 1992; Pinto et al., 1995), as well as positive attitudes and skills in reading (Charmeux, 1992), although it has to be acknowledged that this is not reflected in all research (Genelot, 1996). Johnstone (1999) points out that although the research shows no clear connection between the development of metalinguistic and intercultural awareness at the primary phase and increased success in learning a foreign language in secondary schooling, this does not mean that a connection does not exist, only that as yet one has not been established. Language awareness can also influence pupils' attitudes to language as well as their knowledge about it and skill in using it. Hawkins (1984) argues that linguistic parochialism is deep within our society and that through the study and experience of a foreign language a greater linguistic tolerance can be developed that may help prevent narrowness and prejudice prevalent in some homes. The primary school is well placed to set the learning of a foreign language into the wider curriculum and to make a valuable contribution to the general education of primary children.

The development of social attitudes and motivation to learn languages

In order to learn a language effectively motivation is essential: this is par excellence the subject where 'you can take the horse to water but you can not make it drink'. As a general principle we would suggest that by and large young children can be more easily inspired to want to communicate in a foreign tongue than can adolescents, and they can thus acquire an early confidence in language learning as a result which can make teaching them later as adolescents easier. The findings of the NFER study (Burstall *et al.*, 1974) showed that children who started French in primary school showed a consistently more favourable attitude towards speaking French in comparison with secondary starters, the only substantial advantage identified by this study. A number of studies reflect these findings and show evidence of positive attitudes among pupils at primary school to learning a foreign language (see the review of research in Blondin *et al.*, 1998).

Curiosity is such a strong motivator (Seelye, 1994) which can be used by the primary MFL teacher to inspire an interest that leads to discovery and understanding about the ways of life in another country thereby laying the foundations for tolerance and empathy towards its people. The development of positive attitudes towards foreigners is revealed by some studies to be associated with the development of positive attitudes towards learning the language (Gardner and Lambert, 1972; Schumann, 1978; Mitchell *et al.*, 1992). Hawkins (1987) suggests that the capacity for empathy declines with the onset of adolescence particularly among boys, it can therefore be argued that this essential work has to be achieved before the age of 11, after which insularity and prejudices tend to be more firmly established and consequently more difficult to challenge.

Conclusion

We would therefore wish to assert that it is in these areas of attitudes, values, and socio-cultural understanding that the rationale for the early teaching of MFL is most securely based. In the English context it can be argued that MFL learning makes a significant contribution to personal, social, moral and spiritual education which are statutory requirements of the primary stage of education. On this basis our contention is that the age at which foreign language should begin is at the start of compulsory primary schooling. This is not to say that 4 and 5 year olds in England or elsewhere should be taught formal foreign language structures. It is however most definitely to argue that there should be a properly structured progression of foreign language awareness and linguistic competence development across the primary years as a statutory requirement alongside other statutory curricular provision in primary schools. We would agree with the final report of the Council of Europe's report on language learning for European citizenship which identifies a growing consensus across the Union that 'language learning is now seen as a normal part of education from the child's first socialisation. The question is no longer "whether?" or even "when?" but "how?"' (Council of Europe, 1997: 48).

Editor's note

Sharpe and Driscoll examine the values and purposes of teaching and learning MFLs at an early age. They cite research evidence which suggests that the age pupils begin studying a foreign language has little discernible impact on linguistic proficiency. They note, however, the fallibility of such research, and also recognise the influence of learning in naturalistic settings. The true value of learning MFLs from an early ages they claim, is more attitudinal. Sharpe and Driscoll point out the willingness of young children to accept cultural differences, and indeed, they present a process of acculturation which is facilitated by both the age factor and the exposure factor. Similarly, Sharpe and Driscoll recognise the value of language awareness, as a goal in itself, and suggest that experience and expertise gained through an early start to MFL learning does have a positive impact on pupils as learners of a broad curriculum, and as future citizens.

Implicit throughout their chapter is an assumption that language teaching methodologies should be adaptable to suit the maturational stage of learners' development. One key criticism of research which has failed to note the benefits of an early start is that the teaching and learning methods have been based upon established secondary education principles. Sharpe and Driscoll promote 'primary languages' as a means of improving the education of young people, and not exclusively as a way of improving foreign language skills.

Linked chapters

Chapter 2, Chapter 6, Chapter 18.

References

Asher, J. and Price, B. (1967) 'The learning strategy of the total physical response: some age differences', *Child Development*, 38.

Ausubel, D. (1964) 'Adult versus children in second language learning: psychological considerations', *Modern Language Journal*, 48.

Bailly, D. and Luc, C. (1992) 'Approche d'une langue étrangère a l'école', *Études Psycholinguistiques et Aspects Didactiques*, 2, Paris: INRP.

Bennett, S. N. (1975) 'Weighing the evidence: a review of primary french in the balance', *British Journal of Educational Psychology*, 45.

Blondin, C., Candelier, M., Edelenbos, P., Johnstone, R., Kubanek-German, A. and Taeschner, T. (1998) *Foreign Languages in Primary and Pre-school Education: Context and Outcomes A Review of Recent Research within the European Union*, London: Centre for Information on Language Teaching and Research.

Buckby, M. (1976) 'Is primary French in the balance', *Modern Language Journal*, 60.

Burstall, C. et al. (1974) *Primary French in the Balance*, Windsor: NFER Publishers.

Byram, M. (1989) *Cultural Studies in Foreign Language Education*, Clevedon: Multilingual Matters.

Byram, M. and Morgan, C. and colleagues. (1994) *Teaching-and-Learning Language-and-Culture*, Clevedon: Multilingual Matters.

Charmeux, E. (1992). 'Maîtrise du français et familiarisation avec d'autres langues', *Repères*, 6: 155–72.

CILT (1995) *Modern Languages in Primary Schools: CILT Report 1995*, London: CILT.

Collier, V. P. (1989) 'How long? A synthesis of research on academic achievement in a second language', *TESOL Quarterly*, 23(3) 509–31.

Council of Europe (1997) *Language Learning for European Citizenship: Final Report (1989–96)*, Strasbourg: Council of Europe Publishing.

Dearing, R. (1993) *The National Curriculum and its Assessment*, London: SCAA.

DfEE (1998) *Blunkett Strengthens Curriculum Focus on the Basics – Press Release 006/98*, London: DfEE.

Driscoll, P. (1999) 'Teacher expertise in the primary modern foreign languages classroom', in P. Driscoll and D. Frost (eds) *The Teaching of Modern Foreign Languages in the Primary School*, London: Routledge.

Edelenbos, P. (1990) 'Leergangen voor Engels in het Basisonderwijs Vergeleken', dissertation, University of Groningen, Groningen: RION.

Favard, J. (1992) 'Les langues étrangères à l'école primaire: la problématique française', in D. Arnsdorf, H. Boyle, P. Chaix and C. O'Neil (eds) *L'Apprentissage des Langues Étrangères à l'École Primaire*, Paris: Didier Érudition, pp. 29–38.

Fennes, H. and Hapgood, K. (1997) *Intercultural Learning in the Classroom: Crossing Borders*, London: Cassell.

Gamble, C. J. and Smalley, A. (1975) Primary French in the balance – 'Were the scales accurate?' *Journal of Modern Languages*, 1975: 94–7.

Gangl, R. (1997) 'Learning through interaction – a discourse model for FLT to primaries', manuscript: unpublished doctoral thesis, Karl-Franzens-Universität, Graz.

Gardner, D. B. and Lambert, W. E. (1972) *Attitudes and Motivation in Second Language Learning*, Massachusetts: Rowley.

Genelot, S. (1996) *L'Enseignement des Langues à l'École Primaire: Quels Acquis pour Quels Effets au Collège? Éléments d'Évaluation: le Cas de l'Anglais* (Les Notes de l'Iredu), Dijon: Institut de Recherche sur l'Économie de l'Éducation.

Hawkins, E. (1984) *Awareness of Language – An Introduction*, Cambridge: Cambridge University Press.

—— (1987) *Modern Languages in the Curriculum*, Cambridge: Cambridge University Press.

—— (1996) 'Languages teaching in perspective', in E. Hawkins (ed.) *30 Years of Language Teaching*, London: CILT.

Johnstone, R, (1999) 'A research agenda for modern languages in the primary school', in P. Driscoll and D. Frost (eds) *The Teaching of Modern Foreign Languages in the Primary School*, London: Routledge.

Johnstone, R. (1994) *Teaching Modern Languages at Primary School*, Edinburgh: SCRE.

Karl, P. and Knebler, U. (1996) *Englisch in der Grundschule, und Dann? Evaluation des Hamburger Schulversuchs*, Berlin: Cornelsen.

Krashen, S., Scarcella, R. and Long, M. (1982) *Child–Adult Differences in Second Language Acquisition*, Rowley, MA: Newbury House.

Lapkin, S., Hart, D., and Swain, M. (1991) Early and middle French immersion programs: French language outcomes, *Canadian Modern Language Review*, 48(1).

Larsen-Freeman, D. and Long, M. H. (1991) *An Introduction to Second Language Acquisition Research*, London: Longman.

Lenneberg, E. (1967) *Biological Foundations of Language*, New York: Wiley and Sons.

Long, M. H. (1990) 'Maturational constraints on language development', *Studies in Second Language Acquisition*, 12: 251–85.

Low, L., Brown, S., Johnstone, R. and Pirrie, A., (1995) *Foreign Languages in Primary Schools: Evaluation of the Scottish Pilot Projects 1993–1995 Final Report*, Stirling: Scottish CILT.

Low, L., Duffield, J., Brown, S. and Johnstone, R. (1993) *Evaluating Foreign Languages in Primary Schools*, Stirling: Scottish CILT.

McLaughlin, B. (1985) *Second Language Acquisition in Childhood: volume 2. School-age Children*, second edition, Hilsdale NJ: Lawrence Erlbaum Associates.

Mitchell, R., Martin, C. and Grenfell, M. (1992) *Evaluation of The Basingstoke Primary Schools Language Awareness Project: 1990–91*, Southampton University: Centre for Language in Education Occasional Papers 7.

Morgan, C. (1995) 'Cultural awareness and the National Curriculum', *Language Learning Journal*, 12.

Office for Standards in Education (Ofsted) (1998) *Inspecting Subjects 3–11, Guidance for Inspectors*, London: OFSTED Publications Centre.

Oller, J. and Nagato, N. (1974) 'The long term of FLES: an experiment', *Modern Language Journal*, 58.

Penfield, W. and Roberts, J. (1959) *Speech and Brain Mechanisms*, Princeton, NJ: Princeton University Press.

Pinto, M. A., Taischner, T. and Titone, R. (1995) 'Second language teaching in Italian primary education', in P. Edelenbos and R. Johnstone (eds) *Researching Languages at Primary School Some European Perspectives*, London: CILT.

Radnai, Z. (1996) 'English in primary schools in Hungary', in P. Edelenbo and R. Johnstone (eds) *Researching Languages at Primary School: Some European Perspectives*, London: CILT.

SCAA (Schools Curriculum and Assessment Authority) (1997) *Modern Foreign Languages in the Primary Curriculum*, London: SCAA.

Scarcella, R. and Higa, C. (1981) 'Input, negotiation, and age difference in second language acquisition', *Language Learning*, 32(2).

Schumann, J. (1978) 'From the Acculturation Model for second language acquisition', in R. Gingras (ed.) *Second Language Acquisition and Foreign Language Teaching*, Arlington, VA: Centre for Applied Linguistics.

Seelye, H. N. (1994) *Teaching Culture: Strategies for Intercultural Communication*, 3rd edition, Lincolnwood (Chicago): NCT Publishing Group.

Sharpe, K. (1991) 'Primary French more phoenix than dodo now', *Education*, 3–13 March.

—— (1992) 'Communication, culture, context, confidence: the four 'Cs' in primary modern language teaching', *ALL Language Learning Journal*, 6.

Singleton, D. (1989) *Language Acquisition and the Age Factor*, Clevedon: Multilingual Matters.

Snow, C. and Hofnagel-Hohle, M. (1978) 'The critical period for language acquisition: evidence from second language learning', *Child Development*, 49.

Vilke, M. (1988) 'Some psychological aspects of early second-language acquisition', *Journal of Multilingual and Multicultural Development*, 9 (1 and 2).

Vivet, A. (1995) 'Sens et rôle des langues dans le développement des enfants in Council of Europe', *Report on Workshop 17*, Strasbourg: Council of Europe.

6 The unique contribution of Modern Foreign Languages to the curriculum

Shirley Lawes

Introduction

The issues discussed in this book all contribute to an understanding of what makes modern foreign languages 'special' in the secondary school curriculum. This chapter will examine the three elements of the modern foreign languages curriculum which make the area unique: the teaching of culture and cultural awareness, language awareness and grammar and visits and exchanges abroad. We will consider how the 'uniqueness' of MFLs might be seen as something of a paradox at the present time and how its unique potential is being eroded through curriculum initiatives which are presented as enhancing developments but which, arguably, are the opposite. We will also look at how, in a practical sense, it is still possible for modern foreign languages to be a beacon of universal values in a post-modern world.

In Chapter 3, it was suggested that modern language learning has a key role to play in widening young people's horizons and offers the possibility of breaking down barriers between people from different countries and cultures. This is at the heart of what makes the study of modern foreign languages unique in the school curriculum. It is a traditional view born out of the eighteenth century 'Enlightenment' period during which belief in the progress of human knowledge, rationality, civilisation and control over nature led to unprecedented social, political and scientific advances in society. The Enlightenment project sought to free people from their narrow lives, to bring them together and to promulgate a universal concept of mankind.

'Cultural awareness', by which we mean a knowledge of the country and culture of the language being taught and learned, might be seen as the current expression of the traditional principles of the Enlightenment. Modern foreign languages have the unique potential to be a vehicle for overcoming the barriers between peoples of different countries. However, most interpretations of 'culture' nowadays are anthropological, tending to focus on traditions, customs, folklore and aspects of daily life. Such interpretations of culture nowadays tend to promote ideas about cultural identity which emphasise differences between peoples of different societies and which are more likely to lead to a parochial attitude to the world. This would seem a difficult view to reconcile with a universal outlook.

Modern foreign languages learning offers a unique opportunity to enrich learners' knowledge of how language works. By this, I do not merely mean grammar learning, but the possibility of reflective, comparative analysis which enables learners to gain a fuller understanding of English and of the target language: what we call 'language awareness'. However, there is a danger that the growing emphasis in the school curriculum on 'core' or 'key' skills may paradoxically reduce what should be a richer knowledge of how languages work to basic literacy skills.

School visits and exchanges abroad have long been a feature of secondary school life and are acknowledged as a distinctive aspect of the MFL curriculum. In recent years, however, the popularity of pupil–pupil exchanges, in particular, has declined and perhaps the most important of the unique features of the 'modern languages experience' is under threat. At a time when the European Union is a reality affecting all our lives, it is perhaps difficult to understand such apparent insularity amongst young people.

A relatively recent development in the secondary school curriculum has been the integration of cross-curricular themes, bilingual sections and Information and Communication Technology (ICT) into MFL programmes. Such developments offer exciting prospects for the MFL teacher and learner, but at the same time, run the risk of reducing modern language learning to a 'para-skill' with the result that the study of modern foreign languages is no longer considered as an academic discipline in its own right. In this way, one might argue that such curriculum initiatives ultimately destroy the uniqueness of MFL learning – but does that matter if, foreign languages are spoken by more people in the UK?

Culture and cultural awareness

The consultation materials of the review of the national curriculum in England (QCA, 1999) confirms what it describes as 'the distinctive contribution of modern foreign languages to the school curriculum' by asserting the view that:

> The study of modern foreign languages increases pupils' knowledge, understanding and appreciation of different cultures and people from different countries and communities. It encourages positive attitudes, both at home and abroad, towards speakers of other languages . . .
>
> (QCA 1999: 196)

Chapter 12 looks in detail at the importance of cultural awareness in modern language learning. The focus here is to consider what we mean by cultural knowledge and how we ensure that it does indeed foster positive attitudes of a more universal kind which emphasise common humanity rather than difference.

What do we mean by 'culture'? The word has taken on a much broader meaning nowadays than in the past. As has already been pointed out, the current understanding of the word has anthropological origins which aim to show the difference between people from different countries and cultures and focuses on traditions and customs. Another way of understanding 'culture' is as the best that humanity can aspire to; that is, the greatest, most creative works that an individual or society can produce. This view of culture has been somewhat eclipsed by the anthropological view because it is seen as elitist since in the past only a very small section of society had access to 'high' culture, as it is often called. The reaction to this has been, not to claim 'high culture' for everyone, but to reject it as irrelevant to most young people's lives. For example, A level syllabuses feature much less literature than in the past, favouring more 'relevant' topics such as racism, AIDS or environmental issues. It is interesting to consider whether a discussion of the form racism takes in, say, France or Germany as compared with Britain, will lead to a greater universal understanding of the causes of racism and how it can be opposed, or whether its is more likely to reinforce racist views in itself – our racism isn't as bad as theirs!

In practical terms, this means that learners are much more likely now to be familiar with a whole range of useful knowledge about how people from other countries live in their day-to-day lives, how they celebrate Christmas or other holy festivals, what they do on holiday or how many pets per head of population there are, than to have any idea of the history of the country, know who its most famous artists or musicians are, or have read any of its literature. The emphasis now, therefore, is on possible practical use rather than personal enrichment. There is also a danger that such an interpretation of cultural awareness within modern foreign languages, far from encouraging young people to be more open to other cultures, the celebration of 'difference', reinforces barriers rather than breaks them down.

However, the importance of contextualising language learning within the target culture is now well recognised. It is generally understood that knowledge of the target country, its people and culture makes language learning more relevant and increases motivation in learners. Nevertheless, at the present time, the unique potential that modern language learning offers to initiate young people into anything more than the very superficial is yet to be achieved. Why should this be so?

In the first place, the national curriculum, GCSE and A level syllabuses and school text books all concentrate on the more superficial aspects of other societies and cultures. If cultural awareness is left at this level, learners are more likely to focus on difference and quite possibly have negative, stereotypical attitudes reinforced. Elevation of difference emphasises 'foreignness'; surely it is much more important to encourage young people to recognise and look for similarities and to see apparent differences – like what people eat, what clothes they wear or patterns of daily lives, are only superficial? But more importantly, if we truly want to overcome parochialism and prejudice, we must look beyond the mundane aspects of culture towards cultural achievements that have spread across national boundaries. Kenan Malik (1996) summarises this point well:

> Understanding the richness of human cultural endeavour is a vital and fruitful quest. But contemporary visions of cultural difference seek to learn

about the other cultural forms not to create a more rich and universal culture, but to imprison us more effectively in a human zoo of differences.

(Malik, 1996: 150)

How might it be possible for teachers to initiate all learners in such 'richness of human cultural endeavour', given the constraints under which we work? Teachers are necessarily heavily influenced not only by the requirements of the National Curriculum and examination syllabuses, but also by what appears to be a prevailing belief that young people can only be motivated by that which is immediately relevant and is within their experience. It is questionable whether this is really true. Certainly, learning is likely to be more effective if relevance and the learner's experience are taken as a starting point, but it ought to be possible to move beyond that.

The key is to start as early as possible and in small, consistent steps. For example, we might use famous paintings as flash cards perhaps to introduce colours, or a particular set of vocabulary, descriptions of scenes or people. It would then be possible to talk briefly about the painter, where the painting is exhibited, perhaps even going to see the real thing in an exhibition. Over a period of time, learners would at least be familiar with the names of artists, and know a little about their work. Prévert's poem 'Le Déjeuner du Matin' appears in numerous textbooks as an example of the perfect tense. There are many other accessible poems that could be used for language teaching while at the same time introduce learners to poetry if accompanied by a discussion of the poem itself and the poet.

True cultural awareness, therefore, involves introducing the learner to the cultural achievements of other societies as well as aspects of tradition and everyday life. This is one aspect of the unique contribution of modern foreign languages to the curriculum.

Language awareness

Knowing how languages are structured and how they work, comparing one's own language with those of other countries, learning about the relationship between language and culture has unique potential in modern foreign languages. In 1973, Professor Eric Hawkins, Emeritus Professor at the University of York, first called for English and foreign languages teachers to work together to offer a 'new kind of language apprenticeship . . . in which the space between English and the foreign language would be bridged by the new subject 'language' (Hawkins, 1999). Over the last twenty-five years, Hawkins recalls elsewhere (1996), a number of imaginative 'awareness of language' programmes which brought together teachers from English and modern languages departments. It would be an exaggeration to suggest, however, that language awareness work has really penetrated the mainstream of language teaching.

Today, there is a renewed interest in 'language awareness' on the part of MFL professionals, but the main thrust of future curriculum development in this area is government driven in the form of the National Literacy Strategy. Modern foreign languages, given the very nature of the subject area, are able to contribute in a very distinctive way to learners' general language skills. Knowledge of the structure and pattern of another language can clearly contribute to learners' understanding of their own language. However, there is a sense in which this should be regarded as incidental. Why? Certainly, MFLs are able to make a special contribution in developing learners' knowledge and understanding of how language works and is used which complements the English curriculum. Indeed, MFL teachers often take pride in showing how, for example study of a foreign language helps learners with their knowledge of English grammar and spelling, That is absolutely legitimate. But at a time when the status of MFLs in the curriculum is insecure and there is an increasing importance placed on basic literacy, it is a temptation for teachers of modern languages to attempt to help justify the place of languages in the secondary curriculum on the basis that it is uniquely placed to play an important role in learners' core skills. By so doing, the status of modern languages is in danger of being regarded as a 'support' subject, rather than as a legitimate subject in its own right.

The area of language awareness, therefore, is another paradoxical situation in this sense: what appears to be a real opportunity, finally, to bring English and modern languages teachers together to deepen and broaden learners' knowledge of language and how it works is now more likely to be more restrictive. The current high priority currently given by government to 'core skills' places constraints on what language awareness could and should be. Language awareness could and should have an important place in MFL learning and programmes could and should be devised in collaboration with colleagues in English departments. It is an exciting prospect to plan a programme across the two curriculum areas for learners to compare and contrast languages in terms of sounds, meanings, how words are put together, language patterns, how tenses are used and so on. Hawkins (1988) identifies the following areas that might constitute a language awareness programme: knowledge of structure of our own language; sounds of our own language, alphabet contrasted with others, words as labels, joining words together, doing things with words; talking about the past and the future; word order and meaning. Several of these categories come under the heading of 'grammar' although it would be a mistake to think that what is meant by 'language awareness' is merely a return to old-style grammar teaching. It is not. Language awareness encourages a much richer understanding of the varieties of language, of meaning and contexts. Knowledge and use of both the foreign language and a learner's own language are much enhanced through creative language awareness programmes.

To give a flavour of the sort of activity one might devise for early learners of a foreign language the following extract from Barry Jones' book, 'How Language Works' (1984) offers an idea of the sort of exercise that might be used in the MFL classroom. This example is drawn from a section entitled 'Doing things with words':

A 2-year-old likes to talk about who owns things. This is why she says; *Daddy's garage, Mary's book, Mummy's hairdryer.* A few months earlier she probably began by saying: *Daddy garage, Mary book.* However, the words *Daddy garage* could have meant: *Daddy, (go to the) garage!* (an instruction); *Daddy (is going to the) garage.* (an observation made to someone else); *Daddy('s) garage.* (another observation); *Daddy (is in the) garage* (a *different* observation). Similar confusion occurs with the two words: *Mary book.* In order to make herself clear the child needs to add the 's' sound. What different things could she mean by *Mary book?*

(Jones, 1984: 15–16)

The writer then goes on to contrast how words are put together in Chinese and Hindi to express possession, giving simple examples. He then invites readers to work out for themselves how to say 'my book' in Chinese. Learners are thus encouraged to think about their own language, are introduced to others (which they may have no knowledge of) and then might go on to look at the foreign language they are learning themselves. The book introduces learners to thinking about language in a way that does not generally feature in an MFL lesson and encourages a deductive approach to grammar. This type of work would be most effective if co-ordinated across the English and MFL curriculum. At a time when there is beginning to be a serious re-appraisal of the communicative approach, language awareness is an area of language study which offers great potential in increasing the effectiveness of MFL learning.

School visits abroad and exchanges

Travel abroad in and of itself does not, of course, ensure a widening of experience and broadening of horizons. It is possible to spend time in another country in another country and learn nothing of its language, people or culture. This can be true of badly prepared, so-called 'educational' trips as any other visit. However, where teachers are concerned with providing the best experiences for learners, there can surely be no better way of fulfilling the unique educational potential of modern foreign language learning both in terms of language and culture, than through school trips or exchange visits abroad. David Snow and Michael Byram (1999) talk about 'crossing frontiers' and suggest that '. . . crossing frontiers is a unique educational experience . . . (which involves) not simply a matter of physical displacement but rather the modification and development of richer attitudes and understandings' (Snow and Byram, 1999: 3).

More people, from a wider cross-section of society, now travel abroad for either holidays or work. National borders in Europe are open to all European citizens and it has never been cheaper or easier to travel the world. And yet, school visits abroad and in particular, pupil–pupil exchange visits, are less popular now than in the past. How can we explain this? It is true that taking part in school trips can be a costly business; having a pen-friend to stay means having enough room in the house to accommodate them. The advent of 'languages for all' policies has obviously meant that young people from all backgrounds now have access, at least in principle, to opportunities which were previously reserved for the few selected to learn a foreign language. Teachers have often found that quite apart from the expense of sending their children on school trips, parents often feel uneasy about having a young 'stranger' to stay because they do not consider their home 'good enough'.

However, there are far greater anxieties amongst parents and young people when it comes to going to another country to stay in a family to the extent that many schools no longer arrange this sort of contact. When one talks to young people about why they do not want to take part in school exchanges, in recent years, new sorts of anxiety have emerged. 'Stranger danger' and a fear of the unknown seems to be far greater concerns than in the past, together with a higher level of insecurity about going away from home. Young people seem to have more of a fear of the unknown than a curiosity to try out new experiences. We live in a society where there is a heightened, some might say completely exaggerated, awareness of risk and danger often exacerbated by sensational reporting. Isolated cases of a child murder or child abuse are exaggerated to the extent that irrational scare campaigns lead parents to be over-cautious and over-protective towards their children. Young people as a result are becoming less adventurous, less experimental and less open to new experiences.

Frank Füredi, in his book *Culture of Fear* (1997) provides a wide-reaching analysis of what has become known as the 'risk society'. Füredi claims that safety and caution have become overwhelming concerns in British society, which he sees as essentially conservative and especially damaging to young people's development. He points to several studies (114–6) into a variety of ways in which young people's lives are more restricted nowadays and the detrimental effect this has on the way they live their lives and the adults they become. Armed with such insights, the modern languages teacher can set out, in a small way, to counter this 'culture of fear'. In relation to school exchanges, greater preparatory work needs to be done to motivate pupils and convince parents of the benefits of such projects. For example, instead of relying on the traditional pen-friend link, there are effective school exchange projects which get underway by exchanging videos of the schools, towns, pupils and their families so that participants know what to expect. Recent developments in technology mean that email contacts between learners or even 'virtual meetings' through video-conferencing between exchange groups and their parents mean that fears can be allayed. However, such 'virtual' trips and contacts must not be seen as a substitute for the real thing, but merely a preliminary to what should be memorable life experiences. If there are practical problems or an initial reluctance to accommodate an exchange partner, it might be preferable to organise a short stay on 'neutral' ground at a residential centre of some kind. Many local authority education departments own either a camp site or residential centre either in this country or abroad which would make an ideal venue. This sort of activity might also be used to breathe new life into an existing exchange link.

An alternative to pupil-to-pupil contacts and exchanges, and equally valuable are field or study trips to the target country. Snow and Byram (1999) explore thoroughly the enormous potential of such trips both in linguistic and cultural terms. Some very interesting cross-curricular projects are also possible. The role of the school exchange or study visit in providing an opportunity of putting classroom learning into practice and enabling access to the people, history and culture of another country is unique to modern foreign languages.

Yet, as we have seen, trips abroad and exchanges are perceived as more of a 'risky business' than they used to be. Teachers are not exempt from the 'risks' involved in taking young people abroad since they bear a far greater burden of responsibility as a result. However, these concerns are also largely exaggerated: for every unfortunate incident of an accident, or in one extreme case, a murder on a school trip abroad, thousands of young people have trouble-free, enriching experiences. To fall victim to the exaggerated sense of caution and obsession with safety that currently exists in society is to reinforce parochialism. More importantly, we deny young people vital opportunities to develop into independent, open-minded, confident individuals and we contribute to a diminished sense of what it is to be an adult.

Languages across the curriculum – threats or opportunities?

A recent trend in modern foreign languages, promoted in the national curriculum, has been towards the application of language skills to other curriculum areas, and the integration of non-language skills and subject matter into the MFL curriculum. Cross-curricula themes and dimensions (soon to include education for citizenship and democracy), information and communication technology skills and to a lesser extent the use of the foreign language to teach other subjects are the main focus of this development. Many teachers, trainers and commentators see this as a progressive development which will help to enhance the status and purpose of modern languages in the secondary curriculum. However, there are inherent problems in promoting such approaches which we will now examine.

There is currently a very strong emphasis on ICT skills throughout education. There is an apparent consensus that the best way to develop those skills in school is to embed ICT in the subject curriculum. There are many well-rehearsed claims made in favour of this approach in respect of learner motivation, relevant application of skills, presentation of learners' work, the use of the MFL in a 'real' context . . . the list goes on and many of the benefits suggested are undoubtedly true in themselves. Watching learners turn their survey data into pie charts or use graphics to illustrate their word-processed poem can be very satisfying, but we should not allow these activities to dominate or detract from the real business of the modern foreign languages classroom – language learning! What is more, the world wide web presents a fundamental problem for modern foreign languages. The information superhighway has confirmed the position of English as the dominant world language. True, there are foreign language websites, some very useful, but before we herald the Internet as the new source of authentic materials for MFL teaching and learning, we should perhaps consider whether or not there is a certain perversity in encouraging the use of a medium which clearly does not promote linguistic plurality.

Early guidance for the National Curriculum for modern foreign languages advised that, wherever possible, MFL teachers should integrate broader curriculum 'themes' and 'dimensions' into modern foreign language teaching and learning. The non-statutory guidance (1992) suggested the following 'themes': economic and industrial understanding, careers education and guidance, health education, environmental education and education for citizenship. The 'dimensions' identified were: equal opportunities and multicultural awareness.

To a greater or lesser extent, teachers have addressed these issues through existing curriculum content, aiming at reinforcing learners' knowledge and awareness rather than introducing topics in and of themselves. Most textbooks have followed this model. For example, 'health education' might be approached through a language topic on food, which would probably involve presenting some foods as 'good' and some as 'bad', with accompanying advice about healthy diet. The theme of environmental education is generally approached through the National Curriculum area of experience, 'The world around us', within which, issues like litter control in school, conservation or pollution might be incorporated. Cross-curricular work is often the end product of a series of lessons – perhaps a display of the results of a survey on the eating preferences or a poster depicting a 'healthy' diet.

'Equal opportunities' and 'multicultural awareness' are 'dimensions' which are expected to infuse the curriculum for modern foreign languages. Certainly, as we have already seen, the MFL curriculum is able to play a particular role in looking at cultural issues. However, multicultural education is very susceptible to emphasising 'difference' and 'ethnicity', and as such, is the antithesis of a universal outlook that one might want to promote. 'The aim of multiculturalist education policies', observes Malik (1996: 150), 'is to preserve cultural differences as they present themselves in society, seemingly believing that these differences are static and immutable'. In addition, both equal opportunities and multicultural awareness have become minefields of political correctness which, one might argue, cannot be explored in sufficient depth within a modern languages context. Nevertheless, MFL teachers do have an opportunity to deal with issues such as prejudice, stereotyping and discrimination in a natural, non-moralising way due to, as we have already seen, the very nature of the subject area.

'Education for citizenship and the teaching of democracy' is the new, all-embracing form that cross-curricular themes and dimensions takes. Recent government proposals confirm a much higher profile for citizenship education in the school curriculum. The government Advisory Group on Citizenship (1998) recommends a statutory obligation on schools to provide a discreet education for citizenship programme, as well as a cross-curricular approach to citizenship education. Such a programme would focus around three areas: 'social and moral responsibility, community involvement and political literacy'. The advisory group suggests that: 'modern foreign languages (MFL) can offer a contrasting perspective from other countries on national, European and international events and issues'. This would seem no bad thing in itself, but it is difficult to see how real justice might be done to such weighty political issues within an already crowded MFL curriculum.

Cross-curricula themes and dimensions in general, and education for citizenship and democracy in particular, might once have been described as part of the 'hidden curriculum'. There was a time when such aspects of the 'hidden curriculum' were viewed with suspicion by some educationalists who saw them as a way of inculcating received ideas and views about society and reinforcing the *status quo* rather than encouraging young people to question and think for themselves. Even if one accepts the legitimacy of cross-curricular themes and education for citizenship, it is difficult to see how, within a modern foreign languages context, anything but a superficial understanding of very complex issues could be achieved. Does it matter that the cross-curricula theme becomes more important than the foreign language? Is the unique contribution that modern foreign languages could make in this area merely that of attempting to reconcile a world view of citizenship with a more narrow interpretation of what it means to be a good citizen in Britain today?

Curriculum innovations, such as bilingual sections, that is, the learning of other school subjects through the medium of a modern foreign language, and vocational language courses, are partly attempts at making modern languages more appealing to young people at a time when fewer than ever learners continue MFL study beyond GCSE. Teaching other curriculum subjects through the medium of the foreign language has never managed to become a feature of the mainstream secondary curriculum. Yet research evidence suggests that 'language medium teaching dramatically increases linguistic performance and increases motivation without affecting standards in the curriculum subject' (Coyle, 1996). Whatever the practical problems that one might foresee, the question one might raise is, if the foreign language is merely a vehicle through which other subjects are taught, is the language learning subordinate to the history, geography or business studies being learned and is the uniqueness of modern foreign languages thereby diminished?

Conclusion

The theme of this chapter has been to examine the unique potential of MFLs to help people break out of their narrow, parochial, limited by geographical location and to look at how and why, at the present time, the opposite is likely to be true. Four aspects of modern foreign languages were chosen to exemplify the ambiguities and paradoxes of the subject area in the school curriculum at the present time in an attempt to set out some of the current threats to the underlying goal of modern languages to broaden horizons and promote universal values. The chapter has also sought to show how an understanding of what makes modern foreign languages unique, a commitment to MFLs as an academic discipline in its own right and a clear belief in their universalising potential is essential for the future. I have also tried to give a sense of the importance of modern foreign language learning to the all-round education and personal development of individual learners. The aspects selected for discussion here are not exclusive; there are other important ways in which MFLs contribute to the broader education of the individual. It is also useful to consider, for example, how learning modern languages develops aspects study skills; how the communicative modern languages classroom promotes the development of learner autonomy; how effective, purposeful use of role activities is a powerful tool for extending learners understanding of communicative behaviour. These, too, are important aspects of teaching and learning which have unique features within the MFL curriculum. Fernand Braudel, in his book, A *History of Civilizations* (1987) describes his vision of a Europe united by a common culture and complemented by a common educational 'arena for study and research' which 'would promote, of necessity, a modern form of humanism embracing all the living languages of Europe'. Only a flourishing modern foreign languages curriculum in schools has the potential to fulfil such a vision.

Editor's note

Lawes identifies three aspects of teaching and learning of MFLs which comprise the unique contribution the teaching and learning of MFLs make to the curriculum as a whole: cultural awareness, language awareness and the opportunity to learn from trips abroad. Lawes asserts these potential outcomes of MFL teaching and learning are not always met. By cultural awareness, many teachers understand the presentation of tradition and aspects of every day life. Cultural awareness, for Lawes, also means the opportunity for personal enrichment, which she feels can be achieved by the use of high culture as a means of introducing topics. Art, poetry and all literature provide a rich source of imagery and culture which can be used to stimulate language learning at all levels. MFLs provide the opportunity for enquiry and investigations into language structure, through an insight into more than one language system. The dwindling popularity of MFL-based trips abroad must, Lawes argues be addressed if the full benefits of an MFL experience are to be maintained. The use of technology to allay fears and to provide an introduction to foreign life experiences is one means by which Lawes feels young people will feel less threatened and more confident.

Lawes points out that the real benefits of MFL learning have often been accepted as interesting by-products, and that a more overt and formalised approach to these three issues may well contribute to a deeper appreciation than the current situation approach seems to promote.

Linked chapters

Chapter 10, Chapter 11, Chapter 14, Chapter 16.

References

Braudel, F. (1987) A *History of Civilizations*, London: Allen Lane, The Penguin Press.

Citizenship Advisory Group (1998) *Education for Citizenship and the Teaching of Democracy in Schools*, London: QCA.

Coyle, D. (1996) 'Break-out from English', *Guardian*, 5 November 1999.

Füredi, F. (1997) *Culture of Fear*, London: Cassell.

Hawkins, E. (1988) *Awareness of Language: An Introduction* (revised edition), Cambridge: Cambridge University Press.

Hawkins, E. (ed.) (1996) *30 Years of Language Teaching*, London: CILT.

Hawkins, E. (1999) *The Space Between: A New Kind of Language Apprenticeship in Schools*, paper given at Language World Conference: University of York (27 March 1999).

Jones, B. (1984), *How Language Works*, Cambridge, Cambridge University Press.

Malik, K. (1996) *The Meaning of Race*, London: Macmillan.

National Curriculum Council (1992) *Modern Foreign Languages Non-Statutory Guidance*, York: National Curriculum Council.

Qualifications and Curriculum Authority (1999) *The Review of the National Curriculum in England. The Consultation Materials*, London: QCA.

Snow, D. and Byram, M. (1997) *Crossing Frontiers. The School Study Visit Abroad*, London: CILT.

Part 3

Issues associated with pedagogy

7 Teaching and learning Modern Foreign Languages and able pupils

Jane Jones

Introduction

MFL teachers have done an excellent job in defining the needs of and in making provision for less able pupils and for pupils with a full range of special educational needs. Expert provision is well embedded in whole-school SEN policies, supported by a plethora of commercially produced material to complement purpose-designed resources in MFL departments. It remains the case, a case supported by many Ofsted reports over some considerable time, that provision is less well-defined for able pupils in MFLs. The MFL review of inspection findings for 1993/94, for example, commented: 'although some schools provide 'extension' materials for abler pupils, very few planned or catered for the special needs of the most able'.

There are many possible reasons for these failings, some of them relating to practical difficulties, some of them located in the domain of ideology. The comprehensive principle and the pervasive concept of egalitarianism in education are often considered antithetical to any process that may be seen to be promoting forms of élitism and separatism. Thus, special measures for able pupils and, in particular, separate groups in the form of top sets, bands or streams are sometimes deemed to be agencies of élitism, thereby reinforcing societal hegemonic influences. Where special provision impacts unfairly on any other pupils or prejudices their needs in terms of staffing and resources, there would be understandable unease. Similarly as Kirby argues (1996: 2): 'Programmes of study that fail to make adequate provision for the able pupil may therefore be discriminating against a considerable proportion of the student body.' However, this dialectic has given way to the notion of entitlement of appropriate provision for all pupils of all abilities, which is at the heart of the National Curriculum framework. Indeed, in the Common Requirements of Modern Foreign Languages in the National Curriculum (DfEE 1995), in terms of access, it is stated that: 'The programme of study for each key stage should be taught to the great majority of pupils in the key stage, in ways appropriate to their abilities'.

The ERA 1988, which generated the MFL report, is quite clear in its definition of NC entitlement in relation to: (a) the knowledge, skills and understanding which pupils of differing abilities and maturities are expected to have at the end of each key stage.

What is required is truly differentiated learning opportunities, in whatever grouping formations, or in what, for example, Michael Marland, headteacher of the North Westminster Community School calls 'mixed-attainment' classes[1]. The focus on attainment is particularly apposite and useful in shifting attention from ability, be it natured or nurtured (the subject of another long-standing debate) to the attainment of each individual pupil. Able pupils are entitled to teaching and learning approaches that will help them to achieve their maximum potential along their learning curve. The real benefit, however, is for the whole school and its community in its promotion of excellence and the development of all abilities to the full.

How do we identify able pupils?

Within the discourse of 'teacher-talk', we need first to know to which pupil population we are referring. There is, it would seem from general discussion with MFL teachers, an apparent shared understanding of what 'a top set' is, or a pupil who is 'good at languages'. Sometimes the talent is obvious whilst at others, it is the potential which is perceived. It is, perhaps, helpful to think in terms of a continuum of ability on which we can place our pupils' at any given time (Figure 7.1).

The continuum is, however, a shifting concept and allows for evidence of ability at different stages in pupils' lives, according to certain contextual features that may inhibit or promote its development. These features might include the school's culture, individual pupils' attitudes to their talents and parental support. Teachers' attitudes, the learning environment, the age and maturity of the pupil are also variables that may have an impact. Social and cultural factors are potent influences, both externally and within the school setting, where opportunities and the appropriate support are important agencies for converting latent ability or raw but undeveloped talent into achievement.

In accordance with a broader, more fluid definition of ability, there has been a major shift away from the notion of ability being allied narrowly to a single criterion of IQ and a move towards a multidimensional framework 'which includes personality and creativity as well as cognitive, motivational, social and environmental perspectives' (Montgomery, 1991: 23). Howard Gardner's theory of 'multiple intelligences' (1983) postulates that all learners have the capacity to develop at least seven types of intelligence wherein learning is not just about

> *less able* > *able* > *more able* >

Figure 7.1 Continuum of ability.

cognition. Learning also partly depends upon emotional intelligence that emphasises self-awareness and self-motivation. Linguistic intelligence is one of the seven. However, a very good starting point in attempting to define the common understanding referred to previously is the pooling of ideas and sharing of performance definitions by teachers, drawing on the range of data available to them and common sense knowledge based on experience and intuition.

What teachers say

For the purposes of this chapter, I surveyed twenty experienced MFL teachers and asked them to define the characteristics of an able pupil (in MFL) in terms of learning behaviour or otherwise. The characteristics are listed below in order of frequency of mention:

- the ability to pick things up quickly
- a good memory
- able to perceive and understand patterns/rules/the logic of language
- the ability to reapply such rules
- keen to speak and to use the target language creatively (not just in response to the teacher's questions)
- good attention span
- a good 'ear' and an intuitive feel for language
- good pronunciation and a willingness to imitate language models
- unafraid to experiment with language in a more complex way and to take risks
- keen to go beyond 'core' learning and to do additional tasks
- the enjoyment of a challenge
- the evidence of ability in speaking and writing
- interested in the mechanics – 'the grammar' – of language
- presentation and quality of written work
- able to draw on L1 and knowledge of other languages as a support and inferential strategy
- motivated to learn
- generally bright – general language ability
- results of NFER tests may be indicative
- 'you just know it'

There was a very large measure of agreement with the first ten items mentioned in some way or other by all teachers interviewed. The last comment made by a teacher of long standing was evidence of what I referred to earlier as that seemingly 'implicit understanding' amongst teachers, an understanding which undoubtedly develops from the experiences and engagement with pupils of differing abilities and which allow one to make such confident generalisations.

Eschewing the use of tests, whether school-based or the available standard-ised language aptitude tests (only one interviewee mentioned this method as a theoretical possibility), the teachers surveyed have based their defining indic-ators on the observable features of the learners in the MFL classroom, using their professional judgment.

What the research says

Interestingly, these definitions, gleaned from a random group of teachers, also have considerable resonance with the findings of writers and researchers who themselves have attempted to identify and to define the construct of ability, especially high ability, sometimes in general terms, sometimes in relation to language learning. I begin first with more general categories. Ogilvie (1975) quoted in Kerry (1981) drew up a very comprehensive list of behavioural criteria based on research into able pupils in school and it is from this list that I have selected certain criteria which will be recognisable by many MFL teachers:

- display of initiative
- independence
- imaginative forms of expression
- ability to be absorbed in work
- speed of thought
- ability to make and understand analysis
- ability to move to the abstract
- curiosity and desire to question
- good memory
- reliability and dependability
- suggestion of musical ability

There are important implications for learning deriving from these criteria. This is one interpretation of possible learning scenarios and others are, of course, possible. In a subject such as MFLs where a premium is placed upon creative language use, the assertion that pupils may be relied upon to use their initiative and to be imaginative puts them in pole position, for the pupils are likely to want and to be able to move, with ease, from language reproduction to production. Thus, are the learners likely to be fuelled by confidence and motivation to engage in language creation. Furthermore, this drive would seem to be potentially underpinned by 'an understanding of how the language works', based on the ability to perceive meaningful patterns and, thus, creating a powerful and insightful cognitive basis for learning. Learning data, Ogilvie suggests, are processed rapidly by able pupils, the force of memory being used for the effective retrieval of information, as and when required. How then might we concretise the profile of the able MFL learner with reference to these criteria? First, the learner appears driven in particular ways to want to know and to learn, based on an understanding of what is happening and why. Questions from able pupils are often of the 'why' kind and, in all probability, the ensuing explanations will aid the learner to structure her/his learning. When the learner feels confident, and the indications are that that is likely to be sooner rather than later in the learning sequence, and possibly with fewer examples and less exposition to language required than by other pupils, the pupil could be relied upon to take the initiative, for example, in modeling language in whole class activity or in group and pair activity. With the undeniable support of good memory drives, language production may well be enriched by wide reference to and intermeshing with previous learning.

Some of the other criteria suggested by Ogilvie may also serve to enhance learning. If only all learners demonstrated the 'ability to be absorbed in work'! The able pupils with such a propensity for concentration and application will, if motivated, surge ahead paying attention to detail, overall quality and a general quest for 'perfectionism'. When resources are available, able pupils can, therefore, be encouraged to use their initiative and to undertake responsibility for a good measure of their learning through independent means and in individual ways.

The earlier but complementary findings of Carroll (1969) identified certain key features correlating with successful language learning. These included:

- good auditory discrimination
- the ability to link sounds correctly to written notation
- the ability to recognise the grammatical function of language
- the ability to identify quickly the meaning of new words

From this list can be deduced a logic of linguistic discovery beginning with the ability to make sense of sounds – 'a good ear' – the connecting of sounds with the written form of language and the deciphering of semantic forms; all in all, a powerful conduit to rapid and successful language – learning.

And finally, with reference to French (and by extension to other foreign languages) Denton and Postlethwaite (1985) constructed their profile of good ability by analysing the following nine areas of performance:

- attitude
- aural/oral skills
- oral response
- control over sound/symbol correspondence
- self-confidence
- memory
- mastery of English
- flexibility to use language
- ability to put language together

Denton and Postlethwaite's (1985) profile elements are contained within Table 7.1, and have been amplified to clarify the MFL-specific extensions.

Gardner's concept of 'linguistic intelligence' roundly complements this table and it is worth quoting the definition of it as interpreted by Kosh and Casey

Table 7.1 Denton and Postlethwaite's findings (1985) adapted and extended

Area of performance	D and P's amplification	Comments
Attitude	Enthusiasm: sees the relevance of the learning; cultural interest	High motivation; intra- and inter-disciplinary learning links. Dimensions of PoS Part 4
Aural/oral skills	Good discrimination and articulation	Use of aural texts with greater redundancy; attention to 'form' as well as 'content' in oral communication
Oral response	Alert oral response	Use pupil to model responses and to provide exemplars: 'quick fire' questioning; more searching questions
Control over sound/ symbol correspondence	Good pronunciation (not perverted by L1)	Pupil can model spoken language; independent written work
Self-confidence	Good retention; not 'embarassable'; enjoys trying sounds	Pupil as model in class revision; frequent testing to hone this ability
Memory	Clear evidence of good memory	Memorisation and recall
Mastery of English	Aware, for example, of parts of speech and linguistic nuances	No concession necessary by teacher in terms of metalinguistic discourse
Flexibility	Can adapt rules; thinks in the target language	Tasks which allow for analogy-making; maximum engagement with target language
Ability to put language together	Can form new combinations; creative use of structure	Open-ended activities and tasks which allow for maximum creativity

(1997: 19) in this respect. 'Those who possess this intelligence appreciate the order, meanings and rhythm of words. They are likely to enjoy the challenge of decoding the rules of grammar, inventing a new language, playing with words and enjoying communication.'

A profile of the able pupil may be seen to be emerging from the evidence base utilised. There are, I suggest, key features pertaining to cognitive skills common to all the checklists to which I have referred, and others, as illustrated in Figure 7.2 below.

There are obvious implications for teaching approach which involve the harnessing of the capabilities of the able pupil to an appropriate range of learning activities in the school setting and beyond.

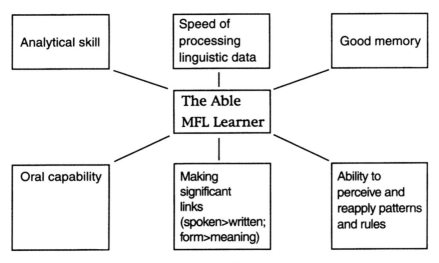

Figure 7.2 Key characteristics of the able MFL learner.

Teaching able language learners

Independent learning has been proposed as a panacea for solving the problem of the need to make provision for able pupils. It is, in fact, part of a solution, one of a range of strategies to be employed. Differentiation, in all its guises, comes into operation, the teacher differentiating, for example, by activity, by task and by outcome in each of and across the four skills. Able pupils can be targeted for the first line of interrogation in question-and-answer work and subsequently with more complex questions. They can also be relied upon to provide models for other pupils. This satisfies many of the intellectual needs of the able pupils in one teaching technique alone. Listening, reading and writing can all be differentiated through, for example, a graded incline of difficulty with different starting and cut-off points, allowing fast-tracking, i.e. leaving out simpler exercises and a speedy entry into more open-ended, creative language-using activities and tasks. This is surely very familiar to MFL teachers. The difficulty is in the implementation of such individualised differentiation which will inevitably require the creation and cataloguing of suitable materials, the identification of appropriate activities and tasks and the detailed concretising of such within schemes of work. Time will need to be invested in identifying the necessary teaching strategies, the resources and the learning activities for able pupils which can be accommodated within the whole-class framework, just as, over the years, the needs of less able pupils and pupils with special educational needs have been accommodated, with success, in the compulsory framework of MFLs.

Ogilvie also found that able pupils enjoyed interaction with adults. In the MFL classroom, it could be possible for the teacher to role-play sometimes with the pupils and for the foreign language assistant to be utilised very productively in the classroom by providing targeted support and extension. Able pupils, it seems, like to do extra and independent work. We need to ensure a rich variety of resources to include texts and tapes of all kinds for independent work, reference books for research and a range of authentic or authentic-construct multimedia materials for extensive listening and reading in particular as well as for enjoyment. The idea of listening, reading and viewing corners or areas to be found in some classrooms or resources rooms is a commendable one.

A point about any independent learning is that there needs always to be an element of direction from, and some negotiation, with the teacher. All learners, however able, need guidance and support as well as periodic feedback about their learning progression.

ICT can become a really meaningful learning experience in this context. The new wave of software materials includes many packages where pupils can log on at different levels, automatically cutting out low level exercises and games that would not stretch the able pupil. Some of the programmes are more word rather than icon-dependent, and in the target language too, which thereby provides a more challenging interaction. All the functions of computer-assisted language learning can provide extended learning opportunities.

Not only are we informed repeatedly by research findings and by the common sense knowledge of classroom practitioners that able pupils can understand a language's system of rules but that they may enjoy the exercise of constructing and reconstructing language according to the rules, enjoy the challenge of discovery and have no fear of abstraction. The use of grammatical terminology and of comprehensible grammatical explanations with able pupils will not therefore be intimidating; on the contrary, this is likely to serve as another element in scaffolding the pupils' learning, of providing opportunities for them to consider and to test hypotheses and to provide a means both of consolidation and extension of learning.

Course materials are resources for teachers to use in whatever way they wish, selecting and rejecting from the available content. A criterion for evaluating a course book would normally include the potential for differentiated learning and provision for able learners. It is perhaps the case that too often there is inadequate provision for able pupils with dull, even pointless, suggestions for 'more of the same'. Sidwell (1994), in a set of inset notes she prepared, makes a very important point about the need for 'quality not quantity' of enriched and extended learning opportunities, with continuous challenges, not just more chances to practise the same. Supplementary, free-standing materials are particularly useful for this purpose and obviate the need for the teacher, whose time is limited, to have to create purpose-designed materials all the time. Whilst there is some potential for using rather 'drier', more grammatically focused texts with able pupils, there is no reason why the challenging tasks and materials I am advocating should not also be interesting and lively, even fun, at times. Games are not the prerogative of less able pupils but can be purposefully selected and organised to provide linguistic challenges at a variety of levels. Experienced teachers are able to dress up the endless repetition and recycling of language required for classroom-bound learning in all manner of interesting guises. One way of challenging pupils in terms of speed of recovery and production of language, for example, is to 'hot-spot' them by asking for specified information within a tight time limit. Thus, for example, might a pupil be asked to introduce themselves and their families within a time limit of 10 seconds. This can be further tweaked downwards to 9, 8, 7 seconds (or less!). Almost any output can be set to a time-limit, other pupils being involved by monitoring and noting down the output, stopwatches set, negotiation to take place in the target language.

Whilst 'hot-spotting' is a way of revising and of helping the pupil to memorise and internalise language, able pupils can excel in the domain of creative language use. Leaving aside the functional so-called 'every day' use of language that seems so much part of the National Curriculum diet, the pupils can be encouraged to use their imagination in such a way that will also consolidate and fix certain language patterns. Poems, for example, can be written in Prévert style, based on a repetitive frame, drawing on the topics of import and the heroes and heroines of the day; text or dialogues can be written to accompany a video shown without sound, all activities predicated upon the imaginative re-use of known language in new contexts, extendible as far as the pupils are able.

Many of the learning features referred to concur with the largely positive findings of Dobson (1998: 6) citing good practice in a section of a school's MFL OFSTED report:

> Listening and speaking skills are developed through plenty of opportunities to communicate with the teacher and with other pupils in a wide range of games, surveys and role plays. Short sessions, when pupils say as much as they can on a chosen subject, extend abler pupils but boost the confidence of all to speak from memory. Reading skills are developed through matching tasks and later by skimming more complex and authentic texts for details and gist. Reading extended text is less developed. Writing skills are fostered through an imaginative variety of tasks and through practice in redrafting, at times using the word processor

A focus on the learner

I have placed considerable burden on the MFL teacher for, for example, employing differentiated teaching strategies and for providing a wealth of materials and opportunities to learn. In recent years, there has been a shift of focus towards the learner and an attempt to identify learner-oriented and learner-driven effective language learning, drawing on the established but somewhat dated work of researchers but also on up-to-date classroom observations and recent research such as Graham (1997) and Naiman et al. (1996). All findings are speculative and specify the need to take into account contextual features. The research of Naiman *et al.*, for example, suggested the following as essential for successful second language learning. The learner must:

1   be active in his/her approach to learning and practice
2   come to grips with the language as a system
3   use the language in real communication
4   monitor his(her) interlanguage
5   come to terms with the affective demands of language learning

Whilst this research was aimed at identifying the 'good' language learner as opposed to the 'able' learner, these are nonetheless generalisations which resonate strongly with the various checklists discussed previously. All in all, there is strong emphasis on the learners taking an active role in their own learning. It is an emphasis that posits the teacher in complementary roles; that of model and director but also of supporter and facilitator in the language classroom, and indeed beyond, to the sites of independent study, wherever they may be. As Graham writes in her exploration of effective language learning:

> In even the most student centred classroom, where perhaps learning is based on self-access to materials, the support and guidance of teachers is still likely to be needed. This is especially true as far as the development of effective learning strategies in students is concerned.
>
> (op. cit. p. 124)

At this juncture, I am postulating certain key features in a teacher approach for able pupils which will revolve around a central construct of active learning strategies and which are summarised in Figure 7.3 below.

Commentary

The development of research and reference skills

Pupils will benefit from an understanding of the processes involved in research and reference and an orientation towards resources to help them follow their lines of enquiry. Dictionary skills are very obvious requirements, particularly the extended and elaborated versions on CD-Rom that allow for much greater in-depth exploration of words in contexts. Other reference materials such as Le Petit Robert type-tomes, the Bescherelle series (for French, with similar items for other languages), selected applied linguistic texts, books and software on cultural issues, not forgetting human resources possibilities such as language teachers and other individuals with a knowledge of foreign languages, the Internet and the various language learning supporting institutions and networks. Modes of accessing, the ability to evaluate resources critically and to be able to utilise them for specific purposes are skills which will need to be taught.

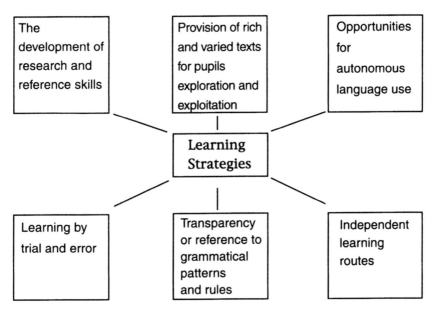

Figure 7.3 Learning strategies for able pupils.

Provision of rich and varied texts for pupil exploration and exploitation

This is closely allied to the previous section but is extended further by resources for both directed intensive learning across the whole learning programme and for extended learning with, for example, purpose designed readers, authentic reading materials (magazines, teenage reading), video and audio tapes, which can also be accessed just for the pleasure of reading or listening.

Opportunities for autonomous language use

This implies, essentially, providing opportunities – in the classroom and outside in other sites of learning – for able pupils to use the foreign language in their own ways for their own purposes. Nonetheless, as noted previously, the teacher has an important role in guiding, framing and supporting autonomous language use.

Independent learning routes

The concern here is to consider the needs of individual pupils, to be aware of their strengths and weaknesses and to direct and plan their learning in such a way as to maximize their strengths whilst, at the same time, enhancing less well developed skills. Work targets can be negotiated which are varied and challenging and can be worked upon over a period of time. Psychological factors may be involved such as encouraging able pupils to take leadership or tutoring roles and to engage more in collaborative styles of learning. Occasionally, able pupils can be asked to 'coach' other pupils within this context.

Transparency of reference to grammatical patterns and rules

There is no need for coyness on the part of teachers when needing or desiring to make explicit a certain grammatical rule. The nomenclature is not in itself off-putting but is a useful naming and classification of 'the bits' of the language. Similarly, an explanation of rules, when appropriate, serves to demystify what can otherwise appear to be baffling and arbitrary linguistic phenomena. This meets the needs of able pupils who 'want to know'.

Learning via trial and error

The independent learning dimension being advocated will invariably involve strategies such as hypothesis testing, informed guesswork and attempting 'best fits' where the stakes include the possibility of error. 'Having a go' should be encouraged by the teacher and the usefulness of error exploited by the teacher.

Learning from error

The role of error, as a learning indicator, merits further consideration. From the teachers' point of view, what is formally called error analysis and recognisable more informally as a teacher's sensitivity in the classroom to errors and mistakes for diagnostic purposes, error in the language classroom provides useful data which may relate to the efficiency of teaching procedures and to the interlingual competences of the learners. In the active, risk-taking approach being advocated for the able learning, the autonomous role of the learner is likely to involve error making as a strategy in learning. This certainly requires a re-conceptualisation of the process and also of the way error is visibly perceived and utilised constructively in the classroom by the teacher and by the learners. Very few learners would actively wish to put themselves in a position where they are castigated or ridiculed for making a mistake. The familiar look of a teacher who has heard an error uttered by a pupil in good faith during oral work, for example, the raised eyebrow, the pointed finger keeping the pupil 'on hold' whilst a correct answer is sought, these are intimidating body language responses likely to inhibit further responses or at least spontaneous attempts at trying to get it right.

School-based research that I undertook with colleagues in a girls' comprehensive school in 1988 about the needs of able pupils, clearly identified the fear of failure as both a negative as well as a potentially positive force. The negative connotations arose both out of a desire not to look foolish in front of peers but also from a strong desire to get it right in the first place, the strive perhaps for 'perfectionism' identified in Ogilvie's research findings referred to earlier. It can be a positive driving force in the hands of an error-sensitive teacher and in a learning climate that encourages spontaneity and boosts the confidence of the pupils. This is what Naiman *et al.* (op. cit.) mean in part by 'coming to terms with the affective demands of language learning'. Graham (op. cit. p. 39) writes of the need for the 'management of affective demands, e.g. learning to laugh at oneself'. Error *per se* is not intrinsically amusing but a non-threatening approach to the treatment can be productive given appropriate feedback. In the research referred to by Jones (see above), able pupils expressed a desire to know the criteria for success and a need for detailed feedback on their performance so that they could actively engage in improving their performance based on an understanding of the nature of their errors. Informed, constructive feedback is also a strong motivating force.

Attitude to learning and motivation

The teachers' responses in my survey indicated a keenness on the part of able pupils to engage actively in learning process evidenced in the desire to speak and, very importantly, a willingness to experiment with language, to take risks, i.e. with the possibility that mistakes and/or errors might be made. As one teacher put it: 'able pupils will just go for it.' As previously discussed, learning from mistakes as well as the reinforcement of correct responses of course, are potentially very effective learning strategies.

The teachers also spoke of able pupils wanting to do additional work, relishing work of a challenging nature. Ogilvie wrote of absorption and curiosity, strong scaffolding learning supports, whilst Denton and Postlethwaite stated unequivocally that attitude is a key factor. Where the appropriate stimulus in whatever context is provided for able pupils, they will thrive and progress. When this is not the case, boredom is likely to ensue and the pupils' drive sapped with a resultant lack of effort, interest and motivation. Ogilvie, for example, observed able pupils who, when bored with mundane tasks, spent their time daydreaming, withdrawing or sometimes attention-seeking in rather more disruptive ways. The switched-off able pupil is not, I would contend, an unfamiliar sight in some MFL classrooms. It would seem, then, essential to maintain interest and motivation through the establishment of high expectations supported by an appropriately challenging teaching approach.

The implications for teachers are challenging too. Good teachers of able pupils will need to understand the pupils' learning needs and be able to respond in an *ad hoc* way and in longer term planning. They require secure subject knowledge competence and pedagogical expertise. An example of this is of the need for teachers to be able to construct higher order questions and tasks that require inference, deduction, analysis and comparison. Teachers also need to be aware of the emotional and psychological needs of able pupils who often suffer from being identified as able, designated as 'boffs' by peers and faced with a range of negative responses. They are also subject to intensive pressure by both teachers and parents to excel and to periods of anxiety and self-doubt since their very ability makes them acutely aware of their limitations and failings. Above all, teachers need to 'encourage all pupils to recognise the value of hard work and special achievement'. (Kirby, op. cit. p. 24) in a climate where able pupils have the personal confidence to make the best use of their talent and where all pupils can seek to develop their own special ability. The creation of such a climate can be detailed in a whole-school policy.

A policy for able pupils

A whole-school policy can construct its own definition of ability that is commensurate with and supportive of the school's overall objectives and ethos. However, policies need to be detailed and practical to be really effective. There are some good examples of policies in Kosh, V. and Casey, R. (op. cit.) and Eyre, D. (1997) for example. They are not MFL-specific, but could be easily adapted.

Whilst identification procedures, provision and the co-ordination of teaching approach for able pupils may be articulated in general terms, subject areas need to consider further subject specific checklists, subject resources and the planning and implementation of teaching and learning strategies to meet the needs of able MFL learners. Finer differentiated distinctions may be needed according to the level of ability of individual pupils. A school policy, therefore, will need to embrace these three levels (Figure 7.4).

Eyre comments that policy making and implementation ought really to be an extension of curriculum planning already *in situ* since: '. . . provision for the most able is an extension of existing systems' but that '. . . if systematic departmental

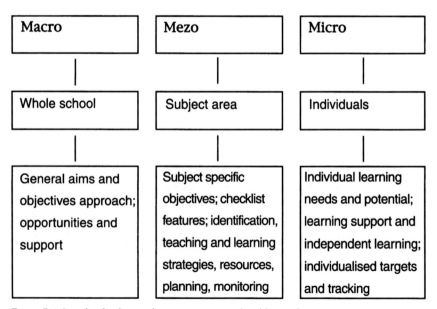

Figure 7.4 Levels of policy making on provision for able pupils.

planning is not well established, then it is impossible for that department to achieve extension planning'(op. cit. p. 100).

The concept of 'extension' has a stretching, 'moving beyond' dynamic which requires the MFL teacher to be absolutely clear about learning outcomes in order to be able to propose possible progression routes through the programmes of study. Kirby (op. cit. p. 80) proposes the following main types of study programme for able pupils:

1   Extension – depth of coverage
2   Expansion – breadth of coverage
3   Supplementary – reinforced learning
4   Acceleration – rapid coverage
5   Peripheral – tangential links with the set curriculum

I have already touched upon extension, supplementary and the concept of acceleration in this chapter. Expansion is a useful notion in that, in MFL terms, it envisages the exploration of language outside of the topic area or area of experience being studied, involving language or cultural content beyond the national curriculum framework, for example. It may be pupil-selected or negotiated with the teacher.

Peripheral elements of a study programme might include after-school clubs enrichment programmes, special language-focused events and competitions. One head of an MFL department explained that she allocated the responsibility of putting together the possibilities of a support and extension programme to the foreign language assistant. As a matter of principle, all events were offered to all pupils as part of an enrichment programme although some pupils obviously demonstrated more ability and interest than others did.

Whatever the details of extension programmes for able pupils, it would be helpful to designate a member of the languages department to elaborate these and to monitor their implementation. This important co-ordinating role would also involve providing training for staff and collecting examples of good practice, both in one's own school and in other institutions and disseminating it. Teachers would be supported in the identification process, share the processes of planning and devise ways of evaluating and recording the progress of able pupils with the establishment of appropriately challenging targets.

High attainment by all

I conclude this chapter by stating that much of what has been discussed in this Chapter arises out of a very broad canvas of consideration of good practice, not just for able pupils, but for all pupils learning a foreign language in school. The teacher, nonetheless, needs to acknowledge differences in ability and in capability and to understand the need for differentiated '*points de départ*' and '*points d'arrivée*' in individual pupils' learning. Many of these the teacher will be able to co-ordinate into major curriculum routes in terms of groups of pupils through the learning programmes, normally but not exclusively linked to National Curriculum criteria and level descriptions. Informed assessment of levels of attainment and detailed quantitative and qualitative profiles of each pupil will provide 'snapshots' of attainment and indicate the potential to excel. This will provide data to inform planning for differentiated teaching and learning and help teachers to set targets for individual pupils at their own rates and in their own ways. It thus reaffirms the right of equal opportunity for all pupils to develop their talents and abilities to the full, including the more able.

Note

1 An opinion provide by Mr Marland in a discussion with PGCE students, Autumn 1998.

Editor's note

Jones commends the MFL teaching profession for the provisions made for less able learners, but also cites evidence that the needs and potential of more able learners have been neglected in recent years. Jones draws on research in order to define the qualities and attributes of able learners as a prerequisite to recommending activities and approaches to cater for such learner types. Jones does not condemn the communicative approach as a language teaching methodology, but does see the need to add to it in order to develop linguistic understanding and mastery. This does not imply a return to former approaches, but serves as a recognition that aspects of learning, notably of grammar, are not to be dismissed on ideological grounds. Jones notes the value of language production and a wish for creativity in the able learner, which demands that imaginative extension exercises are designed and supported by the teacher. She provides a guidance framework, with practical suggestions for stretching able learners, which has the effect of challenging the restrictive constraints of adhering to the communicative approach as it is understood by many teachers.

Linked chapters

Chapter 2, Chapter 16, Chapter 3.

References

Carroll, J. B. (1969) 'Twenty-five years of research on foreign language aptitude', in K. C. Diller (ed.) *Individual Differences and Universals in Language Learning Aptitude*, Rowley, MA: Newbury House.

Denton, C. and Postlethwaite, K. (1985) *Able Children: Identifying Them in the Classroom*, NFER: Nelson.

DES (1988) *Education Reform Act* (ERA), London: HMSO.

DfEE (1995) *Modern Foreign Languages in the National Curriculum*, London: HMSO.

Dobson, A. (1998) *MFL Inspected. Reflections on Inspection Findings 1996/97*, London: CILT.

Eyre, D. (1997) *Able Children in Ordinary Schools*, London: David Fulton.

Gardner, H. (1983) *Frames of Mind*, 2nd edn, London: Fontana Press.

Graham, S. (1997) *Effective Language Learning*, Clevedon: Multilingual Matters.

Kerry, T. (1981) *Teaching Bright Pupils*, London: Macmillan Education Ltd.

Kirby, M. (1996) *Supporting the Able Pupil. A School Plan*, London: Pearson Publishing.

Kosh, V. and Casey, L. (1997) *Effective Provision for Able and Exceptionally Able Learners*, Cheltenham: Hodder and Stoughton.

Montgomery, D. (1996) *Educating the Able*, London: Cassell.

Naiman, N. *et al.* (1996) *The Good Language Learner*, Clevedon: Multilingual Matters.

Ogilvie, E. (1975) *Gifted Children in Primary School*, London: Macmillan (quoted in Kerry above).

OFSTED (1995) *Modern Foreign Languages. A Review of Inspection Findings 1993/94*, London: HMSO.

Sidwell, P. (1994) *Extension Activites for Able Pupils*, INSET notes, Cheshire County Council.

Suggested further reading

There is a dearth of MFL specific up-to-date research and writing about able pupils in MFLs. However, a spate of books has recently been written about able pupils generally which have sections with considerable transfer value. In addition to those already referred to, the following have useful sections:

Davis, G. A. and Rimm, S. B. (1989) *The Education of the Gifted and Talented*, London: Prentice Hall.

George, D. (1992) *The Challenge of the Able Child*, London: David Fulton.

8 Mixed ability grouping in Modern Foreign Languages teaching

Ana Redondo

Introduction

This chapter examines the issue of student grouping in modern foreign languages (MFL) teaching and learning framed by findings from educational research.

The political context

The question about the most effective organisational, i.e. grouping, arrangements for students[1] for educational purposes has been a key concern for some time now, but particularly since the comprehensivisation of the education system in Britain from the mid 1960s. Whilst the 1944 Butler Act put in place an organisational structure characterised by streaming into different types of secondary schools, i.e. the grouping of students by age, aptitude and ability into grammar schools, secondary modern or technical schools, the so-called Crossland Circular encouraged Local Education Authorities to set up a comprehensive system bringing together students from different social strata, with students with special educational needs being educated in special schools. This move was motivated by ideological as well as social considerations, 'using bright middle-class children as an asset for the educational system, to be distributed like fertiliser to help the poorer children grow' (Davies, 1999b).

Whilst a thorough examination of the debate about the introduction of comprehensive schools in Britain is beyond the scope of this chapter, it does seem necessary, nevertheless, to allude at least to some of the issues pertaining to comprehensive schooling as the question of whether students best be taught in mixed ability groups at the micro level, i.e. within schools, is inextricably linked to organisational principles at the macro level, i.e. the types of schools students attend.

With the introduction of the National Curriculum and national testing, the education system in England and Wales (though not necessarily that of Scotland) has seen a move towards greater standardisation and central control since the late 1980s, in particular since the 1988 Education Reform Act and there has been a concerted effort by central government to break up the powers of Local Education Authorities to co-ordinate educational provision at a local level by introducing Local Management of Schools (LMS) and (seemingly) striving for diversity and parental choice as well as, with it, competition amongst schools.

Also, there has been a move since the 1991 and 1993 Education Acts towards the inclusion of children with special educational needs into mainstream schools. At the same time many of the brightest 20–25 per cent of students continue to be educated in private schools. This has led to the average intake of comprehensive schools being skewed, sometimes considerably, towards the bottom end of the ability spectrum. Therefore, the question arises whether some comprehensive schools and the teachers within them have ever been given a real chance to prove whether comprehensive education really works.

Throughout much of the 1990s, educational policy-making has been pre-occupied with school improvement and the raising of standards. School improvement research shows that, despite the socio-economic background of pupils presenting an important factor in deciding academic results, schools can make a difference. However, 'there (are) limits to how much and . . . it (is) not sensible to try and run an entire system on the basis of what exceptional schools (manage) to achieve' (Mortimore, 1999: 6). Davies (1999a) points out that government decided to ignore the importance of students' socio-economic background in their policy making despite assertions from researchers that at most schools could hope to achieve an increase of 8–10 per cent in results, because not only are they relatively cheap and completely absolve central government of all responsibility for failure, but they also promise to deliver results quickly. These measures include league tables which take little or no account of value-added measures or external OFSTED inspections based on a set of seemingly undifferentiated criteria and measuring against national averages potentially leading to the 'naming and shaming' or even the closure of schools.

The underpinning structure of the National Curriculum, namely the notion of clearly defined stages and levels of attainment, as well as the tiered system of the national standardised examination, the GCSE, has been commented upon as being in conflict with mixed ability teaching. Indeed, the recent government White Paper 'Excellence in Schools' (1997: 38) stipulates that '(unless) a school can demonstrate that it is getting better than expected results through a different approach, we do make the presumption that setting should be the norm in secondary schools'. The White Paper justifies this assertion by stating that setting had proved to be effective in many secondary schools *inter alia* for mathematics, science and languages.

The introduction of 'market forces' in education and the emphasis on the comparatively easily measurable, i.e. (academic) achievement published in the form of examination results, has had a major effect on secondary schools. In a bid to maintain and increase pupil numbers to sustain economic viability, schools have had to focus on maximum attainment in league table terms. On the basis of their study of relevant research, Sukhnandan and Lee point out (1998: 47) that under such pressures, the two most cost-effective strategies schools have at their disposal are selection, i.e. to gear their intake towards pupils who are likely to do well against the prevailing measures (A*–C GCSE passes), and ability grouping in a bid to raise students' achievements in terms of examination results.

The active encouragement by government and researchers of parental involvement in schooling and policies aimed at parental choice make demands on schools in terms of ability grouping:

> [research] suggests that there is a strong perception within schools that middle-class parents with 'able' children (i.e. those pupils who are likely to perform well in tests) are more likely to choose schools that implement ability grouping than those which do not.
>
> (Sukhnandan and Lee, 1998: 47)

Discussing mixed ability grouping in its wider context serves to underline that to examine the advantages and disadvantages of grouping by ability from an idealised educational vantage point and as an abstract ideological concept, is of limited use. Instead, decisions about the grouping of pupils need to be taken in consideration of the challenges faced by education and schooling at the beginning of the twenty-first century, i.e. considerable political and societal pressure on schools and teachers to raise standards measured in terms of improvements of examination results, as well as in response to local needs.

All these factors make the discussion of mixed ability teaching highly complex. The topic is highly politically charged as the educational achievement of the nation's children is at stake. Unsurprisingly, therefore, the debate about mixed-ability teaching has tended to be influenced by political dogma as much as by empirical evidence, with concerns for social engineering or the raising of levels of achievement being of particular importance (see e.g. Carvel, 1996).

Decisions concerning the organisation of pupils in schools are not easy to take. They can be seen as an important aspect of a school's ethos and as an expression of educational philosophy. However, as schools find themselves operating in the context of the normative constraints of the National Curriculum framework with centrally prescribed policies enforced through rigorous inspection and the publication of examination results in league tables, pragmatic solutions to the challenge of the raising of standards need to be found. Not least because there is a particular danger that the needs of those who fall significantly below the GCSE C to D grade borderline might be marginalised, decisions about pupil grouping need to be handled sensitively and fairly, ensuring equal access to good quality teaching.

Mixed ability teaching and other forms of organising pupils in comprehensive schools – an MFL perspective

An important premise to the discussion of mixed ability teaching in MFL has to be that the findings from studies investigating the grouping of pupils have tended to be inconclusive (see e.g. Sukhnandan and Lee, 1998: 3).

Above and beyond systemic considerations, as teachers we need to be sensitive to the fact that students, regardless of the nature of a school's intake, are:

> individuals with different needs. No group of pupils is ever homogeneous. Differences in areas such as ability, gender, self-concept, self-esteem, social class, ethnic background or creativity can, for instance, determine pupils' degree of progress, achievement or participation.
>
> (Pachler and Field, 1997: 173)

Research suggests that students tend to perceive, interact with and respond to a learning environment in a relatively stable way, i.e. that they have preferred learning styles of which teachers need to be aware in order to be able to set appropriate work (see Ellis, 1994: 499, and Pachler 1999). Widely heterogeneous classes pose a particular challenge in MFL in this respect to which schools and teachers have reacted in a number of ways.

First, differentiation has been widely used as a key strategy in catering for pupil differences and a variety of pupil needs in heterogeneous classes. For a detailed discussion of differentiation in MFL, see e.g. Convery and Coyle, 1993 and 1999, or Pachler and Field, 1997: 173–203; for a discussion of how best to meet the needs of able learners, see e.g. George, 1993 and 1994.

Second, teachers have been engaging in teaching students about learning strategies and target setting with a view to enabling them to understand better their own learning preferences and thereby maximise their learning gains by making deliberate choices in their learning during and out of lessons. For a pragmatic approach to learning strategies, see e.g. Harris, 1997.

Third, teachers have adopted within-class grouping on the basis, for example, of pupil differences and their learning preferences in order to avoid conflicts between teaching and learning styles, as well as to cater for a diverse range of preferred learning styles in any one group. D-az Maggioli (1996), for example, advances a classification of learners by sensory preferences distinguishing visual, auditory, tactile and kinaesthetic learners with corresponding lists of preferred activities.

Students are widely thought to have multiple intelligences and that, therefore, some are better at certain things than others. MacGilchrist, Myers and Reed (1997: 23–4), for example, stress the importance of the work of Howard Gardner who holds that learners are potentially able to develop at least seven types of intelligence:

1 linguistic: the intelligence of words
2 logical-mathematical: the intelligence of numbers and reasoning
3 spatial: the intelligence of pictures and images
4 musical: the intelligence of tome, rhythm, and timbre
5 bodily-kinaesthetic: the intelligence of the whole body and the hands
6 interpersonal: the intelligence of social understanding
7 intrapersonal: the intelligence of self-knowledge

From the above follows for me that there is a strong educational rationale to be advanced for grouping students homogeneously. As well as many other things, one important requirement for maximising learning outcomes is for the teacher to know her students as best she can, in particular in relation to their learning styles, learning preferences, personal strengths and of course, their ability. In the context of inevitably large class sizes, it stands to reason that homogeneous groupings are more likely to allow the teacher a greater opportunity to meet the individual needs of her students. Mixed ability grouping, conversely and due to the wider range of ability of students in any one class, often makes unrealistic demands on teachers' pedagogical skills. Whilst it should attract a more favourable staff–student ratio, in practice this rarely if ever happens:

> in principle, [mixed ability grouping] provides all pupils with equality of opportunity, in terms of curriculum, instruction and resources, and reduces the negative consequences often associated with homogeneous grouping. However, the effective implementation of individualised teaching makes considerably greater demands on teachers, in terms of planning, than teaching homogeneous groups.
>
> (Sukhnandan and Lee, 1998: 4)

The negative consequences referred to above and associated with setting are on the whole about misbehaviour of pupils in lower sets and their feelings of demotivation. Kellaway (1996: 17) concludes from her research into teachers' attitudes towards mixed-ability teaching 'that modern language teachers do not reject mixed-ability teaching as such but rather the inadequate resources with which to carry it out' and Sue Hallam (1996: 5) reports that '(teachers) appear to dislike teaching lower ability groups because of the pupils' negative attitudes towards school and their poor behaviour in the classroom'. Both approaches, ability grouping and mixed ability grouping, have advantages and disadvantages. Grouping learners homogeneously by taking into account a range of factors including intelligence, learning styles and preferences, etc., in addition to ability goes towards addressing the main challenge of setting as perceived by teachers, namely the formation of lower ability groups and all the obvious consequences this might entail in terms of classroom management and pupil misbehaviour.

It is in particular the ideological dimension of equality of opportunities which has made mixed ability teaching an important consideration and an emotional and controversial issue, particularly in the context of a supposedly comprehensive system of schooling. Hallam (1996: 4) notes that whilst there is a general tendency for children to mix with others of similar ability, social class and gender, there is also evidence to suggest that more mixed friendships occur in mixed ability classes with the form unit providing the basis for friendship groups. Mixed ability grouping, therefore can allow teachers to address educational issues beyond academic attainment and ensure that students participate fully in the curriculum.

I concur with Hallam about the need to address educational issues beyond academic attainment and endorse the principle of comprehensive education for the reasons stated above. Indeed, MFL has a very strong contribution to make in this area. In my view these goals can be achieved more efficiently by teaching MFL to homogeneous groups of pupils. For example, students could engage in whole-class or small group discussion in the target language on issues related to GCSE topics, e.g. 'young people and smoking' or 'cultural traditions' such as bull-fighting. In order for such an activity to be successful, students require a certain cognitive understanding, prior awareness of issues, an ability to form and express opinions, a degree of experience of participating in group discussions and of listening to the opinions of others as well as a certain linguistic knowledge and expertise. Homogeneity of teaching groups allows the teacher to carry out such an activity more effectively by ensuring that those students who have the requisite cognitive and linguistic skills can be immediately presented with the discussion task whilst those students who have not, can be taken by the teacher across a number of prerequisite learning steps before they too can fully participate in the same task, albeit not at the same level. It is important to stress that all students need to access a similar type and range of work and activities but realistically not always at the same level. This is more feasible in homogeneous groups where the teacher can offer sufficient scaffolding for those children who need it as well as stretching the more able. In that way students of all abilities can develop skills of a higher order, accessing the same intellectually challenging topics, albeit in different ways and at different levels of complexity.

In their recent review of the (non-subject specific) research literature on mixed ability grouping Laura Sukhnandan and Barbara Lee list a number of advantages and disadvantages of mixed ability grouping (see Figure 8.1). Please note that arguments in both columns are not directly opposed to each other.

When analysing the points made on both sides of the argument, it is significant to note that emphasis on factors such as social development and behavioural control seem to emerge as the perceived advantage of mixed ability grouping. Clearly, equality of opportunity and equal access to a common curriculum, teachers and resources need to be addressed at a whole school level, but, as I have noted above, I would argue that mixed ability grouping in MFL teaching in secondary schools is not always the most effective way of ensuring students benefit from a learning experience of equal worth. A particular problem with mixed ability grouping appears to be the difficulty for (MFL) teachers to ensure that students with higher ability are sufficiently stretched whilst it seems that, on the whole, those of average and those with lower ability and learning difficulties are often well catered for.

Mixed ability grouping poses particular difficulties in MFL, a subject in which the learning and memorising of words and phrases as well as the understanding of often complex linguistic structures and grammatical features only develop over time, are very important in ensuring progress is made. Students need to develop across listening, speaking, reading and writing as well as in terms of grammatical and cultural understanding and their application coupled with social skills in order

Advantages of mixed ability grouping	Disadvantages of mixed ability grouping
• Mixed ability teaching improves equality of opportunity providing all pupils with equal access to a common curriculum, teachers and resources.	• Mixed ability teaching makes greater demands than traditional forms of teaching because teachers need to ensure that they cater for the full ability range through individualised teaching.
• It addresses the negative social consequences of homogeneous grouping by encouraging cooperative behaviour and more effective social integration.	• Teachers have to complete a great deal of preparation, obtain a range of materials and develop assignments which match pupils' needs and are also motivating.
• It avoids the problems associated with allocating pupils to homogeneous groups.	• Teachers spend most of their time managing pupils' activities and responding to pupils' demands rather than teaching.
• Mixed ability teaching promotes the matching of individual pupils' needs and encourages teachers to assess pupils in relation to their own potential.	• Teachers frequently resort to whole-class teaching or worksheets, which means that lessons tend to be taught at a uniform pace and at a level pitched at pupils of average ability.
• Mixed ability teaching allows for continuity in learning styles between primary and secondary schools.	• Ineffective implementation can result in the failure to meet the needs of high and low ability pupils.
• Mixed ability classes promote good relations amongst pupils and between teachers and pupils.	• Mixed ability teaching can have a negative impact on high ability pupils' level of motivation and achievement.
• Mixed ability classes reduce competition and the labelling of pupils, allowing pupils to learn at their own pace.	• Because teachers spend most of their time working with individuals, the majority of the class is often poorly supervised.
• In mixed ability classes, low ability pupils may benefit from having high ability models, especially in relation to their attitudes and behaviour.	

Source: © Sukhnandan and Lee, 1998: 58.

Figure 8.1 The advantages and disadvantages of mixed ability grouping.

to carry out pair work and group work effectively. Inevitably, students in the same age group are often at a very different level of skill development. In MFL teaching and learning, students' ability to work independently is crucial as there is a considerable need for the release of the teacher from whole-class activity in order to be able to attend to individuals to correct mistakes, address possible misconceptions, help with pronunciation, provide one-to-one support for students, etc. The more homogeneous a group is, the more effectively a student's level of ability and individual academic need can be catered for. In my experience, more able students in particular can be seen to benefit from not constantly being asked to complete greater amounts of work than their less able peers. Also, they should not be expected to support their less able peers for disproportionate amounts of lesson time, to work in unequally matched pairs and groups for most of the time or to persistently have to wait for the teacher's attention.

As mentioned above, recognising the drawbacks of mixed ability grouping has led teachers to adopt strategies to counterbalance the ability gap amongst students in large heterogeneous classes, i.e. differentiation and within-class grouping.

> Research has . . . revealed interesting variations between the effects of different types of within-class grouping and pupils of different ability levels. For example, Lou *et al.* (1996) found that while low ability pupils learned significantly more in heterogeneous groups, average ability pupils learned more in homogeneous groups. In contrast, group composition (homogeneous or heterogeneous) had little effect on the levels of achievement of high ability pupils. The authors suggest that this might occur because low ability pupils gain more from a heterogeneous environment in which they can be provided with assistance from their peers, while average ability pupils gain more through participating in the giving and receiving of explanations.
>
> (Sukhnandan and Lee, 1998: 17–18)

Lou *et al.* (1996) also suggest that pupils' attitudes towards the subject is positively affected by within-class grouping.

Planning and producing differentiated work as well as working with small groups in class on a regular basis is not only very demanding on the teacher but also highly difficult to sustain for long periods of time across a number of groups regardless of the degree of professional experience or language expertise of teachers. In MFL learning there is a particular need for learners to assimilate and accommodate new language and to receive regular feedback and corrections. Given the artificiality of the classroom context as opposed to the linguistically rich environment of the target country this makes the role of the teacher in catering for individual students' needs paramount. Classes of 30 plus (in Key Stage 3) are, therefore, far from ideal. Classrooms of 30 or more children of vastly different ability levels make the task for the MFL teacher even more daunting. Homogenous groups can allow teachers to target and match resources, teaching styles and pace to students' needs more easily and effectively in subject-specific terms and afford them relatively more easily manageable demands in terms of planning and classroom management.

There is therefore a strong case to be made for setting in MFL. Departments clearly need to be aware of some of the challenges associated with homogeneous groupings, namely the difficulty of allocating students to the appropriate teaching group which necessarily deserves careful consideration. Also, care needs to be taken that no stigma is attached to certain groups, that certain social groups are not discriminated against, that the pace of teaching is appropriate in all groups and that the system of group allocation is sufficiently flexible to allow for students to move groups if necessary. Hallam (1996: 3) notes that 'the effects of ability grouping on self-esteem are mediated by the behaviour of teachers and peers'. From this I conclude that the ethos of a school in promoting high achievement and tolerance among other noble aims plays an important role in enhancing the effects of student grouping.

Needless to say, homogeneous student grouping is not in conflict with a policy of 'languages for all'. It is because I fully endorse and promote 'languages for all' that I argue here in favour of homogeneity in student grouping as it provides students with the most satisfactory context in which the needs of the whole ability range is met and yet it allows for high quality pedagogical activity to take place. All students are entitled to have access to a modern foreign language and to reach their full potential in it. Teachers can use materials, as well as teaching styles and pedagogical approaches more effectively when classes share a greater similarity of learning qualities and characteristics.

In terms of policy thinking, I feel it might be time to consider the scope of differentiated aims and objectives for different groups of learners according to individual differences such as, for example, motivation, interest and career aspiration as well as ability. This assertion is based on my belief that we need to be realistic about what can be achieved in the time available in secondary education and it reflects my concerns over the limitations of the current GCSE. In a context where MFL teachers in many schools are desperately trying to maintain a diversified MFL curriculum, often invariably on 'borrowed time', i.e. by teaching two foreign languages in the time allocated for one and the increased workload this entails, e.g. in terms of a larger number of teaching groups and a significantly higher planning, preparation, marking, report writing load, etc., mixed ability grouping often adds unnecessarily to teachers' workload, which tends to be detrimental to the effectiveness of MFL teaching and learning.

Conclusions

Having examined much of the evidence available on pupil grouping, I would advocate operating a flexible system in which the most appropriate form of grouping is implemented according to local needs and that overcomplicated systems should be avoided in order not to jeopardise class cohesiveness and students' sense of belonging (see e.g. Alexander et al., 1992 or Edwards and Woodhead, 1996). Whilst some might not necessarily agree with setting on ideological grounds, in the context of the current educational climate and the characteristics and demands of MFL as a (curriculum) subject, I suggest here to consider 'homogeneous groups' and 'within-class grouping' as pragmatically feasible options. Seated group work, collaborative project work, co-operative learning (see e.g. Slavin 1990), flexible learning (see e.g. Anderson et al., 1991; Eraut et al., 1990; TVEI Flexible Learning and Teacher Support Unit, 1989; or Waterhouse, 1990), task-based learning (see e.g. Skehan, 1996) or carousel work can all be applied in various different ways to ensure academic and social learning. Greater flexibility and consideration of students' individual learning styles could be achieved through learner independence and access to ICT (see e.g. Hallam and Toutounji, 1996; Pachler, 1999; and Pachler and Field, 1997).

However, in the debate about the most effective way of grouping students it is important not to forget that:

> [there] appear to be complex interactions between grouping, teaching methods, teacher attitudes, the pacing of lessons and the ethos of the school. The grouping of pupils is only one of several factors affecting the learning environment of the classroom. The quality of instruction and the curriculum are central.
>
> (Hallam, 1996: 2)

Quality of teaching, appropriateness and effectiveness of teaching approaches, teachers' pedagogic and didactic skills remain the key in maximising student achievement, attainment and enjoyment in MFL learning; nevertheless and in order to provide all students with the opportunity to achieve excellence and reach their full potential in MFL learning, homogeneous, cohesive and sensitive student grouping is primordial.

Note

1   The term student be used in this chapter to denote secondary pupils aged 11 to 18.

Editor's note

Redondo places the issue of setting versus mixed ability teaching in a broader context, noting the need to take into account arguments associated with comprehensivisation, equal opportunities and personal and social development. This gives the chapter a philosophical and political dimension. Redondo draws on research to demonstrate which pupils benefit from which type of grouping, and she also presents the demands made on teachers. She recognises advantages and disadvantages, but explains why she favours setting as a means of striving towards the demands made on teachers at this point in time. However, Redondo does not accept necessarily that the criteria by which pupils are setted are objective and fair. She argues for features other than perceived ability to be taken into account, such as pupil motivation, preferred learning styles and career aspirations. This, Redondo suggests must be accompanied by an awareness of the impact of grouping/setting on pupil motivation and attitudes, and must therefore be dealt with with great sensitivity.

Linked Chapters

Chapter 7, Chapter 15.

References

Alexander, R., Rose, J. and Woodhead, C. (1992) *Curriculum Organisation and Classroom Practice in Primary Schools: a Discussion Paper*, London: DES.

Anderson, J., Harris, V., Stanyer, H. and Walker, G. (1991) *Flexible Learning Project*, London: Goldsmiths College.

Carvel, J. (1996) 'Blair rejects mixed ability teaching', *Guardian*, 8 June 1996.

Convery, A. and Coyle, D. (1993) *Differentiation – Taking the Initiative*, London: CILT.

Convery, A. and Coyle, D. (1999) *Differentiation and Individual Learners*, London: CILT.

Davies, N. (1999a) 'Writing on classroom wall was ignored', *Guardian*, 14 September 1999.

Davies, N. (1999b) 'Mixture of talent makes or breaks a school', *Guardian*, 15 September 1999.

D-az Maggioli, G. (1996) 'The good, the bad, and the ugly. Learning preferences in EFL', *English Teaching Forum*, 34(2). Also available at: http://e.usia.gov/forum/vols/vol34/no2/p32.htm.

DfEE (1997) *Excellence in Schools*, White Paper, London: The Stationery Office.

Edwards, S. and Woodhead, N. (1996) 'Mathematics teaching in primary school: whole class, group or individual teaching?' *Primary Practice*, 6: 4–7.

Ellis, R. (1994) *The Study of Second Language Acquisition*, Oxford: Oxford University Press.

Eraut, M. Nash, C., Fielding, M. and Attard, P. (1990) *Flexible Learning in Schools*, University of Sussex: Institute of Continuing and Professional Education.

George, D. (1993) 'Meeting the challenge of the able child', *Topic 10*, Windsor: NFER-Nelson.

George, D. (1994) 'Provision and strategies for teaching more able children', *Topic 11*, Windsor: NFER-Nelson.

Hallam, S. (1996) 'Grouping pupils by ability: selection, streaming, banding and setting', *Viewpoint 4*, London: Institute of Education.

Hallam, S. and Toutounji, I. (1996) 'What do we know about grouping pupils by ability?' *Education Review*, 10(2): 63–70.

Harris, V. (1997) *Teaching Learners How to Learn. Strategy Training in the ML Classroom*, London: CILT.

Kellaway, C. (1996) 'Mixed-ability foreign language teaching: a survey of teachers' attitudes', *Languages Forum 5*, London: Institute of Education, pp. 15–18.

Lou, Y., Abrami, P., Spence, J., Poulsen, C., Chambers, B. and d'Apollonia, S. (1996) 'Within-class grouping: a meta-analysis.', *Review of Educational Research*, 66(4): 423–58.

MacGilchrist, B., Myers, K. and Reed, J. (1997) *The Intelligent School*, London: Paul Chapman.

Mortimore, P. (1999) 'Does research matter?' *Education Journal*, October 1999, pp. 6–7.

Pachler, N. (1999) 'Theories of learning and information and communications technology', in M. Leask and N. Pachler (eds) *Learning to Teach Using ICT in the Secondary School*, London: Routledge, pp. 3–18.

Pachler, N. and Field, K. (1997) *Learning to Teach Modern Foreign Languages in the Secondary School*, London: Routledge.

Skehan, P. (1996) 'A framework for the implementation of task-based instruction', *Applied Linguistics*, 17 (1): 38–62.

Slavin, R. (1990) 'Achievement effects of ability grouping in secondary schools: a best evidence synthesis', *Review of Educational Research*, 60(3): 471–99.
Sukhnandan, L. with Lee, B. (1998) *Streaming, Setting and Grouping by Ability. A Review of the Literature*, Slough: NFER.
TVEI Flexible Learning and Teacher Support Unit (1989) *Flexible Learning. A Framework for Education and Training in the Skills Decade*, Sheffield: Employment Department.
Waterhouse, P. (1990) *Flexible Learning. An Outline*, Bath: Network Educational Press.

9 Why are girls better at Modern Foreign Languages than boys?

Kit Field

Introduction

It is almost futile to present statistics to demonstrate that girls out perform boys in MFLs. Many research findings read as truisms to teachers of MFLs, who need no reminder that girls' results are better than those of boys. Table 3.1 (see Chapter 3) provides evidence of this at GCSE, and Ofsted (1999) demonstrates no shift in more recent years. There is Ofsted claim, a 16 per cent difference between boys and girls getting the highest grades. A glimpse into teaching rooms where MFLs are setted by ability, in A level classes and indeed in university lecture theatres simply serves to reinforce the view that not only are girls better at MFLs, but they also enjoy the subject more.

The purpose of this Chapter is not to accept, but to question why MFLs might be more appealing and more attractive to females. The statistical and anecdotal evidence, must be placed in context. Questions need to be asked, as to whether the gender imbalance is inevitable, avoidable, 'addressable' or necessary. Several writers (e.g. Dunbar, 1987 and Riley, 1994) comment on the widening gender divide in co-educational schools. Dunbar notes a polarisation in terms of the popularity of MFLs in mixed schools, and Riley, that in general girls and boys perform better in single sex schools. Evidently, boys and girls do influence each other in terms of attitude and performance outcome when learning MFLs.

This apparent impact of comprehensivisation and emergence of co-educational schools supports Abraham's (1995) argument that most education reforms reproduce and amplify class and gender differences which exist in society outside the school gates. Certainly teachers need to be aware of these influences – at times MFL teachers have to battle against xenophobic tendencies and sexist bias with regard to promoting their own subject.

MFLs must not be taken in isolation. Halpin, in the *Education Guardian* (1999) notes that girls do better than boys in almost all GCSE subjects, and that whereas only one quarter of boys gain two 'A' level passes or equivalent, the same rate of success is achieved by one third of girls. Indeed educational success in general can be seen to be dominated by females and that this tendency is simply more marked in MFLs than in many other subjects. Certainly to examine the possible causes of girls' success and boys' failure may well provide indication of more general application.

Already, the reader will note the dangers of presenting arguments in a generalised fashion. Extracting interesting conclusions drawn from teacher research run the risk of creating a bias when attempting to identify possible causes. Thornton's (1999) brief aside that boys lose concentration more easily when lessons are conducted in the target language is a case in point. The issue is of interest, and underlying causes for the loss of concentration need to be examined, rather than teachers assuming that to avoid using the target language is a means of re-dressing the balance. This is not meant as a criticism of Thornton but more a warning to teachers with an interest in the matter. Indeed by reporting a serious research, a journalistic interpretation runs the risk of missing the key points. Rudduck (1994) makes the point that: 'Gendered inequalities cannot be easily combated, unless the structures that sustain them are understood' (p 130).

It is essential to appreciate, then, that the often, apparently stereotypical outcomes of research into gender and MFLs are the reporting of symptoms, not the causes. Teachers and educators reading this chapter, for example, must look beyond the obvious in order to avoid a process of a self-fulfilling prophecy. As Askew and Row (1989) point out, an acceptance at face value of stereotypical traits is extremely dangerous, as it leads to limiting expectations and the internalisation of myths, which in turn can lead to an acceptance of these myths as the norm.

In raising the issue of gender differences it is then my intention that teachers consider how affective, motivational and behavioural factors, which Grenfell and Harris (1997) state influence learning, can be tackled. Researchers have indeed identified truisms, but these must not be accepted at face value. Harris, Nixon and Rudduck (1993) note that girls are more conscientious than boys; Clark and Trafford (1996) acknowledge that girls present their written work in a neater way. Evidently these issues raise the question of whether teachers of MFLs motivate boys, or show equal respect for boys' attributes as they do girls.

I am not presenting a hypothesis that boys are let down by teachers of MFLs. I am drawing on sociological research findings which attempt to show how differences in performance can be seen to stem from factors including curriculum materials, pupil–teacher interaction, peer group pressure and pupil anxiety (see Abraham, 1995). This, albeit adapted list, is not so different from the findings of writers reporting MFL specific research. Dunbar (1987) identified key factors, such as the image of a subject in school, the development of appropriate study skills, the curriculum content, assessment methods, and the respect teachers have for gender-identifiable, pupil behaviour patterns.

My own presentation of issues is structured differently. First, I intend to present the obvious (to teachers of MFLs) differences in behaviour and learning styles between boy and girl learners. Second, I raise questions in terms of how teaching MFLs to pupils at an age when gender differentiation is most marked.

These factors inevitably influence the third section of my argument, pupil motivation. Lastly I question how MFLs are taught, and suggest that the methodology may serve to reinforce the gender-based judgements pupils make about MFL learning, which lead to a gap between boys' and girls' levels of enjoyment and performance.

Obvious gender differences

Dunbar (1987) identifies the image of MFLs in school as a factor contributing to the feminine ethos of the subject. There are though factors outside school which undoubtedly have an influence on the view pupils have of the subject. Myers (1985) recognises that children are aware of and use stereotypes by the age of 3. By the age of 5 or 6, Myers claims children undervalue the role of females in society. An extension of this argument is that concepts and constructs associated with femininity will also be devalued. Abraham (1995) states clearly that parents perceive French and one assumes other MFLs as a girls' subject. In England and Wales, MFLs are a subject not studied until the age of 11, and consequently we can assume that the view of French as a less than necessary school subject is well entrenched.

It would be unfair to apply such a generalised theory to all pupils. However, in combination with other factors, this hypothesis may well have an effect on pupils' pre-learning attitudes. The Cockroft Report (1982) asserts emphatically that girls perform better in verbal reasoning tests from the earliest age, and the argument follows that boys have limited verbal interaction skills. Not only is the attitude of boys vis-à-vis foreign language learning an inhibiting factor, but so is, it is argued, the potential for positive learning, in a subject which requires developed verbal reasoning skills.

The issue of whether the potential for language learning is a natural, gender-related concern, or an outcome of conditioning is hotly debated. For teachers concerned with differentiating according to need, the issue is almost unimportant. What is of interest is to understand factors which contribute to inequality and to provide a curriculum which raises the achievement levels of learners who are less favoured.

Parental support is crucial for educational success. Abraham (1995) suggests that success in language learning is directly related to the encouragement young children receive when learning to read. Once again, this factor weighs heavily in favour of girls. Parents, Abraham proceeds to argue, offer girls more encouragement in this area.

Licht and Dweck (1983) wrote at a time when girls were seen to be under-performing in schools. They did, however, recognise the potential for girls to outperform boys: 'If anything, girls should come to expect greater academic achievement, since in the primary years they receive consistently higher grades' (p. 77).

If girls are actively encouraged to develop their linguistic intelligence and competence, and demonstrate greater educational ability, while boys receive negative views of MFL teaching and learning, it comes as no surprise that girls enjoy greater success in MFLs at secondary school.

Ted Wragg (1997) adds a further explanation by drawing on the 'nature' side of the 'nature/nurture' argument. Wragg believes that in MFL lessons, girls have both halves of their brain activated, whereas boys rely on one half alone. The logical, spatial thinking is therefore complemented, and enhanced by the expressive and creative half of the brain, supposedly more developed in girls. The combination of thinking styles has a powerful impact and inevitably improves the likelihood of success in MFL learning.

The causes of boys' failure may not be physiological. A volume of evidence (Clark and Trafford, 1996; Grenfell and Harris, 1997; Reynolds, 1995) points towards boys lacking in confidence in reading skills in comparison with girls. Confidence, whether overt or subconscious, is inevitably an influence on boys' attitudes to language learning in general.

Many teachers would prefer the explanations for boys' relative failure to learn towards affective factors. Such explanations enable action to be taken to redress the balance. Spender and Scott's (1980) research findings further complicate the issue. They concluded that boys attitudes are more rigid, and that they are less willing than girls to take on unfamiliar and unattractive tasks. Almost by definition, learning a foreign language, requires learners 'to take on' the unfamiliar. In general terms language-related activities represent to boys, tasks which they find difficult, and they undervalue. Again, foreign language learning can appear distasteful. For girls, following Spender and Scott's line of argument, language learning represents a far less unattractive and more appealing progression.

Boys' rigidity of thought can be interpreted in a different way. Grenfell and Harris (1997) note that boys attribute bad learning to fixed reasons, such as a lack of relevance to their own personal agenda. In short boys learn if they want to, and if they perceive personal gain. With low motivation deriving from a sense of failure and from external perceptions of MFLs as a 'low value' subject, boys are at a greater risk of rejecting the subject. Girls, Grenfell and Harris continue, are more in control and are able to respond to 'bad learning' by drawing on the newer developed language learning strategies built up over a long period of time. Girls are also more tolerant, the writers claim. As a consequence, girls compensate for uninteresting teaching by activating language learning skills, whereas boys reject the subject, blaming boring teaching styles.

Tolerance levels and a higher boredom threshold also favour girls' learning in many schools. Clark and Trafford (1996) attribute boys' losses of concentration to long lessons in a subject which requires variety and regular contact. Concentration and application to talk are, Clark and Trafford claim, characteristic of female learners. This view that boys' lose concentration is supported by Spenders' (1982) findings that boys receive two thirds of teachers' attention during lessons, and that the majority of this attention is negative. This observation is explicable in two ways.

First, we could assume that boys are bored and distracted, or second that teachers do not respect the contribution of boys in lessons. Whatever the cause, the relationship between teacher and male learners is not positive.

Various writers (Dunbar, 1987 and Kruse, 1992) have examined the study skills required for successful language learning, and have related these to the study skills teachers generally associate with boys and girls. Dunbar (1987: 193) lists traditionally male and female attributes and invites the reader to decide whether each favours language learning. The assumption is that traditionally feminine study skills of perseverance, neatness, carefulness, conscientiousness, diligence, thoroughness and consistency support the process of MFL learning more than the noisiness, boisterousness, rebelliousness, aggression, assertiveness, inventiveness, energy and initiative normally associated with boys.

Such an assumption may well be overgeneralised however. A closer scrutiny of Dunbars' lists reveals feminine traits to include passivity, docility and compliance. For boys, she includes competition, leadership and originality. To decide which qualities/characteristics least favour foreign language learning is less easy than to identify which list of 'behaviours' are most likely to please teachers.

Kruse (1992) bases conclusions on lesson observations. These observations can be seen to have a more direct impact on teaching. The concentration span of girls is almost double that of boys. Girls prepare well for lessons, and remain focused on the content. Boys are active, but in an anarchistic way, prepare badly and seek to 'broaden the subject beyond the teachers' wish'. Girls respect others right to speak, boys are more impulsive and interrupt. Follow up to such observations revealed that girls view language lessons as a shared venture, whereas boys demand that they are of individual interest.

Boys and girls behaviour patterns are very different in MFL lessons. The precise causes are unknown. However the attitudes of beliefs imparted to learners at a young age gather momentum. Attitudes to MFLs become entrenched and teachers of MFLs face such problems, almost after they become irreversible. It is then no surprise that teachers and researchers are compelled to draw and simplified conclusion such as:

> Indeed, certain academic tasks, and certain academic areas in general may possess characteristic that are compatible with girls' achievement orientations, and that should facilitate their performance.
>
> (Licht and Dweck, 1983: 83)

Age related (maturational) factors

The fact that Dale (1974) and Beswick (1978) note that gender differences are more marked in mixed comprehensive schools, and that girls' superiority in academic study, may be, at least in part, due to the fact that their studies are based on secondary schools. The same point may apply to Dunbar's (1987) conclusions, given that her propositions relate specifically to MFLs, which are based on secondary schools. The studies involve research of adolescents, and it is a common assumption that girls reach adolescence before boys. The development changes that occur during adolescence are not restricted to physical changes. Adolescence incorporates emotional, social and cognitive development. Erikson (1971) builds on Piaget's early works on phases of development, and therefore if girls develop more quickly, it comes as no surprise that they should attain greater academic success earlier in their teenage years. Indeed, this suggestion is supported by the view that bias and imbalance is less obvious in single sex schools, as there are no internal yardsticks against which comparisons can be made.

Social developments compound the issue. Educators have addressed the issue of female underperformance at school, prevalent in the 1970s and 1980s (Spender and Scott, 1980; Askew and Row, 1989). Indeed, Kruse (1992) claims that girls have learnt to be less passive, and are no longer prepared to let boys dominate the classroom. More developed and more assertive girls are assuming a position of academic superiority, which can be seen as simply fulfilling their potential.

Clark and Trafford (1996) and Grenfell and Harris (1997) look at the issue from a different angle. All conclude that boys do little to help by adopting a minimalist approach to study as adolescence kicks in. By rejecting aspects of academic study which they do not perceive to have an immediate personal gain, is to put themselves at a disadvantage. The quest for personal benefits, Graham and Rees (1995) claim, means that boys fail to develop appropriate study skills at a crucial stage of MFL acquisition. Boys they argue, find vocabulary learning boring in the short term, and therefore fail to undertake this necessary task. The cumulative effect, in comparison to girls, is of course that they fall behind. Teenage boys are not as conscientious as teenage girls. Again Clark and Trafford observe that boys do considerably less homework, again arguing that boys do not acknowledge the purpose and value of reinforcing language work covered in class. These attitudes represent an immaturity in terms of cognitive development. Boys fail to conceptualise, and see the long-term impact of study, abstracted from their current, day-to-day environment. MFLs are difficult and require continuous effort and application, which is, inevitably, an observation which falls on deaf ears as far as adolescent boys are concerned.

This difficulty level is often seen as the reason for boys rejecting the subject. Graham and Rees (1995) note that in general terms boys respond to perceived failure to attain a recognisable (to them) standard by giving up. The research also suggests that a typical female response to failure is, first anxiety, and second an attempt to work harder – often through rote learning. In the early stages of MFL learning, rote learning (repetition, copying, substitution exercises) are the means by which teachers encourage pupils (see Pachler and Field, 1997).

MFLs is a school subject, in which pupils are very often placed in ability sets. Arguments against setting include the demotivating effect of being labelled if placed in the lower sets. The early successes of girls, and relative failure of boys, which may be partly due to a slower rate of cognitive development, is bound to have a negative impact on the motivation of boys. Being placed in a lower set, at an age when success is deemed a prime motivator increases the sense of failure for boys.

MFLs are also a 'cumulative' subject, in that success at any stage of learning requires the successful completion of earlier, related tasks. The spiral curriculum model, recommended in the National Curriculum Non-Statutory Guidance, can therefore be seen to have a negative influence on boys' progress. Revisiting topics and themes, which boys already recognise to be areas in which they have failed in relative terms, is not an effective way of inspiring confidence and motivation.

It is inevitable that boys and girls draw gender-related comparisons during adolescence. Myers (1985) remarks that boys and girls are more vulnerable to stereotyping, and indeed become more sexist in outlook as they seek sexual and adult identities. Social and media pressures actively encourage gender-based stereotyping amongst adolescents, and the positive and negative attitudes vis-à-vis school subjects is inevitable. These external pressures, coupled with the tensions associated with making career choices in their mid-teens, further intensifies gender-based influences. Delamont (1980: 55) comments: 'Boys and girls narrow and restrict their ambitions and expectations as they move towards the school leaving age, retreating into stereotyped masculine and feminine roles.'

The negative impact of adolescence on boys' performance and levels of motivation must not be seen to be insurmountable. The problems associated with adolescent development can and should be pre-empted. First and most generally, the teaching of MFLs should not be restricted to the period of young people's lives when physiological changes will have the greatest impact.

Learners need the confidence, skills and knowledge to cope with such demands. MFL learning should begin before the age of 11 in order to equip learners with the personal skills, and study skills to avoid succumbing to the forces of adolescence. Second MFLs need not be presented as feminine subject (see later) and positive action can be taken to motivate boys to an equal extent, but in a different way to what is achieved with girls. The age of pupils is less important than the level of maturity when planning lessons and schemes of work. This may be perceived as a recommendation that boys and girls are taught MFLs separately, or that teachers extend the range of teaching and learning strategies to provide equal levels of interest and motivation to both sexes.

Motivational matters

The previous section raises the issue of needing to provide higher levels of interest, specific to boys in order to address the imbalance of potential and ability during pupils' adolescent years. On the other hand little guidance is given to identify how this might be achieved, or indeed in what ways current provision fails to achieve this end.

Wragg (1997) simplifies the issue. He points out that boys suffer from low motivation, which leads them to spend less time on the task of MFL learning, which finally results in less learning actually taking place. This simple equation explains why boys reject MFLs – it is a subject they are no good at (Abraham, 1995).

Much attention has been given to boys' failure. Licht and Dweck (1983) explain that the opposite applies to girls. They are more successful at MFLs, because they feel able to channel their efforts into an area of the curriculum in which they feel secure:

> Since girls are generally more likely than boys to foster suspicions of intellectual inadequacies, girls should feel more secure in areas where avenues are available to compensate for their perceived weaknesses. This opportunity appears to be more readily available in verbal, rather than in mathematical tasks.

Clearly boys and girls are motivated by different subjects – those which offer the opportunity for success.

Motivation is both intrinsic and extrinsic. I have already indicated that extrinsic motivation for boys is more likely to be a factor which can be perceived to influence their personal agenda. I have also commented that as external examinations approach boys and girls retreat into stereotyped roles. MFLs do not represent to boys a passport to more gainful employment, nor provide easier access to higher education.

Sullerot (1985) concludes that in most European countries, pupils, and society in general, recognise a cluster of curriculum areas which she labels a 'noble path'. Boys, Sullerot notes are more likely to follow the 'noble path', as these subjects provide access to higher paid jobs and facilitate what is seen to be focused higher education study. Sullerot also, crucially, notes that MFLs do not belong to the 'noble path' particularly in Great Britain.

This explanation stands true today. Thornton (1999) reports that boys do not see MFLs as important, either for themselves or for society in general. Girls, on the other hand, are more liable to opt for MFLs, or indeed to apply themselves to MFLs for intrinsic gain and satisfaction. The net result is that girls enjoy MFLs in comparison to boys, and therefore succeed more. Boys, on the other hand fall into the trap identified by Clark and Trafford (1996), that they do not enjoy the subject, and therefore do not succeed.

The ethos of MFLs is not simply a socially generated image. The very experience of learning MFLs has an impact on pupils' enjoyment (see next section). The assessment methods also impact upon pupils' motivation. Harris, Nixon and Rudduck (1993) comment that boys and girls prepare for assessment in different ways. Boys, they claim, focus more on examinations and despite the boredom factor are prepared to engage in last minute revision when the pressure of external assessment is high. This spirit of conscientiousness does not compensate for the longer-term neglect of continuous work. Girls, Harris *et al.* continue, manifest the opposite approach, working continuously hard. MFLs, I have explained, is a cumulative subject requiring continuous effort and application.

The more recent trend towards continuous assessment therefore favours the girls' approach to learning and further hinders boys' success.

Throughout this section, I have made the assumption that the major motivating forces are success and perceived usefulness. Boys' perceptions are that they do not enjoy the same levels of success as girls and that they quickly see MFLs to be a subject of low value. Boys also do not respect French language and French culture, the most commonly taught MFL. When asked, for the purpose of this Chapter with what do boys associate French, many mentioned romance literature, and food. Germany on the other hand evoked images of football, and war. The challenge in terms of motivation, is therefore to lift boys' esteem, both of themselves and of the subject.

Teaching and learning

The attitudes of learners to MFLs can be seen to have an influence on girls' and boys' motivation and performance. It is also important to examine to what extent the content of MFLs syllabuses and the teaching and learning methods also have on gender-related issues. A first, obvious, point to make is that an outcome of girls higher success rate at MFLs learning, is that the majority of teachers are in fact women. Undeniably the role models represented by teachers, are feminine. However this is the case in many other curriculum areas, and therefore it does not explain the more marked gender differences in MFLs.

Callaghan (1998) researched the views of male and female learners vis-à-vis the content of MFL courses to GCSE level. The findings indicate strongly that the content is of greater appeal to girls. Of twelve topics, six are seen to be 'girl friendly', three 'boy friendly' and three of equal interest. GCSE topics do focus on leisure pursuits in general as opposed to vocationally oriented issues, and indeed encourage communication and co-operation with representatives of unfamiliar cultures. Also of interest is Callaghan's observation that the 'girl friendly' topics feature more frequently in examination papers. The implication is that, when assessed, girls enjoy more of a sense of security and comfort than boys.

The communicative approach, or its application in England and Wales, encourages a collaborative approach to learning. Pair work and group work provide all learners with the opportunity to practise newly acquired language forms, yet Riley (1994) comments that such co-operative teaching and learning styles favour girls. MFLs taught in a communicative way do not encourage the individualistic and competitive learning styles associated with more masculine preferred methods.

Abraham (1995) notes that the authentic materials containing more lengthy reading passages, often emanate from magazines. Abraham does not question whether interesting articles selected by teachers represent their own (more feminine) interests, but simply observes that the content is of greater appeal to girls than boys. Undoubtedly more magazines fit female interests than boys, and the predominance of girls in more able groups will lend teachers to perpetrate this cycle of appealing more and more to girls.

It is worthy of note that teaching materials at the early stages of learning (Key Stage 3) are relatively free of sexist roles, and that at the ages of 14–16, pupils do gravitate in a more obvious way to sexist expectations.

Who teaches MFLs, how they are taught, what is taught and when they are taught to young people must in combination influence the gender imbalances within the subject. Recent work on strategy use and development (e.g. Macaro, 1997; Harris, 1998) suggests that positive action can be taken to redress the balance. Macaro notes that boys, despite being undeveloped in language learning strategies, are more receptive than girls to instruction in this area. This suggestion is consistent with earlier arguments that boys respond more readily to learning opportunities which they see can influence their own personal agenda. Indeed Ofsted (1993: 3) reports 'boys performance improved when they had a clear understanding of the progress they needed to make in order to achieve well'.

The communicative approach focuses on meaning rather than form, which can be seen to lead to greater attention being paid to language use than language learning. Current practice cannot be seen to have aided boys in developing their language learning powers. A more overt, direct approach to helping pupils learn, rather than to expect success through exposure and practice techniques may well begin to address the particular problems boys face.

Conclusions

There is no doubting the superiority of girls in foreign language learning. There is also a mountain of evidence to suggest that girls enjoy language learning more. It is of course defeatist to accept this analysis at face value. Reflective teachers should question the impact of provision, which includes their own methodology and approaches. However, the buck should not stop at individual teachers. The impact of the National Curriculum requirements, the recommended teaching approaches, social attitudes, parental guidance and the impact of the media should all be taken into account. An analysis of the issues which contribute to the gender imbalance must be examined, and the MFL teaching community must continue to explore and experiment to improve the learning opportunities for all learners, without hindering the existing opportunities of favoured groups. Positive action in relation to when MFLs are taught to children, how and what constitutes an accessible curriculum, and how all learners can be motivated through interest and long-term rewards must be considered. MFLs are not a lost cause for boys, and must never become one for girls.

Editor's note

Field accepts the view that girls' level of performance in MFLs is better than that of boys. He proceeds to suggest that a range of factors contribute to this – the fact that girls mature more quickly than boys, that social factors such as sexism contribute to boys rejecting the subject, and the fact that girls are advantaged by the support they receive from parents from an early age. Field does not accept that the difference in performance levels must continue, but acknowledges the harmful impact of perceived failure on boys. Field does not propose firm solutions, but does recommend positive action to support boys' development without harming the success enjoyed by girls. These ideas include equipping boys with appropriate study skills from an earlier age, presenting topics in a more boy-friendly manner and indeed adapting the content of courses to stimulate greater interest.

Linked chapters

Chapter 3, Chapter 11, Chapter 15.

References

Abraham, J. (1995) *Divide and School: Gender and Class Dynamics in Comprehensive Education*, London: The Falmer Press.

Askew, S. and Row, C. (1989) *Boys Don't Cry*, Milton Keynes: Open University Press.

Beswick, C. (1978) 'Mixed or single sex for French', *AV Language Journal*.

Callaghan, M. (1998) 'An investigation into the causes of boys' underachievement', *French Language Learning Journal*, 17: 2–7.

Clark, J. and Trafford, I. (1996) 'Return to gender: boys' and girls' attitudes and achievements', *Language Learning Journal*, 14: 40–49, Rugby: Association for Language Learning.

Cockcroft, W. H. (1982) *Report of the Committee of Inquiry into the Teaching of Mathematics in Schools*, London: HMSO.

Dale, R. (1974) *Mixed or Single Sex School*, London: Routledge and Kegan Paul.

Delamont, S. (1980) *Sex Roles and the School*, 2nd edn., London: Routledge.

Dunbar, C. (1987) *Genderwatch: Stage 3 Languages*, London: SCDC Publications.

Erikson, E. H. (1971) *Identity: Youth and Crisis*, London: Faber and Faber.

Graham, S. and Rees, F. (1995) 'Gender differences in language learning: the question of control', *Language Learning Journal*, 16: 28–34, Rugby: Association for Language Learning.

Grenfell, M. and Harris, V. (1997) *Modern Languages and Learning Strategies in Theory and Practice*, London: Routledge.

Halpin, T. (1999) 'The top grade girls who are left behind when they leave school', *Education Guardian*.

Harris, S., Nixon, J. and Rudduck, J. (1993) 'Schoolwork, homework agenda', *Gender and Education*, 5 (1), Abingdon: Carfax Publishing.

Harris, V. (1998) 'Making boys make progress', *Language Learning Journal*, 18: 56–62.

Kruse, A. M. (1992) 'Single sex settings and the development of pedagogy for boys in Danish schools', *Gender and Education*, 4 (12), Abingdon: Carfax Publishing.

Licht, B.G. and Dweck, C.S. (1983) 'Sex differences in achievement organisations: consequences for academic choices and attainments', in M. Marland (ed.) *Sex Differentiation and Schooling*, London: Heinemann.

Macaro, E. (1997) 'Gender differences in strategy use', paper given at the CILT Research Forum 'Strategies in Language Learning', 22 February.

Marland, M. (1983) *Sex Differentiation and Schooling*, London: Heinemann.

Myers, K. (1985) 'Inequality – the curriculum: how to fail most of our pupils without really trying', *Comprehensive Education*, 1985: 14–17.

Ofsted (1993) *Boys and English*, London: HMSO.

—— (1999) *Standards in the Secondary Curriculum 1997/98*, London: HMSO.

Pachler, N. and Field, K. (1997) *Learning to Teach MFLs in the Secondary School*, London: Routledge.

Reynolds, R. (1995) 'Boys and English: so what's the problem', *The English and Media Magazine*, 33: 15–18.

Riley, K. (1994) *Quality and Equality: Promoting Opportunities in Schools*, London: Cassell.

Rudduck, J. (1994) *Developing a Gender Policy in Secondary Schools*, Milton Keynes: Open University Press.

Spender, D. (1982) *Women of Ideas and What We Have Done to Them*, London: Routledge and Kegan Paul.

Spender, D. and Scott, M. (1980) (eds) *Learning to Lose: Sexism and Education*, Oxford: The Women's Press.

Sullerot, E. (1985) *Diversitifation of Vocational Choices for Young and Adult Women*, Synthesis Report, Brussels: EE2 V/1817/84 En Org Fr.

Thornton, K. (1999) 'Teenage boys lost in French', *Times Educational Supplement*, 8 October 1999.

Wragg, T. (1997) 'Oh Boy!', *Times Educational Supplement*, 16 May 1997.

10 Teaching grammar in the Modern Foreign Language classroom

Jane Jones

Introduction

The teaching of MFLs is sensitive, perhaps like no other subject, to regular pendulum swings in terms of methodological and pedagogical redefinition. Hawkins' (1996) review of thirty years of language teaching captured the flavour of the ebbs and flows in recent times whilst Kelly's epic review (1969) covered twenty-five centuries. Whilst a 'communicative' framework has been remarkably constant as a backdrop for some two decades already, this is itself defined variously and idiosyncratically. Grammar has always had a central focus although its role in language learning has been highly contested. The role of grammar within communicative methodology is elusive, sometimes excluded as an irrelevance, sometimes 'done' latently in classrooms, sometimes reinvented in what is deemed to be a more accessible, palatable format and centring on a discourse that focuses on language as 'patterns'.

This is reflected in the National Curriculum Programmes of Study (PoS) Part 1. Thus, in Strand 3, Language–learning skills and knowledge of language can be found, for example, the requirement for pupils to be able to: (f) understand and apply patterns, rules and exceptions in language forms and structures.

However, the indications from OFSTED reports, for example, are that PoS 1 has been less well integrated and elaborated in schemes of work and lesson plans than PoS part 2 and its 'areas of experience', the latter more evidently informing and shaping curriculum learning in secondary schools. Course materials have also tended to focus on the 'areas of experience' in their topicalisation of chapters, with an inordinate influence on many MFL departments' schemes of work. However, the 'great grammar debate' (see Klapper, 1998) has continued to run and seems usefully prioritised once again in the present re-evaluation and restructuring of the National Curriculum. The role of grammar in language teaching and learning is high on the agenda as is a deconstruction of the meaning and purpose of 'grammar'. It is no longer a question of whether grammar is taught but of how, why and, furthermore, where it fits into the broader curricular landscape of literacy and language, across and as an underpin of the whole curriculum. In this chapter, I do not attempt to resolve the massively debated dichotomies that hallmark the theories on language teaching and learning, especially concerning grammar teaching, but I assume a role of sorts for grammar in the MFL classroom teaching and learning arena. As Carter asserts:

> It is not tenable to claim that there is no connection between explicit grammar study and enhanced language performance in spite of research evidence (largely pre-1970s) disavowing such a connection, not least because such research investigated grammar teaching based on 'old-style' descriptive methodologies.
>
> (1997: 32)[1]

A confusion of terms

The debate concerning the role of grammar is further made fuzzy by a lack of agreed definition of terms and a sometimes indiscriminate interchangeability of terms which are, arguably, in certain contexts, quite distinct. This is perhaps surprising, for as Stern (1983: 9) opines:

> One would assume that as a language-conscious profession we (language teachers) had our own house in good order and would use terms that are neatly defined and totally unambiguous. But far from it. The ironic fact is that the terminology we need in language pedagogy is often ambiguous and sometimes downright confusing.

There is a distinct lack of clarity and widespread disagreement in language teaching discourse concerning 'language acquisition' and 'language learning'. Language acquisition has tended to be associated with a learner's first language and all that that connotes in terms of biological and maturational processes. Language learning, on the other hand, is used more in terms of reference to its social construction and, in schooling contexts, as a tutored and oriented activity in the classroom. Table 10.1 below compares and contrasts typical L1 and L2 learning contexts. The classroom learning scenario that derives from this table is one restricted by time, syllabus parameters, and psycholinguistic and motivational factors.

Table 10.1 L1 and L2 learning contexts compared and contrasted

	L1 Non-tutored	L2 Tutored from 11+
Use of target language	Constant	Variable
Exposure	Massive	Limited
Word play	Willingness to play with and enjoy sounds	No such joy
Trial and error	Permitted, encouraged	Controlled
'Whole' language	No grading or selecting	Restricted and graded content
Motivation	Driving force to meet needs	Limited, sometimes nil
Maturation	Learner matures with language	Maturity ahead of language
Goals	Immediate	Distant

However, one major problem with this distinction is that neither acquisition nor learning takes place in hermetically sealed environments and that it takes no account of the complex interaction of language developmental processes. Clearly, language acquisition also takes place, fostered by communicative learning opportunities, for example, by the provision of appropriate 'comprehensible input' or by successful learner strategies used by individuals. The 'controlling' function of the classroom context can be usefully exploited to provide a rich 'exposure environment' for learning as well as an 'intake environment' (Ellis, 1986: 232) for acquisition purposes. The role of the teacher remains crucial according to Cook (1996: 129) who suggests that:

> An important element in L2 success appears to be how learners are treated: the teaching method used with them, the language they hear, and the environment in which they are learning. The purpose of language teaching in a sense is to provide optimal samples of language for the learner to profit from – the best 'input' to the process of language learning.

The purpose of the chapter, however, is not to go over this well-trodden ground, but to consider the place of grammar within these paradigms.

By and large, the activities and processes that take place in the MFL classroom are more to do with language learning. It is the stuff of those time-tabled slots of school time, although not exclusively so. The sites of learning are additionally beyond the classroom; at home, for example, when travelling and in a variety of social contexts inside and outside the school environment. Similarly, whilst the teacher usually provides the initial model of language use, it is deemed good practice to ensure a variety of models in varied contexts using a wide range of media model presentations, some of which the pupils select and access themselves. Nonetheless, the special responsibility of the classroom language teacher is to construct an appropriate programme of study to frame the pupils' learning. National Curriculum requirements will constitute part of the framework as will a clearly thought out and carefully sequenced grammatical framework. There are several kinds of 'grammar'-descriptive, prescriptive, trans-formational-generative, traditional and structural grammars to name some – but teachers will normally have recourse to a 'pedagogical grammar' for purposes which are relevant in the classroom learning context and which will be principally needs-related.

The concept of a pedagogical grammar

It is the view of many teachers that a scientific, descriptive grammar is not one which meets the need of the pupil in the modern foreign language classroom, although it may provide the basis for a selection of linguistic data which the teacher will, nonetheless, need to modify in order to meet the needs of the learners. Noblitt (1972), whose analysis resonates roundly with current thinking on language curricular and planning concerns, quoted in Stern (1983: 175) bases his conception of a pedagogical grammar on a potentially useful five-fold analysis:

1   descriptive and contrastive data and concepts
2   ordering of the information in terms of the four skills

and

3   in terms of levels of achievement
4   evaluation procedures bearing in mind specified learning objectives
5   the educational settings for which the grammar is intended.

This analysis envisages an appropriate selection of linguistic data (grammatical structures), an effective logical sequencing, an integrated assessment framework and due regard for the learning environment. It is an analysis that envisages progression and provides a template for curriculum planning, the sort of planning which is already embedded in the best and most useful departmental schemes of work. In these cases, course materials are used selectively to resource the planned programme and do not themselves constitute the learners' grammatical syllabus. But what then does constitute the grammatical syllabus?

Constructing a pedagogical grammar in a scheme of work

It may be useful to begin with an exploration of the 'descriptive and contrastive data and concepts' that Noblitt proposes. Traditionally, courses have tended to focus initially on the learner's personal situation and concerns (description of self, family, home, friends) and have progressed outwards towards 'the world of work' and the world at large (including professions, future plans, foreign travel and the like). The grammatical structures which have been deemed necessary in the early stages, traditionally the present tense of 'to be' and 'to have' and adjectives including possessives, for example, and in the later stages of learning, future and conditional tenses and a wide range of language functions and notions, have a certain common sense logic based on a simple to more complex input and learning continuum.

Nonetheless, it is widely recognised that this widely contested linear view of learning does not automatically provide opportunities for revision, revisiting of structures or spiralling strategies, nor does it in any way reflect real language use which is, of course, much more varied and complex. More importantly, linguistically stranding learners in the present tense does not, for example, allow them to speak or write about what they are probably keen to speak and write about which is typically their latest weekend activities or their short-term plans for the next weekend. Instead of relegating past tenses to, say Year 8 or 9, a familiarity needs to be developed with selected past tense structures (I went, I saw, I ate, I bought . . .) almost right from the start. In our pedagogical discourse, there is a rhetoric of 'linguistic revisitation' and of 'spiralling' but this appears very limited in practice. It is not unknown to examiners for Year 11 pupils to have either forgotten or to confuse the personal details learnt in Year 7 when asked simple personal questions in the oral examination because of insufficient recycling and incomplete internalisation.

Interestingly, Noblitt also refers to 'contrastive' data whereby, for example, L1 and L2 language features can be contrasted, and where contrastive items within L2 can be used as an aid to learning, such as the paired learning of, in French, *sur* with *dans* as opposed to the confusing introduction of *sur* with *sous*. Less adherence to the traditional grammatical dinosaurs of textbooks of old (and some newer ones) and more a judicious selection of grammatical structures with a high indicator of usefulness and of generative potential are called for.

Noblitt's second analytic strand is that of 'ordering of the information in terms of the four skills'. The way I suggest we interpret this is as follows. Not every structure we present to learners will be introduced in the same way, nor to the same level of competence in all four skills. Whilst the so-called natural order of listening, speaking, reading and writing remains a useful guiding principle, school-allocated learning time does not allow for the presentation of all new language items in this way, nor is it always necessary to do so. Older, more experienced language learners can and should be encouraged to take 'short cuts' and to use their greater range of cognitive strategies to, for example, draw inferences. However, the teacher will need to decide for each major input of new or revisited linguistic data, i.e. the structures, through which skills the structures will be presented and practised, how much exposure will be required in each skill and how many instances of production will be required before the structure may be considered 'learnt', albeit in the first stage of learning. Of course, a great deal more practice and consolidation at later stages will be required before a pattern may be considered fixed. This attempt at quantific-ation is very much in line with the present preoccupation with the identific-ation of detailed learning outcomes and, although this scientific precision may jar with notions of fluency and creativity of language use, is nonetheless useful in the establishment of some observable benchmarks in language learning. The concept allies itself strongly to Noblitt's third stand concerning levels of achievements and his fourth strand concerning assessment.

It is useful to locate achievement within a ladder of progression so that whilst 'benchmarking' achievement for recording and feedback purposes, it remains forward-looking towards a range of defined targets. In order for these targets to be measurable and concrete, some grammatical definition would be in order to complement language task and functional objectives. Noblitt's final point is a consideration for 'the educational settings for which the grammar is intended'. There are many factors which come into play which could include the amount of time timetabled to cover the programme of study, the age and ability range of the learners including special learning and support needs, the learning accommodation, resources, journeys and exchanges, any special purpose needs, class organisation (sets or mixed-ability, for example) and special features such as bilingual programmes or early examination entry. All of these factors, and there will be others, will have an impact on the planned programme in terms of scope and potential, constraining and limiting the grammatical content. Whatever the constraints, Bussman's criteria (1998: 194) for an adequate grammar might be critically applied. The criteria are: applicability, simplicity, completeness, explicitness, coherence, and lack of contradiction.

These criteria refer not only to the grammatical content but lead into considerations of teaching approaches where grammar is concerned, the subject of the next section.

Teaching grammar: some pragmatic considerations

The planning and constructing of a pedagogical grammar gives the teacher an 'ownership' of the core content to be presented and frees her/him from the tyranny of the course book, although this remains as a resource when it is deemed suitable. What, then, are the principles which might guide the teaching of grammatical structures and patterns? Deciding what to teach is the first consideration.

Selection

Within the overall schematic picture of a typical five-year learning programme, the teacher needs to select structures that will be useful in terms of transfer value as regards other structures and other contexts in order to maximise their generative capacity for the learners. In other words, it is useful to teach structures which can be used elsewhere, in different combinations, in conjunction with other structures and as springboards for independent language use. These would include a selection of commonly used verbal structures in present, past and future tenses, expressions of like, dislike, the ability to formulate questions and what Lee (1999) calls 'core' language items such as prepositions and linking words.

Sequencing

Considering language as a 'system of systems', the meaning of given items is partly dependent on the relationship in other patterns. Traditionally, for example, at the beginning of a secondary school foreign language course, a range of concrete vocabulary items is taught in conjunction with the indefinite article, quickly followed by the definite article (or sometimes the other way round, depending on which course materials are in use). A natural and common extension is to then incorporate qualifiers introducing a variety of adjectives. It is the role of the teacher to help the learners to make the connections through a mixture of inductive and deductive approaches, with massive exposure, and opportunities to practise making the link. What I am theorising in this instance, for example, is to do with establishing the concept of gender. When pupils fail to perceive the connections, 'article' use is no more than haphazard guesswork, a kind of linguistic lottery, and the errors will be compounded as the language becomes more complex.

Recycling

Whilst the constraints and needs of classroom learning necessitate some drilling of discrete items as an aid to internalisation, it is helpful to the learners to be shown how a structure learnt in one context may be recycled in another one. A decontextualised *il a*, for example, which learners have some difficulty with, can be seen to have immense recycling value when used variously thus:

> *il a 2 frères* . . .
> il a mal à la tête
> il a mangé dans un restaurant.

Recycling, then, can be planned both in repetitive and in progressive cycles.

Moving from 'form' to 'function'

To borrow the phrases of Wilga Rivers (1988), this involves a shift from 'skill-getting' to 'skill-using' and envisages the learner moving from a stage of very conscious attention to the language form to a more unconscious use for real communication purposes. This process is hugely disputed and is certainly not guaranteed. Nonetheless, this shift is more likely to occur if abundant opportunities for use are provided and may be greatly facilitated by the pupils' understanding of the way the pattern works. This is not a simple one-way process but the reality of classroom learning, with its gaps and disruptions, will require frequent teacher interventions for the purposes of revision, for example, or for corrective purposes and refocusing on 'form' as the need arises. Carter poses this as a 'pedagogic challenge' for teachers to 'find ways of teaching grammar which are sensitive to a continuum of implicit to explicit knowledge and which recognise that appropriate and strategic interventions by the teacher are crucial to the seven processes of making implicit knowledge explicit' (op. cit. p. 32).

Grading of input

It is sometimes useful to restate a very obvious principle such as this assertion that, as well as a sufficient quantity of examples, teachers need to present appropriately graded examples to the pupils. In this way, the first examples will be easier, straightforward and contradiction-free and thus susceptible to helping the learners to infer the pattern(s) and thus to be able to test their hypotheses. Thereafter, the spiral of progression can be used more flexibly, backwards as well as forwards and introducing more complex variations as appropriate.

Use of terminology

Unfortunately, the issue of grammatical terminology has become pathologised as something considered so abstract as to be beyond pupils' comprehension. This is, I would suggest, a little condescending. It is the quality and timing of a presentation and explanation of a grammatical structure that is important and not the terminology *per se*. As Carter cogently argues: 'It is not taught for its own sake but to provide an economic and precise way of discussing particular functions and purposes' (op. cit. p. 24). Such is the continuing pace of educational change that whatever one's views on this issue, it is likely that new Year 7 pupils will bring with them a certain and surely welcome familiarity with grammatical terminology as a consequence of the primary literacy initiative. This will provide a powerful axis for learning and a basis which the MFL teacher can extend and exploit, devoting more time to the practice and consolidation of the language items themselves. It is likely that a new, inclusive discourse of grammar will be the outcome of these changes and its accommodation within MFL teaching methodology.

Applying these principles: an example

Let us take as a concrete example teaching pupils how to tell the time in French. There can be little dispute about the usefulness of this language function.

It comprises various grammatical features such as part of the verb 'to be', agreement, singular and plural and word order as well as potentially confusing issues of pronunciation. The pupils will need to revise numbers thoroughly so that insecure knowledge of numbers does not impede the establishing of the time-asking and time-telling patterns. It is also conceivable that young learners, and some with learning difficulties, may not be totally adept at telling the time in English, especially in this era of digital time-watching.

Most teachers usually then proceed to the presentation and practice of 'on the hour' which is relatively problem free. It approximates to the pattern already existing in the pupils' mindset in English and can thus be accommodated. This balance is so easily upset when the panoply of quarter past, half past, minutes to the hour, special words for 12 o'clock and so on come on-line. Very careful pacing and sequencing are required and much more graded input than is usually given. The capacity for recycling is, nonetheless, promising. Asking the time regularly at the beginning and end of lessons, as well as during lessons, will help to develop automaticity and the structure can be recycled in contexts of travel, entertainment, daily routine and opening and closing times. Far from being a simple structure to teach, the time is, in fact, quite complex with additional internal inconsistencies as in *une heure cinq* but *une heure et quart* and a pronunciation issue concerning the liaison in *deux heures* usually after months of drilling *deux* with a silent 'x'. It seems to me that this single structure alone comprises so many features to remember that a written pupil-friendly summary in exercise books is a useful, indeed necessary, aid and support to learning, a theme I develop in the next section.

Whilst this is most certainly 'old hat' to experienced teachers, for less experienced teachers, it shows the considerable pedagogical scaffolding needed to teach a structure successfully. It also demonstrates what a 'false friend' an apparently simple (on the surface) structure can be and underlines the need to evaluate the 'difficulty for learning' factor of structures and to be prepared with pre-emptive strategies.

Learning the rules

The secondary age pupil is, advantageously, already in possession of linguistic knowledge and learning strategies that the teacher can exploit. The pupil's extensive knowledge of L1 – and in some cases other languages too – needs to be considered as a resource, for comparative and contrastive purposes, for example, and as a vehicle to use for purposes of explanation and clarification. This is not suggesting a reversal to 'gardening [in L2] in a gale of English', as Hawkins (1984) expressed it so memorably but rather to boost the L2 learning path by judicious incursions into the L1 jet stream, to continue the meteorological metaphor. We should key into the learner's cognitive maturity and the considerable dependence on the aids of literacy, including for example, the consolidating function of the written word and the ability to engage in metalinguistic discourse. Reading and writing provide mechanisms of support to provide useful reinforcement of what has been practised orally, and to help establish the concepts through the process of reflecting upon the written forms and conventions, some of which are not evident in oral codes, such as agreement of adjectives and past participles. Unfortunately the issue of explaining the rules and the conscious learning of grammar has been trapped in a dialectic between opposing and influential language learning theories and between stereotypical methodological constructs of 'grammar–grind' and 'learning by osmosis'. This polarisation is unhelpful to teachers and responsible, very probably, for a decade or so of hesitation and uncertainty about the role of grammar in 'communicative methodology'. Approaches that may be more helpful include the following:

- Rutherford (1987), advocated grammatical 'consciousness raising' in teaching, focusing the learner's attention on significant features of the target language.
- Riley (1985) quoted in Cook (op. cit.), who proposed 'sensitisation' of the learners by reference to features of L1 to help them understand the target language.
- Hawkins (1984) who suggested 'grammar approached as a voyage of discovery into the patterns of the language rather than the learning of prescriptive rules'.
- Grauberg (1997) whose view is that 'Learning rules is a cognitive process because it involves understanding concepts and the relation between them. But there is also an action quality about rules: calculations have to be made, problems solved, language forms chosen'.
- Rivers (1988) who insists that pupils 'must not only understand the grammatical concepts they encounter, but also appreciate how each, like a link in a coat of chain mail, interrelates with all the others in one fabric – the French language system'.

These assertions illuminate crucial features about MFL learning in the classroom. Rutherford's point is a powerful reminder of how teachers, through their choice of teaching presentation examples, learning activities and materials, can orientate the learners towards the perception of patterns and the grammatical structures which are the subject of instruction. Without this focusing, there is the danger that the pupils, or some of them, may not see the point at all or may leave the lesson in a fog of confusion, subsuming mistaken hypotheses or unable to make any connections at all from the linguistic data presented in the lesson. Riley's proposal is in similar vein although he explicitly suggests the use of the mother tongue as a point of comparison and/or contrast. Hawkins, in the context of a discussion on language awareness, continues the theme but focuses on learners' exploratory investigations of the data. Grauberg's view is also one which emphasises the pupils' constructivist contribution to their learning based on their discoveries and insights. Rivers reminds us of the need to enable pupils to understand linguistic connections within the whole system and not simply of discrete grammatical items. In very concrete terms, the implications of these features for the MFL classroom are:

- a defined grammatical focus in schemes of work and lessons;
- carefully selected language examples which illustrate the focus clearly;
- opportunities, e.g. in the selected activities and choice of materials, for pupils to explore the possibilities and to have findings confirmed or otherwise;
- comparative/contrastive data to help the pupils work through their hypotheses, using both intralingual and L1 references;
- connections to other structures, as appropriate, and location within the larger coherent 'whole' construct of language.

These are features which may help to emphasise 'meaningful' learning, defined by Ausubel (1967), quoted in Stern (1996: 307) as 'a clearly articulated and precisely differentiated conscious experience that emerges when potentially meaningful signs, symbols, concepts or propositions are related to and incorporated within a given individual's cognitive structure'. In teacher–talk, it is the point when the pupils have 'got it' or when 'the penny has dropped' and will be evidenced in progression of learning and the ability to re-apply the structures learnt in new contexts. It is thus a crucial stage of learning and one which needs to be promoted in a variety of ways, including the learning of grammar as 'a protocol that has to connect the ear, the mouth and the mind' (Pinker, 1994: 125).

Grauberg proposes six readily adaptable stages in rule learning that he elucidates and exemplifies. He stresses the importance of the selection of texts and contexts '. . . where form and function are brought out clearly and without distortion to normal use' (1997: 103–4). Crucially he also concludes that at the end of each micro-learning cycle, pupils should be given the opportunity to demonstrate their learning '. . . made possible or enhanced by the learning of the new forms and rules and maintaining, if possible, some personal element' (ibid. p. 140).

Practical support for grammar learning

Included in the teacher's battery of teaching techniques, at carefully chosen moments, and designed to consolidate the learners' understanding of connections, will be the articulation of the rules, sometimes in the target languages, sometimes in English, sometimes in both. Dictating a set of meaningless notes or reciting the declarative knowledge from a textbook have, quite rightly, been discredited by the critically reflective practitioners of today. Observation of effective teachers leads me to propose the following as useful consolidatory techniques:

1   asking the pupils to deduce the rule(s) after a period of extensive practice. Individual pupils can be asked to write down their understanding of the structure or this could be debated in pairs. Where pupils work in a comfortable learning environment, a pupil could be asked to explain her/his understanding to the class. Pre-prepared prompt cards or OHT pieces could be supplied by the teacher to enable the pupil to demonstrate visually the understanding, e.g. word order, agreements, composite tenses.
2   Simple, non-contradictory notes, with examples, for pupils to record in a grammar or language notebook, or file, or any suitable alternative, so that the pupils build up a written record for personal reference whenever this may be needed. Pupils can personalise these notes with their own idiosyncratic notes, mnemonics and visuals. It is essential that this written record accompanies the pupils throughout their school language careers, unlike other notebooks that are so often jettisoned after each year of learning.
3   Continuing the theme of reference materials, ideally each MFL classroom or, perhaps, centralised resource area, would contain a good range of reference materials which, as well as the usual dictionaries, thesauri and grammatical reference books and CD-ROMs, might include grammar books written for French pupils in their learning of French as mother tongue. The written explanations in these books whilst quite formal, are clear, precise, colour-coded and well exemplified.
4   Taking a leaf out of such publications, every effort should be made to help consolidate learning by appealing to the learners' 'mind's eye'. Examples of this include the now very common and useful colour-coding of significant features; boxing-off of significant features and juxtaposing these to other boxes to help pupils to categorise and then to select from categories and to visualise word order; spraycharts and spidergrams which are frequently used in other subjects and therefore have transfer-value as an aid to learning. Verbs are more easily learnt in star formation than as a paradigm by some pupils with learning difficulties, for example, as is shown in Figure 10.1 below.

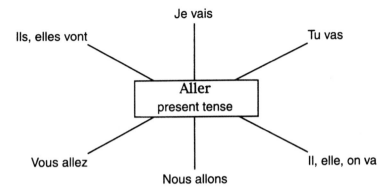

Figure 10.1 Verb star.

Mind-maps, which are simply visual representations of linguistic data, are especially useful for presenting a large amount of data. I have, for example, seen an A3 sheet for pupils that contained a large number of commonly used verbs in all tense formations.

5 The use of *aide-mémoire* charts, hanging 'clouds' and mobiles and notices strategically placed around the classroom walls and hanging from the ceiling, depicting commonly used verbs, sentence starters, question formations, key vocabulary and so on. Some of these items can be more or less permanent, others changed according to the topics and structures being practised, the classroom being presented as a site of multisensory learning and reference, redolent of the learning-supportive environments of many primary classrooms.

The key themes, by way of summary, are:

- Negotiating meaning with the pupils
- Creating purpose-designed user-friendly reference notes
- Providing complementary commercially produced reference materials
- Visual prompts as an aid to learning

Course materials and grammar

Almost all course materials include 'grammar' in some guise or other, to different degrees of formality. Modern course materials have tried valiantly to present the grammar in a pupil-friendly way but the kind of 'flash-grammar' approach has resulted in fragmentation and a lack of connectedness between the 'chunks' presented, denying opportunities for revision and recycling which have depended to a large extent on the teacher's pedagogical intervention. Interestingly, some of the more traditional materials continue to be the most popular choice by teachers as main course book because, as one teacher expressed it: 'at least I can make sense of what is going on and I think the pupils can'. Within the context of a certain renaissance in MFL teaching which is reconsidering the definition and role of grammar (the tone of recent texts and articles on methodology, pronouncements and general discourse at conferences, messages emanating from the QCA[2] for example), the latest publishers' catalogues include unashamedly grammatically focused supplementary materials for pupils at all levels and all abilities. O'Connor's INSET notes (1998) for teachers on teaching grammar in MFLs, locate the NC PoS1 as the central focus in an MFL department's planning, encompassing a common strategy for the teaching of grammar. In this increasingly grammatically sensitive culture of MFL teaching and learning, teachers may feel encouraged to develop and share their ideas, enveloped in a growing collaborative culture of effective grammar teaching in MFLs.

A developing paradigm of grammar teaching

This developing cultural sensitivity is no re-hash of failed methods of old but represents no less than a potential paradigm shift in thinking about MFL teaching methodology. An important question that has generated fresh thinking is the following: What do pupils need to know about grammar to a) be able to communicate effectively, in speech and in writing, and b) to understand comprehensively, both spoken and written texts?

Lee, based on his research with Buckland (Lee *et al.* 1998) investigating pupils' learning and understanding in MFL lessons, suggest that more attention be paid to 'core language . . . defined as those items and aspects of language which are not topic-specific: it includes (a) language essential to building sentences (points of grammar, key verbs, inflexions, patterns, etc); and (b) the small but essential language items of general use (e.g. words for 'but', 'if', pronouns, gender markers, and everyday adjectives and adverbs)'. As they continue: 'the concept is a useful one on the way to more formally defined points of grammar'.

This more formal definition emanates also from the literacy initiative in primary schools, with newly embedded literacy practices, which, as noted previously, will bring generations of Year 6 pupils into secondary schools who are already familiar with basic formal terminology and the ability to reflect upon language at word, sentence and text level. The work that English teachers undertake regarding text analysis has much that MFLs can share and their code-framing strategies, developed in research, for example, to determine what makes an effective text is of direct relevance to MFLs. Text and discourse cohesion and coherence are just as important in MFL narrative and non-narrative and in communication generally as are more technical issues of spelling and sentence structure for example. This is 'grammar-talk' but of a more enlightened kind. The overarching purpose of this talk is to help pupils to develop grammatical competence as complementary to communicative competence so that pupils are linguistically emancipated; emancipated from the set phrases in which the pupils are so often constrained, phrases which have no apparent generative potential because the pupils do not know what to generate nor how.

Grammar teaching: a practical focus

Aware of the need to avoid a new rhetoric of grammar teaching, I conclude by considering the implications of the concerns and issues raised for MFL teachers in the classroom. We need:

- a new, improved, pedagogically inclined and progressive grammar, with better descriptions; a grammar which considers and distinguishes between spoken and written language; one which is sensitive to language variation and culture; one which frames the school MFL programme of study as a coherent whole; one which is enabling and not inhibitive of pupil learning and language use; one which complements what learners already do with grammar.
- to identify the grammatical focus in schemes of work, lesson plans and in the detailed specification of learning outcomes, sharing these in appropriate terms and in a positive, achievable way with the pupils.
- to encourage case studies and classroom learning research, especially by teachers themselves, in order to identify and to disseminate effective strategies and techniques for teaching grammar in a variety of different ways.
- to move away from the over-dependence on and over-presentation of lexis and concentrate more on sentence, text and discourse levels, what Carter also calls 'stretches of language' (op. cit. p. 168). This might involve using a greater variety of materials and differentiated learning activities in order to provide a rich exposure and diverse opportunities for language investigation and use at all levels of learning.
- to continue an emerging shared discourse with colleagues: English teachers, EAL practitioners and all colleagues involved in developing language education for school pupils. Twenty five years on from The Bullock Report (1975), there is an urgency, desire and commitment to redefine and actualise 'language across the curriculum'.
- an attitudinal shift as well as a methodological shift. This is a critical feature that emphasises the role of teachers as agents of change in a process which envisages the strengthening and not the undermining of communicative methodology. We must stop telling pupils that grammar is 'very difficult' or ' the boring bit' and use our resourcefulness to find ways of presenting grammar in such a way as to be 'a puzzling and challenging phenomenon and as a subject of worthwhile and fascinating study' Stern (1996: 131). Inspectors, advisers, mentors and trainers will have a role to play in identifying, supporting and praising effective practice.

Conclusion

Grammar has been described by Purcell (1997: 53) as 'only a means to an end. The end is to be able to use the language. Grammar is a tool to enable us to do this'. We have in the past decade made much of the need for and desirability of learners taking a measure of responsibility for their learning, of using language creatively and for their own purposes. We need grammar-inclusive teaching approaches based on common sense and the realities of classroom learning which take on board theoretical assertions where these are well grounded but are in no way subservient to them. It is intended that such approaches will enable learners to become grammatically skilled and to develop 'monitors' of their own in order to be able to 'edit their own language performance' (Ellis, 1986: 263). In this way, grammatical competence can empower learners to use language selectively, independently and purposefully.

Notes

1 Carter writes primarily from an English-teaching perspective, but his assertion reflects similar concerns in MFL, especially given the recent and welcome 'rapprochement' between English and MFL teachers.
2 QCA: Qualifications and Curriculum Authority, government-funded agency responsible for the revision and exemplification of the National Curriculum.

Editor's note

This chapter does not look back to a golden age of grammar teaching, yet Jones does lament the neglect of grammar teaching and learning, which has accompanied the development of the communicative approach. Jones examines the place of grammar in the language learning process, presenting aspects of it as the means by which learners can transfer the content of one unit/topic to another. Indeed she recommends a model of teaching which focuses on elements which cross topic boundaries, enabling learners to say, understand and write what actually interests them. Jones also looks forward to new cohorts of MFL learners, who will be active participants in the discourse of grammar, having experienced new literacy strategies in their primary schools. Jones sees a need for a new model, one which engages learners in identifying and articulating patterns and structures, and one which enables creative language use. Placing grammar at the core of schemes of work, and empowering teachers to select, sequence, present and exploit will increase the potential for generative language competence by learners.

Linked chapters

Chapter 2, Chapter 3, Chapter 7, Chapter 18.

References

Bussman, H. (1998) *Routledge Dictionary of Language Learning and Linguistics*, London: Routledge.
Carter, R. (1997) *Investigating English Discourse*, London: Routledge.
Cook, V. (1996) *Second Language Learning and Language Teaching*, 2nd edn., London: Arnold.

DES (1975) *A Language for Life* (The Bullock Report), Londom: HMSO.

Ellis, R. (1986) *Understanding Second Language Acquisition*, Milton Keynes: Open University Press.

Grauberg, W. (1997) *The Elements of Foreign Language Teaching*, Clevedon: Multilingual Matters (recommended for further reading).

Hawkins, E. (1984) *Awareness of Language*, Cambridge University Press.

—— (1996) *30 Years of Language Teaching*, London: CILT.

Kelly, L. G. (1969) *Twenty-Five Centuries of Language Teaching*, Rowley, MA: Newbury House.

Klapper, J. (1998) 'Language at school and university: the great grammar debate continues (ll)', *Language Learning Journal*, 18: 22–8, Rugby: Association for Language Learning.

Lee, J. (1999) *QCA Grammar Conference Notes*, January 1999.

Lee, J., Buckland, D. and Shaw, G. (1998) *The Invisible Child: The Responses and Attitudes to the Learning of Modern Foreign Languages Shown by Year 9 Pupils of Average Ability*, London: CILT.

Noblitt, J. S. (1972) *Pedagogical Grammar: Towards A Theory Of Foreign Language Materials Preparation*, IRAL 10, quoted in H. H. Stern below.

O'Connor, J. (1998) *Grammar in Modern Language Teaching*, Leamington Spa: LCP Training Matters.

Pinker, S. (1994) *The Language Instinct*, London: Penguin.

Purcell, S. (1997) *Teaching Grammar Communicatively*, London: CILT.

Rivers, W. (1988) *Teaching French. A Practical Guide*, Illinois USA: National Textbook Company.

Rutherford, W. E. (1987) *Second Language Grammar: Learning and Teaching*, Harlow: Longman.

Stern, H. H. (1983) *Fundamental Concepts of Language Teaching* (9th impression), Milton Keynes: Open University Press.

11 Developing cultural awareness

Barry Jones

Introduction

'. . . It would be nice if we are studying the language to know a bit more about the country and what people are like there'.

(14-year-old boy)

Many teachers of Modern Foreign Languages would agree that developing an awareness of the culture of the people whose language is being taught is integral to teaching a Modern Foreign Language. The original proposals for the National Curriculum for Modern Foreign Languages in England and Wales for ages 11–16 (DES, 1990: 36) make this intention quite explicit (NB examples printed in italics are non-statutory):

> The promotion of understanding of and respect for other cultures is one of the most important aims of modern language studies. It should be inherent in course activities and materials, wherever possible through discussion in the target language. Learners should therefore have frequent opportunities to:
> - work with authentic materials deriving from the communities/countries of the target language and especially from links with schools abroad, *for example objects, audio and video recordings or excerpts from newspapers and magazines*
> - come into contact with native speakers in this country and where possible abroad
> - from these materials and contacts, appreciate the similarities and differences between their own and cultures of the communities/countries where the target language is spoken
> - identify with the experience and perspective of people in the countries and communities where the target language is spoken
> - use this knowledge to develop a more objective view of their own customs and ways of thinking.

There are, however, problems with trying to understand cultural identity. The first is that it is multifaceted, complex, and at times provisional. The second is that the process of defining the cultural identity of others involves an understanding of oneself and one's own identity. This chapter attempts to explore these problems and to identify issues for debate.

Cultural identity: a definition

A person's cultural identity may be defined from two perspectives which may or may not complement each other. If I define my own cultural identity, such a definition will be based on my personal understanding of who I am. This may be independent of or influenced by who you think I am. Given a dynamic of time and experience this is provisional and liable to change. There are three interrelated processes which enable us to define the culture of others. We:

1 look at how others define their own cultural identity both individually and collectively
2 see how such definitions resonate with what we think of as the cultural identity of 'others'
3 define our own cultural identity and relate how we define ourselves to 1 and 2.

We may start with 1 and continue with processes 2 and 3 or we may start with 3 and continue with 1 and 2. The three processes must be included if the definition is not to be deficient.

I will use an example here (Jones, 1995) to illustrate these three processes in action. Two classes of 14-year-old pupils were involved in an interculture project; one class was in a secondary comprehensive school in Cambridgeshire, the other in a secondary school in Bulgaria. The Cambridgeshire pupils put into a shoebox items which they thought represented their cultural identity, or, in their words 'what it was to be English'. The box was sent by post to the 14-year-old Bulgarian pupils, who, in their turn, filled a shoebox with items which they felt conveyed a picture of how they saw themselves as Bulgarian. On receipt of the box the English class discussed what the contents seemed to reveal about 'what it is to be Bulgarian'.

The English pupils' conclusions were sometimes common to the whole group but often differed. When they differed they did so for several reasons as the evidence could be perceived as:

• an amalgam of ways in which members of the group defined themselves but which might not correspond to the cultural identity which any one individual in the target country would agree with.
• an agreed consensus which may or may not be reliable in a wider sample.
• interpretations which might be influenced by what the Bulgarian children, independently or collectively, wanted them, as an English audience, to believe; such interpretations might have been reactions to stereotypes or reported perceptions of a Bulgarian cultural identity which the Bulgarian pupils wished to deny or confirm for reasons of pride or even of perceived accuracy.

The desire to present an idealised representation was evident on another occasion during an exchange of photographs chosen by a class of 13–14-year-old English children to depict 'daily life in their small town'. Some pupils wanted to include a photograph of a large, detached house covered in roses because this was an image of 'the kind of house English people lived in'. They felt such a representation was appropriate for a 'foreign' audience. Only some of the children lived in houses of this kind. They were thus defining their cultural identity in a way which was influenced by how they wanted to be perceived; they were letting others define to some extent the identity they wished to project.

After discussion, the Cambridgeshire children decided that, on reflection, they preferred to be more honest. This resulted in them not discarding the house covered in roses but adding photographs of other kinds of houses in which they lived and enclosing a survey of exactly what kind of house each pupil lived in. They had begun to explore their own cultural identity and to realise its diversity. They had, too, in adding to the variety of photographs, thought about the stereotypes which others may have had about them as English children. They had also considered that evidence of this kind needed to represent all the members in a class and that even this may be a limited sample. They had begun to understand that if, as was to be the case, a shoebox with a collection of photographs was to be sent from Bulgaria, they may need to be circumspect about such evidence. Cultural awareness was thus taking into account the three processes outlined above.

An analysis of the contents of such exchanges of cultural representations picks out the variety of elements which may constitute cultural identity. These seem to include an interplay of some or all of the following aspects:[1]

Gender

This was exemplified by, for example, advertisements, articles from magazines aimed specifically at teenage boy or teenage girl readers.

Generation

Just as some publications are aimed at a teenage readership others are for older people. The pupils who put the shoebox contents together unsurprisingly collected a category of items which they felt categorised their identity as teenagers. These also reflected social practices which they associated with a younger generation such as certain sports (mountain-biking, skate boarding, motorcross etc).

Class

Photographs and descriptions of where they lived, their homes, rooms in their houses, clothes, food, meal times, Christmas menus – these would all be markers of certain ways of living which may (or may not) indicate for members of such groups within a society class divides or differences which to outsiders would not be appreciated or even noticed.

Family

In some societies there would appear to be importance given to family which transcends class. Such an aspect of cultural identity seems to merit consideration as a separate feature.

Religion

Religion either practised or underlying group behaviour can mark cultural identity which if not shared by another culture can lead to misinterpretation and misunderstanding. Teenagers are frequently unaware within their own class group in school of cultural differences and similarities which can be ascribed to shared or different religious backgrounds or histories.

Schooling

Common school experiences can create shared understandings which to an outsider appear alien and exclusive. Pupils often use such shared language and experiences to create an identity specific not just to one school but to a particular group within a school. Such an identity is particularly powerful but not always perceived in an explicit way. Many pupils are unaware of more subtle differences and similarities which together may or may not form part of their perceived identity.

School practices, such as French handwriting, are also markers of cultural identity. More subtle are perhaps ways of thinking which have their origins in common practice within a national school system.

The urban and the rural

During an exchange of descriptions of where they lived some English secondary school pupils who lived in a fenland, farming area told their French teenage counterparts about the horses their parents owned and which they rode. The French teenagers with whom they exchanged these descriptions lived in flats near the Opéra in Paris. To the French teenagers the English families were perceived as well off and privileged. This was not a view which the English children had of themselves, nor was it one which they wished to portray. The urban and the rural mark cultural identity in ways often not realised by those who live in such settings and by those who do not.

The regional

A regional identity was seen by several pupils as a significant component of what they consider themselves to be. This was particularly marked with a group of 17-year-old sixth form students in Willesden, North London, who when asked, were clearly aware of and saw as significant their Irish roots not just perceived by them in general terms but as being based in one specific region or even town in Ireland.

National heritage

When asked to say in a questionnaire what they felt the English liked a majority of Polish respondents wrote 'the Queen'. This opinion was not shared by a group of English 14-year-old children. However, the same group of English pupils was content to agree to include a photograph of the Queen's State Opening of Parliament as a representation of English heritage. There would appear to be an image which if designed for others in another country is acceptable and at times even desirable as a way of marking nationality. For any one individual in the home country, however, such markers may be less acceptable or even rejected.

Beyond national borders

There is evidence from many children of them espousing a cultural identity which transcends national frontiers. This is often manifest in the wish to be part of a global, or at least international culture, represented particularly by such transnational companies as McDonalds. A McDonalds' menu in a shoebox from Bulgaria prompted reactions amongst 14-year-old pupils which expressed relief that a transnational identity was possible. When the evidence came from another culture it was seen as less of a threat than that which was country specific and more integrative when evidence about cultural identity was being transmitted to 'others'.

To see that pizza were available in other countries prompted similar feelings of relief and reassurance, pizza in these contexts not being identified as Italian. Indeed when asked to list 'typically Spanish foods' a 12-year-old Spanish girl included pizza, spaghetti, hamburgers and lasagne in her list of nineteen foods, the rest of which were more readily associated with Spain.

Within this heading, mention should be made of the media and modes of communication such as the Internet. Cultural identity included definitions of self which referred to identification with well known, international film and TV stars. The lifestyles, fashions, and attitudes represented by the stars of some TV programmes, and the world of sport, broadcast across the world were mentioned as shared by some learners, and were part of their identity.

Approaches to practice: becoming interculturally competent

Given the complexity of interrelated elements which constitute cultural identity one of the first observations which others have made (most helpfully Byram, 1997: 38) is that there are different skills and forms of knowledge involved in becoming culturally aware. Byram defines four components or four *savoirs* of intercultural competence as:

Savoir être: an ability to abandon ethnocentric attitudes towards and perceptions of other cultures, and to see and develop an understanding of the differences and relationships between one's own and a foreign culture; this involves affective and cognitive change in learners.

Savoir apprendre: an ability to observe, collect data and analyse how people of another language and culture perceive and experience their world, what beliefs, values and meanings they share about it; this involves practical skills and a readiness to decentre and take a different perspective.

Savoirs: the knowledge of aspects of a culture, a system of reference points familiar to natives of the culture, which helps the natives to share beliefs, values and meanings, and to communicate without making explicit those shared assumptions.

Savoir faire: the ability to draw upon the other three savoirs and integrate them in real time and interaction with people of a specific language and culture.

(Byram, 1997)

The context, in many of Byram's examples, is predominantly, but not exclusively, that of visits abroad. Visits undeniably provide opportunities for learners to experience and reflect upon what it means to live in another country and to make their own observations, collect evidence and come to their own conclusions. During a visit, provided it is carefully structured, as Byram and others illustrate (Byram *et al.*, 1994) pupils can discover more about people who live in the other country and how they convey their cultural identity.

Driscoll and Frost (1999: 143) add a fifth *savoir*, '*savoir s'engager*' which ensures that the acquisition of cultural awareness has an educational dimension. Foreign language learners compare and evaluate foreign behaviours, beliefs and meaning by contrast with their own. The language teacher should '. . . ensure that learners are conscious of the criteria that they are using in their evaluation, and are able to turn their critical evaluation on to their own culture as well as that of others. Foreign language teaching thus develops a "critical cultural awareness" in learners...'

The emphasis, as is illustrated here, is on first hand experience and reflection and shows very convincingly the potential of an approach based on experiential learning. The original proposals for the National Curriculum published in 1990 (DES, 1990) appear to support such an approach and would seem to develop these five *savoirs*.

In order to outline an approach to developing cultural awareness the context and considerations discussed above will be analysed since they prompt a number of key questions. These are:

1   Given that a Modern Languages' teacher accepts that developing cultural awareness is integral to teaching a language, what is the relationship

between the teaching of language and the development of cultural awareness?

2   If cultural identity is as multifaceted as has been shown how can we as teachers build up an increasing awareness of its complexity over time? Is there a progression within such an understanding which teachers ought to be aware of? Are some concepts more difficult to understand than others?

3   Can we capture snapshots of cultural identity at a given moment in a person's or a group's life? Is the provisionality of such a glimpse a problem when learners may see, or tend to consider such identity as being permanent and fixed?

4   Should we relate provisional perceptions of our own identity to the perceptions which 'others' have of themselves, in order to understand those 'others' better?

5   How much can be taught and how much relies on experiential learning? What part can Modern Languages' teachers play in developing the five *savoirs* listed above? Is it not a cross-curricular undertaking? As Driscoll and Frost (1999: 142) point out, the *savoirs* can be considered as leading to 'the acquisition of intercultural competence (. . .) thus part of general education and learning to live in a complex society. (This) can and should be developed in all aspects of the school curriculum'.

6   Are there strategies and means which can develop such awareness more efficiently and effectively than others especially when visits are not possible for all learners? What role do textbooks play in developing pupils' understanding? What can 'handwritten texts, newspapers, magazines, books, video, satellite television, texts from the Internet' and 'sending and receiving messages by telephone, letter, fax or email' (QCA, 1999) achieve?

Let us discuss these questions in turn.

The relationship between using language for communicative purposes and developing a cultural awareness is fundamentally important. Learners need to understand that speaking another language is not merely a question of one-to-one relationships. It is only as a result of such a realisation that they will 'acquire new ways of conceptualising the reality they take for granted as natural' (Byram, 1997: 10). The recognition, for example, that a word in English may sometimes have similar and sometimes different cultural associations when used by speakers of another language is essential if communication is to be achieved without ambiguity. When words have culturally different associations, learners need to anticipate such potential problems to avoid misunderstandings. It is not only the mother tongue and the foreign language which are being brought together but concepts and conceptual systems.

Language and culture are inextricably linked when social relationships are involved. Two cultures may, for example, have politeness forms which not only have to be learned as language but which also have to be used appropriately. Often subtle social and cultural awareness is needed if good human relationships are to be fostered.

Language, too, is integral to understanding cultural difference if, for example, evidence or data are required. *Savoir apprendre* involves the use of language to collect such evidence as well as to understand the cultural dimensions which the evidence reveals. Learners will need to ask questions and seek clarification as well as interpret what they discover.

The second question concerns progression. Since there are concepts within cultural awareness which are more demanding than others for some learners, it seems important here to outline the principles which guide the selection of tasks and experiences for different groups of pupils. Driscoll and Frost are helpful in this respect. They argue convincingly that the selection of appropriate objectives and content can be decided according to the capacities of the learners and suggest, like Bruner (1960), that the key concept is 'learner appropriateness'. They say that, for a start at primary school level:

> the tasks given and the experiences offered must be selected in accordance with the learners' stage of development. They may be cognitively demanding as long as they are concrete; they may be emotionally complex as long as they are experiential; they may be practically exacting as long as they are systematically arranged, i.e. they permit the progression from simple to difficult.
>
> (ibid: 144)

This offers a clear and principled way to approach practice. It serves as a guide when making decisions about tasks and experiences which have as their objective the exploration of the ten listed influences in cultural identity. It reinforces the need to start with the learners and to encourage them to identify what they think of as being 'foreign', because the concept of foreign cannot exist without an understanding of what is 'non-foreign'. The progression is from the concrete and the experiential; it leads from the simple to the difficult.

The third question relates to the provisionality of perceptions of cultural identity. It is possible for most learners of a foreign language to have one or several encounters with the culture of speakers of the language they are learning, from which they can begin to form impressions of otherness. For younger children there may have been, for example, work based on photographs or representations of cultural identity, or songs, or stories (see Martin and Cheater, 1998) designed to: 'provide an opportunity for introducing pupils to aspects of the foreign culture and for celebrating linguistic and cultural diversity'.

Carefully planned and structured projects which involve exchanging messages or other kinds of evidence, or going on a short visit, can serve the same purpose. It is nearly always possible to create opportunities for pupils to meet speakers of the target language and ask questions designed to find out more about how cultural identity is perceived. What they gain from such experiences and subsequent discussion and exploration, especially when orchestrated by a sensitive teacher, often reveals considerable insights not only into otherness, but also into their own culture and self. Such insights are, however, provisional because they relate to a particular moment, as well as to a particular stage in a learner's development and experience, and it is this provisionality which learners sometimes find conceptually problematic. What we are asking learners to do is not just conceptualise the reality they take for granted as 'natural' (Byram 1997: 10) but to see that such reality is not fixed and permanent, and that it may change. Learners need to remain open-minded and curious; we do not want our learners to believe that either positive or negative perceptions are necessarily immutable.

To understand the concept of provisionality we need to reflect on whether the learners' perceptions of their own cultural identity can help them understand others better (question 4).

For example, a teacher asks a group of pupils to define their own cultural identity, to think about and document their understanding of 'being English'. Pupils are asked to bring together a collection of artifacts, printed texts, images and any other items. Class surveys are conducted to show a range of responses relating to the type of food most commonly eaten in the morning, in the evening, on Sunday; what kind of house they live in, with or without a garden; what pets they have; what their favourite leisure activities are. The pupils then discuss and decide collectively what for them is an acceptable representation of 'being English'. Some of the 'evidence' may be discarded as unrepresentative. Lists and photocopies are then made as a record of what is included and what is not.

A group of children is then asked to do an identical task in another contrasting part of England (not Britain). The 'evidence' in its entirety is then exchanged between schools and comparisons are made. The identity, so often fixed in time and space in the pupils' minds, is challenged.

By engaging in a project such as this – and there are others which serve the same objective – teachers can encourage their learners to situate their own often locally defined identity within a national context. They can lead them to see that such an identity may be interpreted differently by individual members of one peer group in the same school, by older students, by their teacher, by parents, by the local community, by the media. What they believe at one moment may thus be modified by others within the same community, and previously fixed notions and perceptions of their own cultural identity are liable to change. The realisation that one's own cultural identity may be interpreted in a number of ways can sensitise learners to problems related to defining others, and to how those others perceive themselves and are perceived.

The relative effectiveness of teaching as opposed to experiential learning, highlighted in question 5, poses a methodological problem. The 1999 (and latest version) of the National Curriculum in England for Modern Foreign Languages (QCA, 1999) appears to move away from learning to focus on teaching:

> Pupils should be taught (my emphasis) about different countries and cultures by:
>
> (a) working with authentic materials in the target language including some from ICT-based sources (*for example handwritten texts, newspapers, magazines, books, video, satellite television, texts from the Internet*);

(b) communicating with native speakers *(for example in person, by correspondence)*;
(c) considering their own culture and comparing it with the cultures of the countries and communities where the target language is spoken;
(d) considering the experiences and perspectives of people in these countries and communities.

This shift from learning to teaching raises the question: is cultural awareness something that can be taught or does it rely more on learners exploring aspects for themselves, where the role of the teacher is to create experiences, provide evidence, challenge beliefs, question assumptions, act as facilitator in a subtle way rather than to impart specific knowledge.

If teachers are to develop the five *savoirs* there are elements which undoubtedly can be taught. There are practical skills associated with *savoir apprendre* which need instruction, such as the use of language and the linguistic competence required to carry out an investigation or prepare a report. Similarly the sociolinguistic competence of understanding the relationship between language, meaning and context can be taught. In the more general *savoirs* there is an assumed knowledge base – schools and school systems, national customs, eating habits etc where appropriate information is required – meaning also takes for granted what is left unsaid.

However, the greatest emphasis underlying all five *savoirs* is on experiential learning and reflection. *Savoir être* involves affective as well as cognitive changes in learners, and can best be developed through learners' experiences of otherness and their willingness to be open to and accepting of cultural difference. It is about behaviour, as Byram (1997: 11) illustrates, which manifests an interest in others and 'a willingness to relativise one's own cultural viewpoint and system of values'.

Savoir être is linked to personality and to a learner's perceived place and role in society. It evolves over time. Similarly, in order to compare and evaluate how we see ourselves and how we see others *savoir s'engager* involves a growing understanding of self and of personal identity.

Developing the *savoirs* is not so much about teaching, in the sense of imparting knowledge, as developing understanding and awareness, fostering curiosity, encouraging openness, challenging attitudes, making beliefs explicit. Teachers of other subjects as well as Modern Language teachers, are, by the nature of their role in school, involved in developing cultural competence since, in a more general sense, living with and understanding others is part of a child's general education.

The special and unique feature of Modern Language learning is the interplay between the learner's communicative competence, linguistic competence, cultural awareness, identity and personality, all operating simultaneously. This interaction requires the selection and combination of appropriate language in ways which follow syntactical, semantic and grammatical rules. Cultural features also need to be taken into consideration to avoid ambiguity or offence as must the personality of the speaker or writer.

In addition, there is the realisation that communicating with someone from another country challenges perceptions of personal identity: are the practices of others strange; do our own practices appear strange to them? When speaking for the first time to a native speaker from another country learners find themselves talking not just as themselves but as someone who is English. They are representatives of something bigger than themselves.

Because Modern Languages' teachers have had experience of the complexity of such interaction they can best explain it. They also understand how to offer appropriate learning opportunities, and how to encourage a critical, analytical approach to developing awareness of self and to encounters with others.

The final question relates to strategies and means, the how of making learners culturally aware and interculturally competent. Developing the ability to be analytical relies on reflection and discussion. It is clear that this takes place in English so that an inability in the target language does not impede the expression of often complex ideas. In the UK, however, mostly in response to the revised National Curriculum for Modern Foreign Languages of 1995 Modern Language lessons use the target language as the main means of communication between teacher and learner in the classroom. The possible conflict between using the target language and discussion in English needs resolution.

In recent years there has been a growing recognition that discussion in English should take place in Modern Language lessons to help learners formulate ideas about and make explicit their learning and thinking. In the area of developing language learning strategies Grenfell and Harris's (1999) research frequently asked learners to 'provide an oral commentary while they undertake a task in the target language or to reflect retrospectively after carrying it out'.

In 1999, the requirements relating to the use of the target language as formulated in previous versions of the National Curriculum for England and Wales (DES, 1990; DFE, 1995) were modified to allow discussions in English about grammar and making comparisons between languages. The 1999 version states 'pupils are expected to use and respond to the target language, and to use English only when necessary (for example, when discussing a grammar point or when comparing English and the target language' (QCA, 1999).

It seems justifiable therefore to suppose that a principled use of English to support learning in terms of developing cultural competence would be permitted.

As visits are not going to be possible for all learners in school cultural insights have to be gained in other ways. The use of textbooks as Snow and Byram (1997) point out 'have usually concentrated on giving information about the people and the country involved. There is a need for this but it should not be the kind of factual information which no native speaker knows and learners soon forget'. They are therefore of use as they stand but will only serve a very limited purpose.

'Handwritten texts, newspapers, magazines, books, videos, satellite television and texts from the Internet' as recommended in the 1999 National Curriculum may well be a valuable resource as evidence and data to be used for analysis and discussion. Communication is here predominantly one way. If the post, email, fax, exchanging audio and video cassettes – and even the telephone – are used then interaction, two-way communication and dialogue is possible. The development of cultural awareness and understanding otherness is best served when questions are asked and evidence is provided in response to learners' curiosity and need for information. Often it is the teacher who decides what is provided in school. This is totally justifiable when the objective is to challenge cultural assumptions and show differences as well as similarities, where learners are required to analyse and interpret, as well as make discoveries. It is, however, the on-going interaction between learners and the other culture, facilitated and challenged by a teacher, which best helps develop this awareness and understanding.

Notes

1 The ennumertaion of influences within cultural identity owes its inspiration and origins to an unpublished paper 'Si mon miroir m'était conté' given by Véronica Pugibet at a conference organised by the Association des didacticiens de français langue étrangère at the Université du Littoral, France, on 15 November 1999. The list in this chapter has been amended from that presented at the conference in order to categorise data from original projects reported elsewhere (Jones, 1995).

Editor's note

Jones considers first how foreign cultures are represented through the use of artefacts and realia. The presentation of what constitutes cultural identity raises many issues. The questions of accuracy or appropriateness, commonality and diversity, representation and perception, all serve to illustrate the complexity of cultural awareness as an element of the curriculum. Next, Jones examines the way such a complex concept can be taught and learnt, which is further compounded by the learner's own perceptions and expectations. Jones refers to the new National Curriculum, commenting on the stronger emphasis on teaching. He presents very imaginative teaching methods valuing the provision of opportunities for implicit and experiential learning. Jones highlights the effect of inter-cultural dialogue as a means of offering learning opportunities. Jones is not negative in his presentation; he recognises the opportunity to focus on cultural awareness as a part of teaching and learning communication. He also considers the place of English as a learning tool in MFL lessons. Once again, the issue of developing learners' levels of cultural understanding raises issues beyond the immediate. This process of conceptualising includes an analysis and examination of the current interpretation of the communicative approach.

Linked chapters

Chapter 3, Chapter 9 and Chapter 17.

References

Bruner, J. (1960) *The Process of Education*, Cambridge, MA: Harvard University Press.

Byram, M. (ed.) (1997) *Face to Face Learning 'Language-and-Culture' Through Visits and Exchanges*, London: Centre for Information on Language Learning and Research.

Byram, M. *et al.* (1994) *Teaching-and-Learning, Language-and-Culture*, Clevedon: Multilingual Matters.

DES (Department of Education and Science and the Welsh Office) (1990) *Modern Foreign Languages for Ages 11–16. Proposals of the Secretary of State for Education and Science and the Secretary of State for Wales*, London: HMSO.

DfEE (Department for Education and Employment) (1995) *Modern Foreign Languages in the National Curriculum*, London: HMSO.

Driscoll, P. and Frost, D. (1999) *The Teaching of Modern Foreign Languages in the Primary School*, London: Routledge.

Grenfell, M. and Harris, V. (1999) *Modern Languages and Learning Strategies*, London: Routledge.

Jones, B. (1995) *Exploring Otherness. An Approach to Cultural Awareness*, Pathfinder 24, London: Centre for Information on Language Learning and Research.

Martin, C. and Cheater, C. (1998) *Let's Join In! Rhymes, Poems and Songs*, Young Pathfinder 6, London: Centre for Information on Language Learning and Research.

QCA (Qualifications and Curriculum Authority) (1999) *The National Curriculum for England Modern Foreign Languages*, London: DfEE/QCA.

Snow, D. and Byram, M. (1997) *Crossing Frontiers. The School Study Visit Abroad*, Pathfinder 30, London: Centre for Information on Language Learning and Research.

12 Issues in target language teaching

Ernesto Macaro

Introduction

> the lesson should be conducted through the medium of the target language
> . . . to avoid interference from the sound and *syntactical patterns of the mother
> tongue* . . . [and] to *lessen any desire the pupils may have to engage in the process
> of translation*.
>
> (Department of Education for Northern Ireland
(DENI), 1985)

> *From the outset*, the foreign language rather than English should be the
> medium in which classwork is conducted and managed.
>
> (Department of Education and Science
(England and Wales), 1988: 12)

> *The natural use* of the target language for virtually all communication is a
> sure sign of a good modern languages course.
>
> (Department of Education and Science
(England and Wales), 1990: 58)

> The learner must be '*led gradually* towards distancing himself/herself from
> the mother tongue'.
>
> (Centre Nationale de Documentation Pédagogique
(CNDP, France), 1993)
>
> (All italics are my own)

There would appear to be a considerable theoretical gulf between the first three
quotations above and the last one. Why should this be? For the past 10 years or
so there has been a vigorous, sometimes acrimonious, debate about how much
the foreign language should be used in the foreign language classroom. Why
should this be? Are the answers not obvious? Why should use of the target
language (TL), particularly by the teacher, have become such an over-arching
methodological principle? Have the answers not been provided by our curriculum planners, our teacher educators and by our inspectors?

In this chapter, I will start from the premise that: the answers have not been provided in any great depth; they have not been provided because the issues are complex; the issues are complex because learning a foreign language is not a simple process where reception is automatically followed by production. So, how do we go about exploring the issues and attempting to answer some of these questions? One way forward is to do the following:

1   We can define what is actually meant by 'using the TL'.
2   We can explore why it is an issue at all.
3   We can explore the opinions of authors on the issue.
4   We can explore the case for excluding the L1 from our classrooms.
5   We can explore the opinions that teachers have about TL use.
6   We can explore the reaction of the learners to the use of the TL.
7   We can describe teacher–learner(s) interaction and monitor its effects on learning.

Defining 'use of the target language'

The following brief definition of TL use is arrived at from my own experience of language teaching, from researching into the issues, from observing other teachers and from reading just about everything I have been able to lay my hands on with regard to the topic.

Using the TL does not just mean interacting in the foreign language (L2) when referring to the content of the lesson, that is to say topics such as: travelling around Italy; buying food in France; planning an evening with a German friend. It also means interacting in the L2 about events in the classroom itself: organising language activities; giving information; making requests; asking for clarification; commenting on behaviour and performance; explaining (implicitly or explicitly) the patterns of the L2.

However, the concept of use of the TL goes even beyond this. It becomes a pedagogical tool whereby the exploration of an L2 text, be it oral or written, delivered by the teacher or by published courses, is accessed and exploited through the L2 itself rather than with reference to the learners' L1. Thus any activities connected with a text, be they for comprehension only or for both comprehension and future production, have to find means of achieving their ends other than by translation of any form. Logically, the emphasis is therefore shifted from 'comprehending the whole' of any text to 'working with' the text. As an extension of this pedagogical principle, any tests or exams must reflect not only the means by which the learner's linguistic competence is measured, but also the whole relationship between the learner and an L2 text.

Why use of the target language is an issue

There are two fundamental reasons why TL use, as defined above, is an issue. First, some would argue that this is not, necessarily, the best way for learners to learn. Second, some would argue that it is a difficult principle to implement at the practical level. I shall return to the latter reason under a different heading. I want to argue here that the issue of whether it is a good way to learn arises at an abstract level from the influence that our understanding of L1 acquisition (the way we learn our first language as babies) has had on theories of L2 learning. The degree of acceptance of that influence determines the position that practitioners take on the question of whether an L2 is acquired subconsciously and implicitly or whether it is learned consciously and explicitly.[1] There are six observations to be made here. Each one offers theoretical arguments and counter-arguments at opposite ends of the spectrum.

1   A Language Acquisition Device (Chomsky, 1965), or Universal Grammar (Chomsky, 1980) exists both for L1 learners and for L2 learners. When a child learns its first language some sort of subconscious language processing system is in operation. This 'device' appears to be universal (it works for all languages) and acts as a sort of 'template' which helps the child make patterns with the language as s/he encounters it. This device has been shown to be operational with L2 learners.
    Although the device may be operational, it is superseded, especially with older learners, by high level cognitive skills which have been developed through the L1. For example learners can make connections thanks to greater contextual knowledge, devise their own semantic clusters, use strategies to help them memorise large chunks of vocabulary, learn syntactic patterns by rote, write things down.

2   Natural Sequences in learning a language (or a 'Natural Order', Krashen, 1981, 1987; Mclaughlin, 1987) have been detected both in L1 and L2 contexts. Some rules are acquired early on, others much later. A language can only be 'acquired' (and therefore native-speaker competence achieved) if these sequences are respected.
    Even in L1 acquisition, the sequences can be affected by the learning context. In L2 learning, particularly in classrooms, the context and the teaching affects the sequences a lot. You can certainly learn, retain and use L2 structures encountered out of any 'natural' order.

3   Both in L1 and L2 learners explore the new language by a process of hypothesis testing: 'Mum baked the bread' therefore 'Mum broked the cup'. The hypothesis is then either confirmed or disconfirmed.
    This is true. However, L2 learners also have another resource – their L1. They can compare syntactic patterns of the L2 with their L1 and use both languages to decipher the code of the L2.

4   We can organise the linguistic progress that L2 learners should make (their learning curriculum) in the same way that L1 learners acquire the language. That is, we can proceed from sounds, to single words, to short phrases, etc.[2]
    Language is linked to psychological development. You cannot compare the psychological development stages of a baby with that of a child of 12. L2 learning need not be like this.

5   Teacher Talk in the L2 classroom is like Child Directed Speech in L1. As long as similar input modification techniques are used, the learner will 'pick up the language'.

Even if teacher talk could have the same input and interaction effects, L2 learners would have to be exposed to enormous quantities of L2. A child will have received thousands of hours of input by the age of 2. Most MFL classrooms provide at best 400 hours of input in 5 years.

6   A 'natural' learning environment can be created in the L2 classroom. This can resemble the L1 learning environment or, at least, a second language (living in the Target Country) type of learning environment.

We can try, but can we ever achieve, the secure environment of the home? In the L2 classroom a learner's output inevitably is scrutinised by his/her peers, is commented on by a comparative stranger, the teacher. In any case the need to communicate is much less powerful in an L2 classroom.

The above six arguments and counter-arguments are by no means the only similarities and differences between L1 acquisition and L2 learning. However, they help to frame the controversy regarding TL use in general and the exclusion of the L1 in particular. As an initial conclusion, we would want to argue that the case for learning the L2 'naturally', like babies acquire their L1, is not proven.

What the literature says about using the target language

As we are limited by space, the following is a somewhat crude summary of the positions taken by various authors on the issue of target language use and the reader should go to the originals for more substantial accounts.

There are those authors who are convinced about L2 exclusivity. These include Chambers, F. (1991), Krashen and Terrell (1988), Frey (1988). Chambers believes that the exclusion of the L1 is 'theoretically uncontroversial' (Chambers, F., 1991: 27). That is to say, although problems may arise in the classroom forcing the teacher to have recourse to L1, each instance of recourse is not beneficial to the acquisition/learning process.

There are those authors who strongly promote the use of the target language, but do not comment on the negative effect of L1 as a learning tool. These include Seliger (1983), Macdonald (1993), Halliwell and Jones (1991). They see the classroom as the opportunity for learners to secure for themselves large quantities of L2 exposure; an opportunity to make the language real through the act of communicating in the classroom; a way of providing enjoyment and immediate success. Some see it as the only opportunity to develop negotiating, interpreting and expressing abilities, the very process of learning itself (e.g. Kramsch, 1981).

There are authors who, whilst recognising the possible value of L1 in the classroom, see its pitfalls. These include Pattison (1987), Cook (1991), Ellis (1984). The use of L1 for them may lead to bad teaching and learning habits. L1 use deprives learners of exposure to the target language models.

Dickson (1992) and Macaro (1997), whilst subscribing to the importance of an L2 rich environment, are concerned that the emphasis on the TL as a teaching strategy may be to the detriment of other, equally important strategies.

Some authors recognise some value in L1 use for a variety of reasons. For Cohen (1998, see below) the L1 is the language of thought for all but the most advanced learners and consequently cannot be ignored as a learning tool. Hagen (1992) argues that code switching, is a perfectly natural operation carried out by virtually all categories of bilinguals and is increasingly the practice in multi-lingual business contexts. Harbord (1992) sees a need to allow some L1 in the classroom on humanistic grounds, whilst Hopkins (1989) argues that excluding the L1 may threaten the very identity of the learner. This point is picked up in Phillipson (1992), who sees the L2-only model as an inappropriate transference to a different context of the TEFL dictum of excluding all languages other than English, this leading to a kind of linguistic imperialism.

The conclusion of this section, again suggests that we are far from the position of being able to ban the L1 from the L2 classroom. We are also encouraged by the above views not to take extreme positions on the issue, a view echoed by authors such as Chambers, G. (1992), Cajkler and Adelman (1992), Atkinson (1993), and Westgate (1991).

The case for excluding the L1

Let us explore a little further the case for excluding the L1 by picking up on one of the ideas above. An obvious reason would be because we might want learners to think exclusively in the L2, to create the environment in which the language of thought is the same as the language being studied. As we saw from the quote at the beginning of this chapter, this is partly to avoid interference from the syntactic structures of the L1. For example L1 speakers of English, who are learning French, often revert to the incorrect 'je suis 14 ans' after 3 years of having been exposed to the formulaic 'j'ai 14 ans'. Clearly, interference from the L1 does exist. Discouraging the L1 as the language of thought should enable more communicative exchanges in the classroom as learners would not be constantly monitoring their oral output via potentially erroneous L1 structures. The question to be answered is (given the preceding section), does the L1 interfere sufficiently to counter-balance any beneficial cognitive processes that making links between L1 and L2 might bring about?

Cohen (1998) reports on a mini-project where learners were asked which language they were encouraged to think in by teachers and their response to this. Most said that the teacher encouraged them to think in L2 and most felt that this was beneficial. However, many still reported using the L1 as the language of thought at particular moments. Moreover, in this study most respondents appeared to have lived in the target country at some time before embarking on the course and, in any case, were advanced learners. It would be extremely useful to have data on beginners or intermediate level students regarding their preferred language of thought during oral interaction in the classroom.

Kern (1994) outlines the advantages and disadvantages (reported by learners) of performing some mental translations and L1/L2 associations when reading a French text. The advantages are:

1   The L1 helps with semantic processing and permits consolidation of meaning;
2   The L1 helps with chunking L2 lexical items into semantic clusters, a way of attempting to reduce memory constraints;
3   The L1 helps with thought processes (the train of thought), avoids losing track of the meaning as the reader works through a text;
4   The reader's network of associations can be made richer with L1 use, therefore better integrated and assimilated;
5   The input is converted into more familiar terms enhancing the reader's confidence and lowering affective barriers;
6   Mental translation may help in clarifying the syntactic roles played by lexical items, verifying a verb tense or checking for comprehension.

Kern saw the following disadvantages of L1/L2 associations during a reading task:

1   Mental translation may lead to inaccuracies and miscomprehension
2   Bottom up de-coding (word-by-word) may not assist with integration of meaning;
3   Focusing for too short a time on the L2 forms may diminish the possibility of actual L2 intake.

My own study into learner strategies suggests similar findings (Macaro 1998b). When 15-year-old learners were asked to 'think aloud' how they tackled an L2 reading text, they inevitably (because of the nature of the task) used the L1 as the language of thought. However, their comments suggest that even if they had not been engaged in the think aloud task their language of thought would have been the L1. This is because they invariably scanned the text for lexical items or strings of items which appeared to them as cognates. The difference between the less successful learners (in terms of achieving this task) and the more successful ones was that the latter constantly checked what they understood at any given point with the context and what they had understood so far. This metacognitive combined-deployment of strategies[3] appeared to be undertaken with the L1 as the language of thought. L1 as a language of thought appeared not to be used, however, in another study with Italian learners of English (Macaro, 1998a) where they helped themselves understand the recorded text (from a video they were watching) with the L2 subtitles which this particular video provided. All appeared to be processed in L2. This does raise the issue about exactly what we mean by thinking in L1.[4] Similarly, most memorisation techniques deployed by learners (for example keyword association) involve some association between the L1 and the L2.

In studies on writing in the L2 (see Kobayashi and Rinnert, 1992; Brooks, 1993) there is some evidence to suggest that, for a majority of learners, preparing the intended output in L1 first and then translating it produced better results (particularly in terms of syntactic complexity) than going straight into L2 written production. Interestingly, however, most of the learners said they preferred direct composition to translation because they claimed it was easier. Learners have to make the choice between using only their current store of language, but not extending themselves, or extending themselves by going partly or totally via the L1, and then finding it difficult and/or making many mistakes.

So, what might we hypothesise about the way learners use the L1 to help them learn? Beginners use the L1 to help them decode text. Beginners and more advanced learners use the L1 to help them write text. L1 tends to be the language of thought unless the learner is very advanced or is in the target country (or can relate to) a past event or experience in the target language environment. Different individual learners of the same level of ability use the L1 more or less frequently according to their preferred learning styles. Any progression from formulaic expression to more 'creative' (in the sense of independently created utterances) may well require some recourse to L1 as the language of thought.

Given the discussion in the above three sections, it would be unwise to recommend the total exclusion of the L1 from the foreign language classroom.

Teachers' opinions about target language use

What are teachers' attitudes to their use of the target language and for what purposes do they use the L1?

A number of empirical studies have tried to answer the latter part of this question using a variety of data collection instruments. These are summarised in Table 12.1.

A number of observations can be made from Table 12.1. First, recourse to L1 appears to occur across all learning contexts in which there is a choice of language use. The issue to be resolved here is whether teachers use the L1 because there is a choice of language or because they believe that to use it actually enhances the learning process. To put it another way, in the TEFL classroom with mixed L1 learners where the teacher has no choice of language, are the learners missing out on any possible teaching or learning strategies? There is as yet insufficient research evidence to provide an answer to this question.

Second, in adolescent classrooms, the behaviour of the learners appears to correlate quite strongly with teacher use of L1. The issue to be resolved here is whether poor behaviour triggers teacher L1 use or whether L2 exclusivity encourages poor behaviour from adolescent learners. Later in this chapter we shall provide some indications which begin to give an answer to this question.

Third, 'the teaching of grammar' features strongly, in a number of studies, as a reason for recourse to L1 by teachers. However, it does not feature as a reason in

Table 12.1 Studies of teachers' use of the target language

Study author(s) and date	L2 teaching context	Data collection instruments	Purposes of L1 use by teachers
Wragg 1970	England; secondary	Classroom observation	Criticism of learners; lexical contrasting
Wing 1980	US; secondary	Teacher self report sheets	Discipline; explanations of grammar
Prahbu 1987	India; secondary	Case study	Glossing of lexical items; complex procedural instructions
Mitchell 1988	Scotland; secondary	Interviews and observations	Explanations of grammar; discipline; activity instructions; teaching background
Kharma and Hajjaj 1989	Arabic L1, country not specified; secondary	Questionnaires; classroom observation; interviews	Explanation of complex lexical items; speeding up the teaching/learning process
Hopkins 1989	England ESL secondary and further education	Questionnaire	Instructions and explanations comparison of cultural differences
Franklin 1990	Scotland; secondary	Questionnaire	Discipline; explanations of grammar; discussing language objectives; teaching background
Duff and Polio 1990	US; university	Observations; questionnaires; interviews	Explanations of grammar; speeding up the teaching/ learning process
Macaro 1995	Italy; secondary	Questionnaire; interview	Complex procedural instructions; building up relationships with learners
Dickson 1996	England; secondary	Questionnaire	discipline; setting homework; explaining meanings; teaching grammar
Macaro 1997	England; secondary	Questionnaires; interviews; classroom observation	Complex procedural instructions; discipline; building personal relationships
Neil 1997	Northern Ireland; secondary	Teacher interviews; self reports; classroom observation	Examination techniques; instructions for tests; explaining grammar;
Macaro 1998	England; secondary	Classroom observation; interviews	Discipline; complex procedural instructions; glossing of lexical items

all studies. Why should this be? I believe it to be the case that not all teachers have the same interpretation of the concept of 'teaching grammar'? Some may conceptualise it as explicit explanation of patterns and rules, others as implicit focus on form. The latter are less likely to see it as a reason for resorting to L1. It may also be the case that some teaching contexts emphasise the importance of communication over form more than others and, therefore, teachers quite simply do less of it. It is clear that any research instruments related to answering questions about grammar teaching need to include systematic classroom observation.

Interpretation of the data is also connected with the fourth observation to be drawn from Table 12.1. What do teachers understand by the notion of 'giving instructions' and what effect does that have on the data analysis? In all three studies I have carried out on TL use I have provided for respondents a distinction between routine instructions ('open your books', 'find page 30') and complex procedural instructions (such as setting up a group work activity involving a number of pupil–pupil oral exchanges). It has become quite clear that teachers have no problem and see great value in remaining in the L2 for the former. This is because it is easy to achieve via routine use of the same vocabulary and formulaic expressions and also keeps the general rhythm of target language use going. It gives the feel that the lesson is, essentially, being carried out in L2. On the other hand, attempting to put across complex procedural instructions for an activity is difficult given that the instructional language is usually at a much higher level than the linguistic competence of the learners. A number of teachers have reported that it often becomes an obstacle to that activity taking place. Teachers are then faced with the option of explaining the instructions in L1 or, in future, avoiding complex (but highly valid) learner-centred activities.

Some of the studies in Table 12.1 also collected data on teacher attitudes to TL use as related to variables other than the purpose the language was being put to (the language activity the teacher was engaged in). One very important variable appears to be the ability level of the learners. Studies as contextually far apart as Dickson (1996) and Karma and Hajjaj (1989) report the learners' competence level as a major factor in bringing about use of L1 by the teacher for fear of not being able to put across the meaning, thus leading to demotivation. In Macaro (1997), more than 80 per cent of teachers agreed that pupil ability was a factor in the amount of L2 a teacher could use.

Another important variable is the age of the learners. Most studies agree that it is easier to maintain virtual L2 exclusivity with younger learners. Dickson (1996) reports a diminution in the quantity of teacher TL use between Key Stage 3 and Key Stage 4. He also points to the fact that the very limited repertoire of many pupils at KS3 means that work in the TL is at a trivial level. It is likely, therefore, that a combination of low ability and older pupils leads to the highest amount of teacher recourse to L1. This is because only the younger beginners will be content with remaining within the limited L2 repertoire. As the learners get older, and the repertoire is not correspondingly enlarged, learners are more likely to react against excluding, for relatively long periods (70 minute lessons are not uncommon), the only language in which they can express themselves.

We can summarise the empirical evidence of teacher attitudes and use of TL as follows. In none of the studies I have come across is there a majority of teachers in favour of excluding the L1 altogether. In all the studies there is an overwhelming impression that teachers believe that the L2 should be the predominant language of routine interaction in the classroom. Teachers report that the areas in which they use the L1 are: building personal relationship with learners (the pastoral role that teachers take on); giving complex procedural instructions; controlling pupils' behaviour; teaching grammar explicitly. They also cite time pressures as an important factor. The major variables in teacher recourse to L1 are ability and age of the learners. Many teachers report feeling guilty when they use the L1.

The above summary of empirical studies, however, still only provides us with a small part of the answers we are looking for. One reason for this is that the studies also provide evidence of enormous variation in teacher quantity of L2 use. Neil (1997) reports between 97.5% and 33.1%. Macaro (1998c) records levels of L2 use among student teachers as between 100% and 71.3%. Why should this be? We shall be taking another look at these findings later in the chapter. Another reason is that teachers' attitudes to TL use, as a reflection of their personal constructs, also varies tremendously. I will argue that we can categorise attitudes towards TL use as follows: *The Total Exclusion Position (or 'Virtual' position)*. This position equates L2 learning with L1 acquisition. It sees no pedagogical value in L1 use by the teacher and virtually no value in L1 use by the learner. The emphasis is on input with the teacher's input given a very high status. The overriding images are the 'language bath' and 'total immersion'. The classroom is little different from the natural language learning environment outside (the environment of ESL learners, for example) except that it is more controlled and enabling.

The Maximalist Position. This position states that there is probably no pedagogical value in learner use of L1 and almost certainly none in teacher use of L1. What distinguishes it from the Total Exclusion Position is the recognition that the perfect teaching/learning conditions do not exist. There is, therefore, fear of communication breakdown resulting in: pupils being distracted; pupils misbehaving; pupils being demotivated. It is also associated with teacher competence and teacher confidence. It has a more socio-cultural dependence than a linguistic one. Variables are by learner ability (able learners can cope with more TL) and learner age (younger learners do not mind so much TL). Its potential for increase is halted by the need to build relationships because the MFL classroom has a pastoral dimension as well as a linguistic one. Teachers may feel guilty if recourse to L1 occurs but may not be able to identify the reasons for that guilt.

The Optimal Use Position. This position sees some value in teacher use of L1 and some value in learner use of L1. It relates quantity only to principles of language pedagogy. It relies on knowing when code switching will have a negative impact. The emphasis is more on linguistic principles than socio-cultural ones although the latter are by no means excluded. There is a constant exploration of pedagogical principles. The emphasis is on promoting teacher–pupil and pupil–pupil interaction. It acknowledges that the L2 classroom can operate short cut strategies through the use of L1. The variable is level of competence (the more competent the less L1 needed for learning the L2). Teachers may feel guilty about recourse to L1 but can analyse those feelings of guilt against a theoretical framework.

The reaction of learners to L2 exclusivity

It is not surprising that the reaction of learners to L2 exclusivity is mixed. There is an increasing body of literature which emphasises the differences between learners rather than their similarities.[5] In terms of reaction to teacher use of TL there are those learners who are comfortable with it. They do not get flustered and they feel that they do not need to understand everything the teacher is saying. In the Macaro (1997) study,[6] this category of learners welcomed the teacher's attempts to paraphrase and give context-enhancing clues. However, even these learners forcefully adhered to the position that important inform-ation (e.g. homework or test instructions) should be given in L1 as well as L2. The other category of learners had quite strong reactions to the idea that they could learn if the teacher spoke in L2 even though they could not understand. They wanted a much deeper meaning of words and phrases. This was their way of fixing meaning in short- and long-term memories, perhaps by making L1/L2 associations. They were particularly keen for L1 equivalents when it came to idiomatic phrases. It is important to point out that these differences in reactions did not result from different teaching styles or capabilities. Differences occurred among pupils who had the same teacher.

We should also note that the appearance of comprehension and/or satisfac-tion at TL use amongst learners does not necessarily mean that they have understood or are satisfied with it. Lack of comprehension and dissatisfaction may well be among the factors which lead to demotivation. This point is made by Stables and Wikeley (1999). From the evidence of their study they conclude that the negative attitudes to foreign languages expressed by the pupils were likely to be, in part, as a result of unequal power relationships which are particularly prevalent in language classrooms where the target language pre-dominates. Giota (1995) reports on a study where adolescent learners them-selves describe the amount of teacher talk. In this study, half the pupils indicated that teacher spoke L2 almost all the time and 12 per cent that the teacher spoke all the time. In this study one category of learners (classified, amongst other criteria, as least motivated) complained of not understanding the teacher's L2 and that the lesson was teacher dominated. It should be pointed out that these were Swedish learners of English, comparatively (compared, say, to English learners of French) highly motivated to learn (what is considered by some Swedes) a second language.

Research carried out on learners' reaction to target language use is limited and there is an urgent need to find out more about, for example, what strategies individual learners use in order to decode the incoming Target Language input. In the absence of such research evidence we can, at least, turn to the analysis of foreign language classroom interaction and try to make an informed guess as to its impact on learners.

Describing the classroom interaction between the teacher and the learners

There are many ways in which we can describe the interaction of the foreign language classroom. All have varying degrees of relevance to the issue of target language but, as space is limited, I will go into detail of only a few.

We can describe the way FL interaction differs from naturalistic conversation. For example, we can describe the way that teacher talk is different from native speaker talk. How do teachers change their L2 use in order to accommodate to the language proficiency of their learners? The phenomenon of 'input modification' is extensively documented in the literature.[7] The issue here is to what extent is this modification of target language input merely serving the purposes of comprehensibility (and for that matter classroom management) and to what extent is it leading to intake and future production of language by the learners?

We can categorise language in various ways. We have already made a distinction above between topic language and classroom language. The issue here is what is more real and motivating for the learner, a body of language projected to the future (meeting up with a friend in Italy), or a body of language dealing with the here and now (the language which makes the classroom work)? One is tempted to say the latter until one observes how reluctant many learners are to use classroom language. We can describe the way medium-oriented language (talking about the language being learnt) differs from message-oriented language (providing new information). We would hypothesise that the latter type is more interesting for pupils until we observe that recourse to L1 most often occurs in message-oriented teacher TL (Macaro, 1997, 1998c). The issue here is as follows. Is it the case that message-oriented interaction, through the language of the classroom, produces the range of functions by learners which leads to communicative competence? Or is it the case that learners are restricted by the rules of classroom interaction to repeating, practising and informing such that it is only the teacher who is involved in a range of discourse functions (Kramsch, 1981)? Is the discourse so unequal in its allocation of privileges that adolescent learners react against it?

In order to begin to answer the above issues, we need to explore the ways in which the discourse is actually controlled in L2 classrooms. In many classrooms the teacher controls the following: which language is to be used and when; what topic will be discussed; the content of the interaction, the vocabulary and phrases; the relevance of the language used. The teacher also controls the turn-taking, not only who should speak but also for how long they should speak. They also control the wait-time, the time they allow a learner to come up with an answer before giving the turn to someone else. The teacher chooses when to change the direction of the discourse via discourse markers (by using L2 versions of 'well,' 'ok,' 'right'). The teacher tends to control the discourse plane changes, very rarely being able to refer to work that has gone before or work that is yet to come because of the complexity of the language that this would involve. The teacher controls the structure of the discourse, often by using the well known Initiation, Response, Feedback formula (Sinclair and Coulthard, 1975).

In a project involving the close study of six student teachers (Macaro, 1998c), I observed that those lessons in which the least amount of L1 occurred were those where the teacher exercised a great deal of the discourse control described in the paragraph above. Is this level of discourse control, via the TL, beneficial to the teacher or the learners? Let us look at a few specific results of this research. By video-recording lessons and then 'sampling' the interaction every five seconds, it was possible to build up a fairly accurate picture of what was going on in a way that had not been possible simply by observing. As we noted above, for example, the range of L1 use was never any more than 28.7 per cent as a proportion of total teacher talk. However, what was interesting was that teacher talk in L1 or L2 had very little effect on whether the pupils spoke in L2. For example:

1   High quantities of teacher L2 talk did not lead to high quantities of pupil L2 talk;
2   Higher quantities of teacher L1 talk did not lead to pupils using the L1 more.

Lessons in the same teaching context (same school; same year; same ability of pupils; same topic) were producing different results.

On the other hand, when comparing different learning contexts some overall differences in teacher–pupils interaction were clearly noticeable. The ability of the pupils was, again, a variable. But now the length of the lesson was also an important factor. For example long lessons (more that 50 minutes) had less average pupil use of L2 in teacher-centred activities than short lessons (35 minutes, approximately). In other words, these teachers were starting the lesson with the intention of engaging in proportionally less interaction than teachers starting short lessons. This is an initial finding, based on a limited sample, which needs further research. However, it may well be that it is not simply the case that it is difficult to sustain L2 interaction beyond a certain length of time but that long lessons seem to develop a culture where L2 interaction is comparatively eschewed. When pair work or group work was added to the equation, here too surprisingly, it correlated negatively with longer lessons although the sample was not large enough to achieve significance (Tau= -0.436; p=0.088[8]). Moreover, the use of L1 by both teachers and pupils increased in longer lessons and produced fairly strong statistical correlations (Tau=0.520; p=0.042 (for teachers) and Tau=0.645; p=0.012 (for pupils)).

What was particularly interesting from the analysis of the interaction in this study was that only one instance of pupil use of L1 resulted from the teacher having resorted to L1. By contrast, quite a number of instances of pupil use of L1 led to the teacher using the L1. The pupils appeared to be deciding to wrest control of the discourse from the teacher by switching to their first language, the language in which they could freely express themselves. In some of these lessons a kind of 'L1 threshold' was stepped over by the teacher whereby s/he no longer was able to repair back to L2 interaction and the lesson became, essentially delivered in L1. It has to be remembered that in lessons which are predominantly teacher-fronted individual learners speak the L2 for astonishingly little proportions of the time, sometimes an average of 5 seconds for each individual pupil. We are therefore led to propose that an over-emphasis on teacher use of TL, with long periods of input modification in order to achieve comprehensibility, may well lead to teacher dominated classrooms and do little to develop the learners' use of the L2.

Conclusion

We have explored, in very brief fashion, all the avenues that might provide answers to the target language issues with which we started at the beginning of this chapter. The one avenue we have not explored is the one which considers cause and effect. Does teaching through the target language actually improve learning? Currently we are not in a position to answer this question. In order to do this we would need to compare two sets of teachers, those who used the target language almost exclusively and those who did not. We would need to analyse a considerable range of their lessons. We would have to find ways of excluding variables such as geographical location of the school and socio-cultural background of the pupils. We would need to establish whether those teachers who used the L1 actually put it to a purpose or whether they used it when, for example, they were too tired to use the L2. Only then might we be able to compare the language competence of the learners with the different teaching styles. Until the results of such a study are available we are left with asking the teachers and the learners what they think and do and comparing this with what can be observed in the classroom. However, we should not discount these approaches to answering the still important question of what it means to teach through the target language.

It is with observation that I would like to end my contribution to this book. In doing so I want to re-affirm a basic belief that learners' use of the L2 is conducive to successful learning. Oral L2 use, particularly, leads to the internalisation of the rule system, an awareness of how language is linked to its speech community, how discourse operates between speaker and hearer. Only through the learner using the L2 can s/he achieve strategic communicative competence. The over-arching pedagogical tool should, therefore, be learners' use of the target language, not teacher use of the target language. In a sense, to say that use of the target language for all communication is a sure sign of quality teaching is to hand practitioners too simplistic a teaching tool. It is a strategy which 'in theory' requires little or no reflective practice. So, back to observation. In the lessons I have observed at all levels of teacher experience a number of practices appeared to contribute to the development and maintenance of high levels of learner L2 use. They were lessons in which: routine instructions were regularly carried out in L2 and reactions and simple requests insisted upon in L2. This helped to create a target language atmosphere in the classroom and maintained the rhythm of the lesson. It felt like you were in a foreign language classroom.

Learners were given a deep understanding of the L2 input and help with processing of L2 input. L1/L2 associations were made. Instances of negative transfer from L1 were signalled. They were given the opportunity and time to produce the L2. It looked as if some thinking in L1 may have helped some learners both with memorisation and production.

Learners were encouraged to initiate L2 dialogue thereby giving them some control over the interaction. They were not admonished for finding relief in occasional use of their own language.

Pupils were given the means with which to express themselves in L2. The language of the classroom was taught in the same way that other topics were taught. Clouds hanging from the ceiling and bubbles on the wall were not considered enough. Classroom language was slowly integrated into the interaction.

Rather than the teacher 'getting through the target language race', that is, getting through the lesson without having to resort to L1, the focus was on the pupils increasing, from month to month, the number of target language laps they could achieve. In order to do this an emphasis was put on praising the quality of the language used not just on completion of the task. This objective was explained to the pupils, sometimes in L1.

Learners were given opportunities to engage in L2 interaction by teachers offering them good quality pair/group work activities which were increasingly less structured in terms of the language that could be used. Learners were encouraged to experiment with the L2. Learners were also encouraged (and provided with the means), in these collaborative situations, to organise themselves in L2.[9] Complex instructions for these collaborative activities quite often included quick bursts of L1 in order to 'lubricate' the pending L2 interaction.

Teachers trained learners to use both cognitive and metacognitive strategies. They took short periods of time out from the language topic they were engaged in to discuss how learners could best help themselves to cope with the language, to learn the language and to review their progress. They 'pre-disposed' learners to the target language and target culture by talking to them about the benefits of language learning and sometimes gave pupils a vision of a more integrated Europe. They sometimes did this in L1.

Teachers avoided becoming remote and unapproachable figures by finding time to interact with small groups of learners or on a one-to-one basis with their pupils. Sometimes this was in L2, sometimes in L1. The building up of personal relationships appeared to be facilitated by those teachers who included independent learning activities in their lesson objectives.

At the end of these lessons teachers would not feel guilty for having resorted to the L1. However, as good reflective practitioners, they would question themselves as to the justification for their L1 use and, in the case of no justification being arrived at, they would explore how they could have performed the same activity in the future, this time by using the target language.

Notes

1 For a discussion on Acquisition and Learning see Krashen, 1981, 1987; McLaughlin, 1987; Ellis, 1984.
2 For an example of this progression see the National Curriculum for MFL (England and Wales), Attainment Target 2 (Speaking), (DES, 1991).
3 By this, I mean intentionally and methodically deploying a number of strategies which complement one another in order to achieve meaning.
4 See Cohen (1998) for a further discussion on this.
5 For an overview of research on individual differences, see Skehan, 1991.
6 Focus group interviews carried out with learners aged between 11 and 13.
7 Useful summaries are provided, for example, by Pica and Long (1986), Allwright and Bailey (1991), Tardif (1994).
8 For those not confident with statistical analysis the Tau gives you the strength of the correlation between two variables on a scale from 0–1. Thus a correlation of 0.5 is a medium strength correlation – it looks as if the two phenomena are linked. The 'p' tells you whether the sample allows you to generalise to the 'population' as a whole. In order to do this the 'p' should be less than 0.05.
9 For example, I can remember a lesson when pupils were engaged in oral group work. The teacher recorded the L1 they used to organise themselves. S/he then taught that language the next lesson and did the whole activity again.

Editor's note

Macaro's chapter looks at the issue of target language use from several perspectives. First, a theoretical and literature search reveals sharp disagreement over the issue, and indeed, Macaro concludes that there is no firm evidence to suggest that exclusive use of the target language benefits the learner. Macaro also considers teachers' own attitudes and practice, noting that the use of the mother tongue is often viewed negatively. He also notes when teachers claim the use of the target language is easier and when they believe it to have a positive impact on learning. Perhaps most importantly, Macaro considers the views of learners themselves, and indeed his own observations of learners. His study does reveal occasions when, and reasons for, beneficial use of the target language. Macaro warns against adopting a firm stance on exclusive use of the target language, noting examples when use of the mother tongue appears to be effective. On the other hand, he notes when use of the target language should not be questioned, such as the issuing of routine instructions. Macaro's message is that teachers should refer to good practice, but make professional judgements for themselves, based on sound principles, and not allow themselves to be dictated to by a given methodological proposition. The key underlying principle is that decisions should be made for the benefit of learners, and ability by the teacher to use the target language exclusively should *not* be seen as a means of measuring teacher competence.

Linked chapters

Chapter 3, Chapter 18.

References

Allwright, D. and Bailey, K.M. (1991) *Focus on the Language Classroom*, Cambridge: Cambridge University Press.

Atkinson, D. (1993) 'Teaching in the target language: a problem in the current orthodoxy', *Language Learning Journal*, 8: 2–5.

Brooks, A. (1993) *Translation as a Writing Strategy for Intermediate-Level French Composition*, Nashville, TN: Department of French and Italian, Vanderbilt University.

Cajkler, W. and Adelman, R. (1992) *The Practice of Foreign Language Teaching*, London: Fulton.

Chambers, F. (1991) 'Promoting use of the target language in the classroom', *Language Learning Journal*, 4: 27–31.

Chambers, G. (1992) 'Teaching in the target language', *Language Learning Journal*, 6: 66–7.

Chomsky, N. (1965) *Aspects of the Theory of Syntax*, Cambridge, MA: MIT Press.

—— (1980) *Rules and Representations*, New York: Columbia University Press.

CNDP (France) (1993) *Anglais: Classes de Collège, 6e, 5e, 4e, 3e*, Paris: Centre Nationale de Documentation Pédagogique.

Cohen, A. D. (1998) *Strategies in Learning and Using a Second Language*, London: Longman.

Cook, V. (1991) *Second Language Learning and Language Teaching*, London: Edward Arnold.

Department of Education and Science (DES) (1988) *Modern Languages in the School Curriculum: A Statement of Policy*, London: HMSO.

——(1990) (Oct.) *Modern Foreign Languages for Ages 11 to 16*, London: HMSO.

——(1991) *Modern Foreign Languages in the National Curriculum*, London: HMSO.

Department of Education for Northern Ireland (DENI) (1985) *Good Practice in Education, Paper 2: Modern Languages Teaching in Northern Ireland*, Bangor: DENI.

Dickson, P. (1992) *Using the Target Language in Modern Foreign Language Classrooms*, Slough: NFER.

—— (1996) *Using the Target Language: A View from the Classroom*, Slough: NFER.

Duff, P. A. and Polio, C. G. (1990) 'How much foreign language is there in the foreign language classroom?' *The Modern Languages Journal*, 74(2): 154–166.

Ellis, R. (1984) *Classroom Second Language Development*, Oxford: Pergamon.

Franklin, C. E. M. (1990) 'Teaching in the target language: problems and prospects', *Language Learning Journal*, 2: 20–4.

Frey, H. (1988) 'The applied linguistics of teacher talk', *Hispania*, 71(3): 681–6.

Giota, J. (1995) 'Why do all children in Swedish schools learn English?' *System*, 33(3): 309–22.

188 Ernesto Macaro

Hagen, S. (1992) 'Language policy and strategy issues in the new Europe', Language Learning Journal, 5: 31–4.
Halliwell, S. and Jones, B. (1991) On Target, London: CILT.
Harbord, J. (1992) 'The use of the mother tongue in the classroom', ELT Journal, 46: 75–90.
Hopkins, S. (1989) 'Use of mother tongue in teaching English', TESOL Quarterly, 27(1): 18–24.
Kern, R. G. (1994) 'The role of mental translation in second language reading', Studies in Second Language Acquisition, 16(4): 441–61.
Kharma, N. N. and Hajjaj, A. H. (1989) 'Use of the mother tongue in the ESL classroom', International Review of Applied Linguistics, 27: 223–35.
Kobayashi, H. and Rinnert, C. (1992) 'Effects of first language on second language writing: translation versus direct composition', Language Learning, 42(2): 183–215.
Kramsch, C. J. (1981) Discourse Analysis and Second Language Teaching. Washington: Center for Applied Linguistics.
Krashen, S. D. (1981) Second Language Acquisition and Second Language Learning, Oxford: Pergamon.
—— (1987) Principles and Practice in Second Language Acquisition, Hemel Hempstead: Prentice Hall.
Krashen, S. D. and Terrell, T. D. (1988) The Natural Approach, London: Prentice Hall.
Macaro, E. (1995) 'Target language use in Italy', Language Learning Journal, 11: 52–4.
—— (1997) Target Language, Collaborative Learning and Autonomy, Clevedon: Multilingual Matters.
—— (1998a) 'Learner strategies: piloting awareness and training', Tuttitalia, 18: 10–16.
—— (1998b) 'Learner Strategies: raising awareness; training the learners', in E. Macaro (ed.) Learner Strategies in Modern Foreign Languages, proceedings of a conference organised by the Centre for Languages, English and Media in Education, Reading University: CLEME, pp. 4–13.
—— (1998c) 'An analysis of interaction in Foreign Language classrooms with particular reference to teacher recourse to L1', unpublished PhD thesis, University of Reading.
Macdonald, C. (1993) Using the Target Language, Cheltenham: Mary Glasgow Publications.
McLauchlin, B. (1987) Theories of Second Language Learning, London: Edward Arnold.
Mitchell, R. (1988) Communicative Language Teaching in Practice, London: CILT.
Neil, P. S. (1997) Reflections On the Target Language, London: CILT.
Pattison, P. (1987) Developing Communication Skills, Cambridge: Cambridge University Press.
Phillipson, R. (1992) Linguistic Imperialism, Oxford: Oxford University Press.
Pica T. and Long, M. (1986) 'The linguistic and conversational performance of experienced and inexperienced teachers', in R. Day (ed.) Talking to Learn: Conversation in Second Language Acquisition, Rowley, MA: Newbury House.
Prahbu, N. S. (1987) Second Language Pedagogy, Oxford: Oxford University Press.
Seliger, H. W. (1983) 'Learner interaction in the classroom and its effect on language acquisition', in H. W. Seliger and M. H. Long (eds) Classroom Oriented Research in Second Language Acquisition, Rowley MA: Newbury House.
Sinclair, J. McH. and Coulthard, R. M. (1975) Towards an Analysis of Discourse, London: Oxford University Press.
Skehan, P. (1991) 'Individual differences in second language learning', Studies in Second Language Acquisition, 13: 275–98.

Stables, A. and Wikeley, F. (1999) 'From bad to worse? Pupils' attitudes to modern foreign languages at ages 14 and 15', *Language Learning Journal*, 20: 27–31.

Tardif, C. (1994) 'Classroom teacher talk in early immersion', *Canadian Modern Language Review*, 50(3): 466–81.

Westgate, D. (1991) 'Modern foreign languages 11–16: a too cosy consensus?' *Language Learning Journal*, 4: 20.

Wing, B. H. (1980) 'The languages of the foreign language classroom: a study of teacher use of the native and target languages for linguistic and communicative functions', unpublished PhD thesis, Michigan: Ann Arbor University (cited in Neil 1997).

Wragg, E. (1970) 'Interaction analysis in the foreign language classroom', *Modern Languages Journal*, 54(2): 116–20.

13 It all ended in tiers

Julie Adams

Introduction

> The traditional view of assessment is concerned with tests and exams leading to grading of students' achievement. However, assessment is much broader in scope, coming into play every time a judgement is made about learning. In this conception of assessment, the vital role is that of providing feedback to learners and teachers
>
> (Atkinson and Lazarus, 1997: 31)

Nowadays, operating in an educational system whose boundaries are defined by a curricular framework and explicit assessment criteria, it is easy to assume that the situation was ever thus. The multiple factors of assessment are now considered so important that they have their own acronym: MARRA (monitoring, assessment, recording, reporting and accountability). Even in adult education – where students traditionally take an evening class in a foreign language for holidays, work purposes or just for fun – assessment has taken on a new importance since LEAs allocate funding for a part-time class only if it is linked to accreditation (Ainslie and Lamping, 1995: 1; Hawkins, 1996: 55). All school curriculum subjects feel the impact of this assessment-driven education system, though MFL assessment displays a few particular characteristics and challenges. In 1990 Thorogood pointed out how assessment took on particular importance now that study of an MFL was, for the first time, to be compulsory for all pupils in the 11–16 age range:

> We teach in a climate in which the pupil and the parent alike want to know what we are doing and why. This is not peculiar to modern languages, but we do teach a subject in which British learners have been notoriously unsuccessful and in which aims and methodology have been widely misunderstood. We are about to (in 1990) teach to all 14–16 year olds a subject which less than half of their predecessors continued with after age 14 and less than a third of their parents ever studied at all.
>
> (Thorogood, 1990: 5)

This chapter traces the development of MFL assessment from a 'secret garden' of norm-referenced, elitism to a transparent, criterion-referenced and inclusive system. Main reference is made to assessment from the age of 11 to the 16+ examination, as post-compulsory education and qualifications are dealt with elsewhere (Pachler, 1999). However, ultimately the conclusion is reached that *'plus ça change'* – the more it changes, the more it stays the same; that despite a decade and a half of major change in MFLs and their assessment, in many respects we have returned to the situation that existed in the mid-1980s. Some of the tensions in MFL assessment are explored, such as the difficulty of assessing the oral element. Questions are posed about the suitability of different assessment systems for the language learning process, such as the fact that terminal examinations and continuous assessment, although sometimes offered with complete parity, may in fact measure very different things.

History of MFL assessment

The history of MFL assessment serves as a brief history of modern language learning and teaching in this country. Teachers joining the profession in the mid to late 1990s entered a system where it was compulsory for all pupils to study a language in Key Stages 3 and 4, with the overwhelming majority of them taking the GCSE examination designed to cater for the whole ability range. Although only small numbers went on to study a language at A level, many more studied a language as part of their GNVQ or NVQ (Hawkins, 1996: 388). However, until the advent of the GCSE, languages were always seen as a 'difficult' subject, with it not being uncommon for pupils to achieve a lower grade in languages than they did for other subjects (Bird and Dennison, 1987: 10). Pachler and Field (1997: 142) point out that much of the blame for this might lie with the examination system: the emphasis on formal grammatical accuracy characterising GCE 'O' level and CSE examination syllabuses has been said to have contributed to a lack of pupils' success in MFL and a lack of popularity of the subject amongst pupils at secondary school.

Public Examinations

Until the advent of the GCSE, the universities exerted a strong hold over public examinations via their examination boards which, from 1950, offered the General Certificate of Education (GCE). This exam was designed originally to select those young people who would be successful at the level of undergraduate study. Therefore the GCE Advanced level in foreign languages was a watered-down version of the common language degree content at that time, literature and translation, heavily influenced by the study of classical languages. The GCE Ordinary level in turn was designed to select those pupils who would make good candidates for study at A level, and so was a diluted version of that exam. GCE O levels in languages consisted of tasks centred around the mastery of grammatical accuracy and translation. Although mark schemes and criteria were not made available to candidates or teachers, it was generally well known that marking was conducted by deducting a mark for each mistake. It was, therefore, theoretically possible to receive a minus mark for a task! Although many learners were stimulated by the academic rigour of this kind of learning and assessment, the implication was that language learning was definitely an academic pursuit and the O level was an examination designed to select the elite, rather than having intrinsic benefit (Hawkins, 1996: 108 and 195, and Bird and Dennison, 1987: vii). The examination catered only for the top 20 per cent of the ability range, and the opportunity to study a MFL was offered to only slightly more than this.

The 'syllabus' for the GCE examinations and the language 'skills' examined would barely be recognised as such by newer entrants to the profession, who never studied O levels themselves. This is well illustrated by the scheme of assessment for the 1970 O level reproduced below (Figure 13.1):

The texts featured in the O level were usually pieces of prose written specially for the exam, rather than authentic or plausible material that we would recognise today. The content in terms of vocabulary and structures was not defined as it is for the GCSE, therefore pupils had to be taught everything just in case it 'came up in the exam'. This led to a great deal of decontextualised rote-learning: I can well remember learning the French and German words for ash, beech, birch, etc, for my O levels, even though I was unable to identify those trees in real life. On the other hand it could be virtually guaranteed that candidates would be called upon to use 'exam favourites' such as 'être en train de faire' during the translation or free composition/picture story. The key to examination success was therefore to learn as much grammar and vocabulary as possible, with some judicious guessing about what might be examined:

> Another criticism which is often levelled at the examination boards is the fact that their modern language syllabuses are scanty or non-existent, and that as a result, examination content can only be surmised from a study of old papers, which come to constitute a very imperfect syllabus.
>
> (Utley, Mitchell and Phillips, 1983: 81)

Associated Examining Board O level 1970

Paper I	Translation foreign language into English	30%
Paper II	Questions in foreign language on foreign language passage (use of language)	20%
	Composition	17½%
	Dictation	7½%
Oral test	Reading (aloud) of a passage Conversation on passage and on 'matters of everyday life'	} 25%

Source: James and Rouve, 1973: 54.

Figure 13.1 A scheme of assessment for GCE O level.

The CSE

With the rapidly advancing comprehensivisation of schools after Circular 10/65, most comprehensive schools wanted to include a foreign language in the curriculum in order to emulate the academic rigour of the grammar schools. Although many able learners did well under the methods and assessment systems of the GCE O level, teachers in school – increasingly called upon to teach a modern language to the whole ability range – were dissatisfied with the emphases and purposes of the GCE. Even though by no means all pupils would continue to study a language until the end of their schooling, a new examination was needed to cater for this wider ability range, and not just one which was a 'watered-down' O level. This took the shape of the Certificate of Secondary Education (CSE) introduced in 1965 and designed to test the top 60 per cent of the ability range (Bird and Dennison, 1987: vii). The CSE's highest grade, grade 1, was designated as comparable to the A, B, C 'pass' grades of the O level. However, even the highest grade of the CSE lacked the necessary currency value amongst employers and parents (Figure 13.2).

A popular solution to the dilemma of the CSE's lowly status was to enter borderline candidates for both the O level and the CSE. This seems an expedient, if expensive, solution, but differences in examinations meant that pupils effectively had to prepare for two very different outcomes. The scheme of assessment for the CSE in 1979 reproduced below (Figure 13.3) reveals the significant differences in the skills and type of language needed for success in the CSE, as compared to the O level described in Figure 13.1 above. Indeed,

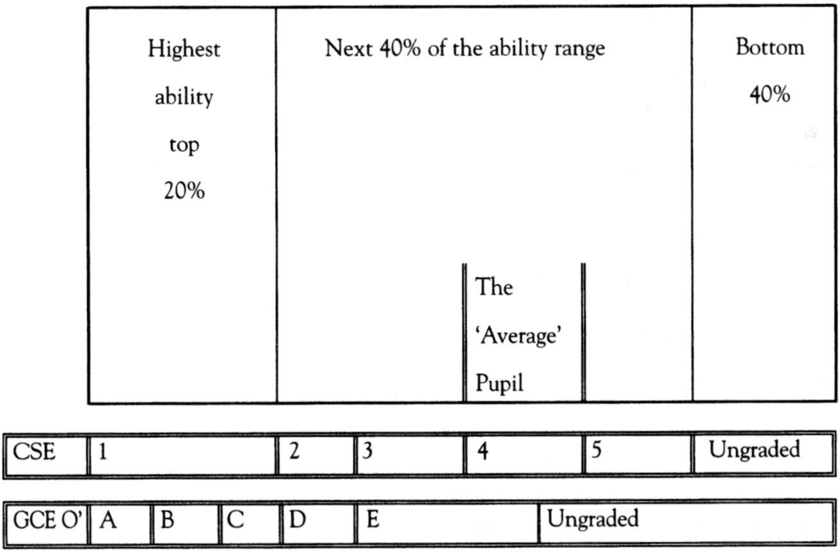

Source: Adapted from Jones, 1994: 20.

Figure 13.2 Comparability of GCE O level and CSE grades.

East Anglian Examinations Board 1979 CSE		
I Oral	Conversation on a single picture	10%
	Role-playing	10%
	Conversation from a set list	10%
II Aural	Listening comprehension, questions and answers in English	25%
III Reading	Written comprehension, questions and answers in English	20%
IV Writing	Composition, short description of 4 unrelated pictures	10%
	Composition, letter to a pen-pal	15%

Source: Moys: 1980, Table 6.

Figure 13.3 Scheme of assessment for CSE.

Whitehead (1996: 202) claims that 'numerous were the candidates for modern languages examinations who obtained a grade C pass at O level, and failed to obtain a grade 1 at CSE level'.

An important difference in emphasis of the CSE boards is that they were set up to serve the needs of schools in their area, rather than the universities. The boards were steered by subject panels consisting of teachers from those schools they served. Schools could enter their candidates for syllabuses and examinations devised by the board, known as Mode I. However, under Mode II teachers also had the opportunity of devising their own syllabuses, from which the board then developed an appropriate exam. In Mode III, teachers could devise both the curriculum and the exam, under the moderation of the board. A figure quoted by Dyson (1970: 25) is that fewer than 10 per cent of French teachers availed themselves of the opportunity to devise their own syllabuses and exams. Dyson puts this down to the large amount of consensus achievable amongst MFL teachers as to what pupils can reasonably be expected to have achieved by the end of five years of study. It is worth pointing out here that teachers are in a good position to judge what constitutes manageability in the examination process, and those teachers devising Mode I and Mode II examinations clearly got it right if only 10 per cent of their colleagues wanted to devise alternatives. It is worthy of note that teacher's autonomy to devise curricula and examinations did not come into question, as at this time there was very little questioning of teacher's fitness to make professional judgements about learning, and few accusations levelled at self-serving professionals.

Nowadays it is all too easy to forget that schools were able to determine their own curriculum, indeed it was argued that the existence of public examinations obviated the need for a centralised curriculum (Bird and Dennison, 1987: vii) – the assessment scheme offered by public examinations *was* the curriculum. But the downside to this was there was often no clear rationale for why pupils should study a certain subject. Teachers interested in the emerging methodologies of audio-lingualism and audio-visualism were dissatisfied with the apparent lack of opportunity in the contemporaneous O level to use the foreign language actively: in the JMB French O level 45 per cent of marks were actually awarded for writing in English, and a further 20 per cent for translation from English (Page, 1970: 8). The 'alternative' O level syllabuses tried to be more progressive by offering a greater element of speaking or reading, at the expense of translation from English.

One of the innovations in trying to develop oral work in the CSE was 'The Hundred Questions.' This was a list of a hundred questions and answers about the pupils' life, interests, etc., prepared by the pupil and learnt by heart, and the examiner selected a few to test in the oral examination. Although all language teachers are aware of the importance of memory in language learning, it is easy to criticise 'The Hundred Questions' as mechanistic rote learning, and indeed there are apocryphal tales of the candidate who managed to transpose wrongly the answers, so that they were 'out of step' with the questions. In the oral test this gave rise to a series of exchanges along the lines of:

Examiner:	Où habites-tu?
Candidate:	Ma matière préférée est la musique.
Examiner:	Quelle est ta matière préférée?
Candidate:	Je voudrais devenir mecanicien.
Examiner:	Qu'est-ce que tu voudrais faire dans la vie?

The rise of the GOML movement

The development of graded objectives and tests was stimulated by a growing feeling that foreign language learning in schools was not proving as successful as many teachers believed it could, and should, be.

(Buckby, 1981: 7)

Even though the CSE was clearly more suited to a wider range of learners, large numbers of pupils still dropped out at the end of year 9, and the CSE examination never achieved the number of entries of the O level (Hawkins, 1996: 381). By the mid 1970s language teachers and HMI shared the concern that:

those pupils who do drop the study of a foreign language after two or three years rarely follow a course which is complete in itself. The DES report (Modern Languages in Comprehensive Schools, HMSO, 1977: 49) recommended that 'precise linguistic objectives should be determined for pupils following the longer and shorter courses . . . taking account of the pupils' aptitudes and need . . .'

(Buckby, 1981: 7)

This heralded the birth of the 'Graded Objectives in Modern Languages' movement (sometimes also 'Graded Attainment in ML'). It is important to emphasise the importance of the GOML movement on the development of modern language education in this country; GOML made language teachers engage with syllabus design, materials production, and more fundamentally, examining the purposes of why pupils were learning a language in the first place. With teachers again at the fore of syllabus and assessment design, they decided that the key features of GOML would be a series of realistic, short-term goals, covering the whole ability range (not unlike the graded music examinations well known in the UK). 'Practical' use of language was a key feature, and like the CSE, pupils were positively marked by receiving credit for showing what they could do in the language, in contrast with the negatively marked O level. Syllabus design centred around transactional language topics, with assessment for each topic. Most GOML schemes permitted pupils to take the test for a particular grade when they felt ready, and some took advantage of mode III CSE to gain accreditation of the higher levels of their GOML courses.

The GOML scheme was tremendously successful not just in this country, but it also influenced the Council of Europe and practice as far afield as Malaysia and Australia (Page, 1996: 102). The practice of setting short-term, realistic targets, with each unit of work rewarded by a certificate not only proved very motivating for pupils, but also engaged the enthusiasm and professional commitment of their teachers, who felt empowered by the scheme (Buckby, 1981: 45). Even more importantly, GOML provided a bridge from the structuralist, norm-referenced, negatively marked O level to the com- municative, criterion-referenced, positively marked GCSE that we would recognise today. It also brought to the fore questions about the benefit of language learning which ranged wider than an effective mode of assessment:

> . . . possibly for the first time, the wider educational – one might say moral – implications of a system like this are set down as quite conscious goals which learners are encouraged to pursue: not only 'coping with problems', 'organising the tasks', ' using pair strategies', but also 'being polite', 'working co-operatively', and 'presenting material neatly'. In this way the planners of the scheme show again that they see pupils not only as language learners but as whole individuals, and language learning as having an effect on their development as individuals.
>
> (Page and Hewett, 1987: 37)

However, the GOML scheme was not without its problems. Buckby (1981: 45) cites the danger that: 'graded tests may come to be used as a sop to pupils of average or below-average ability'. Some teachers worried that the more frequent assessment under GOML might actually heighten tension for pupils, even though pupils were aware that they had an opportunity to retake each test. Most worrying of all was the belief that the topic-based approach of GOML was leaving pupils ill-equipped for language learning at a higher level:

> It was noted also that pupils, except at the simplest level, appeared to be rehearsing language rather than learning how to understand or to manipulate

it in order to create a personal meaning. A similar cause for concern was that in no more than a small number of lessons did abler third year pupils appear capable of producing other tenses than the present and the immediate future.

(Page and Hewett, 1987: 55)

Page and Hewett believe that the lack of a properly conceived methodology for GOML led to the danger that the assessment system became the end in itself (Page and Hewett, 1987: 61). They identified the risk that success was possible in the GOML merely by memory and rote learning:

> . . . GOML schemes run the risk of falling into exactly that danger that HMI identified, that the testing syllabus becomes the teaching syllabus, language practice becomes language rehearsal and implicit restrictions are then placed upon any form of generative or creative language or the transference of items from one context to another
>
> (Page and Hewett, 1987: 61)

This highlights an important issue for MFL teaching and learning: is it necessary to design assessment methods so that they test more than the ability to learn by rote and regurgitate on demand?

Although graded schemes rarely exist in this country now, the GOML movement has left its mark on language teaching in schools, and Page and Hewett believe that the influence of the graded objectives 'philosophy' is to be seen everywhere (1987: 4). Planning teaching around communicative topics is considered to be the norm, and is even enshrined in the National Curriculum Programme of Study and KS3 assessment materials. Teachers nowadays owe a tremendous debt to the innovative spirit and hard work of the groups of teachers who made up the GOML movement.

The advent of the GCSE

There is not room here to analyse the surprising decision of the Conservative government – with its later 'back to basics' movement – to introduce the egalitarian and innovative General Certificate of Secondary Education (GCSE), first examined in 1988. This examination was intended to provide a scheme of assessment for examination of the whole ability range at 16+. The multiplicity of boards were amalgamated into five regional boards: Northern (NEA), Southern (SEG), London and East Anglian (LEAG), Midlands (MEG) and Welsh (WJEC). The GCSE in modern languages, based on a communicative, topic-based approach to learning *authentic* language, was a radical departure from the old O level. Although success in the GCSE still depended on much rote-learning, now it was at least contextualised. The assessment was conducted via four skill areas: listening, speaking, reading and writing, and papers in each skill were offered at both basic and higher levels. However, some boards still jealously guarded facets of the old O level, such as LEAG's picture story which formed part of the writing paper.

The minimum assessable 'core' consisted of the basic listening, speaking and reading papers. The lack of compulsion to be tested in writing is perhaps a hangover from the days of GOML, although omission of the basic writing or any of the higher papers effectively limited the grade a candidate could be awarded. The GCSE was graded on a scale from A to G (the A* grade was not introduced until 1994) and like both the CSE and GOML was positively marked. There were anomalies in the communicative philosophy of GCSE assessment in that the reading and listening papers were a series of questions and answers in English, as were the rubrics for speaking and writing tests. This militated against the use of the target language in the 14–16 classroom which was gaining importance at that time (Ofsted, 1993: 8–9).

It had long been part of staff room lore that to learn how the O level worked, you had to become an examiner. The advent of the GCSE meant that there were no longer any secrets about the way in which marks were awarded: exemplification materials and mark schemes were readily available, and boards held training meetings for teachers. Moreover, boards published syllabuses which contained not just details of the scheme of the assessment, but detailed lists of the vocabulary, notions and functions to be tested at each level in each topic area. In fact, MFL teachers were even trusted to carry out some of the assessment in the oral paper – teachers of other subjects had the option of conducting up to 100 per cent of their assessment via coursework rather than terminal examination. The coursework option was denied modern languages which continued to be assessed via terminal examination until the introduction of a modular GCSE by the SEG board in 1992. The retention of 100 per cent terminal examination in MFL meant that memory and formulaic rote learning still played a huge part in teaching and learning styles in preparing for the GCSE.

Although not without its shortcomings, the GCSE in modern languages was welcomed by teachers who saw it as a fairer and more intrinsically worthwhile mode of assessment. Across all subjects there is some hostility towards the 'profane' GCSE which supplanted the 'sacred' O level (Ball, 1990:45). However, the advent of the GCSE has meant that pupils see themselves as more academic, and are more likely to stay on beyond the age of 16 to study.

The success of the GCSE for modern languages has not increased the numbers of uptake for this subject at A level, though it is common to see a language unit included in both GNVQs and NVQs. Although there is not room here to examine the issues of the 16–19 curriculum, there is an obvious gap between the GCSE and the largely unreconstructed A level, while vocational qualifications lack the credibility of their academic counterparts. If one of the purposes of the GCSE is to prepare for further study, it is worthy of much debate why the GCSE is not successful in this respect.

The National Curriculum

The essence of my argument is the importance of integrating the process of planning, teaching and assessment. Teachers should never lose sight of the fact that they have always prepared, taught, marked, kept a mark book and reported on progress. In principle, the National Curriculum asks little more of them than this.

(Thorogood, 1992: 1)

Teachers had just settled into the demands of the GCSE, which many felt had been introduced with indecent haste giving insufficient time and resources for its implementation (Stoll, 1988: 33), when they were presented with the demands of the first draft of the National Curriculum (in MFL, the 'Harris Report', NCC, 1991). The unwieldy assessment criteria led to fears of 'education by tick-list (Thorogood, 1992: 30). Attainment was measured in ten levels, with teachers commonly claiming that they would be unable to fulfil the demands of the higher levels themselves, especially in their subsidiary languages. This was made necessary by the inclusion of community languages under the umbrella of modern foreign languages. Moreover, it is often overlooked that modern languages are not introduced until KS3 therefore pupils have a shorter length of time to achieve a comparable level of attainment to other subjects. This leads to a fundamental question of the validity of the NC levels for MFL – are the levels awarded in our subject comparable to those in other subjects? Moreover, it is worth considering whether language skills can be assessed independently, as the National Curriculum's four Attainment Targets seems to imply.

Until the Dearing review of the secondary curriculum, all the core and foundation subjects were to be tested via 'standard assessment tasks' (SATs) at the end of KS3. With a list of nineteen languages admissible for study as the foundation subject, the NCC potentially faced the prospect of providing nineteen different SATs every year. For a short period we were promised the apparently farcical solution of 'content-free tests'! Whatever the shortcomings of the original version of the National Curriculum, the principle of profiling pupil attainment expressed positively against agreed criteria in the form of levels of attainment was firmly established. The National Curriculum gave many MFL departments the opportunity to overhaul their schemes of assessment and by 1995 Ofsted were able to report:

> The National Curriculum was influencing the ways in which pupils' attainments were assessed and recorded in Years 7 and 8 in almost all schools. Some relied heavily on assessment materials provided by the commercial course used.
>
> (Ofsted, 1995: 8)

Is assessment in MFL different?

> We all know, of course, that examinations should not influence teaching methods at all. We, the teachers, should aim at teaching our subject to the highest level of competence our individual pupils can attain and external public examinations should arrive as an incidental, objective assessment of that attainment. We all know, equally well, that this is not true.
>
> (Page, 1970: 7)

A common analogy used in talking about assessment, is that it should be the 'obedient servant' since it follows and apes the teaching (Davies, 1968: 5, quoted in Hughes, 1989: 2). Hughes prefers to look upon the relationship as a 'partnership' where testing is 'supportive of good teaching and, where necessary, . . . a corrective influence on bad teaching' (Hughes, 1989: 2). 'Teaching to the test' is a byword for bad practice in the classroom, but this needs to be more closely examined: Hughes lists as desirable qualities of assessment: 'validity, reliability, practicality, and beneficial backwash' (Hughes, 1989: ix). All testing has a 'backwash' effect, i.e. that the teacher's natural inclination is to prepare the learners for what will appear in the test, whether or not this is harmful or what the learners most need to learn (Hughes, 1989: 1 and Davies, 1990: 1). However, there is also a positive side to this effect in that feedback from assessment can have a positive effect on teaching. As has been seen earlier, the shift towards communicative competence demanded assessment more geared towards performance, i.e. the learner's ability to communicate. However, teaching pupils to perform well in such communicative tasks often occurred at the expense of grammatical and structural development. Kalantzis (in de Jong and Stevenson, 1990: 206) proposes that a true measure of communicative competence in the active skills is not just a measure of the overall performance, but also the strategies and skills used in the process of performing that task. It is worth considering whether holistic competence in MFLs can be reduced to separate skills, although the experience of the O level, GCSE, GOML and CSE would seem to dictate that the key skill in examination success is memory and rote learning, whether that is applied to lexis or grammatical constructions.

The NEAB GCSE syllabus includes in its list of aims 'encourage positive attitudes to foreign language learning and to speakers of foreign languages and a positive approach to other cultures and civilisations' (NEAB, 1996: 2).

It also states that some of these 'cannot readily be translated into measurable objectives.' Although it is easy to include some elements of cultural awareness into assessment, how should one assess cultural tolerance? Hawkins' philosophy of 'language apprenticeship' (Hawkins, 1981: 77 and 1996: 121), where learners study a language so they can subsequently apply language learning skills to any language they choose to develop, is an aim to which many teachers aspire. But can language 'apprenticeship' be assessed in tasks simulating 'real' language situations which might be encountered abroad? How, in modern languages, are we to test fairly and reliably the ability to deal with the unpredictable, which is one of the features of communicative competence? Is it possible to test the transferable skills, rather than just vocabulary and structures? However, it remains clear that assessment can make pupils more aware of what they are learning, thereby aiding the development of cognitive skills and the ability to reflect self-critically.

Testing the four skills

Even if we confine ourselves to assessing performance in the four language skills, there are practical difficulties in assessing our subject owing to the large oral/

aural element. Although many of us strive towards the integration of the skills in order to create a more realistic simulation of the use of language, it makes sense to separate out the skills for the purposes of assessment.

The assessment of speaking in particular has long posed problems for MFL teachers: until GOML and the GCSE teachers often felt 'guilty' about conduct-ing oral work: 'in the knowledge that the nearest the student will get to being assessed on such is an unexpectedly difficult or a predictably boring oral (worth 10%)' (Utley *et al.*, 1983: 30). Conducting oral tests in schools for public examinations requires massive amounts of organisation to provide sufficient teacher time, suitable rooms, preparation facilities and supervision for candi-dates etc, and these logistical difficulties have only increased now that more pupils are studying languages up to 16+. However, MFL teachers are supposed to conduct oral assessments regularly, not just at the end of the GCSE course. With a class of 30 pupils, an oral assessment of just 2 minutes per pupil would take a whole hour, and with MFL departments granted on average just 100 minutes or so per week of curriculum time, this amount looks unrealistic. Not forgetting the problem of what to do with the other 29 whilst each individual is being assessed, which even for tutors of adults is an issue (Ainslie and Lamping, 1995: 26). It is also desirable to carry out oral assessments away from the rest of the class, and in 1983 Utley *et al.* suggested that the 'rest of the class are trusted to get on quietly' whilst the teacher is engaged in oral assessment elsewhere (Utley *et al.*, 1983: 66). This suggestion would be unacceptable in the current classroom climate and does not solve the dilemma of finding sufficient time to carry out assess-ments of all the pupils. One solution is to allow pupils to record their oral tasks on to a cassette individually, in pairs or groups, depending on the nature of the task. Although this saves valuable contact time, it still involves a large investment of time and effort on the part of the teacher to mark it. Moreover, if assessment involves being recorded on to cassette, then this should also be a feature of regular classroom activity.

The answer to this dilemma would then appear to be finding opportunities and reliable methods to assess the oral work which pupils are already doing in class. However, even in the heady days of GOML HMI noted: 'with regret that in a majority of schools no oral test was staged on the grounds that it was often felt to be unwieldy' (Page and Hewett, 1987: 55). These problems have still not found a solution in the days of National Curriculum assessment with Ofsted reporting that even in '. . . the best departments, most of the teachers found (integrating continuous assessment into the teaching) difficult, particularly in the case of oral work' (Ofsted, 1993: 12). The long-lived series of course books *Tricolore* 'solved' these problems of oral assessment by asking pupils to write what they would say! (Taylor and Honnor, 1984). Another problem with assessing the conversation element of the oral at GCSE level has been the tendency to regurgitate rehearsed – and often inappropriate – material, satirised by Naomi Adams as a '3,000 word dissertation carefully prepared but sadly never used on 40 different hobbies you've never actually tried (Adams, 1990: 63). Some boards have acknowledged this aspect of learning by incorporating a short prepared presentation in the post-Dearing GCSE oral, a move which has been generally welcomed by teachers.

Speaking is not alone in presenting problems for assessment. As recently as 1983 in the Schools Council study of oral/aural graded tests slightly less than half of the teachers reported that they did not use a tape recorder when conducting aural tests (Utley *et al.*, 1983: 17). Later in the same study (p. 30) teachers argued that there were sound 'educational grounds' for not using recordings of native speakers! However, teachers also complained that, where they existed, the aural tests set by boards were: 'unnatural listening exercises set in multi-choice because it suits the examining board to mark it by computer' (Utley *et al.*, 1983: 30). Whilst it is easy to criticise the examination boards for this 'inept' form of assessment, it does boast the advantage of manageability and ease of marking, both of which are necessary features in any efficient scheme of assessment.

Testing in the target language

> A further paradox arises in the presentation of materials to learners so that they can be assessed. It seems that the more communicative, the more task orientated a test attempts to be, the more English appears on the test paper, assignment sheet or progress card.
>
> (Page and Hewett, 1987: 24)

We have already observed the difficulties of the original GCSE which tacitly discouraged the use of the target language by setting all its rubrics in English. One of the changes in the post-Dearing GCSE was the requirement to have 90 per cent of the answers in the target language. Testing in the target language evokes memories of the O level where it was often possible to render the 'right' answer in comprehension exercises without having understood the text. However, the results of studies by Neather, Woods, Rodrigues, Davis and Dunne (1995) and Powell, Barnes and Graham (1996) would seem to indicate that target language testing has little effect on pupils' ability to cope with the exam. It is worthy of further consideration that the use of target language and rubrics effectively turns any assessment item into a mixed-skill testing environment, i.e. that the candidate has to read and understand the question before being able to attempt an answer. The examination boards indicated from the start that no marks would be deducted in the listening and reading papers for answers written in the target language comprehensible by the sympathetic native speaker. Initial reports of the first cohorts to take the post-Dearing GCSE would seem to suggest that the use of target language rubrics is not presenting undue problems (NEAB, 1997 and SEG, 1997).

Continuous assessment in MFL

> It has been argued on many occasions that performance of the task at any given moment does not guarantee that the learner could still perform the

task at a later date. This is, of course, true of all assessment even of the most traditional sort.

(Page and Hewett, 1987: 29)

The cumulative nature of language acquisition raises questions about the suitability of continuous assessment for MFLs, in addition to those of reliability, flexibility and arbitrary sampling faced by all subjects. Continuous assessment has earned the reputation of being 'necessarily subjective' whilst examinations are seen as 'potentially more reliable especially with "objective" methods' (Palmer, 1970: 56–9). This, however, does not take account of the fact that all decisions on performance are ultimately subjective, whether that decision is taken by a teacher carrying out continuous assessment, an external examiner, or even an Ofsted inspector. Moreover, continuous assessment is frequently misunderstood (Thorogood, 1992: 18, and Page and Hewett, 1987: 24) and instead becomes 'continual testing, which has obvious disadvantages' (CILT, 1970: 70–1). This is best illustrated by Utley *et al.* who cite the following as examples of good practice in continuous assessment: 'Continuous assessment may take a variety of forms, from subjective teacher assessment, through a series of mini- or "waystage" tests, to pupils' progress cards or checklists combined with paired pupil interaction monitored by a teacher/assessor' (Utley *et al.*, 1983: 20).

The current conception of GCSE coursework would appear to be based less on continuous assessment and more on periodic assessment of writing (though this does not mean to imply that either form of assessment has more validity than the other) (Adams, 1998: 3). If the purpose of MFL assessment is to 'assess whether a learner can perform a particular task using language' (Page and Hewett, 1987: 24), it should make little difference whether the candidate is assessed now or later. The main difference here becomes one of memory. In 'real-life' situations a person would usually have the opportunity to look for the necessary words and phrases in a dictionary before embarking on a language 'task' such as describing a problem at the chemists. This raises the question of whether learners should submit themselves for testing in an area when they feel ready, as in the GOML schemes. Again, Page and Hewett:

> Instead of being assessed on a larger amount at the end of the year, the learner is assessed on a series of smaller amounts throughout the year. The tests are still summative but administered at more frequent intervals. In fact, this is the same process that led to graded objectives in the first place: instead of the five year course, a series of shorter courses was suggested.
>
> (Page and Hewett, 1987: 24)

One advantage of continuous assessment is that it can reward 'the process of a learner's learning' (Page and Hewett, 1983: 24 and Palmer, 1970: 57), rather than just the end product. This reflects the view that periodic assessment permits 'assessment motivation' (to be) spread evenly throughout the course and not relegated to the last few months or weeks (Palmer, 1970: 58). If, as Parr says, good practice in assessment usually involves 'gathering evidence over time and making judgements about it based on clear criteria' (Parr, 1997: 2), then continuous or periodic assessment allows the teacher to collect a 'better quality' of evidence. This is reflected in the National Curriculum which now demands a 'rounded judgement' based on the pupil's performance 'across a range of contexts' (SCAA, 1996: 2). However, performance in examination conditions is still seen as being the 'gold standard' of linguistic performance, as one GCSE chief examiner quoted here implies: 'The purist in me says that any linguist worth their salt could write under exam conditions' (Adams, 1998: 3).

Conclusion – plus ça change

Looking at the issues in MFL assessment at the present time, there is an inescapable feeling of 'déja vu'. For example, the recent research on 'The Invisible Child' is reminiscent of GOML as it reveals that pupils leave Year 9 'not well prepared for work in Key Stage 4 and beyond, with its increasing demands on them in terms of knowledge, skills and understanding' (Lee, Buckland and Shaw, 1998: 59). The revised National Curriculum has reinstated the importance of the teacher's professional judgement, but Ofsted (1995: 8) report that in MFL: 'assessment was occasionally being put to formative use (but) there was still much to do'. We still appear to be operating in an environment where the link between assessment and learning is that assessment determines the curriculum – decisions of how a subject is to be tested are made before content and teaching methods are decided.

Practice in KS4 is again in flux since the DfEE's announcement in 1998 that pupils may set aside 'two of MFL, technology or science in order to pursue work-based learning' (DfEE, 1998). This would seem to imply a move away from the hard-fought battle for Languages for All and a return to the study of modern languages reserved for the academically able, at least in KS4. The post-Dearing GCSE also seems to be re-introducing practices of old. The revised GCSE seems divorced from the rest of the NC assessment, using a separate mark scheme, and paying only a passing nod of recognition to the five areas of experience as a way of organising the syllabus. The revised GCSE now puts greater emphasis on the successful application of wider language skills, such as appropriate dictionary use, rather than just rote learning. There is no longer a defined content for higher level, so candidates could theoretically be called upon to read a text or write on the subject of anything. The examination boards are being amalgamated again into even fewer units, although it would appear that boards are still working as before, offering the same exams, but now operate under 'umbrella' names. Tiered testing has been forced on to the examination boards for the GCSE MFL, so regular assessment has gained a new importance in KS4 now that teachers are called upon to take decisions on which tier to enter candidates for in each GCSE paper. The introduction of tiered papers in the GCSE papers is reminiscent of the 'sheep and goats' divide which used to take place in the days of the GCE and the CSE. However, not all teachers are aware that some subjects are exempt from the requirement to offer tiered papers in the GCSE.

To summarise, it would appear that the issues in MFL assessment are many and appear not to have been addressed by the modes of assessment enshrined in the National Curriculum and GCSE: How manageable is it to test regularly in MFL, especially in oral assessment? How far are teachers trusted to take objective decisions in assessment? How far can language competence be described by level descriptors? Do these level descriptors change from one language to another? Do formative and summative assessment in MFL test different skills?

At the classroom level it remains clear that engaging in assessment gives teachers occasion to review not just what we are teaching, but also how and why we are teaching it.

> When attempting to define good practice in managing assessment, we must remember that the purpose of the assessment is entirely dependent on the purpose of learning.
>
> (Ainslie and Lamping, 1995: 20)

Editor's note

Adams demonstrates that teaching and learning styles have been strongly influenced by the assessment methods determined by the government and examination boards over decades. Success rates, and indeed, learner motivation is, at least in part, due to the types and styles of examinations faced by learners. Adams includes an analysis of GCE 'O' levels, CSE, Graded Objectives and GCSE syllabuses, in the form of terminal assessments and as continuous assessment. She is a proponent of continuous assessment, but recognises the need to distinguish between her own preferred approach and the 'periodic' assessment developed by examination boards. What is central to Adams' views is an understanding of the purposes and impact of assessment in terms of the actual learning processes. Assessment must, she argues, serve to improve learning, and as teachers are under pressure to 'teach to the test', the opposite continues to be a risk. Assessment methods do reflect an ideological and pedagogical stance, and it is therefore for teachers to exercise professional judgement if learners are to gain from the assessment process

Linked chapters

Chapter 1, Chapter 10, Chapter 3.

References

Adams, J. (1998) *On Course for GCSE Coursework*, London: CILT.
Adams, N. (1990) 'The German role play, a pupil's view', *Language Learning Journal*, 2: 63.
Ainslie, S. and Lamping, A. (1995) *Assessing Adult Learners*, London: CILT.

Atkinson, T. and Lazarus, E. (1997) *A Guide to Teaching Languages*, Cheltenham: Mary Glasgow Publications.

Ball, S. (1990) *Politics and Policy Making in Education*, London: Routledge.

Bird, E. and Dennison, M. (1987) *Teaching GCSE Modern Languages*, London: Hodder and Stoughton.

Buckby, M. (1981) *Graded Objectives and Tests for Modern Languages: An Evaluation*, London: Schools Council.

CILT (1970) *CILT Reports and Papers 4 – Examining Modern Languages*, abridged proceedings of a conference held at State House, 19/20 March 1970, London: CILT for Committee on Research and Development in Modern Languages.

Davies, A. (1990) *Principles of Language Testing*, Oxford: Blackwell.

DfEE (1998) Letter from Teresa Downing, *National Curriculum: Regulations to Permit the Wider Use of Work Related Learning at Key Stage 4*, 10 September 1998.

Dyson, A. P. (1970) 'CSE Mode III examinations in modern languages', in CILT (1970) *CILT Reports and Papers 4 – Examining Modern Languages:* abridged proceedings of a conference held at State House, 19/20 March 1970, London: CILT for Committee on Research and Development in Modern Languages, pp. 25–9.

Hawkins, E. (1981) *Modern Languages in the Curriculum*, Cambridge: Cambridge University Press.

—— (ed.) (1996) *30 Years of Language Teaching*, London: CILT.

Hughes, A. (1989) *Testing for Language Teachers*, Cambridge: Cambridge University Press.

IEA Education Unit (1988) *GCSE: A Critical Analysis*, Warlingham: Institute of Economic Affairs.

James, C. V. and Rouve, S. (1973) *Survey of Curricula and Performance* London: CILT.

de Jong, J. and Stevenson, D. (1990) *Individualising the Assessment of Language Abilities*, Clevedon: Multilingual Matters.

Jones, B. (1994) 'Modern languages: twenty years of change', in A. Swarbrick, *Teaching Modern Languages*, London: Routledge/Open University.

Lee, J., Buckland, D. and Shaw, G. (1998) *The Invisible Child*, London: CILT.

Moys, A., Harding, A., Page, B. and Printon, V. J. (1980) *Modern Language Examinations at 16+: A Critical Analysis*, London: CILT.

National Curriculum Council (NCC) (1991) *Modern Foreign Languages in the National Curriculum: Initial Advice* (The Harris Report), London: DES.

NEAB (1996) *GCSE Syllabus for 1998 Examinations*, Sheffield: Northern Examinations and Assessment Board.

—— (1997) *GCSE Modern Languages Report on the Examination 1997*, Sheffield: Northern Examinations and Assessment Board.

Neather, T., Woods, C., Rodriguez, I. and Dunne, E. (1995) *Target Language Testing in Modern Foreign Languages*, London: SCAA.

OfSTED (1993) *Modern Foreign Languages Key Stage 3: First Year 1992–93: The Implementation of the Curricular Requirements of the Education Reform Act*, London: HMSO.

—— (1995) *Modern Foreign Languages: A Review of Inspection Findings 1993/4*, London: HMSO.

Oxfordshire Modern Languages Advisory Committee (1981) *New Objectives in Modern Language Teaching*, London: Hodder and Stoughton.

Pachler, N. (ed.) (1999) *Teaching MFL at Advanced Level*, London: Routledge.

Pachler, N. and Field, K. (1997) *Learning to Teach Modern Foreign Languages in the Secondary School*, London: Routledge.

Page, B. (1996) 'Graded objectives in modern languages', in E. Hawkins (ed.) *30 Years of Language Teaching*, London: CILT.

Page, B. W. (1970) 'The influence of GCE examinations on teaching modern languages', in *CILT Reports and Papers 4 – Examining Modern Languages*, abridged proceedings of a conference held at State House, 19/20 March 1970, London: CILT for Committee on Research and Development in Modern Languages, pp. 7–16.

Page, B. and Hewett, D. (1987) *Languages Step by Step: Graded Objectives in the UK*, London: CILT.

Palmer, B. G. (1970) 'The use and efficacy of continuous assessment in CILT', in *CILT Reports and Papers 4 – Examining Modern Languages:* abridged proceedings of a conference held at State House, 19/20 March 1970, London: CILT for Committee on Research and Development in Modern Languages.

Parr, H. (1997) *Assessment and Planning in the MFL Department*, London: CILT.

Powell, B., Barnes, A. and Graham, S. (1996) *Using the Target Language to Test Modern Foreign Language Skills*, Warwick: The Language Centre, University of Warwick.

SCAA (1996) *Consistency in Teacher Assessment, Exemplification of Standards: Modern Foreign Languages: Key Stage 3*, London: SCAA.

SEG (1997) *Chief Examiner's Report Summer 1997 Examinations*, Guildford: Southern Examining Group.

Stoll, P. (1988) 'Two into one does not go', in IEA Education Unit, *GCSE: A Critical Analysis*, Warlingham: Institute of Economic Affairs.

Taylor, G. and Honnor, S. (1984) *Tricolore Assessment Pack 1A Teachers' Book*, Leeds: Arnold Wheaton.

Thorogood, J. (1990) *Recording Progress*, London: CILT.

—— (1992) *Continuous Assessment and Recording*, London: CILT.

Utley, D., Mitchell, R. and Phillips, J. (1983) *Hearsay: A Review of Oral/Aural Graded Tests*, London: Methuen Educational for the Schools Council.

Whitehead, M. (1996) 'Materials and methods 1966–96', in E. Hawkins (ed.) *30 Years of Language Teaching*, London: CILT.

14 Putting technology in its place: ICT in Modern Foreign Language teaching

Stephen Bax

Introduction

Technology is developing apace, to the extent that just when we are accustomed to one device, such as television or the telephone, we find it changing and merging with other forms so as to be unrecognisable. So we can now buy a telephone and email console combined, or a microwave with an integrated computer monitor.

The sheer speed of technological change might be expected to cause unease, even paranoia, but in terms of public attitude the main reaction to these changes has been rather one of enthusiastic adoption, as evidenced in sales of new computers, mobile telephones and similar items. There seems to be a general sense, encouraged by marketing, that technology can solve problems at a stroke, and in general make areas of life easier, more entertaining or more efficient.

In education, too, we are inevitably affected by this 'explosion of modern technology' as Meinhof (1990), puts it and by the accompanying attitude that technology can offer easy solutions. The prevalent assumption appears to be that as technology can solve the problem of entertainment or communication, then it must surely be able to solve the problem of education equally easily. It is seen, in short, as some kind of panacea which will make education quicker, easier and cheaper.

This is not to say that everyone is convinced. Recently, for example, a number of doubts have been expressed about this attitude and about the value of technology, particularly computer technology, in education. For example, Healy refers to the

> unreasonable and unfounded fascination and belief in . . . (computer) technology's educational power at home and school.
>
> (Healy, cited in Haughton, 1999: 2)

She puts forward a number of arguments against the use of computers in education, including the suggestion that 'we are currently spending far too much money (on computer technology) with too little thought' (Healy, 1999: 18), and concludes by saying that

The majority of educational computer use to date has been poorly managed and badly executed.

(Healy, cited in Haughton, 1999: 2)

In short, this kind of argument reminds us that in evaluating the role of technology in education we must resist the popular assumption that it automatically offers easy solutions. To put it another way, we must avoid what I call the 'technical fallacy', namely the tendency, whenever we are faced with a complex human or social problem, to grasp at a single clear solution which appears at first sight to offer the whole answer, but which invariably fails to encompass the complexity of the problem. This is reminiscent of Menchen's well-known remark that:

> . . . there is always a well-known solution to every human problem – neat, plausible, and wrong.

(Menchen, 1920)

The appeal to technology in education could be this kind of mistake.

This does not mean that we should throw technology out altogether. Technology, and 'technical solutions' in general can undoubtedly play some part in educational change. I suggest that in order for them to succeed, however, at least two conditions need to be met, which relate to attitude and action:

1 *Attitude*: those involved in the change (the 'stakeholders') must appreciate the value of technical solutions in general and technologies in particular, but also the limitations. Stakeholders must appreciate the fact that technology can offer at best a partial solution. They therefore need to target technology properly.
2 *Action*: teachers (and others) must attend carefully to all aspects of the change process, including social and interpersonal areas, to ensure that the human elements in the change process are being dealt with as well as the technical.

These maxims have so far not been carefully observed. Healy, already quoted, cites a generally poor result in the use of technology in education, and Meinhof (1990) rightly observes that Modern Foreign Language teaching in particular has not seen as much benefit from technology as might be expected. The principal reason for this, I suggest, has been a failure to tackle the issue of attitude cited above, and a concomitant failure to act in appropriate ways.

This Chapter takes the position, then, that technology (in education in general and in modern foreign language teaching in particular) will only be valuable if it is put in its place. This means, firstly, that it must be seen as only part of the solution – the teacher must ensure that all the other necessary components of the change process are dealt with. Second, we must insist on 'added value' – technology should not merely replace current practice for the sake of novelty, but must contribute to it and improve it. This is particularly true given the fact that technology is often expensive, and that adaptation to it is often time-consuming and difficult.

Against this background, I intend in this chapter to identify ways in which technology can contribute to Modern Foreign Language teaching, and to indicate the other areas of the change process which the teacher must deal with, besides the technology itself – for example, with aspects of the classroom, of methodology, and so on. In other words, I intend to look at how technology can contribute to Modern Foreign Language teaching and how the teacher's role must change and evolve to ensure maximum educational benefit.

I shall structure the discussion according to the principal areas of language teaching as commonly defined, starting with aspects of the language system (grammar, vocabulary and pronunciation), then moving to each of the language skills (listening, speaking, reading and writing). At each point I shall attempt to identify ways in which the technology will mesh with the language teacher's role and ways in which the teacher's role will need to change to accommodate the innovation. Although I shall bear in mind recently expressed reservations about the communicative approach (e.g. Pachler, this volume and Bax, 1999), my discussion will be broadly based within the dominant communicative paradigm familiar to most MFL teachers. Finally, I shall identify particular current technologies which have proved to be valuable (though this area is most likely to date rapidly).

Language system: grammar and vocabulary

Warschauer and Healey (1998), in their cogent and comprehensive analysis of developments in computer assisted language learning (henceforth called CALL) over the last thirty years, divide these developments into three broad phases. The first historical stage is what they term the 'behaviourist' stage, during which the use of computers in language teaching was characterised by drills, repetition and closed question/answer activities – what Healy (1999: 234) calls 'drill-and-practice software', and teachers have been known to call 'drill-and-kill'. Although this has been superseded by what Warschauer and Healey term the 'communicative' and the 'integrative' phases, there is a sense in which much ICT, particularly that which is computer-based, is well-suited to the kind of relatively mechanical 'knowledge-testing' paradigm which typified early CALL software and which still persists, albeit hidden by colour and sounds, in very recent CALL activities. An example is the range of software produced by Syracuse in various languages, another is Linguateach.

How can such approaches assist in the teaching of grammar and vocabulary? A communicative approach to language teaching (see e.g. Mitchell, 1994) would tend to scorn such approaches, but it must be said that they appear to be popular with students, and in terms of reinforcing the learning of grammar and vocabulary they do have a part to play. Just as communicative approaches may have underemphasised the role of grammar (Mitchell, 1994) and vocabulary (Lewis, 1993), so it may unjustly malign relatively mechanical and 'traditional' software. There is surely room here for accommodation, as long as we avoid the 'technical fallacy' described in my introduction, and do not attempt to see this kind of software as the whole solution, but merely one part of the mix, then it can undoubtedly play its part in the teaching of areas of grammar and vocabulary.

In the area of reference works for grammar and vocabulary, technology can certainly add an interesting dimension. CD-ROM dictionaries and thesauri allow learners quickly to access vocabulary, often with spoken pronunciation facilities. The use of hypertext links through which learners can jump quickly to related meanings and contexts has the advantage of speed, and also the added benefit of showing the many ways in which words relate to each other – which is a little more motivating for some pupils that the paper versions. So here there is a clear case for arguing that technology offers something extra.

Such activities must, however, be accompanied by more communicative practice of grammar and vocabulary, and this is where ICT may be less well suited than standard classroom-based activities. Although the World Wide Web (WWW) does offer a variety of grammar practice activities in various languages, such as a 'Grammar Safari' and 'Grammar Quizzes', as well as various vocabulary activities, it is arguable that these are best done orally in face-to-face contexts, in which case the 'live' class may be a better forum for it.

The image we are developing, then, is that of the language teacher knowing the resources available through ICT, and then determining with some precision the ways in which those resources will fit into the language teaching programme, often deciding to do one kind of activity through ICT (such as a relatively traditional grammar or vocabulary practice activity) before or after doing a more communicative activity in the normal classroom, such as a role-play, discussion or communication game to activate the grammar point or the vocabulary item being taught. This may then be followed by a mixed activity, in which some of the class return to the technology (the WWW or CD-ROM, for example) to search for examples of those items in authentic contexts, while others look in newspapers and other non-ICT resources.

Such an approach – already part of much good practice in using ICT in the language class – assumes a 'normalisation', in which teachers and learners treat the technology as merely one of the many learning resources available. It also assumes that the teacher not only has a wide familiarity with available resources but also knows the limitations inherent in the technology, what it can do and what it cannot do, and knows to direct learner activities towards it or away from it at the right times. This is very different from merely adopting the popular view that technology has all the answers, or avoiding ICT altogether – it is putting technology in its place.

Language skills: reading

If we turn to language skills development, we can take the teaching of reading as an example of the attitude and approach to ICT which seems most appropriate for the MFL teacher. As I mentioned above, one criterion to follow when using technology in the classroom is its ability to contribute something different from non-ICT approaches. In the area of reading, although the quantity of reading material available to us is now enormous, via the Internet in particular, this does not necessarily mean that the best approach is to let pupils read on the screen. There is evidence to suggest that with certain kinds of texts this is in fact a cumbersome and relatively unproductive approach, and that on-screen reading is in many ways a skill in itself which students need to develop, and has its own problems (Healy, 1999).

What this tells us is that we need clearly to distinguish the types of reading task we are aiming to practise and develop. If we are aiming at certain of the reading sub-skills as identified by, for example, Grellet (1981: 12–13), we may indeed choose to make use of ICT resources such as the WWW- or CD-ROM-based texts and activities. Skills such as predicting, previewing and scanning, and tasks such as identifying salient points in a text, comparing information and so on, can usefully be done on-line or on-screen. However, other reading skills, particular those involving longer texts, are probably better done on paper. If we look at Grellet's list (Grellet, 1981: 12–13), we could argue that skills which are best taught on paper include reorganising information, reordering events and others. In this case, ICT might serve as a resource for the teacher, with texts being identified and printed, but not used directly.

It is worth noting here the fact that ICT not only now offers different ways to approach the teaching of established language skills – it also requires new skills as well. For example, standard textbooks on teaching reading do not include what is becoming an important new sub-skill, namely that of 'hypertext reading'. This is distinctly different from paper reading as it requires the ability to extract information quickly and to choose in a relatively active way how to proceed on to linked parts of the same text or linked other texts elsewhere, so as to get the required information, and then the ability to go back, further back and then forward again as necessary. When first we sit in front of a hypertext document we realise that this ability requires new strategies, which in fact take some time to acquire, during which period we experience the frustration and waste of time which all readers suffer when learning a new sub-skill. Clearly, this type of reading skill is crucial in this Internet age, and is one which learners must acquire in their own language and in other languages as well. It is a skill which can only be taught through ICT resources, rather than via paper.

This point exemplifies our proposed approach – in the teaching of language skills we need first to devote time to the pedagogical decisions as to which precise sub-skill we wish to develop, which genre to address, which strategy to adopt. Only then can we turn to technology to see if and where it fits with our decisions. A typical plan of action might then end up with these elements, if not in this precise form:

Skimming:
• Start with a long paper-based text on a particular topic.
• Give students three minutes to skim through it then stop them and ask

them to identify three main points or things they found strange (focussing on content rather than form).

- Then turn to the computer terminal and get students to look at a longish text on the same topic on the WWW.
- Again, give them three minutes then stop them and ask them to identify three main points.
- Then ask them, with a partner, to compare the two texts.

(Grellet 1981: 12–3)

This example is not intended to be original, but rather to illustrate in a simple way how a standard approach to teaching skim-reading can be combined in a relatively straightforward way with ICT. It is an example of putting technology in its place – pupils need and will continue to need extensive work on reading paper-based texts, but where technology can offer an additional resource it can fit relatively seamlessly into the procedure, as long as the resources are available.

One area where technology can certainly contribute to the reading classroom is in the range of available texts, the increased variety of accessible text-types, topicality (in the sense of up-to-date materials) and motivation. It is not impossible from a technical point of view to have an 'electronic textbook' in 'digital ink' updated overnight with current affairs materials, chosen in advance by the teacher, for use the next morning in class. It is currently common practice in some schools for the teacher to access new texts, print them out and use them directly. These two practices differ in the extent of reliance on new technology, but they share the feature of offering fresh materials rather than outdated texts which may be less real and less motivating.

While making this point, however, there is a danger that the technological possibilities can push the teacher into the background. Topical texts alone do not teach classes. The success of the procedure depends entirely on the teacher's ability in a number of areas: in identifying the kind of reading skill to be developed and practised, knowing where and how to obtain the right text, devising the methodology for approaching it and setting up and running the activity effectively. These abilities (amongst others) on the part of the teacher are what we need to focus on rather than the technological possibilities in isolation – as Murray and Barnes (1998) put it in the title of their recent article, we need to get 'beyond the 'wow' factor' and concentrate on the pedagogy.

Listening

The general approach which I outlined for reading, in which technology becomes 'normalised' and the methodology and precise skills areas become the key area of focus, seems appropriate for the other skills also. In teaching listening we may follow a standard communicative approach such as those outlined in Rost (1990, 1991) or Anderson and Lynch (1988), but add elements of ICT to increase motivation and authenticity among other things. There are many good listening texts available on CD-ROM (the Language Library series from Vector, for example, or the Entreprise series for French, or The French Experience from the BBC) and now the Internet is a good source for listening texts also.

A typical procedure for teaching listening with ICT resources can be derived from an example of my own practice in teaching English to speakers of the languages. Groups of mixed-nationality adults come to the computerised lab every week for a listening skills lesson based on the news and topical events. In the first week they are shown the technology, particularly how to run and operate the RealPlayer software (from Real Audio, http://www.real.com) on screen. They are then set pre-listening prediction questions about the day's international news such as 'which countries do you think will be mentioned?' After listening to the BBC World Service news summary (http://www.bbc.co.uk/worldservice/ news/) across the Internet they discuss their predictions with the whole class while the teacher elicits and writes notes and vocabulary on the board. After a few more detailed questions the students listen a second time and take notes. Later they might turn to a longer listening text on the BBC World Service Education pages (http://www.bbc.co.uk/worldservice/education/) for more extensive practice.

This scenario is unlike MFL school teaching in some superficial ways – it deals with adults in a well-resourced setting, for example. But as long as the computers are available and connected to the Internet there is no reason why this could not be a regular procedure in school MFL classrooms also. The same news is available on the BBC site and others in all main modern foreign languages, the software is free and easy to use, and the activities are firmly based on standard communicative listening practices (see an interesting example of Real Audio material for French learners: La vie culturelle, http://www.cortland.edu/www/flteach/civ/cultur/cultur.htm)

What the technology is adding are two main things – first students are motivated by very topical authentic material (in the case of the BBC news, updated every hour); second they are able fully to control the speed, volume and so on as in any language lab, so developing a sense of autonomy difficult to achieve when the teacher controls the tape-recorder. They are not simply let loose on the technology as if that is enough – as with the reading example above, what underpins the whole procedure are the teacher's decisions as to text-type, listening sub-skill to be practised, methodological procedure, classroom grouping and so on.

Speaking

Speaking has been given prominence in communicative approaches, and in this area it is arguable that ICT can assist relatively little in MFL teaching. In the case of pronunciation, resources based on CD-ROM or the WWW can help to model the target sound or phrase for imitation, but ICT is generally not reliable enough to replace the teacher in the role of evaluating and then modifying the input to take learners on to the next stage of their pronunciation development.

With regard to general oral skills, if nothing else is clear from communicative language teaching (CLT) it is the point that we learn to speak a language through communication which is as realistic as possible. What this means in essence is communication which is two-way, interactive, evolving in un-predicted ways, with a real purpose and in as real a context as can be provided. These elements are simply unachievable through current technology alone; although some software boasts speech recognition it simply cannot meet the demands which communicative approaches make of it, and in this area the classroom – and human interaction in general – have as yet no technological substitute.

We should not fall into the trap, though, of thinking that since technology cannot do everything in this area, it can therefore do nothing. Some forms of ICT (such as video conferencing, voicemail and so on) which aim not to replace the human element, but merely aim to facilitate interaction at a distance, do allow the teacher to pursue communicative aims with the added motivation of communicating with someone new, to talk about relatively real topics with a relatively real purpose (Butler and Fawkes, 1999). In addition ICT can provide plenty of stimulus for discussion and other speaking activities.

In other words, technology will have a reduced role in the teaching of speak-ing but it may have a role nonetheless – the teacher who is aware of its possibilities and limitations will be able to pull ICT into the lesson appropriately and achieve other aims through more standard classroom work.

Writing

Communicative approaches to the teaching of writing already emphasise the process and the finished product, as well as the audience and their response (see White and Arndt, 1989). Classroom approaches in this model already encourage pupils to write to someone other than the teacher, to offer responses to content rather than form, and to think about the whole process of brainstorming, drafting, responding, redrafting and so on.

In this case technology will only add to the experience if it can contribute something which is not already available, and in fact ICT is in a good position to do this through email and other resources, where the added dimension is that of writing to a real reader in a far more authentic mode than writing for a classmate – the pressing need for real, authentic communication is obvious and motivation is therefore raised (Townshend, 1997).

Besides straightforward email interaction, there are now excellent ICT resources on the WWW for developing writing skills. For example, the EPals website (http://www.epals.com/) offers a forum for schools to contact each other, and even to set up their own private chat areas accessible around the world.

The teaching of writing, more perhaps than the other skills, calls for a longer-term scheme of work in which all participants know their role. The bad old days of 'now write an essay about your holidays', emphasising the product, have generally given way to a more developmental focus on the process, in which students may draft, discuss, compare, rewrite, show to each other, and show to the teacher, over several lessons. The International Writing Exchange (for English – http://www.hut.fi/~rvilmi/Project/IWE/) offers a good example of the tight timetabling and clear choice of topics which are essential if teachers are to feel confident and secure when using a process approach to writing within the new medium, but in addition the teacher needs to have a good grasp of the writing programme and where it is leading and where the students are within it at each stage, to ensure that the huge potential of ICT in developing this skill is properly directed.

Once again, therefore, the vision which seems to offer most promise is of the teacher with a comprehensive grasp of students' language learning needs, a well-elaborated scheme of how those needs can be met over a school term or year, and a precise specification of where and when ICT resources will be called into play to help meet those needs – based on an acute awareness of the strengths and weaknesses of ICT in this area.

The role of the teacher

We have looked briefly at the teaching of the language system, and at each of the four skills in turn, and have emphasised the fact that technology must take its lead from the teacher's decisions about all other aspects of the syllabus and classroom practice. But this assumes that teachers will have a particular attitude towards technology and adopt a particular role towards it – in fact it assumes that teachers will have precisely the attitude and will carry out the actions which I suggested in my introduction are clearly lacking in practice at the moment.

If this is true, it means that the kind of normalisation of technology which I am arguing for, putting technology in its place in language education, is unlikely to happen in the near future, for the simple reason that many teachers probably share the general attitude towards technology which combines excessive respect for its potential with excessive fear of it. To put it another way, the kind of approach I have tried to describe above requires that teachers are knowledgeable about the potential strengths and limitations of technology, and confident in using it to the extent that they can decide on a daily basis to include it in their teaching in precisely the right way and to the right extent.

Few MFL teachers are currently at this level of technological understanding and confidence. This points to the need for some form of teacher development aimed at developing the attitude to ICT referred to above, so that MFL teachers can come to see ICT as a 'normal' resource like any other, to be used in a targeted way for effects determined carefully in advance by the syllabus and methodology.

The wider implications of change

Besides training teachers in the nature of technology, how to be confident in it and how best to integrate it with teaching so that it becomes 'normalised', we need to consider the fact that these changes in current classroom practice will have ramifications in many directions. They will lead to changes in timetabling, resourcing (as I discuss below), attitudes of other staff, attitudes of students and attitudes of parents. As I suggested in my introduction, far from being a panacea, a kind of aspirin which will soothe all pain, technology is rather more like surgery which can have the effect of moving familiar bits to unfamiliar places, necessitating a radical change in attitude and self-perception.

The implication of this is that not only will MFL teachers need to develop their ideas of the place of technology in their work; other staff, students, parents and other stakeholders will also need to change their views, and those in administration and at the heart of this change process will need to be aware of how difficult and slow such attitude change can be, and how they can help the process as 'change agents'. Discussion of how exactly this could be effected would need another Chapter to itself – here it is enough to flag it as an issue which will need attention if ICT is to be truly effective in MFL teaching.

Resources

Another, related issue which our discussion has thrown up is that of resources. My arguments have been based on certain assumptions about the kind of facilities available to teachers. In summary these need to be of the sort that allow the teacher to 'normalise' their use – by which I mean that ICT resources must be available in sufficient quantities, of varied types, with sufficient technical support, sufficient training support, and so on, so that the teacher can in practice, as well as in principle, concentrate on the teaching aspects and simply, naturally, slot the technology into place. An ideal might be the classroom which has computerised and other ICT facilities around the sides so that students can be working on one thing at their desks or tables, then turn at various stages to use the computer or other resources in line with the teacher's plan.

Too often, of course, the technology available is not reliable, not there or not free for use, so that the teacher's preoccupation – as she or he works out how to book that room or beg this piece of equipment – returns to the technical and is dragged away from the teaching once again. With smaller and cheaper ICT equipment now available, the vision of a computerised classroom throughout the school is closer than it used to be, but even when it is on a school's shopping list, it is crucial that those in charge of resourcing have the same vision of how technology can fit into the language classroom as the teacher – for example, they need to see that timetabling the use of ICT once or twice a week is not likely to achieve the kind of integration and normalisation which I have argued for.

Technology in its place?

These are all issues of importance. As I have argued, we need to put technology in its place, to 'normalise' it so that its use assists us in achieving our key pedagogical aims. For that to work, as I have also suggested, we need to ensure that MFL teachers have the right attitude, act in the right way towards the various non-technical areas of change, have the right facilities and the right support from other stakeholders.

But it would be wrong to end on a negative note. There are signs that more teachers are moving towards this normalisation, and are able to resist the false promises of technology on the one hand without rejecting it fearfully on the other. As we get used to new technologies in our daily lives, so we get used to new technologies in the classroom, and as we learn to accept the fact that domestic technology has advantages but also has limitations, so we gradually perceive the value and the shortcomings of educational technology also, and we are then able with more confidence to integrate it into our syllabus and methodological planning, getting beyond the 'wow' factor. This bodes well for the future use of ICT in the Modern Foreign Language classroom since it means that instead of being over-respectful or over-fearful of it we can identify its proper role in our work – which is putting technology in its place.

Editor's note

Bax appeals to teachers to exercise professional judgement when using new technology. He explains that use of computers must add to the value of MFL learning, and not simply serve as a replacement for good teaching. Teachers must too, be prepared to think beyond the constraints of any particular methodology in order to recognise the potential of ICT in the languages classroom. Bax realises the need to develop teachers' own understanding and technical skills, but notes optimistically that school teachers' levels of competence are improving apace. He presents ideas and activities, with reference to software and websites which serve to improve learning. HE relates activities to the key tenets of the communicative approach, and demonstrates the potential for use as part of a process of independent and autonomous learning. The suggestions are not idealistic, in that they are tempered by the need to evaluate and relate current practice as a means of justifying technological change in the classroom. Included with this critical analysis is much practical guidance and support in terms of accessing up to date material and communicative activities.

Linked chapters

Chapter 1, Chapter 15.

References

Anderson, A. and Lynch, T. (1988) *Listening*, Oxford: Oxford University Press.
Anivan, S. (ed.) (1990) *Language Teaching Methodology for the Nineties*, Singapore: SEAMEO.
Bax, S. (1999) 'The end of CLT? A Context Approach to English language Teaching', Conference Paper, IATEFL Conference, Edinburgh, April 1999.

Butler, M. and Fawkes, S. (1999) 'Videoconferencing for language learners', *Language Learning Journal*, 19: 46–9, Rugby: Association for Language Learning.

Grellet, F. (1981) *Developing Reading Skills: A Practical Guide to Reading Comprehension Exercises*, Cambridge: Cambridge University Press.

Haughton, E. (1999) 'Look what they've done to my brain, ma', *The Independent*, education supplement, 3 June 1999, p. 2.

Healy, J. (1999) *Failure to Connect*, New York: Simon and Schuster.

Lewis, M. (1993) *The Lexical Approach: the State of ELT and a Way Forward*, Hove: Language Teaching Publications.

Meinhof, U. (1990) 'Television news, the computer and foreign language learning', in S. Anivan (ed.) *Language Teaching Methodology for the Nineties*, Singapore, SEAMEO, pp. 250–68.

Menchen, H. (1920) *Prejudices: Second Series*, New York: Knopf.

Mitchell, R. (1994) 'The communicative approach to language teaching', in A. Swarbrick (ed.) *Teaching Modern Languages*, London: Routledge.

Murray, L. and Barnes, A. (1998) 'Beyond the 'wow' factor – evaluating multimedia language learning software from a pedagogical viewpoint' *System*, 26: 249–59.

Nuttall, C. (1996) *Teaching Reading Skills in a Foreign Language*, 2nd edn, London, Heinemann Educational.

Rost, M. (1990) *Listening in Language Learning*, London: Longman.

—— (1991) *Listening in Action: Activities for Developing Listening in Language Education*, New York: Prentice Hall.

Townshend, K. (1997) *E-mail. Using Electronic Communications in Foreign Language Teaching*, London: CILT.

Warschauer, M. and Healey, D. (1998) 'Computers and language learning: an overview', *Language Teaching*, 31: 57–71, also available at: http://www.lll.hawaii.edu/web/faculty/markw/overview.html.

White, R. and Arndt, V. (1991) *Process Writing*, Harlow: Longman.

Software and websites

BBC education: http://www.bbc.co.uk/worldservice/education/

BBC news: http://www.bbc.co.uk/worldservice/news/

Epals: http://www.epals.com/

International Writing Exchange: http://www.hut.fi/~rvilmi/Project/IWE/

LinguaTeach : Beaumont Software, Language Support, Nottingham, UL.

Real Audio: http://www.real.com

Syracuse: *Games in English* (and also in Spanish, German, Japanese and French) Syracuse Language systems. Website: http://www.syrlang.com/

Grammar Safari: http://deil.lang.uiuc.edu/web.pager/grammarsafari.html

Grammar Quizzes: http://www.aitech.ac.jp/~itesl/quizzes/grammar.html.

Software

The Language Library – Vector Multimedia, Lancashire.

Entreprise Multimedia Study Pack, OUP/ Wild Strawberry.

The French Experience, BBC Education.

La Vie culturelle: http://www.cortland.edu/www/flteach/civ/cultur/cultur.htm

15 Towards independence in language use and language learning

Vee Harris

The aim is learner autonomy – learner autonomy is the only means possible.
(Dam, 1990: 20)

Those aspects of the Programmes of Study concerned with increasing pupils' independence and encouraging more ambitious use of the target language were largely absent from the work in Years 10 and 11.
(Ofsted, 1993: 8)

Communicative competence and learner autonomy

It is hardly surprising if we read the list of forty statements in the National Curriculum Programme of Study part 1 without pausing to consider in detail the implications of statement 3C; that pupils should have opportunities to 'develop their independence in language learning and use' (DFE, 1995: 3). So it may be worthwhile starting this chapter by exploring if there is a relationship between independent language learning and independent language use; if autonomous learning and communicative competence are somehow inextricably linked. We have seen in earlier chapters that 'knowing' a foreign language has come to mean not only grammatical competence, but sociolinguistic, discourse and strategic competence (see Canale, 1983). A learner cannot be said, for example, to 'know' a language if they are unable to engage in a conversation without whispered prompts from the teacher; or to repair for themselves breakdowns in communication, or to read authentic (rather than 'doctored') materials from the target language country, without constantly needing to resort to a dictionary. Learners may make mistakes, they may not understand everything that is said to them or that they read, but they must have sufficient confidence and competence to be able to choose both what to say and how to say it. And they have to be able to navigate their own way through the complex and unpredictable nature of the language world that surrounds them. In other words learners have to function independently. One might also argue that given 'knowledge' of the language is never perfect and pupils may encounter new contexts in which they must operate, they need also the confidence and competence to continue learning the language independently. This may involve recognising 'gaps' in

their linguistic repertoire and knowing how to go about bridging
by referring to appropriate grammar books or textbooks, liste,
recordings or consulting native speakers.

Given such linguistic and educational autonomy is the ultimate
process of working towards it must necessarily involve the learner in
choices. A pre-packaged diet which involves them in rote learning of p..rases
that the teacher has chosen, and never requires them to engage in the struggle to
find the means to express their own identity, to 'create oneself in and through'
the target language (Grenfell 1991: 7) is unlikely to enable them to develop the
necessary independence either as language learners or language users.

The need for choice not only in the content of what is learned but also the
methods and materials to learn it, is all the more important given what is known
of the language learning process. The debate over acquisition versus learning
has been rehearsed in Chapter 11, but it is clear that whatever methodology is
used, what learners make of the input will vary. For each individual it will be a
messy and unique experience. Pieces of the language only 'slot' into place when
the learner is ready. However much we may drill a particular grammar point, it
will not be acquired until the learner has reached the appropriate stage in terms
of their own internal mental development. As Barnes pointed out as early as
1976, in relation to learning generally:

> To learn is to develop a relationship between what the learner knows
> already and the new system presented to him, and this can only be done by
> the learner himself.
>
> (p. 81)

This is no less true for language learning. We know too that people have a
range of different learning styles (see, for example, Skehan, 1989); what suits
one language learner may be unhelpful for another and each may need a
separate 'diet'. Common to all learners, however, is that it is the personal need
to make sense of and make sense in the target language that drives the
acquisition process forward (see Grenfell op. cit.).

The concern to foster autonomous learning is not limited to the British
secondary school context. The recent publication, Modern Languages: Learning,
Teaching, Assessment. A Common European Framework (Council of Europe
1996) invites users of the framework to:

> consider and where appropriate state the steps they take to promote the
> development of pupils/students as responsibly independent language learners
> and users.
>
> (section 6.7.4.: 94)

The arguments then for autonomous learning, both as a means and an end,
seem convincing. Learners are unlikely to become communicatively competent,
if they are not faced with genuinely communicative demands. Genuinely

communicative demands require them to make choices independently of any support. Why is it then that we feel the need to choose the topic to be learned, predict the language to be used and determine the activities the pupils will undertake? Why is it that we feel obliged to carefully 'spoon feed' pupils with neat, self-contained parcels of language? For this is the picture that emerges whether from the Ofsted report quoted earlier, or Mitchell's observation (1994: 40) that:

> versions of the 'communicative approach' are producing learners who can do little more than reproduce unanalysed global phrases, and have not yet internalised a creative language system (ie a grammar) which will allow them to produce original utterances correctly in situations of open and unpredictable target language use.

Developing autonomous classrooms: the teachers' perspective

The GCSE examination and the National Curriculum

The possible explanations for the current difficulties in fostering independent learning are complex and cannot be fully rehearsed in one chapter. The nature of the GCSE examination may be one factor. On the one hand, the clear identification of topics, tasks and functions was welcomed by many teachers as a significant step forward compared to the traditional O level exam. On the other hand, it could be argued that the very fact that the tasks and topics are predetermined has created a straitjacket for us. Although there are examples of teachers working creatively within the syllabus (see the case study of Christiane Montlibert's classroom in Page, 1992) there is little that actively encourages them to do so. To take one obvious example, assessment of a pupil's oral competence at the end of five years of language learning takes the form of a 'one-off' interview between teacher and pupil. It is often little more than an interrogation, where the teacher has to fire a battery of questions that can be readily answered provided certain stock phrases have been rote learned. The kind of spontaneous interaction discussed for example in Burch (1994), is not a requirement.

The advent of the league tables, where GCSE results are compared across schools, may have compounded our fears of exploring new approaches. Understandably, it can seem 'safer' to work one's way through a coursebook, geared specifically to the GCSE syllabus, than to engage in a constant process of negotiating with the learners both what is to be learned and how. The model that teacher 'input' will lead directly to 'output' from the pupils is also much easier to work with than something that would have to take into account the messy and individual nature of language learning. Similarly, the paradigm of the 'three P's' (Presentation and Practice of the language leading finally to Production), where the class works through the same activities at the same pace, is easier to structure and to organise than a situation where different groups of pupils are working on different activities. It takes a very experienced and confident teacher to reconcile the demands of the GCSE examination with the desire to encourage independent learning.

Although the National Curriculum Programme of Study part 1 includes the need to 'develop their independence in language learning and use' (3C), this is but one in a list of forty other learning opportunities that pupils should be offered. Furthermore, the very presentation of the Programme of Study in the form of a list under four headings (Communicating in the Target Language, Language Skills, Language Learning Skills and Cultural Awareness) makes it harder to see the intimate connections between statement 3C (hidden as it is in the middle of the list) and some of the other opportunities. Table 15.1 attempts to make some of these relationships more explicit.

Although Ofsted inspectors are quick to comment if teachers fail to offer the full range of opportunities in the Programme of Study part 1, not least 3C, preparation for the inspection process itself and the implications of a poor report place heavy burdens on them both in terms of time and stress. It may leave little space for reflecting on the rationale underlying the statements or for the kind of 'risk-taking' implicit in developing a more autonomous classroom.

Motivation

A further inhibiting factor may stem from our anxiety about pupils' motivation. Some would argue that Dam's success in developing her pupils' autonomy is dependent on the fact that they are learning English in Denmark and hence their motivation is higher than British secondary pupils. Many teachers here are anxious to 'keep it simple' in order to avoid pupil disaffection the minute they are faced with a task they perceive as 'too difficult'. We have consequently

Table 15.1 Regrouping some statements in the National Curriculum Programme of Study part 1

Statement number	Statement
Independence in language use	
1e	use everyday classroom events as a context for spontaneous speech
2c	ask about meanings, seek clarification or repetition
2g	initiate and develop conversations
2o	vary language to suit context, audience and purpose
3i	develop strategies for coping with the unpredictable
3g	use their knowledge to experiment with the language
Independence in language learning	
2a	listen attentively, and listen for gist and detail
2n	redraft their writing to improve its accuracy and presentation
3b	acquire strategies for committing familiar language to memory
3d	use dictionaries and reference materials
3e	use context and other clues to interpret meaning

managed to develop a range of what Johnstone (1989) refers to as 'problem-reducing strategies', making extensive use of mime and gesture to ensure immediate comprehensibility of target language instructions, for example. But unless this support is gradually withdrawn, pupils may never learn to infer meaning by listening to clues from the language itself. They may come to rely totally on any native speaker being prepared to engage in a lively 'song and dance' act! Similarly, to avoid pupil embarrassment when they struggle to answer a question, Johnstone (p. 25) notes that we tend to carefully scaffold the interaction; with the result that the pupil hardly produces any language at all:

> Et le meilleur programme pour toi, c'était . . .?
>
> Eastenders
>
> Bon alors . . . Eastenders . . . Tu aimes ça, Paul . . .?

Such scaffolding is unlikely to prepare pupils to cope with the demands of real language use. It is interesting to consider whether this approach, however well meaning, may in fact have been counterproductive in the struggle to increase motivation, particularly by Key Stage 4. With the best of intentions, we may have actually increased pupils' disaffection by presenting them with simplified and often trivial language, that they are well aware bears little resemblance to 'the real world'. After all, it is hardly natural to tell each other what time we brush our teeth.

If the teacher feels such scaffolding is indispensable even for successful whole class interaction, how much more daunting is the prospect of leaving pupils to work on their own? Their fears may appear confirmed when, often prompted by negative comments in an Ofsted report, they embark on 'group work', frequently in the form of a 'carousel' of activities. Here they may immediately be faced with cries from pupils of 'What do we have to do?' and 'I can't do this' which are unlikely to reassure them.

First steps?

I have argued in the past (Harris and Noyau, 1990; Harris, 1996) that the 'carousel' may be a legitimate 'first step' towards autonomy. However in recent years, I have become less and less convinced of its value. My concerns about the 'carousel' stem from five observations:

1   Some teachers find it difficult to move on from the carousel to more genuinely autonomous ways of working. It becomes a final rather than a first step;

2   On a pragmatic level, it usually involves teachers in a great deal of time-consuming work, such as photocopying of resources etc;

3   Even where pupils work their way through a predetermined menu of activities, taken from the textbook, the choice is usually limited to doing an

easier or a harder activity, or working on one skill area rather than another. There may be no requirement for pupils to base those choices on a careful review of their own strengths and weaknesses and an informed under-standing of what will help them most;

4   There may be no outcome or purpose to the menu of activities, such as giving a presentation, writing a booklet for younger pupils or another class or making a video; pupils simply 'do a listening, a reading';

5   Whilst initially pupils enjoy the opportunity to work together, the 'novelty' value may wear off after a number of weeks and they are mechanically working their way through the tasks, as mindlessly as they would in a teacher-directed classroom.

These concerns point in the same direction: pupils are not genuinely engaged; both because they neither have a real 'say' in their learning nor any sense of responsibility for it. These are two sides of the same coin. Autonomy implies freedom to choose; choice implies the ability to make sensible decisions. Such decisions may include 'I am finding x difficult, so I need to do . . .' or 'what area would really interest me, so I would devote proper time and effort to it?' Without some understanding of how to learn, how to monitor your learning and what to do to improve it, responsible decisions are impossible. We will return to this theme when we consider the potential contribution of strategy instruction to the development of autonomous learning.

As a result of these observations, I have come to question how fruitful a 'first step' it is to superficially restructure the way the classroom is organised but without any fundamental changes in who makes choices over what. It may be preferable to retain the familiar teacher-centred structure, but to introduce small elements of genuine choice. For example, pupils can choose a text of personal interest from a magazine and devise a set of questions on it for their partner to answer. Or they can have a choice of three homeworks, one of which is to make a game for a group of pupils to play in the subsequent lesson. Nunan (1995) draws on a number of studies to indicate other ways of moving along 'the learner-centred continuum'. These include inviting learners to evaluate their own progress at the end of a unit of work and showing them how to activate their language outside the classroom.

The introduction of the written form

A final factor that may be holding some of us back from offering more autonomy is a concern over the introduction of the written word. A common assumption held about the communicative approach is that the emphasis should be on oral work (see Mitchell, op. cit.). New language should first be introduced and practised orally, before pupils see the written form. The argument is that it should be withheld until accurate pronunciation has been ensured through careful oral drilling. Of necessity, this means that all the language pupils will use has to be predicted in advance so that it can be practised orally first. One of the problems of a more autonomous classroom is that individuals or groups request French or German phrases that are specific to their own needs and interests. The teacher is understandably concerned that they lack both the time and the means to practise all such phrases orally with the whole class. They would therefore have to resort to writing it down. Little (1997) however describes how Dam and Thomson make use of the written word from the earliest stages of pupils' language learning. In a complex argument drawing on Vygotsky's work, Little argues for the early introduction of writing for two reasons (over and above the fact that most children are already literate in their mother tongue). First, provided it is strongly interactive as in Dam's classroom, it 'requires us (among other things) to internalize the dialogue of social interaction as psychological process' (p. 7). If learning is an internalisation of what was originally a social process, collaborative writing has an important role to play. Second, it encourages a focus on linguistic form and consequently helps foster the development of metalinguistic awareness.

Thus far, we have focussed on possible explanations for the lack of autonomy in our classrooms in terms of teachers' concerns and preoccupations. I want now to turn to the learner. A clearer understanding of how they learn may help to address some of these concerns.

Becoming an autonomous learner: the pupils' perspective

In 1989, I was involved in a project to support a group of London teachers in developing a degree of pupil autonomy in their classrooms. Although pupils' initial responses were promising, we soon began to realise that they lacked a number of key skills, if they were to be able to take advantage of the opportunities being offered, rather than panic at the prospect of tackling language tasks unaided (Grenfell and Harris, 1993). These ranged from basic 'study skills', such as the use of a dictionary, to the ability to infer meaning from the context of a reading text or even to being able to work together in groups collaboratively. Our observations connected directly with research to identify the characteristics of the 'good language learner', that has been taking place over the past twenty years. Much of this research is based in America, often studying adult learners of English (see for example, Stern 1975 and Rubin, 1981). The aim is to identify what it is that successful language learners do that their less successful peers do not; the strategies that they use to tackle the task of coping in a new language. Oxford (1993: 175) defines these strategies as:

> Specific actions, behaviours, steps, or techniques that students employ – often consciously – to improve their progress in internalizing, storing, retrieving, and using the L2.

A number of ways of categorising strategies have been developed. One taxonomy (O'Malley and Chamot, 1990) divides them into metacognitive strategies, cognitive strategies and social and affective strategies. Metacognitive strategies are used to reflect on the learning process, to plan how to approach a task and to evaluate how well one has performed it. Cognitive strategies are involved in grappling with the language itself and include 'inferencing' and 'transfer', as well as what might be termed 'study skills' such as 'note-taking' and using dictionaries and other reference materials. Social and affective strategies involve seeking help from others and managing feelings such as anxiety or the need for self-motivation associated with language learning. Many of the strategies they identify relate to statements in the Programme of Study part 1.

Common to all these studies is the sense that a 'good' language learner is:

> one who takes personal decisions, in an implicit or explicit manner, regarding what to do to facilitate learning in whatever context they find themselves. They know what to focus on and which strategies might apply at any particular stage of the learning experience. They actively seek information, opportunities to practise, and assistance from available resources, including people around them and from printed documentation. This description presupposes an individual development plan, which in many respects is self-determined. The implication of this realisation is that lessons and teaching which are mostly directed by the teacher who chooses what is to be learnt, when and how, runs counter to this form of individualised linguistic development rather than enhancing it. In other words, many of the characteristics of the good language learner are discouraged rather than promoted in the teacher-centred classroom.
>
> (Grenfell and Harris, 1999)

Strategies then add a third dimension to the relationship between the autonomous communicatively competent language user and the autonomous language learner, for the autonomous language learner has at their disposal a raft of strategies to facilitate their learning. Indeed, a number of studies (see for example O'Malley and Chamot, op. cit.) suggest that whereas the high attainer has a wide range of strategies used frequently, the low attainer has a much more limited repertoire and makes use of them less often. Furthermore, high attainers adopt a multipurpose approach, using strategies in combination rather than isolation (see Graham, 1997). It would be misleading to suggest, however, that learners are aware of the strategies they are using. Indeed, one could almost surmise that the more proficient the learner, the more successfully they have internalised strategies to the point that they are able to activate them immediately. They do not need to go through the time consuming process of analysing the task to identify the most relevant strategies to deploy and then consciously putting them into operation. Furthermore, Seliger (1983) argues that it is often only the most articulate and reflective of learners who are able to make explicit how they tackle their own learning.

If learners are not always aware of the strategies they use, if the most successful have a wider range of strategies than their less successful peers, if these allow them to tackle language learning independently, then the issue is raised of whether we should intervene directly and teach learners how to learn more effectively. Would the pupils involved in the Flexible Learning Project for example have benefited from clear instruction in the use of strategies? If pupils are to make sensible decisions as to what to learn, when and how, do they need some support in evaluating their own strengths and weaknesses (metacognitive strategies), in knowing which cognitive strategies to deploy for which task and in developing the social strategies that will allow them to work collaboratively in groups? Could they be enabled not only to understand their own preferred learning styles and the strategies that match them but also even to develop other ways of learning that may help make them more successful in tackling areas where they are less comfortable?

The issue of the potential value of strategy instruction (SI) has not gone uncontested. Some of the debates will be rehearsed towards the end of the chapter. First, it may be helpful to provide an example of what SI looks like in practice. The principles underlying this particular model of SI and its place in the curriculum will then be discussed and related to the debates.

Illustrations of what we have come to call the 'cycle of strategy instruction' across a number of skill areas and levels can be found in Harris, 1997 and Grenfell and Harris, 1999. Here the focus is on memorisation skills. The key role memory plays in communicative competence is evident. Yet we often set pupils the task of learning new words for homework, without knowing how they approach such a task. Research (Low et al., 1993) suggests that while the class as a whole may report using up to fifteen strategies, each pupil may only be employing two or three. Table 15.2 describes the cycle of strategy instruction in relation to memorisation strategies, and explains the context for Table 15.3 and Figure 15.1

From practice to principles: strategy instruction in theory

We have only seen the cycle of SI illustrated with one particular skill area. Nevertheless, it may be possible to begin to identify some of the theoretical principles underlying this model of SI. The most fundamental is that rather than being a 'bolt-on' addition to an otherwise traditional teacher-centred classroom, SI should be part and parcel of a shift towards an autonomous classroom, with communicative competence at its core. It is not a matter of selecting a discrete number of strategies and teaching them in order to improve examination results. As Little (1996: 26) warns: 'Some pedagogical traditions have devoted so much time to the explanation, illustration and memorization of grammar rules that no time has been left to develop communicative ability; much the same danger attends the current obsession in some quarters with "strategy training".'

There is a danger that strategy instruction is seen as an 'instant panacea' to some of the limitations in the current implementation of CLT discussed at the beginning of the chapter. In the worst of scenarios, we would spend a couple of lessons telling pupils about strategies and assume that they would then successfully deploy them. But SI should be part of a process by which learners are empowered to take control of their learning and develop the confidence and

Table 15.2 Strategy instruction in action: memorisation strategies

Step	Activities
1 Awareness raising	In the first step, pupils are set a task 'cold' (such as learning 10 items of vocabulary). Instead of the teacher testing them the next day, they are asked in groups to share the strategies they used to go about memorising the words. An initial checklist is built up on the board.
2 Modelling	This step often leads automatically into the second step of modelling, as pupils demonstrate to each other how 'their' strategies work. There may be other strategies however, that none of the pupils are using so the teacher must be prepared to model them. They may, for example, not be aware of the value of word and visual association. When trying to remember the Spanish for alarm clock, for example, (despertador), I find it helpful to think of someone 'spurting to the door' when the alarm goes and drew a picture to remind me. It is at this point that the teacher also needs to make explicit the purpose of SI, explaining the benefits of widening their repertoire of strategies.
3 General practice	Each group of pupils is assigned a different strategy to use to learn a further 10 words. The groups then compare their experiences. In another lesson, pupils work in pairs choosing a list of 10 words to learn. Each pupil must try out their partner's preferred strategies. In subsequent learning homeworks, pupils have a checklist and tick off the strategies they used to ensure they are still practising them.
4 Action planning	Pupils then select for further focussed practice those strategies that will help address their particular problems. They may need some initial guidance in this (see Table 15.3), since not all pupils appreciate that if their problem is pronunciation, copying the words out over and over again will do little to help them. They then draw up their action plan, which includes identifying how they will know if progress has been made (Figure 15.1).
5 Focussed practice and fading out of the reminders	Opportunities for pupils to practise their particular memorisation strategies can be readily integrated into the lessons. For example, if they finish a worksheet or a speaking task before the others, they identify the five words they think they will find hardest to remember and use the strategies from their action plan to learn them. The teacher gradually stops reminding pupils to practise their strategies, since the aim is that they should reach a stage where they have been successfully internalised and can be drawn on automatically without prompting from the teacher.
6 Evaluating strategy acquisition and recommencing the cycle	At some point, teacher and pupil return to the action plan to judge whether the strategies have been assimilated and progress has been made. If it has, a new action plan can be drawn up. A low attainer, for example, may initially have wanted simply to focus on remembering the meaning of words. S/he can then move on to accurate spelling, or gender. If progress has not been made, then teacher and pupil can discuss what is going wrong and identify possible solutions.

Table 15.3 Guidelines for pupils in selecting strategies for their action plan

Mes difficultés	Les meilleures stratégies
Comment mémoriser les mots difficiles	• Associer à un mot anglais et dessiner une image
Comment mémoriser le genre	• Associer aux couleurs (vert=masculin, rouge=féminin)
Comment écrire le mot	• Écrire mot plusieurs fois • Utiliser la mémoire photographique
Comment prononcer le mot	• Répéter le mot • Inventer une chanson • Écouter la cassette

the competence to operate independently in the target language. Viewed from this angle, certain debates within strategy instruction (outlined in O'Malley and Chamot, op. cit.) appear easier to resolve.

The purpose of strategy instruction should be made explicit to pupils

In 'embedded' instruction, learners are presented with activities and materials designed to elicit the use of strategies but are not informed of the reasons underlying the approach. It is difficult to see however, how such instruction could help pupils develop the metacognitive strategies of planning, monitoring and evaluation discussed earlier. Active involvement in discussing how they learn plays an essential role in deciding what to learn. The action planning step allows them to take personal responsibility for their own progress and to understand themselves as learners better. Furthermore, if it is the case that success depends not on the use of one individual strategy but rather the effective management of a repertoire of strategies, then learners need to be able to make conscious, informed choices. An explicit understanding of learning strategies gives them the freedom to transfer strategies from the training context to any other appropriate settings they may encounter and to develop the ability to choose which strategies are most appropriate to the task in hand without constant guidance from the teacher. Finally making explicit the rationale for SI

Mon Plan d'Action
Nom;
Date;
Je veux développer ....ma prononciation
J'ai choisi les stratégies suivantes; écouter la cassette, inventer une chanson
Je saurai que j'ai progressé parce que j'hésiterai moins pendant les jeux de rôle

Figure 15.1 Action plan.

can do much to improve motivation, particularly for low attainers. As Rubin (1990: 282) points out:

> Often poorer learners don't have a clue as to how good learners arrive at their answers and feel that they can never perform as good learners do. By revealing the process, this myth can be exposed.

Strategy instruction should involve interactive, collaborative learning

If, as Vygotsky asserts, learning is an internalization of what starts as a social process, then learners need regular opportunities to 'borrow each other's consciousness', to share the strategies they use to tackle their language learning, hence the importance in the cycle of group and pair activities. His notion of the zone of proximal development means that pupils also need to interact with the teacher, who can judge the moment at which to fade the reminders. Learning new strategies is no different from learning anything else. When we learn to drive a car, the instructor may tell us how to work the brakes and the clutch but we need constant reminders and feedback before the process becomes automatic. Step 6 where teacher and pupil discuss the success of the action plan provides one context where this feedback can take place. Clearly such one-to-one interaction is harder to organise in the traditional teacher-centred classroom than in one where pupils are used to working on their own.

Strategy instruction should be part and parcel of the modern language curriculum

If the principles above are to be implemented, it follows that strategy instruction should be integrated into everyday modern language lessons. 'Separate' instruction takes place before or parallel to the language lesson. Holec (1996: 99) indicates some advantages of integrated instruction in providing learners with opportunities to: 'draw upon, experiment with and immediately apply in his language learning what he has learnt in learning to learn'.

Again, we are reminded here of the relationship between language use and language learning. However valuable a general 'study skills' course may be as part of personal, social and health education, pupils still need the opportunity to directly apply their knowledge on a regular basis. That said, greater cross-curricular collaboration could help reinforce strategies common across subjects and facilitate the development of a coherent whole school policy.

As much as possible of the strategy instruction should be in the target language

If strategy instruction is to 'pay its way' in terms of feeding into the development of communicative competence, if full advantage is to be taken of the opportunities it provides for collaborative reflection, then a central role must be accorded to the use of the target language. Discussing what and how to learn is, after all, one of the few classroom activities that requires learners, as Clark (1984) puts it, to use 'language for a purpose beyond that of merely practising forms'. A study by Vandergrift and Belanger (1998) appears to suggest that this may be one of the hardest principles to implement, particularly for beginner and intermediate learners. Teachers can, however, translate the checklist into the target language, using pictures to help comprehension. The action plan too can be written in French, if pupils are first involved in drawing up a list of possible expressions from which to choose. With most beginner classes, however, it is likely that the 'awareness-raising' in step 1 and the 'evaluation' in step 6 would have to be in the first language initially. The aim is to get everyone participating. As they become familiar with the process of reflecting on their own learning, they can be taught gradually to make their comments in the target language, especially if the language is kept simple. Burch (op. cit.) provides a wealth of useful ideas for teaching the language of classroom interaction. Posters too, like those used by Dam, could provide much needed support.

Strategy instruction should be geared towards learners' needs

Strategy instruction should be geared toward learners' needs and based on an initial evaluation of the strategies they are already using. It appears (Chesterfield and Chesterfield, 1985) that there may be a developmental order in which strategies are acquired. Basic, receptive, mechanical strategies are acquired first and more complex interactive, reflective and metacognitive strategies later. To state the obvious, there is little point in requiring pupils to use strategies for which they are not yet 'ready'. The 'awareness raising' in step 1 allows the teacher some insight into their stage of development, along with informal observation of the pupils at work. That said, there are dangers in following the developmental order too rigidly, which will emerge when we consider how to integrate strategy instruction into the scheme of work.

The place of strategy instruction in the scheme of work

Strategy instruction is a relatively new area and research results to date are mixed, although the most recent review by McDonough (1999) suggests encouraging results. Certainly in the current concern to 'get through the GCSE syllabus', it may seem impossible to make any additional time available. Yet Allwright's question 'why don't learners learn what teachers teach?' (1984: 3) may be a timely reminder of the gap between our intentions and the actual outcomes.

In Harris (1997), we have indicated how implementing the cycle of SI may only involve an extra one and a half lessons out of a sequence of ten, since many of the activities can become part and parcel of the learning of any new topic. The issue is more which strategies to teach when. In spite of the developmental order discussed earlier, it is not as simple as suggesting that Year 7 pupils learn memorisation strategies, Year 8 move on to reading strategies, etc. It is clear that within the skill areas, some tasks and hence the strategies that are needed are more or less demanding than others. Within reading, for example, using inferencing to guess the meaning of a particular cognate in a hotel brochure is easier than using inferencing to ascertain someone's attitude to environmental issues. Even if we were to resolve this problem by concluding that some reading strategies are appropriate for Year 7, others for Year 9, etc., a fundamental issue still remains. It relates back to the earlier discussion of the most useful 'first steps' to take. On one level, it could be argued that we should take account of the 'natural', developmental order by implementing a spiral model, where more autonomous ways of working are gradually introduced alongside instruction in strategies that themselves become ever more complex and match the new opportunities that pupils are offered. There is a danger that in such a model, the action planning and evaluation steps of the cycle might be omitted with beginner learners. Yet, we have argued that these steps are vital in enabling pupils to take some responsibility for their progress. Furthermore, some initial classroom case studies (Grenfell and Harris, 1999) suggest the significant role these metacognitive strategies can play in facilitating even younger pupils' learning. In the discussion of the carousel, we noted that whilst on the surface pupils appear to be working independently, in fact they have very little control over their learning. There may be a similar problem in adopting a graded and gradual approach to the introduction of SI; namely that it fails to address the same fundamental reluctance to 'let go'. Like the carousel, any 'first steps' may become fossilised, so that pupils are never given the opportunity to move forward. So whilst SI may contribute to reducing pupils' initial panic at working on their own, it may not resolve the problem of our fears of developing genuinely autonomous classrooms.

Teacher autonomy

We started this chapter by arguing that the only way to develop our pupils' ability to function as independent language users was to enable them to be independent language learners. We noted the lack of autonomy offered in most classrooms and outlined some possible reasons, including methodological assumptions such as the paradigm of the '3Ps' and the introduction of the written word. We observed the constraints impinging on teachers' work; meeting the requirements of the National Curriculum and GCSE, competing with local schools in the league tables and preparing for OFSTED inspections. It seems likely that the various new 'standards' for Qualified Teacher Status, Subject Leaders and Advanced Skills Teachers, established by the Teacher Training Agency, will exert further pressures. As one teacher, who preferred to remain anonymous, wrote recently:

> I've been appraised, inspected, observed, interviewed, chewed up and spat out by all manner of experts telling me what to do.
>
> (*Times Educational Supplement*, 1998: 13)

It is not appropriate here to discuss possible explanations underlying the attempts over the last five years, both overt and more subtle, to exert centralised control over all aspects of initial teacher education and further professional development (see Hextall and Mahony, 1998). Nevertheless, in the current educational context, it is hard to see how we can explore ways of developing autonomy in our pupils when our own control over what to teach and how is so severely restricted.

Acknowledgements

This chapter draws extensively on work undertaken over the last 8 years with my colleague, Dr. Michael Grenfell, Southampton University.

Editor's note

Harris argues that the autonomous use of language, implicit in communicative competence, cannot be separated from autonomous language learning. She recognises barriers to this more illuminating approach – GCSE syllabuses, National Curriculum prescriptions, technicist standards for teachers and even the dogmatic interpretation of the communicative approach. Harris recognises that to break from such powerful influences is to take risks, and that often the safer teacher-centred approaches appear to meet teachers' immediate concerns. Harris, however, recommends that learners assume responsibility for learning, which involves making informed choices about content and process. Harris acknowledges the need to provide learners with the understanding and skills necessary to make such choices. She is clear about the goal, and which strategies need to be in place at the end of the process. Harris also presents activities which enable such skills and learning strategies to be developed as a normal part of the learning process. She is less clear, and is appealing for further research and study into which strategies should be introduced when, and of how learners can reinforce, reject or select strategies which work best for them. Learning how to learn should not be separated from language learning, and further work on the integration of the two will serve to improve the outcome of MFL teaching and learning.

Linked chapters

Chapter 2, Chapter 11, Chapter 14, Chapter 18.

References

Allwright, R. L. (1984) 'Why don't learners learn what teachers teach? The interaction hypothesis' in D. M. Singleton and D. Little (eds) *Language Learning in Formal and Informal Contexts*, Dublin: IRAAL, pp. 3–18.

Barnes, D. (1976) *From Communication to Curriculum*, Harmondsworth: Penguin.

Burch, J. (1994) 'Grammar in classroom interaction' in L. King and P. Boaks (eds) *Grammar! A Conference Report*, London: CILT.

Canale, M. (1983) 'From communicative competence to communicative language pedagogy', in J. C. Richards and R. W. Schmidt (eds) *Language and Communication*, London: Longman.

Chesterfield, R. and Chesterfield, K.B. (1985) 'Natural order in children's use of second language learning strategies', *Applied Linguistics*, 6(1): 45–59.

Clark, J. (1984) *Syllabus Guidelines for a Graded Communicative Approach towards School Foreign language Learning; Part 1 Communication*, London: CILT.

Council for Cultural Co-operation Education Committee (1996) *Modern Languages: Learning, Teaching and Assessment. A Common European Framework of Reference*, Strasbourg: Council of Europe.

Dam, L. (1990) 'Learner autonomy in practice. An experiment in learning and teaching', in I. Gathercole (ed.) *Autonomy in Language Learning*, London: CILT.

Department for Education (1995) *Modern Foreign Languages in the National Curriculum*, London: HMSO.

Graham, S. (1997) *Effective Language Learning*, Clevedon: Multilingual Matters.

Grenfell, M. (1991) 'Communication: sense and nonsense', *Language Learning Journal*, 3: 6–8.

Grenfell, M. and Harris, V. (1993) 'How do pupils learn? Part 1', *Language Learning Journal*, 8: 22–5.

Grenfell, M. and Harris, V. (1999) *Modern Languages and Learning Strategies. In Theory and Practice*, London: Routledge

Harris, V. (1996) 'Developing pupil autonomy', in E. Hawkins (ed.) *30 Years of Language Teaching*, London: CILT.

Harris, V. (1997) *Teaching Learners How To Learn; Strategy Training in the ML Classroom*, London: CILT.

Harris, V. and Noyau, G. (1990) 'Collaborative learning: taking the first steps', in I. Gathercole (ed.) *Autonomy in Language Learning*, London: CILT.

Hextall, I. and Mahony, P. (1998) 'Effective teachers for effective schools,' in R. Slee and G. Weimer with S. Tomlinson (eds) *School Effectiveness for Whom?* London: Falmer.

Holec, H. (1996) 'Self-directed learning: an alternative form of training', in H. Holec, D. Little and R. Richterich (eds) *Strategies in Language Learning and Use*, Strasbourg: Council of Europe.

Johnstone, R. (1989) *Communicative Interaction: a Guide for Language Teachers*, London: CILT.

Little, D. (1996) 'Strategic competence considered in relation to strategic control of the language learning process', in H. Holec, D. Little and R. Richterich (eds) *Strategies in Language Learning and Use*, Strasbourg: Council of Europe.

Little, D. (1997) 'The role of writing in second language learning: some neo-Vygotskian reflections', paper given at the symposium 'Prozesse des Schreibens', Hannover, 24–25 January.

Low, L., Duffield, J., Brown, S. and Johnstone, R. (1993) *Evaluating Foreign Languages in Primary Schools*, Stirling: Scottish CILT.

McDonough, S. H. (1995) 'Learner strategies: state of the art article', *Language Teaching*, 32: 1–18.

Mitchell, R. (1994) 'The communicative approach to language teaching; an introduction', in A. Swarbrick (ed.) *Teaching Modern Languages*, London: Routledge.

Nunan, D. (1995) 'Closing the gap between learning and instruction', *TESOL Quarterly* 29(1): 133–58.

O'Malley, J. M. and Chamot, A. U. (1990) *Learning Strategies in Second Language Acquisition*, Cambridge: Cambridge University Press.

OFSTED (1993) *Modern Foreign Languages: Key Stage 3. First year 1992–3; a Review of Inspection Findings*, London: HMSO.

Oxford, R. (1993) 'Research on second language learning strategies', *Annual Review of Applied Linguistics*, 13: 175–87

Page, B. (ed.) (1992) *Letting Go – Taking Hold*, London: CILT.

Rubin, J. (1981) 'Study of cognitive processes in second language learning', *Applied Linguistics*, 11: 117–31.

Rubin, J. (1990) 'How learner strategies can inform language teaching', in V. Bickley (ed.) *Language Use, Language Teaching and the Curriculum*, Hong Kong: Institute of Language Education.

Seliger, H. W. (1983) 'The language learner as linguist: of metaphors and realities', *Applied Linguistics*, 4: 179–91.

Skehan, P. (1989) *Individual Differences in Second Language Learning*, London: Edward Arnold.

Stern, H. H. (1975) 'What can we learn from the Good Language Learner?' *Canadian Modern Language Review*, 31: 304–18.

Times Educational Supplement (1998) 'Dear Mr. Blunkett . . .', 6 November.

Vandergrift, L. and Bélanger, C. (1998) 'The national core French assessment project: design and field test of formative evaluation instruments at the intermediate level', *Canadian Modern Language Review*, 54: 4.

16 Literature in the communicative classroom

Norbert Pachler and Douglas Allford

Introduction

'Why study literature in the modern foreign language (MFL) classroom?'[1] If the question has an importunate quality, refusing to go away until a satisfactory answer has been found, that is evidence of the collapse of old certainties. Until the early 1980s it was widely thought to be self-evident that the study of literary texts should form an integral part of MFL syllabuses at A level[2] and on many undergraduate courses, particularly at the older universities. Now, however, much of what once seemed axiomatic is being called into question. Current uncertainty about the study of literature, expressed in its optional status on many specifications (formerly syllabuses), belongs to a wider debate about the aims of MFL learning and teaching in Britain today, and it is with some of these issues that we shall begin.

The past dozen or so years have seen a major shift within the education system towards MFL courses with a vocational or applied bias (see Allford and Pachler, 1998: 2–3). So great has been the change that today 'a majority of university language students are specialists in disciplines other than languages' (Coleman, 1996: 70). Likewise, students in higher education who might once have specialised in MFLs alone now combine them with, for instance, business studies or computing, conscious that 'employers do not tend to recruit people primarily for their linguistic ability' (Rigby and Burgess, 1991: 8) but expect prospective employees to offer other substantive skills and knowledge besides. The major changes sweeping through the labour market and MFL education have one priority in common: the acquisition of communicative competence in the target language (TL).

The current utilitarian rationale for MFLs has tended to stress not just communicative skills but oral communication at the expense of reading in general and the study of literature in particular (see Allford, 1997; Bayley, 1994: 41; Turner, 1997: 8). There is of course a powerful case for the importance of written texts in MFL study and for the use of literature, as we argue below. Yet establishing practical TL communicative competence as a principal goal signalled a change in priorities from the old grammar-translation model, to which the various sectors of the education system responded at differing rates and with varying degrees of enthusiasm. If an emphasis on communicative skills was most evident first at GCSE (arguably with an over-generous conception of what constituted TL 'communication'), after some delay examination boards at A level instituted change, citing the importance of candidates' social and career needs and acknowledging the fact that not all were aiming for university (see e.g. OCEAC 1996: 1–3). Initially at least, the HE sector was sharply divided in its response to the change. The new universities, usually relying on very limited resources, strove to match their courses to the shifting patterns of demand for vocationally related MFLs (see e.g. Duensing, 1996). The older universities, however, tended to retain course content and teaching methods along traditional lines, with prose translation, essays in English on literary texts and so on (see e.g. Bayley, 1994; Coleman, 1999). The consequent delay in change at A level produced a discontinuity with the rationale of GCSE that stresses TL communicative competence and attaches less importance to grammatical accuracy or the written word. Thus, to many GCSE students the prospect of studying literature at A level and beyond represented merely an unwelcome complication, whose relevance to the everyday use of the TL was quite unclear. And change when it came – partly on an *ad hoc* and partly on a principled basis – resulted in the study of literature being marginalised at A level (see e.g. Turner, 1999) and becoming only one of a range of options, alongside European studies, economics, politics, etc., at undergraduate level.

Scepticism about the practical linguistic usefulness of the study of literature was partly justified. Within the established canon of 'high literature', texts frequently offered precious little that could be transferred directly into a student's own productive language repertoire. Practical competence in the TL, if it was achieved at all, often seemed to be developed in parallel with literary studies rather than as a consequence of them. To conclude from this, however, that the study of literature *per se* cannot contribute to practical mastery of the TL would be mistaken, since literary texts embody the TL in authentic use and can provide insights into social and cultural dimensions of the country where it is spoken.

New approaches to literature at A level and beyond amount to a paradigm shift. The primacy of the foreign language, the integration of skills, together with a focus on contemporary society and the freedom to choose contemporary or recent texts (see e.g. OCEAC, 1996: 3, 18, 22), all tend towards integrating work on literary texts with other language learning activities. Literary texts can now be treated as a 'resource', a means of engaging a student's interest and providing 'linguistic opportunities' (Carter and Long, 1991: 3), rather than being viewed as 'an institutional discipline, . . . the subject of specialist study' (McRae, 1996: 17). The latter model, though now rejected – at least at A level – represented the norm for many years and it will be useful to review that first.

The 'high literature' model

Many of those attitudes which are only now being revised were shaped in the last century by the wish to secure acceptance of MFLs at British universities as a subject worthy of study. In practice, modern languages as a discipline based itself upon the model of Latin and Greek, which meant that teachers and textbook writers 'aped the methods of the classics', and in their enthusiasm to show that the study of French or German was sufficiently 'intellectually demanding' they turned the grammar-translation syllabus into 'a jungle of obscure rules' (Howatt, 1984: 135–6). An accurate knowledge of grammar was held to 'discipline the mind', whereas conversational fluency was dismissed as being 'superficial' (Hawkins, 1987: 113) – priorities which powerfully influenced the study of literature.

MFLs could strive towards 'the rigours of Greats and philology' and transcend the status of English, which was widely regarded as a 'distressingly dilettante subject', being little more than 'idle gossip about literary taste' (Eagleton, 1996: 25). The works of foreign literature to be studied were those of acknowledged stature, typified in French by the neo-classical tragedies of Racine and Corneille and in German by the dramas of Goethe and Schiller, and they tended to have a number of features in common. The language often belonged to a period remote in time or to an elevated register, and only rarely did it correspond to contemporary everyday use. Texts were frequently laced with erudite references and allusions, sufficiently obscure to make annotated editions necessary. Finally, the content was often complex enough to tax the average native reader. If thus restricting the canon made it 'rigorous', it also had other implications, some of which are no longer relevant to A level studies and others which still are (see e.g. OCEAC, 1996: 1–6, 18, 22).

Problems alleviated by changes in A level specifications

1   A focus on 'high' literature alone denied students exposure to other genres such as journalism, historical narrative, semi-technical writing, etc., and gave them only the sketchiest knowledge of contemporary life and institutions in the TL country.
2   To ensure that students had grasped the meaning of a work far beyond their productive competence, a sentence-by-sentence rendering of it into English was often undertaken, which could foster intense resistance to the study of MFL literature. If, in order to alleviate this burden, TL paraphrases were provided, they risked giving the impression that the work could, without loss, have been written much more simply. (It is a different matter to ask the student herself to rewrite a passage from the original in order to highlight certain features of it.)

Issues for specialist study of literature

1   If a work is historically remote from the reader she will possess limited understanding of the society and period for which it was written, or she might be confronted by TL works about whose English counterparts she is ignorant. The remedies for serious students of literature are clear: in the

former case, she would need to consult the relevant secondary literature and in the latter case, before tackling for instance Goethe's *Werther* or Laclos' *Les Liaisons Dangereuses*, she might read an eighteenth-century epistolary novel in English.

2   Using English to discuss and write about MFL texts may be necessary if the priority is to conduct the argument at a certain level of sophistication, rather than to develop TL communicative competence.

Issues relevant to new A level specifications

1   'What linguistic knowledge and general assumptions about life would a native speaker bring to this work?' The student may start with only the haziest notion about these matters and needs repeatedly to ask herself such questions under guidance from the teacher.

2   Whilst making use of editorial notes can be necessary and legitimate, trusting to works of literary criticism as a source of ready-made arguments for rote learning has justly been deplored (see Widdowson, 1992: xiii; Carter and McRae, 1996: xxi); it devalues the student's own responses to a work and may discourage her from exploring what those responses are.

A rationale for literature in the MFL classroom

Three main types of reason for studying literature in the language learning classroom tend to be advanced (see Carter and Long, 1991: 1–4), and these can be conveniently grouped as follows: language; society and culture; personal involvement.

Language

Unlike fragments of TL borrowed or invented in order to illustrate a linguistic point in the classroom, a literary text allows students to explore an entire work in context, since it furnishes much if its own context, and provides them with exposure to language serving actual communicative purposes. The language of a literary text, like that of newspaper or magazine articles, is authentic in that it is produced by a native writer for native readers of the TL. Moreover, a single literary work may make use of various text types (narrative, dialogue, etc.), encompass a range of registers (formal, slang, etc.) and move between different styles (ironic, impressionistic, etc.).

Yet it is worth noting that none of these features is peculiar to literature, which, however much one may value it, is probably undefinable (see Cook, 1996: 151–4). If 'literariness' means 'special uses of language', then these are to be found in literary texts but also in many places outside them (Eagleton, 1996: 5). Creative uses of language appear in puns, advertisements, newspaper headlines and so on, where the language does not simply refer to the world around us but, instead, plays with and shapes discourse 'in such a way as to invite readers to interpret how it represents that world' (Carter, 1996: 6). In this sense reference denotes 'purely informational' language as exemplified by a dictionary definition or 'the instructions how to operate a piece of machinery', whereas representation involves 'shades of meaning, understanding of points of view . . . and elements of uncertainty' (McRae, 1996: 17–20). Representational language is typically to be found in poetry, where meanings can often be both elusive and multiple (see Widdowson, 1992: 16–25, 186–94) but it is by no means restricted to such works.

Non-literary texts provide countless examples of words and images combining to produce complex effects, one such being an advertisement for a savings and investment scheme in a recent issue of *Der Spiegel*. Under a coloured drawing of a four-leaf clover is the headline *Quattro: Viermal mehr für's Geld* ('Quattro: Four times as much for your money'), a claim that is repeated in the body of the text. The advertisement offers the chance to make money and, in attempting to persuade the reader to accept the offer, it uses two closely interwoven motifs: good luck and the number four. Developing the opening headline, the text announces that the reader has 'the freedom . . . immediately . . . to make more' of her money, for *zum Glück* ('fortunately') *Quattro* is now available. Then four aspects of the scheme, each marked by a four-leaf clover, are highlighted as being particularly beneficial to prospective clients. In a text of only 60 words the name Quattro, which is widely known as a component of brand names (e.g. of a power drill), appears four times. The writers seem to be making intertextual allusions to well-established brands, one such being the Audi Quattro car, which they must presume to be generally associated with qualities such as high performance and reliability, and they are thereby attempting to appropriate those positive connotations for the service they are advertising. (In what is highly subjective territory, writers can proceed only on the basis of informed guesswork, and it is quite possible that any individual reader might have strongly negative feelings towards a particular brand name.)

Plainly, the advertisement has been carefully composed. It employs devices such as symbols and repetition to reinforce its message and aims to appeal to the reader at a number of different levels, not all of them obvious. It makes a number of assumptions about the knowledge, linguistic and non-linguistic, that a reader brings to the text: that a four-leaf clover is perceived as a symbol of good luck, possibly that *quattro* is known to be the Italian for 'four' and that the brand name Quattro is familiar and carries positive connotations.

The above text is by no means exceptional, and our discussion of it leads to a more general point. Given that non-literary texts often employ language in ways similar to literary ones and that similar methods can be used to explore both, it can be helpful to supplement the study of a literary work by examining non-literary texts dealing with related topics. In marked contrast to the attitudes fostered by the 'High Literature' model, such an approach acknowledges that we are surrounded daily by an abundance of non-literary texts which may reward scrutiny and may have much in common with literary works.

Society and culture

The view that literature 'enables students to understand and appreciate cultures and ideologies different from their own' (Carter and Long, 1991: 2), whilst widely held, may benefit from some elucidation. More precisely, a work of literature may offer the reader opportunities to understand more about the TL country, and approaches to the text are needed that assist the student in making the most of such opportunities. At a practical level, since the text was written for native readers, students will need to be guided towards relevant supplementary material such as newspapers, magazines, travel guides, maps, Internet texts, etc., chosen so as to supply the background knowledge implied by a particular text.

However, if one wanted a systematic or 'balanced' introduction to some aspect of contemporary society or to a recent period of history in the TL country, a work of creative fiction would usually be a curious starting point. Even where social or historical issues are central to a work, the narrator's standpoint may well be biased, eccentric or otherwise unreliable, for the author is under no obligation to create a 'reliable' text. For a factually accurate exposition of major events, names, geographical locations, dates and so on, the reader should consult the relevant non-fictional sources. There, starting with a body of material which is broadly undisputed, she can progress to contentious issues such as interpretations of the causes of historical events or the assessment of the relative importance of various social or economic factors.

The importance of a knowledge of contemporary life and institutions in the TL country is recognised in current A level specifications, as is a grasp of the social and historical context within which a work of literature is situated. Thus, when tackling a text such as *Das Brandopfer* by Albrecht Goes, it will be enormously helpful for a student to possess some awareness of the experiences of German citizens living through the *Nazizeit* and the political instability and economic crises of the Weimar Republic which preceded it. Given such background knowledge, the reader can gain powerful insights from the text into what life was like for the working wife of a small shopkeeper: hating yet fearing the local Nazi party members; slowly realising that previously useful precepts for the conduct of daily life along the lines of 'business as usual' were grotesquely inadequate to the times through which she was living; and not grasping the significance of the gradual disappearance of Jewish neighbours until it was brought home with dreadful clarity.

Such imaginary worlds consist of the literary text and what the reader brings to it, and there she may experience, vicariously but with great intensity, the emotions and moral predicaments of characters located in a different culture and in different historical circumstances.

Personal involvement

If the study of MFLs is to have an educational rationale, as distinct from a narrowly vocational one, then it may be expected to contribute to the student's general development. Just as planned trips to the TL country can afford an opportunity to outgrow parochial prejudices (see Hawkins, 1987: 43–6), so reading its literature can provide access to its traditions of thought and experience. Moreover, the study of literature can, it is widely argued, by stimulating understanding of society and the people within it, help students to 'grow as individuals' (see e.g. Carter and Long, 1991: 3).

However, such 'growth' should be seen as part of overall intellectual development and be sharply distinguished from any attempt to attribute a 'morally improving' effect to literature. The dangers of equating aesthetic appreciation with ethical or humane behaviour are tellingly exposed by Steiner's observation that the perpetrators of genocide and torture have often been (and continue to be) 'cultivated' individuals (see 1975: 45). Moreover, the notion that literature confers moral improvement has other implications, two of which particularly concern us here. The idea that authors convey the fruits of their 'superior perception or judgement', if they do possess these attributes, by means of language assumes 'a very simple transmission view of communication' (Cook, 1994: 2) – a model quite at odds with the importance we attach here to the reader's own role. Second, the view of literature as a repository of wisdom and moral precepts implies (the probability of) a single 'correct' interpretation, presumably known to the 'experts' and towards which students should strive, whereas in fact literary works typically evoke a wide range of responses and provide students with opportunities to discover a variety of possible interpretations supported by the text (see Bredella, 1996: 8).

If literature does not furnish moral instruction, neither is it in any straightforward sense a source of information. Whilst a literary text may serve in part as a 'cultural lexicon' (Stewart and Cohen, 1997: 245), providing insights into the TL country and its people, it is under no obligation, as noted above, to be factually reliable. Whilst some 'fictional narratives supply us with a mental catalogue of the fatal conundrums we might face' (Pinker, 1998: 543), thereby allowing us to prepare mentally for various crises, this does not account for our interest in the banal (e.g. soap operas) or in stories which can have no direct bearing on our lives (e.g. meeting aliens).

Although no comprehensive theory has been advanced to explain why people seem universally to delight in reading about fictional events (see de Beaugrande, 1987), it is nonetheless possible to predict the kind of texts likely to arouse the curiosity of one's students (see below). Young adults in the process of discovering, and often questioning, the conventions governing social behaviour may well be interested by an 'outsider' such as Meursault in Albert Camus' *L'Étranger* who openly challenges certain such customs. Similarly, as they often feel themselves to be powerless and bewildered in the face of the institutions and structures of an adult world with which they are not yet fully familiar, younger readers may be able to understand the plight of someone who falls victim to them, such as the central figure in Heinrich Böll's *Die verlorene Ehre der Katharina Blum*.

Thus, a reader can be interested by a wide range of narratives, often taking pleasure in those that display linguistic dexterity, which may allow a comparison between literary and everyday uses of the TL. And if literary texts order experience and create meanings out of events that in real life are generally incoherent, they also invite readers to explore what those various meanings may be.

It is worth mentioning that at A level and beyond, all the activities implied under the above headings could be carried out largely or exclusively in the TL.

The study of literature in the MFL classroom

Working with literature can help develop students' literacy skills

Reading is a highly complex and important skill, be it in the mother tongue or in the foreign language, and it needs to be learnt (and taught). It is not merely a matter of information processing and fitting together disparate pieces of information extracted from texts. It involves the making of judgements about the information contained in texts, extracting relevant information, relating relevant bits of information to each other in thematic contexts, ordering them, formulating and testing hypotheses, abstracting meaning, adding information to fill gaps in the text, as well as creating larger entities of meaning with them which we may or may not store in our short- and/or long-term memories. These processes apply equally to mother tongue and foreign language reading but, for obvious reasons, are more difficult for the foreign language learner, who, because of linguistic and cultural 'deficits', is often less able to make (accurate) predictions, to anticipate, select, skim and scan the text for relevant information. This in turn slows down the reading process and can make the act of reading in the TL less enjoyable and more laborious. (see Ehlers, 1992: 7–48).

Thus, helping foreign language readers to identify overarching themes, to choose relevant information contained in the text and to make predictions are important pedagogic tasks for the teacher. This can be achieved, for instance, through guiding students with explicit objectives, through using various types of comprehension checks and engaging students in hypothesis building or through activating and furthering students' knowledge of pertinent linguistic structures and lexical items as well as through working with them on the cultural and historic setting or literary conventions. Work on these process skills for effective reading in the MFL classroom can have a positive effect on literacy skills in the mother tongue, which constitutes a valuable reason for the inclusion of work with literature in MFL teaching and learning, particularly in the current educational climate.

Literary texts, due to their specific characteristics, require certain reading strategies, which need to be taught. Compared with non-fiction, literary texts more readily allow for interpretation and multiplicity of meaning; their connections, themes and topics are not always explicit; the narrative structure tends to be complex; and meaning tends to be subjective and indicative rather than objective and unambiguous (see Ehlers, 1992: 42).

Working with literary texts can facilitate students' involvement and engagement in the learning process

Working with literary texts in MFL lessons enables the initiation of students into the literary world and affords them the benefits of being an active member of this discourse community in terms of personal and social development. It allows students to find out about and learn from autobiographical or fictional experiences of other human beings and how they deal with life, as well as to assimilate and accommodate these experiences for their own lives. Work with literary texts potentially allows students a wealth of personal and emotional responses. Literature can feed students' imagination, creativity and intellectual activity by exposing them to thoughts and ideas and can be a source for enjoyment.

In an interesting article, Jon Stott (1994) asks himself the question why stories attract us. He posits that, like most things created by humans, they presumably fulfil a need and he uses the term 'storying' to describe 'the process of creating (as teller or author) and recreating (as listener, viewer, or reader)'. Storying, to him, 'appears to be a fundamental and uniquely human activity.' (p. 245). Whilst stories can provide (light) entertainment or an escape from the 'real' concerns of life, they can also be seen to transmit moral and social values in an interesting way and, thereby, represent a valuable educational tool. In other words, they help answer two fundamental questions: 'Who am I?' and 'Where do I belong?' (see p. 248). Importantly, for our purposes, Stott also points out that stories can help human beings become members of a larger community (i.e. a culture) and function effectively as a member of this community as stories articulate conceptions in words (see Stott, 1994: 247 and below).

> Storying is an essential aspect of life that explains life by giving its details a sense of coherence and significance. Stories help us to order and understand life more fully and, therefore, to live it better, more fully. When groups ban or burn books of stories, they often do so because they disagree with the interpretations of life these offer. They fear the power of what they consider a bad story and seek, usually unsuccessfully, to destroy it.
>
> (Stott, 1994: 248)

Students may find work with literature difficult because throughout their study of MFL at beginners level they have tended to focus on a narrow range of functional-transactional language and activities and have been socialised into reading to extract information rather than to respond personally to texts. However, we feel it is exactly this potential of literary texts to provide stimuli for students to talk about the here and now rather than to rehearse dialogues scripted to conform with certain notional-functional principles for possible use in future transactions which constitutes a major benefit of literary texts for MFL teaching and learning (see also Butzkamm, 1985: 117). Coherent pedagogical tools are required to allow for successful use of literature in MFL teaching and learning at intermediate level. We suggest that approaches developed around the reader response theory offer workable solutions.

Reader response theory, advocated amongst others by Wolfgang Iser in his seminal books *Der implizite Leser* (1972) and *Der Akt des Lesens* (1976), suggests that the potential of a literary text can only be unfolded through the act of reading since the presence of a reader is implicit in the text. This affords the personal and subjective response of the reader significant importance in the creation of meaning in that it acknowledges certain gaps ('*Leerstellen*') in a text to be filled by the reader according to the conditions surrounding the receptive act. This runs counter to traditional approaches to work with literary texts which tended to strive for a 'canonised' interpretation. In pedagogic terms it means a greater emphasis on student-centred approaches in the reader response tradition compared with more teacher-centredness in traditional, stylistic approaches.[3]

Using literary texts can facilitate students' language-and-culture learning

Traditionally culture used to be defined as 'material' culture for the purposes of MFL teaching and learning, operationalised in the study of written sources, particularly literary texts, and of the institutions of the target countries. As we have shown above, this definition of culture provided a rationale for the inclusion of literature. Literary texts as products of high culture necessitated a particular reading and methodology: the text was seen as a work of art and an aesthetic whole to be analysed and interpreted in a 'text-inherent' ('*werkimmanent*') manner. This school of thought was promoted in particular by Wolfgang Kayser in his book *Das sprachliche Kunstwerk* (1948). Increasingly, though, culture is being seen as what happens between members of a community – the attitudes and beliefs, the ways of thinking and behaving as well as remembering they share. First-hand experiences with TL speakers and TL sources have become increasingly important on the basis that '(culture) in the final analysis is always *linguistically mediated membership into a discourse community, that is both real and imagined* (Kramsch, 1996: 3, italics in original; see also Pachler, 1999). The rationale for the use of literature in this paradigm is quite different: literature becomes a rich repository of authentic language and discourse as well as of target culture thoughts, ideas, beliefs, attitudes, ways of thinking, behaving and remembering, etc. Of course, as we have already pointed out, literary texts are invariably subjective rather than objective and often do not give a truly representative picture of the target culture. Indeed, they often aim to challenge and question, be uncomfortable and get the reader to think critically about the status quo. Therein, we believe, lies their strength and their attraction. These characteristics allow the reader a critical insight into the target culture in its richness and diversity.

Moreover, literary texts are often more authentic than supposedly 'authentic' texts based on everyday life currently dominating coursebooks, which are in fact often linguistically idealised, particularly at beginners level. Real-life utterances are characterised by repetitions, clarification, misunderstandings, uncertainty of expression, ambivalence, etc. In this respect literary texts are more representative of authentic discourse than carefully scripted and clinical coursebook dialogues (see Müller, 1985: 397–9).

Some criteria for choosing literary texts for MFL teaching

According to Bernd Kast (1985: 132) literary texts present a 'burden' for the reader, as they require decoding at three levels: the linguistic-semantic, the linguistic-aesthetic and the cultural-semantic. Stern (see 1985: 34) identifies four inherent difficulties of literary texts: syntactic, lexical, discoursal and semantic. He also discusses possible contextual problems of a cultural, pragmatic or sociolinguistic nature, as well as the dispositions the reader brings to the text: limited or lacking preconceptions about the writer, as well as other presuppositions such as personal literary experience etc. (see p. 36). As MFL teachers we, therefore, need to bear in mind the specific characteristics of texts, ie their difficulty in relation to the criteria listed above, as well as those of the readers when choosing texts for classroom use.

Length of text is, of course, an important selection criterion given the limited time available as is the level of world and target culture knowledge required. Thematic appropriacy such as the search for personal identity, sexuality, friendship, family, ie themes resonating with the intended readership and protagonists with whom students can identify, might help to ensure the success of working with literature in the MFL classroom (see also Chambers, 1991: 38). Teenage fiction, in our estimation, offers a rich source of appropriate literary texts, despite the fact that the literary merit of teenage fiction has been disputed amongst philologists until quite recently.

Research into story structure suggests that both story organisation and amount of TL study influence students' success when working with short stories (see Riley, 1993: 425). Riley notes that action constituents are better recalled than reactions (e.g. internal responses such as thought or emotions) (Riley, 1993: 418). Also, a 'canonical' story structure, i.e. a story conforming to an 'ideal' story type, was found to be more memorable and comprehensible. This would characteristically consist of a 'Beginning Event during which the protagonist encounters a conflict, followed by the Development where the protagonist establishes a goal path to follow in order to resolve the conflict and attempts to achieve the goal' resulting in 'an Outcome, and subsequently an Ending' (Riley, 1993: 417).

> [Text] structure is an important factor in comprehension for 'moderately difficult texts'. If the ideas are fairly unfamiliar, then the text structure is depended upon to determine which ideas are more important than others. If the text is extremely difficult, students won't use structure because they won't have access to it . . .; if the language, concepts, and so forth are simple, then structure may also be less important.
>
> (Riley, 1993: 425)

Story structure and organisation, in particular linearity may, therefore, be another important criterion for choosing literary texts for intermediate level MFL learners. Where the 'ideal' story structure is not present, the teacher will wish to deploy, alongside standard activities to accompany reading, a number of prospective and retrospective strategies, such as advance organisers, pre-reading and post-reading tasks to help students cope with potential difficulties in the narrative:

> it is important to recognise that students expect a story to have structure, and that they look for and use story structure as a basis for comprehension and memory. The structural expectations that readers bring with them to the reading of short stories can be exploited in the classroom setting to enhance comprehension.
>
> (Riley, 1993: 426)

Further, when choosing a text we might consider whether we have access to support material such as film versions, theatre performances or study guides.

Points for reflection

- In this chapter we refer to Jon Stott's notion of 'storying' as a uniquely human activity and as an educational tool. Consider different ways in which the human desire to tell or be told stories could be used effectively in the MFL classroom.
- We noted that literary texts often aimed to challenge and question, to be uncomfortable and get the reader to think critically. Consider how this potential could be exploited in the context of a topic your students are currently studying.
- We suggested thematic appropriacy as one selection criterion for literary texts for classroom use: which themes do you deem to be appropriate for your students and why?
- Does working in the TL place limitations on the ways in which a text can be discussed? Is there scope for using some material in English which can be incorporated into a TL discussion but without it merely being translated?

Notes

1 The following discussion focuses mainly on A level and undergraduate work but should, we hope, be of general interest.
2 For ease of reference we use the term A level to subsume Advanced Subsidiary here.
3 Unfortunately there is insufficient space here to discuss the implications for practical work with literature in more detail, but see e.g. Carter and Long, 1991.

Editor's note

Pachler and Allford argue that a restricted view of communicative competence – associated with GCSE, the growth of narrowly vocational courses and other factors – has resulted in a neglect of literary texts. Although specifications at A level and some undergraduate courses have been revised to take account of radically shifting demands, literature is still largely marginalised, except where it is studied as a specialist subject.

Moving beyond the 'high literature' model, which tends to divide the study of literature from language learning, Pachler and Allford outline a rationale which could integrate the two. Literary texts would be supplemented by non-literary ones in studying the TL in authentic use and in learning about TL society and culture. However, unlike most other types of text, a work of literature has the potential to engage the reader's interest in an unfolding narrative and in the fate of strongly delineated characters.

Pachler and Allford, then, consider more closely how studying literary texts entails the development of a range of interpretative skills, both in a detailed reading of the text and at a broader, strategic level. As well as providing pleasure, literary works crucially require a range of creative responses from the reader and these lend themselves quite naturally to exploration in the TL, thereby developing language competence. This process of engagement with texts can in turn provide access to the TL culture, which, rather than being fixed and monolithic, may more accurately be seen as a multiform and shifting 'discourse community'.

In selecting suitable works, characteristics such as accessibility of language and subject matter are of central importance, along with length of text. Likewise, a clear narrative structure can help to make a text intelligible, especially for less experienced readers.

Pachler and Allford's intention in this discussion is to show that the study of literature can and should be integrated with other language learning activities. Further, whilst they should be studied alongside non-literary texts, works of literature, if carefully selected and exploited, can have a special contribution to make to an understanding of the TL and the countries where it is spoken.

Linked chapters

Chapter 6, Chapter11, Chapter 18.

References

Allford, D. (1997) 'Are we all vocationalists now?', in *Studies in Modern Languages Education*, 5: 38–56.

Allford, D. and Pachler, N. (1998) 'Learner autonomy, communication and discourse', in *The Institution-Wide Language Programmes: 7th National Conference*, Sheffield: Sheffield Hallam University.

Bayley, S. (1994) Literature in the modern languages curriculum of British Universities,' *Language Learning Journal*, 9: 41–5.

Beaugrande, R. de (1987) 'Schemas for literary communication', in L. Halasz (ed.) *Literary Discourse*, Berlin: de Gruyter.

Bredella, L. (1996) 'The anthropological and pedagogical significance of aesthetic reading in the foreign language classroom', in L. Bredella and W. Delanoy (eds) *Challenges of Literary Texts in the Foreign Language Classroom*, Tübingen: Narr.

Butzkamm, W. (1985) 'Literarische texte als Sprachlerntexte', in M. Heid (ed.) *Literarische Texte im kommunikativen Fremdsprachenunterricht. New Yorker Werkheft*, München: Goethe-Institut, pp. 114–31.

Carter, R. (1996) 'Look both ways before crossing', in R. Carter and J. McRae (eds) *Language, Literature and the Learner*, London: Longman.

Carter, R. and Long, M. (1991) *Teaching Literature*, London: Longman.

Carter, R. and McRae, J. (eds) (1996) *Language, Literature and the Learner*, London: Longman.

Chambers, G. (1991) 'A-level literature in the 1990s: a fresh start?', *Language Learning Journal*, 3: 34–40.

Coleman, J. (1996) 'University courses for non-specialists', in E. Hawkins (ed.) *30 Years of Language Teaching*, London: CILT.

—— (1999) 'Looking ahead: trends in modern foreign languages in higher education', in N. Pachler (ed.) *Teaching Modern Foreign Languages at Advanced/Advanced Subsidiary Level*, London: Routledge.

Cook, G. (1994) *Discourse and Literature*, Oxford: Oxford University Press.

—— (1996) 'Making the subtle difference: literature and non-literature in the classroom', in R. Carter and J. McRae (eds) *Language, Literature and the Learner*, London: Longman.

Duensing, A. (1996) 'The customer is always right – foreign language degrees in the 90s', *Languages Forum*, 1(5): 31–5.

Eagleton, T. (1996) *Literary Theory: An Introduction*, 2nd edn, Oxford: Blackwell.

Ehlers, S. (1992) *Literarische Texte lesen lernen*, München: Klett Edition Deutsch.

Hawkins, E. (1987) *Modern Languages in the Curriculum*, revised edn, Cambridge: Cambridge University Press.

Howatt, A. (1984) *A History of English Language Teaching*, Oxford: Oxford University Press.

Iser, W. (1976) *Der Akt des Lesens. Theorie ästhetischer Wirkung*, München: Fink.

—— (1972) *Der implizite Leser. Kommunikationsformen des Romans von Bunyan bis Beckett*, München: Fink

Kast, B. (1985) 'Von der Last des Lernens, der Lust des Lesens und der Lust der Didaktik. Literarische Texte für Anfänger im kommunikativen Fremdsprachenunterricht', in Heid, M. (ed.) *Literarische Texte im kommunikativen Fremdsprachenunterricht, New Yorker Werkheft*, München: Goethe-Institut, pp. 132–54.

Kayser, W. (1948) *Das sprachliche Kunstwerk. Eine Einführung in die Literaturwissenschaft*, Bern: Francke.

Kramsch, C. (1996) 'The cultural component of language teaching', in *Zeitschrift für interkulturellen Fremdsprachenunterricht 1 (2)*. [Online] Available at: http.//www.ualbertaca/~german/ejournal/archive/kiamsch2.htm.

McRae, J. (1996) 'Representational language learning', in R. Carter and J. McRae (eds) *Language, Literature and the Learner*, London: Longman.

Müller, H. (1985) 'Plädoyer für eine Pädagogik der Phantasie', in M. Heid (ed.) *Literarische Texte im kommunikativen Fremdsprachenunterricht. New Yorker Werkhef*, München: Goethe-Institut, pp. 394–405.

OCEAC (Oxford and Cambridge Examinations and Assessment Council) (1996) *Modern Foreign Languages: Oxford Syllabus*, Oxford: University of Cambridge Local Examinations Syndicate.

Pachler, N. (1999) 'Teaching and learning culture', in N. Pachler (ed.) *Teaching Modern Foreign Languages at Advanced/Advanced Subsidiary Level*, London: Routledge.

Pinker, S. (1998) *How the Mind Works*, Harmondsworth: Allen Lane.

Rigby, G. and Burgess, R. (1991) *Language Teaching in Higher Education*, Coventry: University of Warwick.

Riley, G. (1993) 'A story structure approach to narrative text comprehension', *The Modern Language Journal*, 77(iv): 417–32.

Steiner, G. (1975) *Extraterritorial*, Harmondsworth: Penguin.

Stern, H. (1985) 'Literature teaching and the communicative approach', in M. Heid (ed.) *Literarische Texte im kommunikativen Fremdsprachenunterricht. New Yorker Werkheft*, München: Goethe-Institut, pp. 6–46.

Stewart, I. and Cohen, J. (1997) *Figments of Reality*, Cambridge: Cambridge University Press.

Stott, J. (1994) 'Making stories mean; making meaning from stories: the value of literature for children', *Children's Literature in Education*, 25(4): 243–53.

Turner, K. (1997) 'Reading: meeting the demands of the National Curriculum', *Language Learning Journal*, 17: 8–13.

Turner, K. (1999) 'Working with literature', in N. Pachler (ed.) *Teaching Modern Foreign Languages at Advanced/Advanced Subsidiary Level*, London: Routledge.

Widdowson, H. (1992) *Practical Stylistics*, Oxford: Oxford University Press.

Part 4

Broader issues

17 Raising the profile and prestige of Modern Foreign Languages in the whole school curriculum

Do Coyle

Introduction

In retrospect, the 1990s were a time of confusion and 'mixed messages' in the modern language teaching world. At the start of the decade there was an emphasis on the effective implementation of the National Curriculum. Building on communicative principles tried and tested in the 1980s, a steady rise in GCSE entries, a 'languages for all' policy firmly in place and a curriculum which emphasised target language use and explicit grammar teaching, it seemed as though the scene was set for a fruitful period in language learning in secondary schools. Not so! By the end of the decade, language teachers were once again fighting to maintain compulsory language learning to the age of 16, 'A' level entries had decreased and the shortage of modern language teachers had reached crisis level. The National Curriculum had not succeeded in fostering cohorts of motivated adolescent learners who would perceive language learning opportunities as providing them with skills essential to their future working lives. Moreover, against the backdrop of the Nuffield Inquiry into Modern Languages (October–December 1998) aimed at defining in more concrete terms the country's language needs for the following twenty years, the message is clear: Britain's linguistic capability lags behind other countries in Europe. The 1995 European White Paper, which has as one of its priority objectives proficiency in three European language for all its citizens, sits uneasily with national realities. Quite simply many learners are voting with their 'disaffected' feet.

In this chapter I would like to briefly trace the reasons for the demise of foreign language learning in the previous decade in order to lead us towards exploring how a re-conceptualisation of the MFL curriculum may contribute to inculcating more positive attitudes towards language learning in our future work force and bringing about more relevant and satisfying experiences for both teachers and learners alike.

The content and context of the communicative approach

Whilst the Graded Objectives Movement, led by practitioners themselves, laid the foundations for classroom communication and grew out of an 'irresistibility of the idea whose time has come' (Page, 1996), its legacy was to leave the next generation of language learners and teachers 'grappling' with the communicative approach – ill-defined yet very much prevalent in today's classrooms. However, as government attitudes towards the teaching force hardened and support for curriculum innovation waned, so too did teachers' flexibility to sustain areas for development such as those outlined in the 1987 'Languages for Communication – The Next Stage: Recommendations for Action'. One could argue therefore that it is the *status quo* of the communicative approach itself which has led to a small number of topics such as 'house and home' or 'travel and transport' being recycled at regular intervals during a five-year period into a commonly agreed classroom repertoire. It is one thing to deconstruct language into functions and notions which encourage transactional communication in terms of getting things done, but this process bears little resemblance to 'real' communication – as learners soon become aware. Whilst such an approach provides a pragmatic and perhaps essential starting point for teaching purposes, it does not equip a wide enough range of learners to enter the world of genuine and realistic communication by enabling them to function more independently in the future. Armed with a battery of stock phrases directed by the examination syllabus and textbook, prescribed language seems to be the most appropriate route for ensuring examination success and the school's rightful place in the league tables. In other words, transactional language for responding to syllabus-steered topics and predictable classroom activities has been fine-tuned, but this seems to have stopped short of enabling many learners to own the language they are required to use. Why is it that Ofsted reports that with the exception of ICT and RE, progression from KS3 to KS4 in Modern Foreign Languages is lower than all other subjects? 'Pupils in Key Stage 4 are unable to express themselves in the target language in a wider range of contexts than in Key Stage 3.'

Legutke and Thomas (1991) describe a different kind of progression, a disquieting change from enthusiasm, typical of first year students in secondary schools, to lifelessness, as learners become more passive. Theirs is a particularly powerful image of dead bodies and talking heads! So why such passivity when language learning potentially offers so much in terms of creativity and communication?

Clark (1998) in her study of 250 students studying French, suggests that the root of disaffection may lie to an extent with the content of language learning which according to her learners was found to be 'dull, superficial and irrelevant'. 'Some of the stuff we've learnt is kind of pointless, because I mean some of the conversations that we have it's not the kind of thing that you'd have in a conversation with a French person' (Clark, 1998: 8).

Salter *et al.* (1995) concurs with this view when he describes the content of language learning as largely irrelevant to learners in the secondary sector. For young teenagers to be reduced to talking about the colour of their pets and the shops in their town – something which will have been inevitably covered in primary school at KS1 in English – without additionally being empowered to say, albeit it at a simple level, the things they wish to say, then it is little wonder that language learning during the last decade has variously been described as trivial, inconsequential, pedestrian (Salter, 1995) and anodyne (Powell, 1986).

A hard look at foreign language classroom practice does raise questions not only about how students might take possession of the language and 'make it their own', but crucially if they even wish to, given a diet of 'tired' topics and prescribed utterances. Perhaps now is an opportune time to re-conceptualise the communicative approach into an evolving learning environment where the content of language learning provides students with a challenging and relevant context within which to work.

For example, reappraising the content of the school Modern Foreign Language syllabus especially in the second and third years of language learning may well raise some difficult issues – particularly in the field of textbook approaches, assessment procedures and teacher and learner expectations. The tension for teachers seems to lie more in risk-taking by straying from what have now become established as the 'norms' of classroom behaviour and safe practice which may not easily motivate learners but may produce more predictable examination grades. And yet in terms of content, the revised National Curriculum (1999) upon which teachers must statutorily base their teaching can be interpreted as an enabling device offering open-ended guidance as follows:

I would argue that a re-think of the languages curriculum at 14+ is already too late for the majority of learners, whilst the more 'interesting' and engaging issues-led curriculum of the advanced syllabuses remains the reserve for all but a few. No, I call here for a realistic and forward-looking examination of the Key Stage 3 programme. Whilst drawing, labelling, simple role-play and repetitive linguistic formulae have significant pedagogical value, they will not hold the attention of most learners for 2 or 3 years. Moreover, if we are to look ahead to the introduction of foreign language learning in primary school, then the first two years in the secondary sector will by definition take on a different role. Therefore, as the realms and nature of communication rapidly change in our techno-'virtual' world, in line with an 'enabling' National Curriculum, there is a real sense of urgency for linguists to collaborate with colleagues working in other curricular areas, to share in pedagogical planning regarding the content and style of lessons.

Towards a *Thinking Curriculum*: integrating content, cognition and communication

Whilst the notion of a whole curricular approach to learning is already familiar with the Language Across the Curriculum thrust of the 1980s (all teachers are teachers of English) and ICT delivery of the 1990s (all teachers are teachers of ICT!), in essence such an approach to learning is rarely adopted despite the suggested advances in the National Curriculum non-statutory guidance (1990): 'The full potential of the National Curriculum will only be realised if curricular planning involves identifying the overlap of skills and content across the different subjects.'

Interestingly, however, in contrast to current national governmental demands concerning classroom methodology which seem to be increasingly restrictive and prescriptive, there has been a recent shift in pedagogical emphasis from teaching to learning. This has not only brought with it a focus on the role of social interaction in the classroom, where both learners and teachers work together to construct the learning environment, but also experimentation at grass roots level into the development of thinking skills within the curriculum, as students are actively involved in creating meaning and solving problems. As Nisbet (1991) points out:

> The demand for a *Thinking Curriculum* arises partly because of rapid changes in modern society. It is also the result of recent developments in cognitive psychology: the constructivist theory of learning argues that learners create their own framework of interpretation in a search for meaning and understanding. If learning is to be retained and to be readily available for use, then learners must make their own construction of knowledge – make it their own – and must learn to take responsibility for the management and control of their own learning.
>
> (Nisbet, 1991: 27)

Moreover, an important DfEE report by McGuinness published in 1999, entitled 'From Thinking Skills to Thinking Classrooms: a review and evaluation of approaches for developing pupils' thinking', makes the connection between how and what young people learn:

> Standards can only be raised when attention is directed not only to what is to be learned but on how children learn and how teachers intervene to achieve this.
>
> (McGuiness, 1999: 5)

The increased interest in the development of thinking skills is demonstrable in teaching initiatives such as CASE (cognitive acceleration through science education), CAME (cognitive acceleration through mathematics education) and the Thinking Through Geography Programme. What all these approaches share is an explicit emphasis on developing learners' thinking skills through the context of the curriculum. Whilst there are several general taxonomies of thinking skills available, the most common skills include sequencing and ordering; sorting, classifying and grouping; analysing relationships, comparing and contrasting; making predictions and hypothesising; drawing conclusions; generating new ideas and brainstorming and so on. The issue to be addressed is how the learning of a modern foreign language can contribute to the development of such skills. In other words, it is not only the content of language learning *per se* which for me is problematic, but also a perceived absence of inherent cognitive challenge contained within that content – especially in the early stages of the language learning process. As a stimulus for discussion, departments may wish to audit the cognitive and linguistic challenge of class-room activities, plotting a cognitively demanding and undemanding axis against a linguistically demanding and undemanding axis. Tasks which are positioned in the linguistic and cognitive undemanding quadrant should be examined with caution. For me, our challenge as teachers is to explore how we can provide learners with linguistically accessible yet cognitively demanding experiences.

Whilst it could be argued that the assimilation and subsequent use of complex grammar rules is in itself challenging, unless grammar teaching and learning are contextualised through meaningful language use and learners begin to take ownership of the language, then students are likely to 'switch off', since the work is irrelevant to their perceived needs.

From amidst the complexity of current foreign language practice an equation begins to emerge – learner demotivation added to teacher dissatisfaction creates a potentially powerful catalyst for change. The remainder of this chapter will look for ways of harnessing that challenge, whilst retaining what is good, successful and enjoyable and building on what works!

For me, at this moment in time, the challenging questions are as follows: How might the profile of foreign language learning gain credibility and prestige amongst the future workforce? How might Modern Foreign Languages gain its rightful place as a core element in the school curriculum? How can we as linguists respond to Nisbet's claim (1993) that 'before the century is out, no curriculum will be regarded as acceptable unless it can be shown to make a contribution to the teaching of thinking?'

Re-appraising content

There are of course no simple answers, yet to avoid a 'rear-view mirror approach' to exploring a curriculum for the twenty-first century, we might at least start with content and cognition. Building on the premise that we use language to learn as well as to communicate, the regular modern languages curriculum is arguably limited in its learning opportunities to the specific 'new' content areas of grammar and some elements of culture associated with the target countries of the language learnt. The planned inclusion of these elements however, tends to be left up to the textbook writers. From this perspective, language teachers are losing valuable ground – the tried and tested GCSE topics do not usually take the learner into uncharted and motivating territory; uncertainty surrounds the effective teaching of grammar at different levels; and 'culture' if covered at all, tends to remain at the level of curiosity and challenging stereotypes. As a matter of some urgency, there is a need to identify how the potential for content to develop skills and understanding in communication, cognition and culture may be increased, where the learner's attention is genuinely focused on what is being communicated or learnt in addition to either its form or the simulated context. 'Foreign language teaching must be concerned with reality; with the reality of communication as it takes place outside the classroom and with the reality of learners as they exist outside and inside the classroom' (Littlewood, 1981: 84).

A useful starting point for exploring such realities might be to revisit the recommendations of the National Curriculum non-statutory guidance, published in 1990. This suggested a three-tiered approach to curricular linking as a way of encouraging whole curriculum teaching and learning. Potentially this enables the modern languages curriculum to be released from the strait-jacket of out-moded and repetitive topics to include:

- cross-curricular work developed within MFL courses;
- co-operation between MFL and other departments;
- other subjects taught mainly or entirely through the foreign language for a specific period of time.

The three models may have a different focus, but all share at least one common objective – to encourage communication skills by extending language use. Whilst learners clearly need to have an entry point into using language as a means of communication and a vehicle for learning, analysing appropriate content for conceptual and linguistic demands, as well as the language for potential content creates a richer learning environment.

For departments wishing to explore cross-curricular work within the modern languages classroom there are several examples of materials already available which also respond to the National Curriculum requirements: the CILT Pathfinder 'New Contexts for Modern Language Learning: cross-curricular approaches' (Brown and Brown, 1996) provides a useful catalyst for ideas by suggesting ways in which teachers may share approaches and resources across the curriculum; the Charis Project materials (French and German) have a PSE and RE emphasis; the excellent Tacade 'Directions' materials (French, German, Spanish) deal with drug and alcohol education with an emphasis on risk-taking, solving problems and being in control; Development Education Centres are also a useful source of foreign language materials in French, German and Spanish (Mundi) which are explicit in their treatment of global, cultural and social issues.

Whilst in many schools there is a tradition of cross-curricular collaboration ranging from technology and drama to the joint geography or history field visit to France or Germany, in the current climate there is little scope or inclination to analyse the curriculum of other subjects, to identify areas of commonality and share ideas for collaborative teaching across departments. However, if collaboration between departments is seen as valuably adding *to* rather than detracting from the languages curriculum, if it encourages planners to analyse language from a different perspective and discuss a range of teaching and learning styles, then this is surely time well-spent.

For example, the Key Stage 3 Geography National Curriculum contains a list of countries to be studied from selected areas including Europe and Africa (potential source of francophone countries). Geographical thematic studies also covers weather and climate, eco systems and environmental issues – all of which might be reinforced or developed through and in language lessons. History topics including the world wars, dictators and the French revolution are regularly featured on most syllabuses throughout Europe. 'Science Across the World', a project based on global scientific issues such as acid rain, renewable energy, water, waste and so on, offers materials in different European languages. Using a worldwide electronic data base and communications network, schools in Britain can collaborate with schools which are also working on the same science theme – from Burundi to Belgium, Norway to New Zealand. Although the scheme is organised by the Association for Science Education, opportunities for linguistic exploitation are clear – a topic could, for example, be taught in Spanish, or partly in English by the science teacher and partly in Spanish by the linguist when collaborating with a school in Spain or Mexico.

Other examples on a pan-European basis include the Cité des Sciences et de l'Industrie at La Villette in Paris, which regularly runs specialised experiential learning events or 'classes villettes' for learners and teachers by exploring themes such as 'l'électricité', 'roches et volcans' and 'communication'. The Franco-British government initiative Dialogue 2000 project, involved over 100 schools, colleges and lycées in a programme of two-month post-16 student exchanges based on collaboration at joint curriculum level. Common themes selected included for example ethnic diversity in Britain and France, where teachers and students worked together through research, work experience, cultural visits and practical tasks, resulting in 'dramatic improvements' in the foreign language. In fact, with the advancement of European funding through the Socrates Programme, projects such as these illustrate rapidly growing opportunities for international exchanges and electronic and interactive communications networks. One could argue that more than ever before, foreign language use should have gained its rightful place within the international and virtual classroom. And yet, for many schools, initiatives such as these are additional to the realities of classroom life. They are not embedded into the regular curriculum and in terms of learner entitlement remain an optional extra!

Perhaps the most challenging consideration is the delivery of elements of the National Curriculum other than MFL through the medium of a modern language, integrating both the subject and language teaching and learning. Ten years ago, this approach was clearly the domain of the International or European schools with a handful of pioneering enthusiasts in other schools. Although Britain has a successful tradition of bilingual education with the Welsh and Gaelic-medium schools, the teaching of subjects through a European language – which is not a heritage language – has remained peripheral to mainstream education. However, this is fast becoming a growth area as more schools are investigating more innovative methods of immersing students in a language other than English as well as looking to a curriculum delivered in more than one language.

The movement is now well established in other European countries especially in Germany, France, Austria, the Nordic countries and The Netherlands and is gaining momentum in the UK. There is no one model in operation since schools are developing programmes according to individual circumstances. School programmes currently in operation range from a ten lesson module to a term's programme, from a core syllabus lasting two years to a proportion of lessons say two out of three lessons per week – for an extended period of time. Alternatively, it may consist of a Year 7 Foundation Course or GCSE Geography taught in Spanish. An expanding network of schools is working with subjects such as Science, Geography, History, Drama, ICT, PSE, Sport or Business Studies. In such instances, language is used to explore concepts and assimilate new knowledge in contexts where the language itself is not the focus of learning.

To illustrate the point, I cite as a particular example an extract from a transcript of a Year 9 history lesson in French (Coyle, 1999). The learners are in a top ability set in a comprehensive school. This extract is taken from the 'warm-up' stage of the lesson where the students are developing their hypothesising skills.

Teacher:	Bon, essayez de formuler une question sur toute l'histoire étudiée pendant l'année sur de Gaulle. Par exemple, question: *Qu'est-ce qu'il serait arrivé si De Gaulle n'avait pas parlé à la BBC?* Réponse: *Il n'y aurait pas de Résistance*, par exemple. Bon, OK? Alors avec un partenaire essayez de formuler des questions et des réponses . . .
Learner 1:	Qu'est-ce qu'il serait arrivé si Hitler n'avait pas lu les idées de de Gaulle?
Learner 2:	Je ne sais pas! il n'aurait pas gagné la Guerre.
Learner 1:	Oui, mais qu'est-ce qu'il serait arrivée si Hitler avait gagné la Guerre?
Learner 2:	Il 'y avait er aurait moins de personnes juives.
Learner 3:	Qu-est-ce qui serait arrivé si Hilter ne serait pas né?
Learner 4:	Je crois que, peut-etre que l'Allemagne n'aurait pas attaqué parce que Hitler est devenu dictateur . . . ça c'est mon opinion.
Learner 5:	Qu'est-ce qui serait arrivé si Germany er l'Allemagne ne serait pas entré l'Hongrie et Russie
Learner 6:	Si l'Allemagne n'aurait pas envahi la Russe je pense que les Russes ne auraient pas entré dans la Guerre
Teacher:	André, tu peux expliquer à Matthieu *qu'est-ce qui serait arrivé si il n'y avait pas une seconde guerre...*
Learner 7:	Qu'est-ce qu'on fait?
Learner 8:	On dit la phrase et met les mots *qu'est-ce qui serait arrivé si quelquechose n'a pas fait ou si quelquechose etait fait*
Learner 7:	Ah oui oui oui, je pose la question . . . Qu'est-ce que tu non qu'est-ce qui serait arrivé si le Seconde Guerre n'avait pas (stops checks with A – il n'avait pas), s'il'n y avait pas la Seconde Guerre?
Learner 8:	Le pays serait plus riche . . . parce que après la Guerre c'etait l'argent le problème . . . les Etats Unis seraient moins riche mais la Grande Bretagne serait plus riche que les Etats Unis parce que après la Guerre tout l'argent c'est . . . l' économie de les Etats Unis était bien mais mais de Grande Bretagne c'était pas mal mais . . . peut-être il y aurait . . . plus de morts . . . peut-être il y aurait eu plus de morts ou moins de morts?

Learner 7: Moins moins de morts . . . et qu'est-ce que serait, qu'est-ce qui serait arrivé . . . qu-est-ce qui serait arrivé si de Gaulle n'avait pas formé la Résistance?

Learner 8: La Guerre aurait pu durée plus temps – une possibilité . . .

Whilst not all the language is grammatically correct, this transcript demonstrates that learners were working with tenses and vocabulary which would not normally be used in a Year 9 language class. The extract also contains examples of the students gradually trying to express more complex ideas in the language and using language spontaneously in areas beyond the confines of the modern languages classroom to discuss and explore their own views and opinions. The extension of the context in which to use language means that students are able to build on their language learning experiences – the language then becomes a tool for learning rather than the object of learning.

In fact, as more schools become involved, not only is the range of subjects taught extending, so is the age and ability range of the learners. Content teaching is no longer an elite passport for a small group of able linguists, but a pragmatic exploration for creating further opportunities within the confines of the school for learning in a challenging and motivating way. The SALT 2000 initiative (1999) supported by the French and Spanish Embassies and the Goethe Institut, grouped together subject and language teachers from 12 different schools to create modules in three different languages based on the National Curriculum in history, geography, science, mathematics and languages. Investigations include mathematical inquiry, eating and digestion, water, Japan, natural hazards, civilians in war, the Second World War, the Cold War, the Norman Conquest and hurricanes. This particular project however marked a significant landmark for four main reasons:

- subject and language teachers collaborated to create common modules each bringing their respective expertise;
- the themes are rooted in the everyday curriculum and are not dependent on additional funding or time;
- the modules target a wide range of learners;
- teachers planning the modules where appropriate included the development of thinking skills and learning strategies centred within purposeful activities:

A purposeful activity is more than an activity involving meaningful language. It not only uses language that conveys meaning, but also contains some value to the learner . . .

(Burden and Williams, 1998: 87)

Whilst I am not suggesting that teaching elements of other subjects through the medium of the foreign language does not raise some difficult and challenging issues, I do believe that it directly addresses questions of motivation, the content of communication and the provision of a challenging learning environment – whatever the level of the learners, i.e. it makes the value of the learning more explicit. Such an approach relates wherever possible the language to be learned to the content which is used to learn it; considers language as a medium for learning as well as a linguistic system; combines learning to use language with using language to learn; acknowledges the role of interaction at all levels but especially within the classroom – in order to give our young people the skills to become competent and confident communicators.

Case study research (Coyle, 1996, 1999) also supports the view that there are potentially positive outcomes of integrated learning: an increase in learner motivation and confidence as well as linguistic competence, a willingness to communicate and take risks, an acceptance of the normality of working in an alternative language and improved study skills (memory techniques, concentration span, awareness of learning). Working far beyond the transactional, the development of other skills (such as hypothesising, analysing, and discussing) enhances the individual's profile and appears to inculcate positive attitudes to learning. Moreover, such approaches also address whole school concerns – raising boys' achievement (as in the case of working through the medium of French in Science for example), or raising teacher and learner expectations, and therefore can be incorporated into school development plans. As more schools become involved, networks flourish, practice is shared, confidence increases and crucially – support systems are put into place.

Perhaps the most fundamental aspect of planning and monitoring integrated learning is that it puts curriculum development firmly on the agenda and provides a forum for teachers to re-conceptualise their practice:

> Teachers have found that content and language integrated learning is about far more than simply teaching non-language subject matter in an additional language in the same way as the mother tongue . . . (i) is not a matter of simply changing the language of instruction. Rather it is a set of method-ologies in which dual-focused orientation of the learning of the subject and the language is realised.
>
> (Marsh, Enner and Sygmund, 1999: 17)

It also enables teachers and learners to look beyond the current confines of the language classroom to present language learning within a more meaningful context.

> A language is a system which relates what is being talked about (content) and the means used to talk about it (expression). Linguistic content is inseparable from linguistic expression. In subject matter learning we overlook the role of language as a medium of learning. In language leaning we overlook the fact that content is being communicated.
>
> (Mohan, 1986)

From reaction to interaction

Yet, modifying the content of the languages classroom will not automatically lead to an increase in communication skills and more motivating opportunities unless there is also a radical shift in how classroom language is developed and used. In essence this implies a move from learner reaction to interaction, so that language becomes the medium for both communicating and learning.

> Interaction is the process whereby everything that happens in the classroom gets to happen the way it does. Let us make the most of it.
>
> (Allwright, 1984: 169)

'Making the most of it' to me implies defining what I shall call 'strategic classrooms'. To achieve this teachers and researchers will need to work together to collect more detailed evidence of the kind of practice which belongs to strategic classrooms, analyse in detail the moves and transformations which take place and together develop professional confidence in a pedagogy which values social interaction as the nexus of learning. It would seem therefore that strategic classrooms are those where language activities are transformed into learning opportunities and interaction is the basic toolkit of the language teacher and learner.

> As foreign language instructors we need to view our classroom as the social organisation that it is and we need to participate in dialogic activity with learners so that they may achieve cognitive and linguistic self-regulation in ways that are socioculturally appropriate. In short, our task is to enable learners to find their voice, their speaking personality, the(ir) speaking consciousness.
>
> (Holquist and Emerson, 1981: 434)

If social interaction is to be elevated to such a central position in the classroom, then practitioners need to know more about how such interaction works – how students might be encouraged to use language spontaneously regardless of their linguistic competence. The implications are as follows:

- a better understanding of the kinds of classroom interaction between teacher and learners and between learners and learners, which facilitates a wider range of exchanges and interchanges – especially those which can be transformed into exploratory or spontaneous moves with appropriate support;
- a deepening awareness of the role played by regulation or 'control' in the learning process. On the one hand being 'controlled' (i.e. object or other-regulated) contributes to and assists the learner's quest for self-regulation or independence; on the other, over-regulation, especially by the teacher, may preclude such achievements. In this sense, over-regulation may prevent rather than facilitate communication and learning. A hard look at some current practice may reveal that both language used and activities organised are frequently 'over-regulated' by the teacher, textbook or syllabus;

- a more extensive repertoire of classroom tasks which encourages individuals to engage in collaborative learning, working with different groups of peers, problem-solving and task-based learning, as well as an emphasis on tasks which promote cognitive challenge or 'conflict'. Such tasks will engage learners in deploying a range of strategies and reflective skills to make sense of their learning.

Perhaps the most urgent of all is the development of creative and spontaneous language skills within the classroom, where learners progress from speaking to talking and reflecting. For me such a development is founded on the distinction between reaction and interaction. If students are to engage more readily with foreign language learning – a pre-requisite for raising its prestige and profile – then a sense of both purpose and involvement has to be accessible to the majority not the minority.

Whilst the issues discussed in this chapter may appear to hit hard, I have tried to suggest ways forward to challenge commonly held views such as:

> Learners are frequently asked to engage in activities in the target language that are cognitively superficial and unchallenging, merely because the learner does not have a proficient grasp of the language, or in tasks that are boring, childish, too simplistic, unrelated to their interests and often just insulting to their intelligence.
>
> (Burden and Williams, 1998: 87)

I have also tried to create a stimulus for discussion so that teachers as well as learners may play a greater part in deciding what kind of learning belongs in the modern languages classroom – to channel and fine-tune the foundations of good practice into more profitable and satisfying outcomes.

I propose therefore that for language learning to gain its rightful place in the curriculum, there should be a radical reappraisal of the content and context for language use, so that learners experience from the outset the value of developing their language capability in strategic classrooms. Such classrooms will guide and support language learning as well as empower individuals to take ownership of language use. After all, any classroom can be strategic – all classrooms should challenge learners.

Editor's note

Coyle laments the demise of MFLs throughout the 1990s, a decade which began with much hope as the subject became compulsory for all learners aged 11–16. Coyle notes the stultifying effect of the content of an MFLs curriculum on learners, and suggests alternative approaches to stimulate learners and drawing on work and approaches abroad and in other curriculum areas at home. Principally, this involves the study of other subjects, or at least parts of other subjects through the means of the foreign language. This serves two main purposes; to give a reason for learning and using a foreign language, and secondly to reinforce learning in the other subjects. Coyle does not dismiss the relevant parts of a communicative approach, but focuses her attention on the content of MFL learning. Her recommendations, at Key Stage 3 and 4, present strong argument for re-appraising MFL teaching and learning, demanding learners to use the language for the very real purpose of learning cross curricular themes, encouraging co-operation and transferability between subject areas, and the coverage of topics only in MFL lessons. Coyle is not yet challenging the way MFLs are taught and learnt, but is beginning to assess the place of the subject in the curriculum through an analysis of appropriate content.

References

Allwright, R. L. (1984) 'The importance of interaction in classroom language learning', *Applied Linguistics*, 5: 156–71.

Burden, R. and Williams, M. (eds) (1998) *Thinking Through the Curriculum*, London: Routledge.

Brown, K. and Brown, M. (1996) *New Contexts for Modern Language Learning: Cross Curricular Approaches*, Pathfinder 27: CILT.

Clark, A. (1998) *Gender on the Agenda: Factors Motivating Boys and Girls in Modern Foreign Languages*, London: CILT.

Commission of the European Communities (1995) *Teaching and Learning: Towards the Learning Society*, Brussels: DGV.

Coyle, D. (1996) 'Language medium teaching in Britain', in G. Fruhauf, D. Coyle and I. Christ (1996) *Teaching Content in a Foreign Language: Practice and Perspectives in European Bilingual Education*, Alkmaar, Netherlands: Stichting Europees Platform voor het Nederlandse Onderwijs.

—— (1999) 'Adolescent voices speak out – if only they would, if only they could. A study of interaction in classrooms where foreign languages are used', unpublished thesis, University of Nottingham.

DES/WO (1990) *Modern Foreign Languages Working Group Initial Advice*, 'The Green Book', London: HMSO.

Department for Education and Employment, and the Qualifications and Curriculum Authority (1999) *The National Curriculum: Modern Foreign Languages*, London: HMSO/QCA.

Holquist, M. and Emerson, C. (1981) 'Glossary', in M. M. Bakhtin, *The Dialogic Imagination: Four Essays* (edited by M. Holquist, translated by C. Emerson), Austin: University of Texas Press.

Legutke, M. and Thomas, H. F. (1991) *Process and Experience in the Language Classroom*, London: Addison Wesley, Longman.

Littlewood, W. (1981) *Communicative Language Teaching*, Cambridge: Cambridge University Press.

Marsh, D., Enner, C. and Sygmund, D. (1999) *Pursuing Plurilingualism*, Jyväskylä, Finland: University of Jyväskylä.

McGuinness, C. (1999) *From Thinking Skills to Thinking Classrooms: A Review and Evaluation of Approaches for Developing Pupils' Thinking*, Research Report 115, DfEE: HMSO.

Nisbet, J. (1991) 'Projects, theories and methods: the international scene', in M. Coles, and W. D. Robinson (eds) (1991) *Teaching Thinking*, Bristol: Bristol Press.

Nisbet, J. (1993) 'The thinking curriculum', *Educational Psychology*, 13: 281–90.

Nuffield Languages Inquiry (2000) *Where Are We Going with Languages?*, Nuffield Languages Inquiry, PO Box 2671, London W1A 3 SH.

Office for Standards in Education (OFSTED) (1996) *Handbook for the Inspection of Schools*, London: HMSO.

Page, B. (1996) 'Graded objectives in ML(GOML)' in E. Hawkins (ed.) *30 Years of Language Teaching*, London: CILT.

Powell, R. (1986) *Boys, Girls and Languages in Schools*, London: CILT.

Salter, M. (ed.) (1987) *Languages for Communication – The Next Stage*, London: DFE.

Salters, J., Neil, P. and Jarman, R. (1995) 'Why did the French bakers spit in the dough?' *Language Learning Journal*, 11: 26–9.

Project information

Charis Project: Stapleford House, Wesley Place. Stapleford. Nottingham NG9 7BR.

Cité des Sciences et de l'Industrie: 30, avenue Corentin-Cariou, 75019, Paris. E-mail: classes.villette.int@cite-sciences.fr.

Dialogue 2000 project: Central Bureau for Educational Visits and Exchanges (British Council)10, Spring Gardens. London SW1A 2BN.

Tacade, Directions Project: 1 Hulme Place, The Crescent, Salford M5 4QA.

SALT 2000 Project (Subjects and Language Teaching): contact Michèle Bouygue, French Embassy Cultural Services, 23 Cromwell Road, London SW7 2EL.

Science Across the World: ASE, College Lane, Hatfield, Herts. Contact http://www.ase.org.uk or saw@bp.com.

MUNDI: Mobile Unit for Development Issues, School of Education, Jubilee Campus, University of Nottingham, Nottingham. NG8 2BB.

18 Language transfer and the Modern Foreign Language curriculum

Cathy Pomphrey

Most MFL teachers at some moment in their career ask themselves the question 'What is the point of teaching MFLs?' Earlier chapters have already considered the academic and vocational value of MFL study. This chapter aims to encourage further reflection on the broad educational value of this subject and in particular the contribution which learning an MFL can make to the overall language development of the learner, not just in the specific language being taught but in the L1, the L2 and further FL learning, and the resulting influence on the learner's broad perception of what language is. Such reflection cannot take place without considering the other language learning experiences which school students undergo, including experience of the mainstream English curriculum and its relation to the MFL curriculum. Nor should it be forgotten that large numbers of school students in Britain are already bilingual, some of them learning English as an additional language (EAL). In most school classrooms it would be common to find diverse experience of languages and language varieties other than Standard English contributing to the learners' overall perception of language.

Some important questions to be addressed are:

- How does knowledge of one language affect the learning or acquisition of others?
- Are skills and concepts gained in the L1 transferred to the learning of further languages later in life (either as an L2 or an MFL)?
- What are the implications of such links for the MFL curriculum in schools?

There are no easy answers to these questions, but a wide range of studies from various fields of language research suggest that there are important links between L1, L2 and FL learning processes. The precise nature of these links is not always as clear as we would wish, which sometimes makes it difficult to draw appropriate conclusions for the school curriculum. MFL teachers in this country, however, have so far made very limited use of the insights gained from these studies and the MFL curriculum still tends to stand apart from other areas of the school curriculum, even from areas which have a focus on language such as mainstream English. Thus this chapter will look at a selection of studies related to the integration or transfer of language skills and knowledge and raise questions about their relevance to the work of MFL teachers in Britain. Because the circumstances are so different from MFL teaching in other parts of the world or the teaching of other subjects in the curriculum, MFL teaching in Britain can have a tendency to be very insular. For this reason I have selected studies whose relevance to the day-to-day work of the MFL teacher in Britain is not always very direct. I have done so with the deliberate intention of opening up a broad discussion and looking at familiar issues from less familiar perspectives.

In looking at these studies it is important to bear in mind relevant features of the social and political context in which MFL teachers work in Britain. In other contexts, where English is the main FL learned, utilitarian justifications for MFL study are so obvious that questions about its purpose or place in the curriculum seem strange and inappropriate. Everyone understands the importance of being able to use English for access to many spheres of communication, including the media, the arts, business, industry and technology as well as academic spheres. As seen in earlier chapters, the power and status of English as a world language has an enormous impact on learners' motivation, on the choice of language or languages for the school curriculum and on attitudes and approaches to foreign language learning and to bilingual learners and their languages. Thus, in the British context, questions about the purpose of MFL study cannot be avoided.

Language awareness

The British Language Awareness movement was founded during the 1980s and arose from the work of Eric Hawkins and others who were interested in developing an integrated approach to discussion about language, making a bridge between different areas of the school curriculum such as MFL, mainstream English, E2L and Heritage and Community languages. Most of the work carried out under the umbrella of Language Awareness was aimed at curriculum development. In 1981, Eric Hawkins expounded an 'apprenticeship model' as a rationale for MFL teaching in the British context, where English is the predominant language and there is no obvious choice of specific foreign language for the school curriculum which is likely to be widely used by learners in the future. This model sees the school curriculum for MFL as providing a foundation of preparation for learning any language needed in the future. Following this broader perspective on the aims of MFL teaching, Hawkins later developed ideas for a further broadening of perspective on language teaching across the curriculum in his seminal 'Awareness of Language: An Introduction' (Hawkins, 1984). Hawkins' work has at its heart a concern for the lifelong overall language development of the learner, not just in MFL but also in mainstream English and other L1 learning. Hawkins makes a clear case for including what since the Kingman report (DES/WO, 1988) has been referred to as 'knowledge about language' in the curriculum. If learners never have the opportunity to use the language taught in the MFL in later life, at least this knowledge (in addition to the skills developed) can be applied to other languages met later as well as to the L1 to develop a broader perception of what language is.

Despite its undisputed influence as a champion of MFL as a vital part of the school curriculum, Hawkins' call for greater integration of language learning experiences in school has never really materialised for a variety of reasons. In particular, MFL and mainstream English teaching have remained very separate activities. Although there were a few exceptions (see, for example, Anderson, 1991), curriculum development activities tended to take the form of bolt-on Language Awareness courses run by modern languages departments as some form of preparation for MFL study rather than cross-curricular innovations. Such courses were criticised by the DES survey of 1990 as showing little evidence of contributing to progress in MFL and interest in this approach dwindled as a result. The focus in the ensuing NC for MFL on use of the target language, the development of skills and use of language rather than knowledge about language made it very difficult for Language Awareness courses to survive. (For an argument in favour of Language Awareness within the National Curriculum for MFL, see Pomphrey, 1993.)

The British Language Awareness movement did result in a number of calls for greater integration of language learning experiences across the curriculum, such as Brumfit's 'Charter of Language Rights' (Brumfit 1989). The Association for Language Awareness is still a strong international force for the study of language in its broadest sense, summarised by James and Garrett's five domains of Language Awareness namely the affective, the social, the power, the cognitive and the performance domains (James and Garrett, 1991). In this country, however, for a variety of reasons, MFL teaching has tended to tread a narrower path by focusing on the use of one foreign language for most learners. As a result MFL and mainstream English departments have rarely come together to discuss their separate treatment of these broad domains of language study. This is demonstrated in the findings of a project carried out at Southampton University (Mitchell *et al.*, 1994). The project found the perceptions and activities of English and MFL teachers in the area of 'knowledge about language' to be widely differing and found little evidence of dialogue between English and MFL teachers. Although language is central to the NC of each subject, the interpretation given to 'knowledge about language' in each does not seem to facilitate collaboration between the two departments.

Studies related to bilingual learners

The British Language Awareness movement was largely concerned with curriculum structures and curriculum development rather than language learning processes. Another area of research which is relevant to the concerns of this chapter comes from studies of language learning and teaching processes related to working with bilingual learners learning an L2 within the relevant language community. Although this is a very different context from the MFL classroom, there are some useful findings for MFL teachers arising from such studies. A key figure in recent research in this area is Jim Cummins who worked with bilingual learners in the USA and Canada. In 1980, Jim Cummins produced his 'iceberg analogy' which hypothesised a Common Underlying Proficiency linking L1 knowledge and skill with L2 development (Cummins, 1980). Cummins' hypothesis proposed the likelihood of transfer of skills and concepts from the first language to further languages learned later. Thus a student with strong literacy skills in the L1 is likely to transfer much of this skill and knowledge to the L2, with what Cummins refers to as the 'surface features' of the new language needing to be added to the underlying understanding already in place. Similarly communication skills can be transferred, as well as much implicit knowledge.

Cummins makes a strong case for teachers in all curriculum areas to familiarise themselves with the detail of learners' L1 strengths and difficulties, as well as to support the development and maintenance of the bilingual learner's L1 to provide a sound foundation for further language progression in any language. It is all too often the case that MFL teachers have little awareness of what learners know or can achieve in English or other L1s or of the relevance of such knowledge to the learner's progress in MFL.

Another useful outcome of Cummins' work is his distinction between Basic Interpersonal Communication Skills (BICS) and Cognitive Academic Language Proficiency (CALP) (Cummins, 1984). Although Cummins warns against the dangers of an over-literal use of this distinction to categorise learners' use of language, it does give a useful reminder to MFL teachers, who are often (understandably) so concerned with developing the surface features of basic communication in the language that some of the more cognitively demanding aspects of language learning which engage learners in the language learning process can be neglected, to the dissatisfaction of many. This is a point made by Mike Grenfell (Grenfell, 1991) in his discussion of some of the dangers of a transactional interpretation of a communicative approach to MFL teaching. Arising out of the BICS and CALP distinction is Cummins' curriculum framework which relates the cognitive demand of curriculum tasks to a context which is meaningful to learners. The matrix below shows the framework (Figure 18.1).

High cognitive demand

E.g. putting a picture story in correct sequence following a text	E.g. writing a narrative from memory

Context embedded   **Context reduced**

E.g. matching pictures to words or simple sentences	E.g. copying, imitating decontextualised words with no visual or other support for meaning

Low cognitive demand

Figure 18.1 Cummins' framework applied to MFL tasks.

A context can be provided by incorporating learners' previous experience such as experience of the rules of a game or of a well-known story or the layout of a piece of text, as well as through visual or gestural support, all of which are very familiar to MFL teachers. This framework has been used in L2 teaching as a curriculum planning framework, a device for differentiating tasks, an assessment aid and a diagnostic tool. It has proved a very useful structure for EAL teachers in helping them to balance the learner's need for clear contextual support when embarking on a task in an unfamiliar language with a need for an appropriate cognitive demand which will engage and challenge the learner while enabling the activation of skills and concepts already acquired in the L1.

When Cummins talks of cognitive demand and transfer of concepts and skills, he is addressing issues of entitlement and access for bilingual learners at their own cognitive level to the whole curriculum rather than a specifically language-focused curriculum. The concepts in this case are usually related to other subject areas such as Science, Mathematics or Humanities. However there is no reason why the broad message of Cummins' work should not be applied to subjects such as MFL and English dealing with 'knowledge about language' where language is the knowledge content as well as the medium for developing concepts.

Cummins' theories also lend support to the case for undertaking study of other subject areas in the target language (as in immersion courses or 'sections bilingues'), whereby the cognitive demand can be provided by the concepts of the subject content as well as the opportunity for the transfer of concepts and skills from the L1 to the target language.

Contrastive analysis and language transfer

One of the problems with applying Cummins' theories to MFL teaching is that they attempt to deal with broad universals and thus to cover any language combination when looking at transfer of proficiency and knowledge from one language to another. In these theories, Cummins does not distinguish between the characteristics of specific languages. Thus, for example, the transfer of literacy skills between an ideographic language such as Chinese, and an alphabetic language such as English, is likely to involve some different processes and issues than between German and English. Linguistic research in the area of contrastive analysis, however, is directly concerned with such distinctions.

The term 'contrastive analysis' was used by Robert Lado (Lado, 1957) to describe comparisons made between linguistic and cultural features of the student's L1 and the new language to be learned with the specific aim of identifying the likely areas of difficulty or 'interference' for a speaker of a specific L1 learning to use a specific L2 or FL. Contrastive analysis would predict, for example, that a native speaker of English would find the use of 'être' with subject agreement of the past participle to form the perfect tense in French difficult because of the lack of an equivalent in English, whereas a native speaker of Italian would find this structure relatively easy to learn in

French because of the similarity with Italian. Most accounts of Lado's work particularly focused on what is now termed 'negative transfer', namely the features of the language and culture which are very different from the learner's L1, and therefore assumed to be more difficult to learn and where transfer of knowledge from the L1 would cause errors. Such features were largely identified through analysis of learners' errors. This information would enable language teachers to give extra emphasis to these areas of difficulty to prevent 'negative transfer' from the L1. This early form of contrastive analysis was allied to a behaviourist interpretation of the process of learning a new language which saw language learning as a process of developing new habits of response to replace the habits acquired in the L1. The L1 habits had to be replaced by the habits of the new language through extensive drills. Contrastive analysis fell into disrepute when the behaviourist theories of language learning with which they were linked were discredited by Chomsky (Chomsky, 1959) in favour of theories which gave a more cognitive explanation of language acquisition and a more participatory and creative role to the learner. As a result, L2 learning and acquisition theories allied to Chomsky's Universal Grammar became more popular than contrastive analysis explanations. Dulay and Burt's 1974 study of learners' L2 errors found these to be following a universal pattern regardless of the L1. The errors made by learners were described as developmental rather than arising from the L1 system. The study concluded that L2 acquisition processes were the same as L1 processes and that L1 knowledge was not an important factor in L2 acquisition. This study has lent force to arguments for reproducing, as far as possible, in L2 and FL teaching the conditions for developing the L1 such as comprehensible input (see Krashen, 1985), focus on meaning rather than form, avoiding explicit instruction and learning through consistent communicative use of the language. Although the study has had its critics (for example see Hatch, 1978) it has been very influential and for a long time tended to divert interest away from the L1 as a source of knowledge for L2/FL development.

In recent years, however, there has been a questioning of the L2=L1 hypothesis. Ellis (1985: 73), in raising this question concludes 'Certainly the L2=L1 acquisition hypothesis has not been proven in its strong form, although similar processes appear to operate in both types of acquisition'. Although current theories still tend to stem from notions of Universal Grammar and developmental learning sequences, the over-simplistic conclusion that the L1 plays no part in L2 learning or acquisition has been seriously challenged. With this has come a revival of interest in comparing languages with a view to understanding more about language learning processes. A number of studies focus on 'positive transfer' or those features of the L1 which are similar to or in some way help the learning of a new language. Researchers have considered all aspects of language development, including pronunciation, acquiring vocabulary, grammatical understanding, oracy and literacy skills, as well as discourse and cultural features. Studies such as Ringbom (1987) found significant differences in the rate of learning according to the similarity or dissimilarity of the L1 and the FL being learned. A useful summary of studies of language transfer can be found in Odlin (1989). Odlin presents a much more complex picture of language transfer than the earlier contrastive analysis would allow. Most studies relate transfer processes to the Universal Grammar at the heart of Chomsky's theories and to the Inter-language theory of Selinker (1972).

Thus features which are common to all or most languages (for example in all but a few languages the subject comes before the object) are likely to be trans-ferred easily between languages and internalised early on in the learner's interlanguage, whereas more specifically 'marked' features will take longer to internalise, even when learners have received target language input and/or explicit explanation of these features. For example the simple preverbal negative in Spanish (as in 'no tengo', etc.) is relatively easy to learn because it is more universal as a language structure than the English, German or French negative forms (see Felix, 1984). Thus even though it is very different from the L1 form, an L1 speaker of English, German or French will learn the Spanish negative relatively easily. Odlin shows how languages which make finer distinctions or 'marking' of linguistic features present greater conceptual challenges for L1 speakers of languages which do not make such distinctions. For example, in the area of vocabulary, the distinction in French between 'savoir' and 'connaître' presents a conceptual challenge for an English speaker learning French because English uses only one verb 'to know' to cover both concepts.

It is important at this point to emphasise that most of the recent explor-ations of language transfer have been concerned with the transfer of implicit rather than explicit knowledge of the L1. Most studies describe language transfer processes as involving unconscious use of implicit knowledge of the L1 in constructing an 'interlanguage' which combines the learner's incomplete knowledge of the L2 with assumptions based on the sounds, structures and cultural features of the L1. Thus native speakers of English might assume that adjectives in French will come before the noun or that there is only one pronoun to translate 'you' into French until, through experience of the L2, they acquire a different set of knowledge. Even after having met the French version, slips and inconsistencies in spontaneous conversation will show that this new knowledge about the L2 has not yet been sufficiently internalised to become part of the learner's communicative use. Bialystok (1983) lists borrow-ing from the L1 as an important communicative strategy for L2 learners. This is a much more developmental interpretation of the role of language transfer from that of Lado and his followers.

It is not appropriate to delve deeper into the detail of language transfer studies within the confines of this chapter, however the brief account given shows that there is now a widely held assumption that cross-linguistic influence is a powerful aspect of the L2 and FL learning process. These studies also warn against an over-simplistic interpretation of what language comparisons can contribute to the learning process and of what might be classed as 'easy' or 'difficult' for language learners.

Future directions

How can the widely ranging studies described above help us to develop an approach to MFL teaching which takes account of the realities of language transfer without returning us to sterile and outdated Grammar Translation or audiolingual approaches? The studies quoted are all on the margin of the usual MFL teaching context in Britain, nevertheless it is possible to apply them to some strategies or directions which should be possible for teachers in this context.

Links with the English curriculum

The first suggestion is to establish links between MFL and English departments in schools. There is a long tradition of separation between these two curriculum areas in British schools and this is clearly not going to be easy to change. However, the time is right for a re-assessment of this situation. The Language Awareness movement called for cooperation between English and MFL departments largely because of its interest in looking at explicit knowledge about language. There is plenty of current political support for such a focus in the curriculum, with the very explicit metalinguistic terminology used in documents such as the national literacy strategy (DfEE, 1998a) or the ITT curriculum for English (DfEE, 1998b). Following the Kingman report (1988) the English National Curriculum includes extensive reference to 'knowledge about language' and the MFL teaching community is looking for ways to incorporate more conscious approaches to the teaching of grammar within a communicative framework.

It is probable that what is most hindering collaboration between English and MFL teachers in Britain is linked to their differing perceptions of the importance of explicit knowledge about language. Mitchell *et al.* (1994) found that English teachers did not believe there was a link between pupils' proficiency in using language and their explicit knowledge about language, whereas most MFL teachers in their study believed there was a strong link. In a small-scale study of the perceptions and attitudes towards knowledge about language of PGCE students of English and MFL conducted at the UNL (Pomphrey and Moger, in press), a good deal of tension surrounded open discussion of broad language issues. In particular there was tension on the part of the English specialists in talking about formal language structures. The PGCE English students often felt inadequate in their knowledge of appropriate metalinguistic terminology and decried their inability to articulate their implicit knowledge of the structure of English or even of other first languages among students who were bilingual. The difficulty of being explicit about the structure of the language most closely associated with the individual's identity was very evident in this study. A similar anxiety was found even among language professionals by Deborah Cameron when she administered a grammar judgement test to colleagues who were English specialists at the university where she worked (Cameron, 1997). If English and MFL teachers are to share their differing perceptions, it is important to face the emotional, as well as the intellectual tensions this involves. The distinction between metalinguistic terminology and metalinguistic concepts also needs to be clear, so that teachers who have not learned the labels attached to familiar concepts are not discouraged from engaging in dialogue about language forms. English teachers have a great deal to impart to MFL teachers about text level structures while MFL teachers usually have greater awareness of sentence level or word level forms from which their English teaching colleagues could benefit.

Transfer of implicit knowledge

In the studies described we can see that there is extensive evidence of a link between the two curriculum areas in terms of the transfer of implicit knowledge from the L1 to the L2/FL. Cummins' theory of Common Underlying Proficiency, as well as the language transfer studies mentioned above, suggest that teachers of English, MFL and of Heritage and Community languages could gain a much more complete picture of learners' overall language proficiency, both actual and potential, were they to collaborate. At the very least, MFL teachers would be more aware of the limits of the learner's L1 competence so that, for example, difficulties with oracy or literacy in the L1 might help to explain L2 or FL learning difficulties.

Transfer of explicit knowledge

In this post-Chomsky era, it is difficult to find much convincing evidence of a direct link between explicit knowledge about a language and proficiency in using that language (for recent studies, see Youngju Han and Ellis, 1998 and Alderson *et al.*, 1997). Perhaps instead of arguing on the basis of questionable links between explicit knowledge and language proficiency in relation to learning a specific language, it would be more useful to consider whether knowledge about language is worthwhile as an educational experience which opens up broader perspectives and paths to further understanding. For example, explicit knowledge about adjectival agreements and collocation in French may be much less effective than input and practice in developing the English speaking learner's spontaneous use of this aspect of French. However, in terms of the learner's understanding of how languages are organised as systems, it provides a useful challenge to implicitly held assumptions based on the L1. Explicit knowledge of this kind could trigger a different set of future expectations about adjectives as a knowledge base for further language learning. At the same time this experience can make the learner more aware that there is a pattern to adjectival use in English.

Transfer from FL to L1

Looked at in this way, the potential for collaboration between teachers of the two subjects could be easier. A person who has never had the experience of using a second or foreign language could be forgiven for perceiving language as an unconscious 'given' for making meaning in the world rather than a phenomenon with an underlying structure or system. This is clearly a rather distorted perception if an understandable one. The very act of consciously learning a language in the classroom implies a distancing of the self from the usual unconscious habits of everyday communication. This means that explicit knowledge about language as a system is likely to be more easily extracted from the foreign language learning experience than from learning which takes place in the L1. In L1 use, the strong links between the language used and the individual identity of the user make such objective contemplation of structure and system more challenging. Seliger (1979) claims that a learner's explicit knowledge is likely to be simpler and less complete than the same person's implicit knowledge of a language. If this is true of a developing L2, it is even more likely to be the case for knowledge of the L1. If we believe that enabling learners to look objectively at language is a valid educational experience then perhaps we should look more closely at the powerful contribution that the foreign language learning experience can make to this 'knowledge about language'. In other words, while language transfer from the L1 to the L2 is more likely to be implicit, unconscious and difficult to track, there is scope for the transfer of explicit knowledge about language from the L2/FL to the L1. MFL teachers are constantly bemoaning the fact that their pupils do not know anything about the structure of English; perhaps we should look at this the other way round and suggest that learning a foreign language helps learners to stand back from implicit language use and thus enables learners to look more objectively at the forms of their first language. The explicit knowledge gained from the FL learning experience can thus be applied to and compared with the L1. In suggesting this I am not advocating teaching the MFL via explicit explanation of language forms (as in the Grammar Translation method), but rather reflecting on what has been learned in the FL and in doing so attempting to articulate explicitly the developing implicit knowledge gained through practice and communicative use in the FL.

The MFL teacher's role

One of the problems arising from the isolation of MFL in the school curriculum is the over-specialisation of the teacher's role. If Hawkins' apprenticeship idea is a suitable motivation for MFL teaching in Britain, then a rethink of the MFL teacher's role as a language educator rather than a language instructor is called for. This implies abandoning the 'blank slate' approach to starting MFL study in the secondary school and trying to find ways of incorporating pupils' previous linguistic experience, including knowledge of different languages and language varieties, into MFL classroom activity. A language educator is more likely to be interested in the learner's broad knowledge about language as well as use of a specific language. Such a role also implies considering the contribution of the MFL experience to overall language development, including the development of literacy and oracy skills and the ability to talk about the forms and structures of language in relation to meaning.

Opportunities for reflection

The interest in independent learning has led many MFL teachers to incorporate opportunities for occasional reflection by learners on the language learning process in the MFL classroom. This is often accompanied by self-evaluation of achievement, as well as explicit articulation and development of strategies for improving language learning. Such activity is not seen as posing a major threat to the communicative basis of classroom activity. Such reflection could usefully incorporate comparisons of linguistic features across languages. This could be word-level comparisons or reflections on sentence or text level grammatical structures, as well as social or cultural aspects of language. Comparing linguistic forms is an exercise which could usefully take place in a number of subjects on the school curriculum. For example, comparing a standard English text with a dialect version or comparing a formal technical written account of a science experiment with a more descriptive, informal account. The skills of 'noticing' modifications or patterns of language in this type of exercise could easily be applied to cross-language comparisons. Learners could be helped to identify similarities between languages which can aid comprehension strategies and speed up production of new language, thus developing the learner's awareness of some appropriate language learning strategies. Reflection on negative transfer, errors or differences between languages can be useful in aiding the learner's perception of how language works and often throws light on the patterns and structures of the first language.

One of the arguments against such reflection is that it can only take place rather superficially in the target language until a reasonable level of Cognitive Academic Proficiency (to use Cummins' term) has been reached in that language. It is important to weigh up the benefits to be derived from brief moments of such reflection, even if not carried out in the target language, in terms of cognitive challenge, language transfer possibilities, broadening the learner's perception of how language works, contributing to strategy training and self-evaluation compared to the disadvantage of losing a few moments of target language input or practice. It is often this kind of reflective experience which encourages a curiosity about language and a questioning which can enhance future language learning of the L1 or other languages.

Conclusion – the goals of the MFL curriculum

An examination of cross-language transfer does challenge assumptions about the goal of MFL learning in the school curriculum in this country. A goal which ignores the sociolinguistic context in which the FL is taught is of questionable value. Prior to the introduction of the National Curriculum, the Harris report (DES/WO, 1990) stated that MFL study 'exposes learners to new experiences and enables them to make connections in a way that would not otherwise be possible, and this in itself deepens their understanding of their mother tongue'. The National Curriculum for MFL which followed this report was very skills-focused and based on the use of the target language rather than on a concern for explicit knowledge about language, contemplation of the L1 or making connections between languages. If this is the aim it seems logical to provide opportunities for the contemplation of explicit knowledge side by side with experiences of lively, interactive language use in context so that learners can be helped to make connections and transfer concepts, both implicitly and explicitly. Together with this, reflection on the development of language skills and strategies as suggested in Chapter 15 provides a sound basis for Hawkins' 'language apprenticeship'.

While the experience of absorbing target language input and of developing the skills of communicating in a new language must remain central to the MFL curriculum, nevertheless this experience in isolation from the rest of the language curriculum cannot in itself provide a sufficient educational goal. Some reflection on the broad educational purpose of the MFL experience is called for, together with a review of the place within MFL study of explicit 'knowledge about language' and a rethinking of links with the English curriculum. The MFL experience could have a much bigger impact than it has had so far on the mainstream English curriculum and as a more explicit preparation for the study of further languages, if some of the connections and deepening of awareness hinted at in the DES 1990 report were explored more thoroughly.

Editor's note

Pomphrey praises the work undertaken in the 1980s on language awareness, and laments its demise due to the post-Chomskyan attacks on behaviourist approaches to MFL teaching methods, and the overcrowded National Curriculum. She advocates a more eclectic approach, recognising the advantages of such work, and even of some aspects of a more traditional grammar translation methodology. This is not to say that she is recommending a return to some sort of golden age, but that a wholesale adoption of any one particular approach, namely the communicative approach, has led to the neglect of an appreciation of language in its broadest sense. Obvious links between English teachers and MFL teachers have never materialised, and the gains of learning MFLs beyond the development of communicative competence have not been fully exploited. The comparison of writing styles, the intercultural learning, the development of metacognitive and metalinguistic skills can only be rewarded if they are articulated and serve as foci within the curriculum as a whole. Pomphrey, therefore, sees the role of the mother tongue in MFL learning, and the place of MFLs in the learning of English and the learning of other subjects as vital, mutually complementary components of learning. This inevitably involves a questioning of the communicative approach, and offers greater potential for the teaching and learning of MFLs in the wider curriculum.

Linked chapters

Chapter 3, Chapter 11, Chapter 17.

References

Alderson, J. C., Chapman, C. and Steel, D. (1997) 'Metalinguistic knowledge, language aptitude and language proficiency', *Language Teaching Research*, 1(2): 93–121.

Anderson, J. (1991) 'The potential of Language Awareness as a focus for cross-curricular work in the Secondary school', in C. James. and P. Garett (eds) *Language Awareness in the Classroom*, Harlow: Longman.

Bialystok, E. (1983) 'Some factors in the selection and implementation of communicative strategies', in C. Faerch and G. Kasper (eds) *Strategies in Interlanguage Communication*, London: Longman.

Brumfit, C. J. (1989) 'Towards a language policy for multilingual secondary schools', in J. Geach (ed.) *Coherence in Diversity*, London: CILT.

Cameron, D. (1997) 'Let's hear it from the linguists: a vote of no confidence: SCAA's grammar test', *The English and Media Magazine*, 36: 4–7.

Chomsky, N. (1959) 'Review of 'Verbal Behaviour' by B.F. Skinner', *Language*, 35: 26–58.

Cummins, J. (1980) 'The construct of language proficiency in bilingual education', in Georgetown University Round Table on Languages and Linguistics 1980, Georgetown University Press.

—— (1984) *Bilingualism and Special Education; Issues in Assessment and Pedagogy*, Clevedon: Multilingual Matters.

DES/WO (1988) *Report of the Committee of Inquiry into the Teaching of English Language* (The Kingman Report), London: HMSO.

—— (1990) *A Survey of Language Awareness and Foreign Language Taster Courses*, London: HMSO.

—— (1990) *National Curriculum Modern Foreign Languages Working Group: Initial Advice* (The Harris Report), London: DES.

DfEE (1998a) *The National Literacy Strategy: Framework for Teaching*, London: HMSO.

—— (1998b) *Teaching: High Status, High Standards. Requirements for Courses of Initial Teacher Training Circular 4/98*, London: HMSO.

Dulay, H. and Burt, M. (1974) 'Natural sequences in child second language acquisition', *Language Learning*, 24: 37–53.

Ellis, R. (1985) *Understanding Second Language Acquisition*, Oxford: Oxford University Press.

Felix, S. (1984) 'Two problems of language acquisition: the relevance of grammatical studies in the theory of interlanguage', in A. Davies and C. Criper (eds) *Interlanguage: Proceedings of the Seminar in Honour of Pit Corder*, Edinburgh: Edinburgh University Press.

Grenfell, M. (1991) 'Communication: sense and nonsense', *Language Learning Journal*, 3: 6–8.

Hatch, E. (1978) 'Acquisition of syntax in a second language', in J. C. Richards (ed.) *Understanding Second and Foreign Language Learning*, Rowley, Mass: Newbury House.

Hawkins, E. (1981) *Modern Languages in the Curriculum*, Cambridge: Cambridge University Press.

Hawkins, E. (1984) *Awareness of Language: An Introduction*, Cambridge: Cambridge University Press.

James, C. and Garett, P. (1991) 'The scope of Language Awareness', in C. James and P. Garett (eds) *Language Awareness in the Classroom*, London: Longman.

Krashen, S. D. (1985) *The Input Hypothesis: Issues and Implications*, London: Longman

Lado, R. (1957) *Linguistics across Cultures*, Ann Arbor, Michigan: University of Michigan Press.

Mitchell, R., Hooper, J. and Brumfit, C. J. (1994) *Final Report: 'Knowledge about Language', Language Learning and the National Curriculum*, Occasional Papers 19, University of Southampton.

Odlin, T. (1989) *Language Transfer: Cross-Linguistic Influence in Language Learning*, Cambridge: Cambridge University Press.

Pomphrey, C. (1993) 'The "knowledge about" and "use of" dichotomy', *Languages Forum*, 2(3): 8–10, London: Institute of Education.

Pomphrey, C. and Moger, R. (1999) 'Cross-subject dialogue about language: attitudes and perceptions of PGCE students of English and modern languages', *Language Awareness*, 8(3 & 4): 223–236, Clevedon: Multilingual Matters.

Ringbom, H. (1987) *The Role of the First Language in Foreign Language Learning*, Clevedon: Multilingual Matters.

Seliger, H. (1979) On the nature and function of language rules in language teaching, *TESOL Quarterly* 13: 359–69.

Selinker (1972) Interlanguage, *International Review of Applied Linguistics* X: 209–30.

Youngju Han and Ellis, R. (1998) Implicit knowledge, explicit knowledge and general language proficiency, *Language Teaching Research* 2(1): 1–23.

Index